Ludwig Klages and the Philosophy of Life

This book provides a unique overview of and introduction to the work of the German psychologist and philosopher Ludwig Klages (1872–1956), an astonishing figure in the history of German ideas. Central to intellectual life in turn-of-the-century Munich, he went on to establish a reputation for himself as an original and provocative thinker. Nowadays he is often overlooked, partly because of the absence of an accessible and authoritative introduction to his thought; this volume offers just such a point of entry. With an emphasis on applicability and utility, Paul Bishop reinvigorates the discourse surrounding Klages, providing a neutral and compact account of his intellectual development and his impact on psychology and philosophy.

Chapter 1 offers an overview of Klages's life, visiting the major stations of his intellectual development. Chapter 2 examines in turn nine major conceptual 'tools' found in Klages's extensive writings, aiming to clarify Klages's terminology, to demystify his discourse, and to sift through Klages's credentials as a psychological thinker. Chapter 3 consists of extracts from Klages's writings, thematically oriented; these showcase the aphoristic and lyrical, as well as psychological and philosophical, qualities of Klages's writing, including his interest in aesthetics. Taken together, all three chapters constitute a vitalist 'toolkit' – to build a fuller, richer life.

Drawing on previous studies of Klages that have only been available in German, *Ludwig Klages and the Philosophy of Life* provides a non-polemical account of Klages's life and work, with explanations and commentaries to guide the reader through extracts from his writings. The book accessibly explains the most important ideas and concepts found in Klages's work, including soul, spirit, character, expression, will, and consciousness, and it reveals Klages to be a serious figure whose thought remains relevant to many disciplines today. It will stimulate interest in his work and create a new readership for his remarkable worldview.

Paul Bishop is William Jacks Chair in Modern Languages at the University of Glasgow and a Fellow of the Chartered Institute of Linguists. His previous publications include *On the Blissful Islands with Nietzsche and Jung, Analytical Psychology and German Classical Aesthetics* (2 vols), and, as editor, *The Archaic: The Past in the Present* and *Jung in Contexts: A Reader* (all Routledge).

Ludwig Klages and the Philosophy of Life
A Vitalist Toolkit

Paul Bishop

LONDON AND NEW YORK

First published 2018
by Routledge
2 Park Square, Milton Park, Abingdon, Oxon OX14 4RN

and by Routledge
711 Third Avenue, New York, NY 10017

Routledge is an imprint of the Taylor & Francis Group, an informa business

© 2018 Paul Bishop

The right of Paul Bishop to be identified as author has been asserted by
him in accordance with sections 77 and 78 of the Copyright, Designs and
Patents Act 1988.

All rights reserved. No part of this book may be reprinted or reproduced or
utilized in any form or by any electronic, mechanical, or other means, now
known or hereafter invented, including photocopying and recording, or in
any information storage or retrieval system, without permission in writing
from the publishers.

Trademark notice: Product or corporate names may be trademarks or
registered trademarks, and are used only for identification and explanation
without intent to infringe.

British Library Cataloguing in Publication Data
A catalogue record for this book is available from the British Library

Library of Congress Cataloging in Publication Data
Names: Bishop, Paul, 1967– author.
Title: Ludwig Klages and the philosophy of life: a vitalist toolkit /
Paul Bishop.
Description: New York: Routledge, 2017. | Includes bibliographical
references.
Identifiers: LCCN 2017023450 (print) | LCCN 2017040784 (ebook) |
ISBN 9781315522494 (Master E-Book) | ISBN 9781138697157
(hardback) | ISBN 9781138308510 (pbk.)
Subjects: LCSH: Klages, Ludwig, 1872–1956
Classification: LCC B3279.K64 (ebook) | LCC B3279.K64 B57 2017
(print) | DDC 193–dc23
LC record available at https://lccn.loc.gov/2017023450

ISBN: 978-1-138-69715-7 (hbk)
ISBN: 978-1-315-52249-4 (ebk)

Typeset in Times New Roman
by Wearset Ltd, Boldon, Tyne and Wear

In memoriam
Dietrich Jäger (1928–2010)

Figure 1 Ludwig Klages.

The point of life is life.

(Goethe, letter to J. J. Meyer, 8 February 1796)

O humankind, become essential!

(Angelus Silesius, *The Cherubinic Wanderer*, book 2, §30)

Go beyond 'you' and 'me'! Experience cosmically!

(Nietzsche, *Kritische Studienausgabe* 9, 11[7], 443)

Contents

Preface	xi
Acknowledgements	xxvi
List of abbreviations	xxviii
Glossary of Klagesian terminology	xxix

1 Life   1

Childhood and early years 1
Schwabing years 3
The 'main business' 17
Klages and Nietzsche 20
Celebrity ... and catastrophe 28

2 Works and key ideas   51

Conceptual tool #1: science of 'expression' 51
Conceptual tool #2: study of 'character' 56
Conceptual tool #3: theory of the will 62
Conceptual tool #4: genesis of consciousness 70
Conceptual tool #5: the doctrine of 'the reality of images' 73
Conceptual tool #6: the opposition of 'spirit' and 'soul' 89
Conceptual tool #7: 'Schablonisierung' 94
Conceptual tool #8: images are elementary souls 99
Conceptual tool #9: specific happiness 103

3 For advanced readers – selections from Ludwig Klages   120

Life: what could be more vital? 121
The symphony of the rhythms: living to the beat 127
The reality of images: what's real is what works 134
Distance and ancestral worship: how the past persists in the
*   present 151*

x   *Contents*

All-embracing love: 'this kiss for the whole world' 158
Writing and poetry: it's a kind of magic 163
Anthropology and the guidance of souls: we are truly blessed 174
Final thoughts 190

Further reading   206
Index   210

Preface

In *Hopscotch* (*Rayuela*, 1963), a novel set in Paris and Buenos Aires by the Argentinian novelist and essayist, Julio Cortázar (1914–1984), one of the founders of the so-called Latin American Boom, we find an exchange between Horacio Oliveira, a disgruntled intellectual, and Ossip Gregorovius, a fellow-member of the Serpent Club (a meeting-place for artists and thinkers). Oliveira declares that it is imperative humans keep looking for 'the beyond', lamenting the way in which culture has led modern humankind into a 'blind alley' and into 'scientific barbarism'. To which Gregorovius replies with the lapidary observation that Klages had already said all that.[1]

Who is Klages, the man who has said it all? And what is it exactly that Klages has already said? These two questions will serve as the guiding-thread for our journey into the labyrinth of Klages's psychological and philosophical thought, allowing us to penetrate to its core – and to find our way back to the world again. According to the ancient Greek myth, the labyrinth harbours a monster in its centre. Sometimes, it can seem as if there is something monstrous about Klages, given the way he is often talked about, if he is talked about at all. But we should remember that the claim about the monster is only a myth ... yet it was not always this way, and one does not have to look far to find numerous plaudits and expressions of appreciation for Klages's work.

In 1924, the German novelist Hermann Hesse (1877–1962) offered the following generous praise of a work by Klages that had appeared a couple of years earlier, describing Klages as 'renowned as the brilliant creator of a doctrine of expression and a graphology found on real intellectual depth'. Klages's new book, *Of Cosmogonic Eros* (*Vom kosmogonischen Eros*), had 'such psychological depth and rich, fruitful atmosphere' that it had moved Hesse 'more deeply [...] than the writings of a Spengler or a Keyserling', thus placing Klages *above* such contemporary figures as the Baltic German philosophers Oswald Spengler (1880–1936) and Hermann Graf Keyserling (1880–1946). For, so Hesse wrote, in some pages of this book, *Of Cosmogonic Eros*, 'something almost inexpressible has found the right words'.[2]

In 1927, the German philosopher Karl Löwith (1897–1973), a former student of Heidegger, declared that, 'in the narrow context of philosophical works written on Nietzsche, the work by Klages' – he means Klages's monograph of

xii *Preface*

1926, *The Psychological Achievements of Nietzsche* (*Die psychologischen Errungenschaften Nietzsches*) – 'can be ascribed without any hesitation an outstanding significance'.[3] And in 1928, Max Scheler (1874–1928) observed in *The Human Place in the Cosmos* (*Die Stellung des Menschen im Kosmos*) that Klages was

> the one who provided a philosophical foundation in Germany for the *pan-Romantic* way of thinking about the nature of the human being, representatives of which we can find today among many researchers in different disciplines, for example, [the palaeontologist] Edgar Dacqué [1878–1945], [the ethnologist and archaeologist] Leo Frobenius [1873–1938], [the Swiss analytical psychologist] C.G. Jung [1987–1961], [the psychiatrist and art historian] Hans Prinzhorn [1886–1933], [the philosopher] Theodor Lessing [1872–1933], and, to a certain extent, Oswald Spengler.[4]

In a letter to the scholar Gershom Scholem of 15 August 1930, the German philosopher and cultural critic, Walter Benjamin (1892–1940) was able to write that Klages's 'major work', *The Spirit as Adversary of the Soul* (*Der Geist als Widersacher der Seele*) (1929–1932), 'is without doubt a great philosophical work' – even if he felt obliged immediately to add, 'regardless of the context in which the author may be and remain suspect'.[5] In a letter to Wolf Goetze of 16 January 1930, the German philosopher of history Oswald Spengler – the author of *The Decline of the West* (1918–1922) to whom Hesse had compared Klages – remarked that 'in the field of scientific psychology, Klages towers over all of his contemporaries, including even the academic world's most renowned authorities',[6] even if on other occasions Spengler sought to distance himself from Klages.[7] In short, all these writers would have agreed with the assessment of the Austrian artist Alfred Kubin (1877–1959) in 1926: 'Klages is a fascinating phenomenon, a scientist of the highest rank, whom I regard as the most important psychologist of our time'.[8]

Nor was this assessment limited to the German-speaking world. In the seventy-fifth of his *Cantos* (composed between 1915 and 1962), the American-born Modernist poet, Ezra Pound (1885–1972), declared:

> Out of Phlegethon!
> out of Phlegethon,
> Gerhart
> art thou come forth out of Phlegethon?
> with Buxtehude and Klages in your satchel, with the
> Ständebuch of Sachs in yr/luggage
> – not of one bird of many[9]

– referring in these lines to the flaming fire in Hades, Phlegethon; to the contemporary Dresden pianist and composer, Gerhart Münch; to the Danish-German Baroque composer and organist, Dieterich Buxtehude; to a collection of illustrations

Preface xiii

to the songs of the medieval German *Meistersänger*, Hans Sachs; and, of course, to Ludwig Klages.[10]

True, academic critics and reviewers in the English-speaking world more often found it hard to assess the importance of Klages; not surprisingly, since so little of his work was translated and published in English. The only one of Klages's works to be translated into English was *Die Grundlagen der Charakterkunde*, published in 1929 as *The Science of Character*. Writing in *Mind* in 1929, the British philosopher and psychologist, W. J. H. Sprott (1897–1971), began his review of this work by confessing that 'Prof. Klages is difficult to place', and he continued: 'He is a mixture of scientist and philosopher, and he is a philosopher according to the common acceptation of the term', i.e. he is 'involved in his subject' and has 'strong feelings about it', he 'does not stand aloof like a pure scientist and describe and hypothesize', and he 'has some kind of message' – one which has, in Klages's own words, ' "aroused such enthusiastic echoes in the souls of the young that we should hesitate to omit" an extract from a previous work "although it does not fully agree with our present view" '.[11]

And writing in the *Psychological Bulletin* in 1933, the American psychologist Gordon W. Allport (1897–1967) noted that 'American students of personality' had given 'scant attention' to the writings of Klages, 'which at first sight seem so neologistic and strange, and from the academic point of view, so unpleasantly heterodox'; nevertheless, Allport added that 'it must be confessed […] that many of the most original contributions to the study of personality have come through "irregular" channels', and Klages 'ranks high among the provocative and influential non-academic writers of Europe'.[12] Rightly, Allport emphasized that graphology 'plays a relatively small part in [Klages's] doctrine of characterology', and he categorized Klages's approach to psychology as 'explicitly personalistic': 'The problems of individuality, [Klages] holds, are much greater, richer, and more manifold than can be treated with the meager and discordant formulas of the traditional school of psychology'. For this reason, Allport concluded, if Klages's indictment of psychology seemed 'unnecessarily harsh and malapropos' and 'an anachronism', this was only because psychologists had 'spontaneously adopted some of the problems which for many years Klages has been calling to their attention', and had 'even commenced in a tentative way to admit some of his principles into their horizon'.[13]

And in a critical survey of different kinds of literary criticism, first given as a paper at the 51st Annual Meeting of the Modern Language Association held in Philadelphia in 1934, Martin Schütze (1867–1950), a Germanist at the University of Chicago, considered the role of letters and the arts in a philosophy of culture in relation to what he termed a 'modern humanism'. Taking the thesis of 'rationality-irrationality' as his starting-point, Schütze considered three figures: the German historian and hermeneutic philiosopher, Wilhelm Dilthey (1833–1911); the Swiss psychoanalyst, C. G. Jung (1875–1961); and Ludwig Klages. In the case of Dilthey, this rational–irrational dualism becomes extended to the dualism of *Erlebnis* (i.e. experience) and *Dichtung* (i.e. poetry), or to the

xiv *Preface*

event of an actual experience and the poetic expression of it; in the case of Jung, a psychology of the unconscious turns into 'a mystical doctrine – [...] almost a religion' – of the unconscious, centred around 'the "Urvision" or absolutely primary, unanalyzable, indefinable vision of an ultimate reality', serving as a 'real symbol' in which 'the limitation of temporal, individual consciousness finds a 'needed compensation'; and in the case of Klages?[14] Schütze describes the doctrine founded by Klages, and subsequently adopted by Ernst Bertram (1884–1957) and by Hans Prinzhorn, as the doctrine of 'Bios-Eros-Soul' as the antagonist of 'Logos-Reason (*Geist*)', and he went on to argue:

> This is a deliberately irrationalistic, biological-mystical doctrine which has appropriated many of Nietzsche's antirationalistic theories. It rests on the old dialectic antithesis of reason and feeling (logos and soul) and of spontaneity and mechanism, and is therefore, after all, in spite of its strange terminology, only another variant of minus-rationalism.[15]

As an example of how Klages's ideas might work in literary-critical practice, Schütze cited the analysis of Schiller's poetry and philosophy offered by one of Klages's followers, Werner Deubel (1894–1949), in an article first published in the *Goethe-Jahrbuch* in 1934.[16] On Deubel's account of Schiller's famous poem, 'Ode to Joy' (as summarized by Schütze), 'enthusiasm becomes "orgiasm"; "joy[,] ecstasy", and the expansive vision of a rapturous Olympian fervor is sensationalized into a Dionysian fury'.

Yet if the reception of Klages in the fields of psychology and literary criticism in the English-speaking world was limited, his influence in the world of German-speaking psychology was much greater. Some of these psychologists who found themselves, to a greater or less extent, in agreement with Klages were discussed by Frederic Wertham (1895–1981), the German-born American psychiatrist (and critic of mass media), in one of a series of articles published in 1930 on 'Progress in Psychiatry' in *Archives of Neurology and Psychiatry*.[17] (The other articles in the series examined 'industrial psychiatry', the 'active work therapy' of Hermann Simon [1867–1947], experimental type psychology, and eidetic phenomena and psychopathology; the entire series provides a useful insight into vanished traditions of research in the field of psychology in the early twentieth century.) Wertham noted that, 'in recent years', the psychology of Klages had 'exerted an apparent increasing influence on German psychiatry', and he cited the work of the German neurologist and psychiatrist Ferdinand Adalbert Kehrer (1883–1966), *The Predisposition to Psychological Disturbances* (*Die Veranlagung zu seelischen Störungen*) (1924), co-written with the psychiatrist Ernst Kretschmer (1888–1964), as an example of how Klages's outline of the personality could be made 'the basis of the study of major and minor personality disorders'.

Other thinkers who, on Wertham's account, had taken on board Klages's ideas to a lesser degree included the German-Jewish psychiatrist, Arthur Kronfeld (1886–1941); the psychiatrist and psychotherapist, Johannes Heinrich

Schultz (1884–1970) (the founder of a system for self-hypnosis called autogenic training); the psychiatrist, Kurt Schneider (1887–1967) (known for his work on schizophrenia and on personality disorders), who accepted Klages's distinction and characterization of the three zones of the personality or the character; the German psychiatrist and neurologist, Hermann Hoffmann (1891–1944) (known for his work – now controversial – on genetic biology), who drew on Klages in his study of the problems of character formation (*Das Problem des Charakteraufbaus*, 1926); the psychiatrist and neurologist, Gottfried Ewald (1888–1963), whose *Temperament and Character* (1924) had been influenced by Klages's discussion of temperament; the psychiatrist, neurologist, and researcher into *Kriminalbiologie*, Johannes Lange (1891–1938), who used Klages's scheme of personality traits to diagnose paranoid psychoses; the paediatric psychologist, August Homburger (1873–1930), and the child psychologist, Else Voigtländer (b. 1882), who applied this scheme to children with behaviour disorders; and the German psychologist and psychiatrist, Eugen Kahn (1887–1973), who drew on Klages's understanding of hysteria as a condition characterized by a diminished capacity for expression accompanied with a strong impulse to expression.

Indeed, in his *General Psychopathology* ([1]1913; [2]1919; [3]1922; [4]1942; [7]1959), the German-Swiss psychiatrist and philosopher, Karl Jaspers (1883–1969), paid tribute to Klages for having made 'the most effective attempt to bring some order into personality-structure'; Klages's study of personality, Jaspers believed, 'outstrips all previous efforts'.[18] And as far as the historical study of symbols is concerned, Jaspers compared Klages to Jung in this respect:

> Nowadays it is Klages and Jung who have become known as the interpreters of symbols. What Burckhardt termed 'archaic images' ('urtümliche Bilder'), Klages termed 'images' and Jung 'archetypes'. But there are certain essential differences between Klages and Jung. Klages's interpretation has a fascinating vividness. His presentation of the symbols of poetry and art remains as perhaps the really lasting contribution in all his great work, in which he brings forward rather doubtful evidence for the development of a strange, precritical philosophy through a synthesis of rationalism and gnosticism.

In fact, Jaspers goes so far as to regard Klages's work on symbolism as superior to Jung's –

> Jung on the contrary lacks the impressive vividness of Klages and his work has nothing like the same weight. He is the deft master of all the means of interpretation but the inspiration is missing. Klages has inspiration, in as much as he is the true successor of Bachofen, whose work he rediscovered. Jung's expositions become tiring and irritating because of the many undialectical contradictions. As the reader emerges from many of Klages's pages, he is struck by a winged quality which is lacking from the work of Jung who favours a worldly scepticism.

xvi *Preface*

– even if Jaspers ultimately remained unconvinced by both men's efforts:

> The present day is poor in symbols and both these men are anxious to discover primary reality. Jung's efforts strike me as a fruitless new start through the exploitation of what is old, while Klages's attempt, as he appears to have felt himself, seems a rather hopeless recollection of the lost depths of history.[19]

This positive view of Klages's contribution, at least on a theoretical level, was matched on the therapeutic level by the German psychiatrist and art historian, Hans Prinzhorn (1886–1833), who turned Klages's teaching into the basis for a presentation of psychotherapy in his book, *Psychotherapy: Presuppositions, Essence, Limits* (*Psychotherapie: Voraussetzungen, Wesen, Grenzen*) (1929), and his article entitled 'The Founding of a Pure Characterology by Ludwig Klages' (1927).[20] For the German psychiatrist Martin Reichardt (1874–1966), the director of Würzburg Mental Hospital who conducted research into the importance of the brain stem for psychiatry, the distinctions made by Klages between instincts, strivings, and volitional tendencies offered an important basis for understanding somatopsychic (i.e. mental-physiological) relations.[21] And when Albrecht Langelüddeke (1889–1977), a pioneer of forensic psychiatry, wrote his groundbreaking article on rhythmic expression in both healthy and mentally diseased patients, he made use in part of Klages's theory of expression.[22]

Klages played a role, in other words, in the history of clinical research; its exact extent is undetermined, a study of the reception of Klages's ideas in the fields of psychology and psychiatry being a major desideratum of Klagesian research. And his wider contribution to the history of ideas was still being recognized towards the end of his life. According to the German philosophical anthropologist, Erich Rothacker (1888–1965), writing in the *Frankfurter Allgemeine Zeitung* in 1954, '*The Spirit as Adversary of the Soul* by Ludwig Klages ranks with Heidegger's *Being and Time* and Hartmann's *The Foundation of Ontology* as one of the three greatest philosophical achievements of the modern epoch',[23] thus placing Klages in the same philosophical league as the German existential phenomenologist, Martin Heidegger (1889–1976), who is still very famous, and the Baltic German existentialist philosopher, Nicolai Hartmann (1882–1950), who is in the meantime considerably less so, arguably being even more forgotten than Klages himself.

In 1956, shortly after Klages's death, the German philosopher and member of the Frankfurt School, Jürgen Habermas (b. 1929), published an obituary in the *Frankfurter Allgemeine Zeitung* with the title, 'Ludwig Klages – outdated or untimely?', expressed admiration for the way in which Klages had tapped into 'the foreign experiences of that underground German philosophy, which flowed over Jakob Böhme, the Swabian Pietists, and Romanticism into the worldview conditions of the Historical School'. And Habermas noted that he himself had, thanks to his philosophical teacher, Erich Rothacker, learned to see how Klages

Preface   xvii

unfolded [...] a myriad of observations that should not be obscured by the veil of an anti-intellectual metaphysics and an apocalyptic philosophy of history: above all, anthropological and speech-philosophical observations that are perhaps untimely, but then in Nietzsche's sense – not superseded, but rather need to be realized [*einzuholen*].[24]

There was civic recognition of his services to some extent as well. In 1932, Klages was awarded the Goethe Medal for Art and Science; in his lifetime, he was the recipient of not just one *Festschrift*, but two, on the occasion of his sixtieth and seventy-fifth birthdays in 1932 and 1947 respectively; and in 1952, he was sent congratulations on his eightieth birthday by the German Bundespräsident, Theodor Heuss. In this year, the German weekly paper *Die Zeit* devoted an article to his life and work, picking up on a passage where Klages once described himself as 'the most plundered author of the present age'.[25] Nevertheless, perhaps the greatest honour bestowed on him was the formal edict placed on his biocentric approach by the National Socialist German Workers' Party – i.e. the Nazis.

Yet it is clear that, in the meantime, something strange has happened to Ludwig Klages. For he has disappeared. Even though his work was hailed by numerous contemporary thinkers as a landmark in twentieth-century thought; even though he earned the highest of praise, not just from such philosophers as Karl Löwith and Max Scheler, but from such literary figures as Hermann Hesse and Alfred Kubin; and even though his main work, *The Spirit as Adversary of the Soul*, was ranked alongside Heidegger's *Being and Time* and Nicolai Hartmann's *The Foundation of Ontology* as 'one of the three greatest philosophical achievements of our time', Klages has completely disappeared from cultural scene in general and the philosophical scene in particular.

Yet even Erich Rothacker's statement manages, in its way, to say it all. For, after all, who today remembers Nicolai Hartmann and his work, *The Foundation of Ontology*? And Heidegger, while advancing to a remarkable prominence, thanks not least to the analysis of his work by the French postmodernist Jacques Derrida (1930–2004), has become tainted with a sulphurous reputation in some quarters, thanks to Heidegger's membership of the NSDAP (National Socialist German Workers' Party). And the recent publication of Heidegger's *Black Books* (*Schwarze Hefte*) has only damaged his reputation further. Indeed, Klages – if he is mentioned at all – is usually only ever named in order to be swiftly dismissed for his alleged right-wing (and, more specifically, anti-Semitic) views. For instance, in July 2006 an article published in the UK left-of-centre political magazine, *New Statesman*, described Klages as a 'German ideologue' and an 'anti-Semitic crank',[26] and in 2008 an article in the popular US conservative new magazine, *National Review*, referred to him as a 'proto-Nazi philosopher (and rabid anti-Semite)'.[27] In an article published in the *Frankfurter Allgemeine Zeitung* on 1 August 2012, Alexander Grau rehearsed an argument presented in a recent journal article on Thomas Mann's novel *Joseph and His Brothers* to the effect that the figure of Joseph embodied a literary protest against Klages's claim

xviii *Preface*

that 'Christianity was the cause of modern logocentrism and intellectualism', dismissing Klages as a proponent of '*irrationalistische Geistfeindlichkeit*'.[28] And on 5 September 2016 Berthold Neff gleefully reported in the *Süddeutsche Zeitung* of how efforts had been frustrated to place a commemorative plaque on Leopoldstraße 53, where Klages – 'an ardent anti-Semite' – had lived in Munich.[29]

Within the academy, the rush to condemnation is equally in evidence. Such is the case with the British Germanist, Ritchie Robertson, for example, who in a review of a biography of Stefan George describes Klages as belonging to the 'weirdest cultists' who believed that 'the irrational forces of the blood should conquer the arid intellectuality of the spirit'.[30] Then again, in his study of the reception of Bachofen, another UK-based Germanist, Peter Davies, claims that Klages's system 'provides an intellectual justification for anti-Semitism'.[31] Most recently, and in more detail than previous critics, the US intellectual historian Nitzan Lebovic has presented the case for viewing Klages as an 'anti-Semite' and as the promoter of a 'Nazi biopolitics'.[32]

Of course, none of this is new. Such critics are doing no more than repeating the line of attack opened up earlier by such Marxist critics of Klages as Ernst Bloch (1885–1977) and Georg Lukács (1855–1928), both of whom unhesitatingly assigned to Klages a position on the extreme of the political Right. That said, the sheer contempt of Bloch's attack – his dismissal, along with C. G. Jung as 'the fascistically frothing psychoanalyst' and the 'imperialist' Alfred Adler, of such 'sentimental penis poets' as D. H. Lawrence and such 'complete Tarzan philosophers' as Ludwig Klages – might signal that a certain caution is required before aligning oneself with his views; after all, is it really the case that 'there is nothing new in the Freudian unconcious'?[33] And the huge bulk of Lukács's *The Destruction of Reason* suggests that almost anyone could be read as paving the way to Fascism. Even Klages is by no means singled out for special discussion in a separate chapter, but considered – along with the novelist, Ernst Jünger (1895–1998); the philosopher and pedagogue, Alfred Baeumler (1887–1968); the philosopher, Franz Josef Boehm (1903–1946); the writer and pedagogue, Ernst Krieck (1882–1947); and the National Socialist ideologue, Alfred Rosenberg (1892–1946) – as an exponent of 'pre-Fascist and Fascist vitalism'.[34] Yet the Left could also be more nuanced in its approach to Klages: in *Eclipse of Reason* (1947), for instance, Max Horkheimer (1895–1973) provides a detailed critique of pragmatism, and only touches on reactionary cultural convervatism, on the revival of pagan mythology in Germany, and on *Lebensphilosophie* as sources of that 'eclipse'.[35]

It has certainly not helped that some of Klages's friends come from an end of the political spectrum with which I, for one, have no sympathy. Such is the case with the website 'The Biocentric Metaphysics of Ludwig Klages', containing translations of Klages by Joe Pryce, on a website that promotes the work of the extreme conservative American professor, Revilo P. Oliver (1908–1994); or with the selections of Klages's texts, again translated by Pryce, that have been published by the Arktos publishing-house in London.[36] (Presumably named after Arktos, a centaur who fought against the spearmen of the Lapith tribe, this

Preface xix

publishing-house describes itself as aiming to be the principal publisher in English of the writings of the European 'New Right' school of political thought, whose exponents include Alain de Benoist, Guillaume Faye, and Pierre Krebs; at the same time, its catalogue includes works by such Traditionalist thinkers as René Guénon, Julius Evola, and Frithjof Schuon.) And when the original German text of Klages's main work, *The Spirit as Adversary of the Soul* (*Der Geist als Widersacher der Seele*), is made available on the website of the right-wing 'cultural association', Thule Italia, at www.thulia-italia.net, I can understand why people become suspicious. Why should one waste one's time on a thinker associated with occultism, Nazi-ism, or any number of combinations of both?

So Klages is, it seems, a thinker whom it would be safer for one to avoid (and, in terms of career development in modern academia, one would be doubtless wise to do so!). He seems to be a thinker whom one should read, if at all, wearing protective gloves – or reading with one hand, while the other is used to hold one's nose. One gets the impression that he is a thinker who is, in the phrase used by Lady Caroline Lamb to describe Lord Byron, 'mad, bad, and dangerous to know'. It's an open-and-shut-case: never mind 'forget Foucault' (as Baudrillard combatively titled his study of the French sociologist), 'forget Klages'! Or is it really so open-and-shut? And should we really forget him?

In this short introductory study, the first of its kind in English, I shall try and present an alternative view to the prevailing consensus that Klages has nothing to say to us. I shall do so, because I believe that Klages is *not* a fundamentally anti-Semitic thinker, *not* a right-wing philosopher, and *not* a Nazi. This is not to say I agree with everything that Klages wrote, said, or thought; it does not mean I subscribe to every one (or even most) of his philosophical tenets; and it does not mean that I may not be entirely wrong about Klages's outlook, its significance, and its implications. But it strikes me as, in a way, a kind of confirmation of the validity of some of Klages's central arguments that today he is either attacked or ignored; after all, as Lance-Corporal Jack Jones so often observed in the BBC comedy series *Dad's Army*, 'They don't like it up 'em', and one would expect any system to try and neutralize its critics by ignoring, vilifying, or otherwise seeking to dispose of them.

Against the consensus view of Klages stands the challenge of his actual writings. Collected in nine large volumes, they represent an act of defiance to anyone who seeks to dismiss his contribution to philosophy. And there is a substantial body of commentary on Klages's works, from a large variety of scholars, as well as the ongoing work of the Ludwig-Klages-Gesellschaft e.V., a society whose mission is to promote, not Klages's work *tout court*, but informed discussion of it. The Gesellschaft's journal, entitled *Hestia* (after the goddess of the hearth, and a figure dear to Klages's thinking), consists of academic articles that try to explicate and explore his rich and – to be fair – difficult philosophical prose. Over the years I have profited a good deal from the lively discussion at the LKG's bi-annual conferences, and from the welcome it has extended to new members interested in Klages.

xx *Preface*

In particular, as seasoned readers of Klages will be aware, I am indebted in this presentation of his life and thought to two earlier accounts: first, the catalogue of the exhibition on Klages held in the Deutsches Literaturarchiv, Marbach am Neckar, in 1972 on the occasion of the centenary of his birth, prepared by Hans Eggert Schröder (1905–1985). In its turn, this account draws extensively on Schröder's multi-volume biography of Klages, using materials from the Klages *Nachlass* in Marbach, and which will remain the standard work in the field – until, that is, the publication of the new biography currently being prepared by Heinz-Siegfried Strelow.[37] Second, I have been greatly helped by the account of Klages's thought given by Robert Josef Kozljanič in his introduction to the history of vitalist thought, itself an immensely helpful guide to this suppressed (or, at any rate, forgotten) tradition in Western thought.[38] To this extent, I should like to see this short study of Klages as, in its way, a contribution to the kind of project of recuperation that, on a much larger scale, Michel Onfray has been undertaking over recent years in France to write a 'counter-history' of philosophy.

In addition, I am grateful for two further sources: first, the extremely useful selection of passages from Klages's collected works, edited by one of his closest followers, Hans Kern (1902–1847), and published with extensive additions by another Klagesian, Hans Kasdorff (1908–1993, under the title *On the Sense of Life: Words of Wisdom from the Collected Works.*[39] And second, the fascinating collection of anecdotes about Klages, compiled from first-hand accounts, edited by Hans Eggert Schröder together with Annelise Krantz-Gross under the title *The Image that Falls into the Senses: Memories of Ludwig Klages.*[40]

This book describes itself as a toolkit,[41] and it is one in two senses: first, because it provides us with the conceptual tools required to understand Ludwig Klages's *Lebensphilosophie* or philosophy of life; and second, because those concepts in turn can be used to construct a life based on vitalist principles. As a toolkit, it consists of three chapters: each part can be read independently from the others, and they can be read in any order. But it is recommended to read them in order they are presented:

- Chapter 1 – offers an overview of the life of Ludwig Klages and his intellectual trajectory;
- Chapter 2 – considers some of the fundamental concepts of Klagesian philosophy;
- Chapter 3 – offers a selection of more advanced passages, illustrating the breadth and depth of Klages's thought.

Klages's writings are notoriously difficult to translate, for reasons that have long been recognized. In part, this is because Klages creates a good number of new psychological terms and, in part, because he sometimes uses words in a specific technical sense, whose meaning is not always obvious.[42] (And maybe they are difficult for reasons that have not been so readily recognized). Wherein lies the

Preface xxi

difficulty of translating Klages from German to English? First, there is his grammatical and syntactical complexity: put simply, Klages belongs to another epoch in terms of his grammatical sophistication, and on some places even the so-called native speaker has difficulty in following the sense of a sentence. To this extent, Klages is a child of another age, albeit one who has mastered the German language to an extraordinarily high degree. Second, this difficulty is in part deliberate: much as such members of the Frankfurt School as Theodor W. Adorno cultivate an obscure, hieratic style in order to force the reader to slow down and think carefully, Klages is trying to encourage us to see the world and ourselves in an entirely new light – the light of his central thesis about the antagonistic relationship between spirit (*Geist*) and soul (*Seele*). Third, and as a result, the grammatical and syntactical difficulties evinced by his language embody precisely this antagonistic relation, representing in linguistic and rhetorical form the metaphysical conflict of spirit and soul.

At the same time, there are passages which reveal Klages as a great essayist and stylist, and it is these qualities which the longer passages selected for study in Chapter 3 are intended to exemplify. For instance, Klages invents some remarkably striking images to convey his ideas, such as a master or signature image of body and soul as

> *poles* of the life-cell which belong inseparably together, into which from *outside* the spirit, like a wedge, inserts itself, in the endeavour to split them apart, to 'de-soul' the body, to disembody the soul, and in this way finally to kill all the life it can reach
>
> (*GWS=SW* 1, 7)

– the concluding scenario of his survey of the 'prehistory of the discovery of the images' where he describes how, in the 1890s, the final vitalist wave of this epoch has faded away and left with a (post)modernity summed up as follows: 'The earth gives off smoke as never before from the blood of the slain, and all that is apelike struts with the spoils plundered from the shattered temple of life' (*GWS=SW* 2, 923); or for that matter the apocalyptic landscapes infused with fantasies of death and destruction that one finds in some of his early prose or poetic sketches, such as the fragment which offers the following vision of 'The End of the World':

> He had traversed the fields of night and was approaching the coast of destruction. Feebly across suspicious distances there flickered the bluish signals which surround the restless realm of the living. In front of him, however, from mists wavered immeasurably uncertain expanses, which massed together in the distance into dreadful darkenings. [...] And suddenly the shivers of ultimate solitude came over him. [...] Thus broke in him the part of being human that no-one can preserve across the threshold of silence: the power to wish and to hope. [...] And now the darkness began to brighten: a terrible, unpleasant greyness, and the naked skeletons of trees

Figure 2 Klages in Kilchberg.

Preface xxiii

that towered as high as the stars shot up out of it. [...] And the forest opened up and he was standing on the shores where existence ends. [...] And, first gently, and then increasingly audibly, rose from the unfathomably monstrous night a hoarse roaring noise: And now he knew: that is beyond the furthest cliff, and all the beings that life was able to bind: there the fall crushes them. But only for heroes or gods was this death destined; for no-one else would be able to bear the closeness of that noise that already rose up with a deafening rattle and called out resoundingly into a timeless darkness.

(*RR*, 233–234)

Yet the passages found in Chapter 3, the choice of which has been largely, but not exclusively, guided by that made by Hans Kern and Hans Kasdorff, have not been selected simply for aesthetic reasons, but are included out of the conviction that, whatever the hindrances – conceptual, cultural, historical, or ideological – to understanding his thought, Klages nevertheless has so much to say to us today. Or as the German sculptor, Wilhelm Hager (1921–2006), wrote in his tribute to Klages:

Whoever immerses oneself with dedication to the doctrine of the 'reality of images' will be transformed in every respect: one's spiritual existence undergoes something like a complete 180 degree turn. One's views and perspectives are suddenly changed, so that one believes one is looking at the face of a newly created world.

(*CAK*, 191)

Notes

1 *Hopscotch: A novel*, tr. G. Rabassa, New York: Pantheon, 1966, p. 445.
2 H. Hesse, 'Über die heutige deutsche Literatur' (1924), excerpted in *CAK*, p. 78.
3 K. Löwith, 'Nietzsche im Lichte der Philosophie von Ludwig Klages', in *Reichls philosophischer Almanach*, vol. 4, *Probleme der Weltanschauungslehre*, ed. E. Rothacker, Darmstadt: Reichl, 1927, pp. 285–348 (p. 293).
4 M. Scheler, *The Human Place in the Cosmos*, tr. Manfred S. Frings, Evanston, IL: Northwestern University Press, 2009, p. 60. For discussion of the contrasting approaches of Klages and Scheler to the concept of the spirit, see K.-A. Sprengard, 'Geist – Widersachervorwurf und Geistvertrauen in Lebensphilosophie und Neuer Anthropologie: Gedanken zu Ludwig Klages' Misstrauen und Max Schelers Zutrauen', in K. Broese, A. Hütig, O. Immel, and R. Reschke (eds), *Vernunft der Aufklärung – Aufklärung der Vernunft*, Berlin: Akademie Verlag, 2006, pp. 305–317.
5 W. Benjamin, *The Correspondence of Walter Benjamin*, ed. G. Scholem and T. W. Adorno, tr. M. R. Jacobson and E. M. Jacobson, Chicago and London: University of Chicago Press, 1994, p. 366. For further discussion of Benjamin's interest in Klages, see J. McCole, *Walter Benjamin and the Antinomies of Tradition*, Ithaca and London: Cornell University Press, 1993, pp. 234–240; R. Block, 'Selective Affinities: Walter Benjamin and Ludwig Klages', *Arcadia* 35, 2000, 117–136; W. Fuld, 'Die Aura: Zur Geschichte eines Begriffes bei Benjamin', *Akzente* 26, 1979, 352–370; W. Fuld, 'Walter Benjamins Beziehung zu Ludwig Klages', *Akzente* 28, 1981, 274–287; and M. Großheim, 'Archaisches oder dialektisches Bild? Zum Kontext einer Debatte zwischen Adorno and Benjamin', *Deutsches Vierteljahrsschrift für Literaturwissenschaft und*

xxiv *Preface*

Geistesgeschichte 71, 1997, 494–517; as well as M. Pauen, *Dithyrambiker des Untergangs: Gnostizismus in Ästhetik und Philosophie der Moderne*, Berlin: Akademie Verlag, 1993, pp. 139 and 187–189 (on Benjamin), pp. 139–140 and 189–190 (on Adorno).

6 O. Spengler, *Briefe 1913–1916*, ed. A. M. Koltanek and M. Schröter, Munich: Beck, 1963, p. 605. For further discussion, see M. Pauen, 'Affinität und Antagonismus: Zum Verhältnis von Ludwig Klages und Oswald Spengler', *Hestia: Jahrbuch der Klages-Gesellschaft* 19, 1998/1999, 192–209.

7 Compare with Spengler's letter of 3 October 1927 to Elisabeth Förster-Nietzsche:

> What you write about Klages coincides entirely with my opinion. He is basically a real professor and wishes to reduce Nietzsche to a level from which he can represent him as his own predecessor. Lastly it is a misunderstanding of Nietzsche's work, if one sees nothing in it except a system of psychology.
> (O. Spengler, *Spengler Letters 1913–1936*, tr. A. Helps,
> London: Allen & Unwin, 1966, p. 223)

8 A. Kubin, *Dämonen und Nachtgesichte*, Dresden: Reissner, 1926; in *CAK*, p. 82. For further discussion, see P. Bishop, '"Mir war der 'Geist' immer eine 'explodierte Elephantiasis'": Der Briefwechsel zwischen Alfred Kubin und Ludwig Klages', *Jahrbuch der Deutschen Schillergesellschaft* 43, 1999, 49–98.

9 E. Pound, *The Cantos*, London: Faber & Faber, 1986, Canto LXXV, p. 450.

10 C. F. Terrell, *A Companion to 'The Cantos' of Ezra Pound*, Berkeley, Los Angeles, London: University of California Press, 1983, pp. 388–389.

11 W. J. H. Sprott, [Review of] '*The Science of Character*. By Ludwig Klages. Translated by W. H. Johnston. [...]', *Mind* [NS] 38, no. 152, October 1929, 513–520 (p. 513).

12 G. W. Allport, [Review of] 'Klages, Ludwig. *The Science of Character*. Translated by W. H. Johnston. [...]', *Psychological Bulletin* 30, no. 5, May 1933, 370–371 (p. 370).

13 Allport, [Review of] 'Klages, Ludwig. *The Science of Character*', p. 371.

14 M. Schütze, 'Toward a Modern Humanism', *Publications of the Modern Language Association* 51, no. 1, March 1936, 284–299 (p. 286).

15 Schütze, 'Toward a Modern Humanism', p. 287.

16 W. Deubel, 'Umrisse eines neuen Schillerbildes', *Jahrbuch der Goethe-Gesellschaft* 20, 1934, 1–64; reprinted in W. Deubel, *Im Kampf um die Seele: Wider den Geist der Zeit: Essays und Aufsätze, Aphorismen und Gedichte*, ed. F. Deubel, Bonn: Bouvier, 1997, pp. 163–198. For further discussion, see P. Bishop, 'The "Schillerbild" of Werner Deubel: Schiller as "Poet of the Nation"?', in N. Martin (ed.), *Schiller: National Poet – Poet of Nations: A Birmingham Symposium*, Amsterdam and New York: Rodopi, 2006, pp. 301–320.

17 F. Wertham, 'Progress in Psychiatry III: The Significance of Klages' System for Psychopathology', *Archives of Neurology and Psychiatry* 24, no. 2, 1930, 381–388 (p. 383).

18 K. Jaspers, *General Psychopathology*, tr. J. Hoenig and M. W. Hamilton, Manchester: Manchester University Press, 1963, p. 436.

19 Jaspers, *General Psychopathology*, p. 334.

20 H. Prinzhorn, 'Die Begründung einer reinen Charakterologie durch Ludwig Klages', *Jahrbuch der Charakterologie* 4, 1927, 115–132.

21 M. Reichardt, 'Brain and Psyche', tr. F. I. Wertham, *Journal of Nervous and Mental Disease* 203, no. 10, October 2015, 390–396.

22 A. Langelüddeke, 'Rhythmus und Takt bei Gesunden und Geisteskranken', *Zeitschrift für die gesamte Neurologie und Psychiatrie* 113, no. 1, December 1928, 1–101.

23 E. Rothacker, 'Ludwig Klages neu gesehen', *Frankfurter Allgemeine Zeitung*, 7 August 1954.

24 J. Habermas, 'Ludwig Klages – überholt oder zeitgemäß?', in *Frankfurter Allgemeine Zeitung*, 3 August 1956, p. 8; translated in A. D. Moses, *German Intellectuals and the Nazi Past*, Cambridge: Cambridge University Press, 2007, p. 117.

Preface xxv

25 R. Ibel, 'Der meistgeplünderte Autor des Gegenwart: Zum 80. Geburtstag des Kultur-philosophen Ludwig Klages', *Die Zeit*, 11 December 1952.

26 E. Skidelsky, 'The Ideas Corner: A Less than Perfect World', *New Statesman*, 31 July 2006. Compare with his comments on Klages in *Ernst Cassirer: The Last Philosopher of Culture*, Princeton and Oxford: Princeton University Press, 2008, pp. 174–180. Yet, as Skidelsky notes, 'Cassirer was not […] entirely hostile to Klages's *Kulturkritik*' (p. 180).

27 J. Goldberg, 'A Half Century's Slander: It Isn't Conservatives Who Must Answer for Fascism', *National Review*, 28 January 2008.

28 A. Grau, 'Auf humoristische Weise mystisch sein', *Frankfurter Allgemeine Zeitung*, 1 August 2012, N3; cf. J. Rohls, 'Die Theologie von Thomas Manns "Joseph und seine Brüder"', *Zeitschrift für Neuere Theologiegeschichte* 19, no. 1, 2012, 72–103.

29 B. Neff, 'Einspruch', *Süddeutsche Zeitung*, 5 September 1916.

30 R. N. Robertson, 'Maximin and the Master', *Times Literary Supplement*, 18 April 2008.

31 P. Davies, *Myth, Matriarchy and Modernity: Johann Jakob Bachofen in German Culture 1860–1945*, Berlin and New York: de Gruyter, 2010, p. 288.

32 N. Lebovic, *The Philosophy of Life and Death: Ludwig Klages and the Rise of a Nazi Biopolitics*, New York: Palgrave Macmillan, 2013. For a review of this title, see P. Bishop, 'Fashionable Ideas', *Times Literary Supplement*, 5 November 2014.

33 E. Bloch, *The Principle of Hope*, tr. N. Plaice, S. Plaice, and P. Knight, Oxford: Basil Blackwell, 1986, pp. 59, 61, 72.

34 G. Lukács, *The Destruction of Reason* [1962], tr. P. Palmer, Atlantic Highlands, NJ: Humanities Press, 1980, pp. 522–539.

35 M. Horkheimer, *Eclipse of Reason* [1947], New York: Oxford University Press, 1947, pp. 41–53 (pragmatism), pp. 54, 56, 164 (cultural conservatism), p. 65 (pagan revival), and pp. 171–172 (*Lebensphilosophie*). Nor are his examples of the domina-tion of nature – his critique of the ego, and the modern habit of thinking of the moon 'in terms of ballistics or aerial mileage' – far removed from Klages's own critique of modernity, *Eclipse of Reason*, pp. 92–127 (domination of nature), pp. 105–106 (critique of the ego), pp. 101–102 (the moon). For further discussion, see Vincenzo Martella, *Dialetics of Cultural Criticism: Adorno's Confrontation with Rudolf Borchardt and Ludwig Klages in the 'Odyssey' chapter of 'Dialektik der Aufklärung'*, inaugural dissertation, Justus-Liebig-Universität Gießen, 2012. I am grateful to Christian Kerslake for this reference.

36 L. Klages, *The Biocentric Worldview: Selected Essays and Poems*, tr. J. D. Pryce, London: Arktos, 2013; and *Cosmogonic Reflections: Selected Aphorisms*, tr. J. D. Pryce, London: Arktos, 2015. I have reviewed these two volumes in the following journals: 'The Woods are Alive', *Times Literary Supplement*, 18 October 2013 (review of *The Biocentric Worldview*); and *Journal of European Studies* 46, no. 1, 26, 83–84.

37 Klages' autobiographical notes, which amount to some 120 manuscript pages of hitherto unpublished material, are currently being edited by Heinz-Siegfried Strelow under the provisional title *Ludwig Klages – die Autobiographie*, together with a critical com-mentary by Strelow.

38 R. J. Kozljanič, *Lebensphilosophie: Eine Einführung*, Stuttgart: Kohlhammer, 2004, pp. 149–196.

39 L. Klages, *Vom Sinn des Lebens: Worte des Wissens aus dem Gesamtwerk*, ed. H. Kern, rev. H. Kasdorff, Bonn: Bouvier; Grundmann, 1982.

40 H.-E. Schröder and A. Krantz-Gross, *Das Bild, das in die Sinne fällt: Erinnerungen an Ludwig Klages*, Bonn: Bouvier; Grundmann, 1986.

41 For the notion of a toolkit in this context, I am indebted to David Bodanis, who gave a lecture course authorized by the Social Studies Faculty Board in Hilary Term 1992 entitled 'An Intellectual Tool-kit: Concepts in Social Thought'.

42 Wertham, 'The Significance of Klages' System for Psychopathology', p. 383.

Acknowledgements

In the words of Goethe (as translated by Walter Arndt), 'He who still grows will ever render thanks' (*Ein werdender wird immer dankbar sein*) (*Faust I*, l. 183). In the years leading up to the preparation of this toolkit on Ludwig Klages, I have accumulated a number of debts of gratitude, which I should like here to mention.

It is now some fifteen or so years since I was invited to participate in the annual conference of the Klages-Gesellschaft, held in the Seidlvilla, in München-Schwabing, in June 2003. The invitation followed an article I had published in *Oxford German Studies*, examining Klages's early reception of Nietzsche, and I soon discovered that there was a relation of inverse proportion between the number of delegates at the conference – or, perhaps better, symposium – and the depth and seriousness of the papers given. The topics ranged from genetic research and ancient experiences of ecstasy to myth and tragedy; gothic, baroque, and rococo art; the pathos of religious Protestantism; and a comparison between vitalist and evolutionary concepts of nature in relation to rhythm.

So the greatest debt I owe is to the members (present and former) of the Klages-Gesellschaft, many of whom have offered personal friendship or professional support over the years (even if not all of them are still members of the society): Michael Großheim, Olivier Hanse, Hans-Ulrich Kopp, Thomas Rolf, Heinz-Siegfried Strelow, and in particular I would like to thank Robert Josef Kozljanič, for whose *Jahrbuch für Lebensphilosophie* it has been a pleasure and an honour to write contributions, and above all Catrina Trippel, whose time-consuming work as the secretary of the Klages-Gesellschaft and personal support are extremely valuable.

I first came across the figure of Ludwig Klages in the context of my research into Nietzsche and C. G. Jung, a doctorate at the University of Oxford supervised by Richard Sheppard. Following an attempt to win a Junior Research Fellowship on the strength of my interest in Klages, where the examining committee for the post plainly had no idea who Klages actually was, Richard told me (and I remember the phrase) that 'no one realizes how important Klages really is'; over the following years of searching for funding into Klages, how right those words would prove to be! For the original encouragement and inspiration to continue work on a figure whose importance few seemed to realize, I remain grateful. During my time at Glasgow, I benefited from numerous conversations

Acknowledgements xxvii

with my predecessor as the William Jacks Chair of Modern Languages, Roger Stephenson, who remained unfazed by his younger colleague's enthusiasm for the problematic, even controversial, figure of Ludwig Klages; support for which I likewise remain deeply grateful.

I should like to thank the Klages-Gesellschaft for permission to cite in translated form extracts from the *Sämtliche Werke* of Ludwig Klages, the rights of which lie with the Klages-Gesellschaft and which have been published in a beautiful, eight-volume edition by Bouvier Verlag, whose current managing director, Thomas Grundmann, I should also like to thank for his interest in this project at an early stage. My colleague at the University of Sheffield, Henk de Berg, has kindly sent me secondary literature on Klages over the years, and to him, as well as to Andrew Samuels of the University of Essex and Charles Bambach of the University of Texas, I should like to express my thanks for their support for this project. And I cannot thank enough Helen Bridge for her patience when, at the dinner table, I ask her for her view on how to translate some utterly untranslatable Klagesian phrase into English. Her suggestions are always as wise as they are perceptive.

Finally, I am grateful to the reviewers of the book proposal submitted to Routledge for their enthusiasm and helpful suggestions; and, last but not least, at Routledge I should like to thank Susannah Frearson, for finding a place in the Psychology list for an introductory work on Klages.

This volume is dedicated to the memory of Dietrich Jäger, Professor of English Literature at the University of Kiel, who died in September 2010 and who had kindly invited me to participate in the conference in München-Schwabing all those years ago.

Picture credits

All photographs of Ludwig Klages © Deutsches Literaturarchiv, Marbach am Neckar.

The photographs in this book are reproduced with the kind permission of the Deutsches Literaturarchiv, Marbach am Neckar. Funding for reproduction costs was generously provided by the Ludwig-Klages-Gesellschaft e.V., Marbach am Neckar.

My thanks to Jens Tremmel and Tanja Fengler-Veit of the Deutsches Literaturarchiv and to Catrina Trippel and Heinz-Siegfried Strelow of the Ludwig-Klages-Gesellschaft.

Reproduction of Böcklin's *Im Spiel der Wellen* © bpk/Bayerische Staatsgemäldesammlungen.

Arnold Böcklin's *Im Spiel der Wellen* is reproduced with the kind permission of the dpk-Bildagentur and the Bayerische Staatsgemäldesammlungen.

Text credits

'Canto LXXV' by Ezra Pound, from *The Cantos of Ezra Pound*, copyright © 1948 by Ezra Pound. Reprinted by permission of New Directions Publishing Corp.

Abbreviations

CAK	Hans Eggert Schröder, *Ludwig Klages 1872–1956: Centenar-Ausstellung 1972*, Bonn: Bouvier Verlag Herbert Grundmann, 1972.
GWS	Ludwig Klages, *Der Geist als Widersacher der Seele*, 6th edition, Bonn: Bouvier Verlag Herbert Grundmann, 1981 = *SW*, vols 1 and 2.
ME	Ludwig Klages, *Mensch und Erde: Gesammelte Abhandlungen*, Stuttgart: Kröner, 1973.
RR	Ludwig Klages, *Rhythmen und Runen: Nachlass herausgegeben von ihm selbst*, Leipzig: Johann Ambrosius Barth, 1944.
SW	Ludwig Klages, *Sämtliche Werke*, ed. Ernst Frauchiger, Gerhard Funke, Karl J. Groffmann, Robert Heiss and Hans Eggert Schröder, 9 vols, Bonn: Bouvier, 1964–1992.
Erinnerungen	Hans Eggert Schröder and Annelise Krantz-Gross, *Das Bild, das in die Sinne fällt: Erinnerungen an Ludwig Klages*, Bonn: Bouvier Verlag Herbert Grundmann, 1986.
Sinn des Lebens	Ludwig Klages, *Vom Sinn des Lebens: Worte des Wissens aus dem Gesamtwerk*, ed. Hans Kern, rev. Hans Kasdorff, Bonn: Bouvier Verlag Herbert Grundmann, 1982.

Glossary of Klagesian terminology

In his translation of the fifth and sixth editions of Klages's *The Science of Character*, W. H. Johnston offers a translator's note in which he lists the following equivalents of German terms used in a technical sense by Klages. In this *Toolkit*, the terminology of this glossary has been used as a guide and, where appropriate, adopted.

Antrieb   impulse
Artung   nature
bindender Antrieb   bond
Erinnerung   recollection
Gedächtnis   memory
Geist   spirit
Leben- [compound nouns]   vital
lösender Antrieb   release
pathisch   pathic (note by W. H. Johnston: *pathisch* describes 'that passive disposition of the soul by which the man in whom it exists is made susceptible, while his spirit is stimulated to profound intuitions'.)
Pathiker   pathos
Pathos   pathic type
Streben, Strebung   striving
Sucht   passion
Trieb   drive
Willensakt   act of will
Wille   will
Wollen   volition
Wollung   event of willing

1 Life

Childhood and early years

Ludwig Klages was born on 10 December 1872 in Hanover, the son of a business man, Friedrich Ferdinand Louis Klages, and his wife, Marie Helene née Kolster. Although the house in which he was born, Warmbüchenstraße 23, was later pulled down, a plaque on the wall of the house that replaced it commemorates the location as the birthplace of this forgotten philosopher.[1]

Then, as now, Hanover is an important yet attractive small city, located at the crossing-point of important transport connections. Today it is the capital of the federal state of Lower Saxony, but in Klages's day it was the capital of the Prussian province of Hanover, after it had been annexed by Prussia in 1866 during the Austro-Prussian War. Although the city was a target for bombing in the Second World War, the architecture that survives (or has been rebuilt) gives one a sense of the its nineteenth-century splendour.

Klages's father had been born in a village called Gladeback, situated in the valley between the towns of Hardegsen and Göttingen. Louis Klages had been a professional soldier, but following the demobilization of the Kingdom of Hanover's army in the wake of annexation by Prussia, he became a businessman, dealing in cloth. He settled down and established a family, moving with his wife and their four-year-old son to a larger house, Hildesheimer Straße 225.

In 1878, the family grew: a sister, Helene Klages (1878–1947), was born. Throughout his childhood (and in fact throughout his life), it is said that the relationship between these two siblings was always a close one. (Certainly, Helene shared her brother's interests, and later on she became a graphologist.) Perhaps this close relationship with his sister was intensified by the loss, when Klages was just nine years old, of his mother on 19 March 1882. The cause of death is thought to have been pneumonia, and her unexpected death can only have made a deep impact on her son.

(For those of a psychoanalytic persuasion, the roots of Klages's later fascination with the figure of the *magna mater* or 'Great Mother' might be traced back to this loss. In a letter, Klages once commented that his mother had been 'more the object of a raving fantasy than a real experience'.[2]) Before she passed away,

2   *Life*

Marie asked her sister, Ida Kolster, to help look after her children, and she soon moved into the family house in the Hildesheimer Straße.

By now Klages was attending school, going to the Ratsgymnasium (or, as it was then called, the Lyceum) on the Georgsplatz in Hanover, where he received an education with a traditional emphasis on the classics and the humanities. He was a keen pupil, and one in whom a strong imaginative flair was beginning to express itself. In notebooks he recorded his first poems and prose sketches, and at the age of fourteen he developed the plan to write a tragedy. Its subject was to be Desiderata, one of the daughters of Desiderius, the King of Lombardy and the ruler of the Germanic tribe who dominated Italy from the sixth to eighth centuries. In order to form a political pact between the two states, she was married in 770 to Charlemagne, the King of the Franks, but the annullment of this marriage a year later led to the war in 774 between the Franks and the Lombards that resulted in the defeat of the Lombards at the Battle of Pavia.

Here we see one of Klages's two main interests: the history of the Germanic tribes in Europe. The other one was mythology: he developed a system for relating the various ancient Greek gods, and later the deities of Germanic mythology. These interests are likely to have been encouraged by one of his teachers, who used the classes set aside for religious instruction to educate the pupils in his charge in all manner of historical, geographical, and cultural matters. Thanks to this teacher, Klages became introduced to the work of Wilhelm Jordan (1819–1904).

Jordan is an extraordinary figure in German political and literary life in the nineteenth century. A theologian-turned-journalist who had been converted away from religion by the writings of G. W. F. Hegel (1770–1831) and Ludwig Feuerbach (1804–1872), Jordan served briefly as a member in the Frankfurt Parliament before becoming an advisor to the Reichshandelsministerium, where he was involved with building up Germany's naval fleet. But he was also active writer of poems and plays, enjoying particular fame for his version of the legend of the Nibelungs. In 1867, he published his epic poem, *The Nibelungs* (*Die Nibelungen*), written in a special kind of alliterative verse called *Stabreim*. In his version, Jordan combined the ancient sources of the Old Norse saga and the Old High German *Lay of Hildebrand* with a modern psychological interest; Klages was deeply impressed with the work. He was to write many years later:

> It can have been no more than a dozen alliterative verses that plunged the fifteen-year-old [...] into a turmoil, and I cannot decide whether it was more like a fainting fit or more like the explosive forces of a daimonic feeling of power.[3]

Klages's enthusiasm for Wilhelm Jordan was shared by his friend during his years at school, Theodor Lessing (1872–1933). Despite their many years of friendship (and a set of common interests), their amical relationship came to an end in 1899; the complicated nature of their relationship is captured well in a detailed study of it by Elke-Vera Kotowski, who calls them 'hostile Dioscuri', a pair of twins at war with each other.[4] Lessing hated the *Gymnasium*, and the shared enthusiasm with Klages for mythology, antiquity, and the world of the imagination played an important role in the intellectual development of both. So why did their friendship end? For some, the break in his relation with Lessing, a Jew, is an indication of anti-Semitic tendencies on Klages's part, but it is likely that the reasons were more complex than that. As Lessing himself once wrote, Klages was his 'most painful chapter':

> Yes, yes, yes, I admire his work immensely and yet I feel – once that was in the blood and now it's only a doctrine, and there is also a lot of human vanity mixed in. Two stars from a single sun: he became a fixed star; I remained a wandering comet.[5]

In 1891, when both came to the end of their school education, Lessing and Klages chose paths that took a similar trajectory. Lessing chose to study medicine in Freiburg im Breisgau, then Bonn, then Munich, where he changed his subjects to literature, philosophy, and psychology, completing a dissertation on the Russian-Ukrainian philosopher and logician, Afrikan Spir (1837–1890).

For his part, Klages ended up in Munich, too; but not before he had spent two semesters studying chemistry and physics in Leipzig (1891–1892) before returning to Hanover for a semester at its Technische Hochschule (1892–1893). In Munich (1893–1900), Klages completed his degree as a chemist and he went on to do research, publishing in 1901 his *Attempt at a Synthesis of Menthone*. This work was carried out in the Chemisches Institut, a laboratory founded at the Ludwig-Maximilians-Universität in Munich in 1875 by Adolf von Baeyer. (In 1905, Baeyer was awarded the Nobel Prize for his work into the synthetic production of organic dyes.) In 1893, the year that Klages joined the Institut, chemistry had moved from being a subject in the Medical Faculty to a subject in the Philosophy Faculty, and he was about to undertake a similar shift himself.

What is menthone? Naturally occurring as an organic compound, and belonging to the group of organic compounds known as ketones, mentone has applications as a cosmetic and as a perfume (but it can also be used as a pesticide). Klages's research, which was supervised by the chemist Alfred Einhorn (1856–1917), gave him a doctorate as a scientist, but his interests had long since moved away from chemistry towards a different kind of 'science' – graphology.

At this point, it is worth reflecting on Klages's career to date: the exemplary school pupil had become an empirical scientist, working in the lab amid the test-tubes and retorts. Yet he had also been a child with an intense imagination, secretly recording the poems that his parents and teachers forbade him to write. Although his career to date pointed in the direction chemistry, living in Munich had broadened his horizons – and introduced him to some rather unusual people.

Schwabing years

In 1895, Klages moved into a new flat, one owned by someone called Frau Bernhard. She had four children, three sons and a daughter, and it was with Frau

4   *Life*

Bernhard's daughter, whom Klages called 'Putti', that he began an intense sexual relationship. Yet it is not so much the fact that a tenant was sleeping with his landlady's daughter (and, it seems, with his landlady's approval) that we would today regard as the problem, but the fact that Putti was, when the relationship began, twelve years old. So can one add to the accusation that Klages was a Nazi, the charge that he was also a paedophile?

Clearly from our current standpoint, Putti was very young. Maybe it is worth noting that, in ancient Rome, it was a legal requirement that a bride be at least twelve years old, and the Catholic Church followed this age limit in the medieval period. And, as Nitzan Lebovic has pointed out, Sophie von Kühn (1782–1797) was twelve years old when the German Romantic poet, Friedrich von Hardenberg, better known as Novalis (1772–1801), began his relationship with her in 1794, and became engaged to her in 1795, before her death a year later in 1797. In his biography of Novalis, his friend Ludwig Tieck (1773–1853) described Sophie von Kühn in the following terms:

> Even children give an impression which – because it is so gracious and spiritually lovely – we must call superearthly or heavenly, while through these radiant and almost transparent countenances we are struck with the fear that it is too tender and delicately woven for life, that it is death or immortality which looks at us so penetratingly from those shining eyes, and only too often a rapid withering motion turns our fear into an actual reality.[6]

Could it be that Putti exercised a similarly fascinating attraction on Klages? Or should one simply regard him as a sexual predator? (In which case, was Novalis a sexual predator, too?)

Whatever the case, it would be entirely wrong to think that Klages was only attracted to younger women. For his years in Schwabing, the bohemian quarter in the northern part of Munich where Klages – along with other intellectuals, painters, and writers – lived, stand under the sign of the famous 'Bohemian Countess', Fanny Liane Wilhelmine Sophie Auguste Adrienne Gräfin zu Reventlow, better known simply as Franziska zu Reventlow (1871–1918). While the exact nature of the relationship between her and Klages – i.e. how far was it Platonic and how far was it erotic? – remains a matter for conjecture, her conversations with Klages and other members of the so-called Cosmic Circle (see below) informed her famous *roman à clef*, called *Herrn Dames Aufzeichnungen: oder, Begebenheiten aus einem merkwürdigen Stadtteil* (which can be translated as *The Notebooks of Mr Lady, or Occurrences in an Unusual Part of Town*), published in 1913. In these pages, her conversations with Klages are transmuted into utterances by a character called Hallwig. (This was not to be the only literary incarnation of Klages, for he was also to feature in a Modernist novel by Robert Musil (1880–1942) (see below). Reventlow's works have recently been republished, and there is renewed interest in her specific approach to feminism).[7] Reventlow satirically refers to Schwabing as *Wahnmoching*, a name that suggests more than a little eccentricity; and behind

Schwabing years 5

this caricature of Klages and the Cosmic Circle lies an important stage in Klages's intellectual development.

For during his second semester in Munich, i.e. in 1894, Klages met Hans Hinrich Busse (1871–1920), a poet, painter, and sculptor who had just opened an institute for graphology. Nowadays graphology, or the study of handwriting, is seen as something of a fringe subject (although arguably less so in Germany, where it can even be used in recruitment processes, than in the Anglo-American world). Can, one wonders, there be any legitimacy to the claim that handwriting can say anything reliable about an individual's character or personality? Surely this is a pseudoscience, to be dismissed along with astrology, phrenology (the study of the skull as a means of personality evaluation), and eugenics (the improvement of society through 'purifying' the genetic pool); or, for that matter, along with ESP (extra-sensory perception), NLP (neuro-linguistic programming), and all manner of homeopathic practices (many of which are nevertheless still in vogue in Germany today...)?

In Busse's case, the thinking behind graphology had much to do with his lack of success in the academic world (just as, in the case of Klages, it was bound up with his sense of dissatisfaction with empirical science). By founding the 'Institute for Scientific Graphology' (*Institut für wissenschaftliche Graphologie*), Busse was attempting to open a new career for himself – much to the horror of his parents, it seems, who wanted him to continue his academic studies.[8]

Now there already existed a tradition of graphology, stretching back for centuries, and the 'subject' had been revived in the nineteenth century by Jean Hippolyte Michon (1806–1881), Jules Crépieux-Jamin (1859–1940), and Alfred Binet (1857–1911). Busse sought to 'professionalize' the field, by holding courses on graphology, publishing papers, and producing analyses of handwriting (sometimes, incredible as it seems, as an expert witness in legal cases in court!). Busse was responsible for translating two major studies of Crépieux-Jamin into German, his *Practical Treatise of Graphology* (1885) and his *Handwriting and Character* (1888), and he wrote his own introductory textbook, entitled *Study of Handwriting* (*Die Handschriftenkunde*). Did Busse make a lot of money out of graphology? Apparently not, around 50 Marks a month, that barely allowed him to scratch together a living. But he pursued his graphological interests with a passion, and this is doubtless what attracted Klages to him.

Another graphologist came, like Klages, from a scientific background. Georg Meyer (1869–1917) had a training as a medical doctor, specializing in psychiatry: his major publication in this area was *The Scientific Foundations of Graphology* (*Die wissenschaftlichen Grundlagen der Graphologie*) (1901). Together with Meyer and Klages, Busse founded on 24 November 1896 – exactly twenty-five years after the publication of Michon's *System of Graphology* – a new organization called the German Graphological Society (*Deutsche Graphologische Gesellschaft*). Among its first members were, aside from Crépieux-Jamin, some prominent and up-and-coming figures of the time: the classical archaeologist, Ludwig Curtius (1874–1954); the English-born scientist and father of behavioral embryology and child psychology, Willhelm T. Preyer (1841–1897);

6 *Life*

the Czech-born writer, Robert Saudek (1880–1935) – and Nietzsche's sister, the infamous Elisabeth Förster-Nietzsche (1846–1935)....

Before turning to Klages's own publications in the field of graphology, let us pause and reflect on graphology's ambitions. Needless to say, this is not the place to debate (let alone try and defend) the tenets of graphology, but what could possibly have attracted Klages to this pseudoscientific area? Part of its attraction may be seen to lie in the kind of analysis it offered of handwriting – an analysis akin to an aesthetic one. For instance, when in 1901 Busse made a bronze sculpture of Goethe's head for the Goethe Society in Frankfurt, Klages wrote the following appreciation of a copy of it:

> Busse's mask of Goethe is trying to elaborate *this* side of Goethe's being in the most penetrating way. It wants to recapture by means of sculpture what Goethe – containing his being into a few verses – said in the primal words he described as Orphic. Here we see the *fateful fate* of the Apollonian: it is not the daimonic fatedness of the earlier world, nor is it the power of 'external circumstances' – but it is *the* necessity that emerges out of the *innermost* (beyond every conscious will) *individuality of the individual being.*[9]

In other words, what Klages saw here in Busse's sculpture of Goethe (and with reference to Goethe's late, great poem, 'Primal Words. Orphic')[10] was what graphology, or at least graphology as Klages understood it, was trying to interpret about the individual whose handwriting lay before it for analysis. So what were Klages's views on graphology itself?

Looked at today, Klages's decision to abandon chemistry and embark on a career as a graphologist looks like a return to the poetic – or at least non-scientific – mode of expression he had cultivated in his childhood. For Klages, however, it was a decision to replace one form of science (chemistry) with another (graphology). In fact, Klages never abandoned graphology as (in his view) a scientific discipline, and over the course of the next five decades he wrote several treatises, delivered numerous lectures, and gave various instructional courses on graphology. In 1905, he went so far as to establish in Munich his own 'Psychodiagnostic Seminar' (*Psychodiagnostisches Seminar*). A brochure from this period gives as an idea of how he presented his subject, for it includes the following lecture themes:

- handwriting and character;
- the influence of one's temperament on one's handwiting;
- the feeling of personal space in handwriting;
- expressive movement (*Ausdrucksbewegung*) and its physiognomic evaluation;
- temperament and character;
- the psychology of the criminal;
- the main psychological tenets of Goethe;
- the psychological achievements of Nietzsche;
- on the psychology of the folksong.

Schwabing years 7

Subsequently, these lectures got written up, revised, and published as articles, or they fed into the monographs that Klages now began to publish.

Thus, within his work as a graphologist, Klages sought to combine his teaching and research in the same way that a traditional academic used to do, except that, following the completion of his doctorate, he was now working (and for the rest of his life would continue to work) outside the university establishment. To a certain extent, in fact, the Psychodiagnostic Seminar was conceived as a potential rival to the university, and Klages even developed plans, never realized, to turn it into a kind of private college.

Despite its status outside the academic establishment, the Psychodiagnostic Seminar was attended by lecturers at the university in Munich as well as by a wide range of other academics and intellectual figures. Those who are known to have attended lectures and courses at the Seminar included the cultural critic and academic, Ernst Bertram (1884–1957); the pedagogue and theorist of gymnastic dance, Rudolf Bode (1881–1970);[11] the art historian, Otto Fischer (1996–1948); the doctor and optician, Gustav Willibald Freytag (the son of the novelist and playwright Gustav Freytag, 1816–1895); the psychiatrist, Viktor Emil von Gebsattel (1883–1976); the calligraphist, Ernst Glöckner (1885–1934); the neurologist and psychoanalyst, Hans von Hattingberg (1879–1944); the literary scholar and (re)discoverer of Hölderlin, Norbert von Hellingrath (1888–1916); the poet Alfred Walter von Heymel (known as Spectator Germanicus and Alfred Demel) (1878–1914); the psychiatrist and philosopher, Karl Jaspers (1883–1969); the classical philologist, Walter F. Otto (1874–1958); the translator and writer, Heinrich Steinitzer (1869–1947; Herta Wedekind;[12] and the Swiss art historian, Heinrich Wölfflin (1864–1945). This list reads like a roll-call of a selection of prominent thinkers of the time, some of whom have been forgotten, some of whom (especially Jaspers and Wölfflin) have not. The contribution of Klages's Psychodiagnostic Seminar to the intellectual development of contemporary thinkers is one of the unwritten chapters of Klages's reception.

As well as lecturing in Munich, Klages went on lecture tours and gave talks at various venues in German-speaking Europe. (It is hard for us today, in an age of television and internet, to appreciate the extent to which it was an evening's entertainment to go and listen to a lecture. Yet in bourgeois circles and in working-class circles alike, the lecture was a genuinely popular form of instruction; one thinks with some surprise, for instance, of the innumerable lectures given to working-men's associations by the indefatigable founder of anthroposophy, Rudolf Steiner [1861–1925].) Over time Klages built an entire network of contacts or a lecture circuit, delivering around fifty lectures in thirty different locations every year. And there were a couple of locations where Klages was particularly well-received or where he felt he was especially at home.

One of these place was Stettin (now Szczecin in Poland), where he had been invited to lecture by Walter Riezler (1878–1965), a classical archaeologist who served as the director of the Municipal Museum from 1913 to 1933/1934. Riezler had known Klages from his own days in Munich. Among the audience on Klages's first visit was Erwin Ackerknecht (1880–1960), the Director of the

8 *Life*

Municipal Library and the local Volkshochschule, who became a lifelong promoter of Klages's work and one of his close friends.

Another of the places where Klages scored a success with his lectures was Vienna, still at the height of its *fin-de-siècle* splendour (as indeed, as we shall see, was Munich too). In the latter half of the nineteenth and in the first two decades of the twentieth century, Vienna had expanded rapidly, both in terms of new architecture (the Ringstraße incorporating into the city what had formerly been suburbs) and in terms of culture: at the time when Klages was visiting, Vienna had established itself as one of the major European centres of Modernism. Klages's contacts in Vienna included a professor of music and his wife, Gustav Donath (1878–1965) and Alice Donath, in whose home Klages met Robert Musil,[13] as well as the Austrian writer and graphic designer Rudolf von Larisch (1856–1934). Every year Klages gave talks at the Urania, and at the invitation of Sigmund Freud (1856–1939), he even gave a paper at the Viennese Psychoanalytic Society.[14] Klages also attended the Congress of the International Society for Medical Psychology and Psychotherapy, when it was organized by Eugen Bleuler (1857–1939) and held in Vienna in September 1913.

Finally, Klages gave lectures in Winterthur, where he had been invited to visit by the writer and theologian, Johannes Ninck (1863–1939), who was in charge of the local committee responsible for inviting prominent speakers to come and give talks.[15] Here again, Klages soon became a personal friend of Ninck and his family, in whose house in Brühlhof he stayed when lecturing in Winterthur. These contacts in the north and south of Europe testify to Klages's persuasiveness as a speaker as well as to his personal charm, which led to him being a welcome guest in so many homes. Both these aspects of his personality are confirmed by Freytag in his recollections of Klages:

> Klages had long ago discovered his talent as a speaker. The circle of his disciples and admirers increased and encouraged his public appearances. I, too, could help him in this respect in the context of a lecture course which I was organizing in Munich. Later he was able to undertake great lecture tours at home and abroad, including in Eastern European countries, in the Balkans, etc., which brought in not only his fees as a speaker, but a small amount of money through the steadily increasing sales of his books. Unfortunately it was entirely used up later on by his long-term illnes with the result that he ended up with not inconsiderable debts. Yet he had the good fortune to find his new home country friends who generously supported him in his hour of need.
>
> In other respects Klages lived extremely frugally. If he treated himself in the evenings at home to one or more bottles of lager, then it was, at a price of 12 Pfennings a bottle, certainly no great luxury. Besides he needed the beer mainly as a soporific drug, even if he did so erroneously. For as a doctor one has to think of the strain on the heart brought about by large amounts of liquid which, if one is no longer as young as one was when a student, is certainly not something that promotes sleep. Klages's modest

life-style was also displayed on his travels. He always travelled third class, even on overnight journeys, sitting on a small cushion. He rarely made use of second class, and probably never went in the sleeping-car. These were certainly great strains, added to which there were the lectures and dealing with many people in foreign countries, to which he had to be attentive especially since he was frequently a guest in people's homes. And all this on often ridiculously small amounts of sleep!

(Erinnerungen, 40)

Because of the reputation of graphology as a pseudoscience, this aspect of Klages's work – reflected in volume 7 of his *Sämtliche Werke* – has not helped *his* reputation as a thinker at all. Yet, setting aside the problems surrounding the 'discipline' of graphology, these lectures offered a chance for Klages to 'think himself into' his own philosophy, reflected in the shift of interest away from actual handwriting analysis to what he called 'characterology' (*Charakterkunde*).

This shift is tied up with the way in which a new term comes to prominence in Klages's thinking, 'expression' (or *Ausdruck*). So the years between 1901 and 1914 represent an opening-up of Klages's intellectual development to an entirely new set of concerns, reflected in a new set of philosophical concepts:

- from his investigation into 'expression' as reflected in handwriting Klages developed an entirely new discipline, the science of expression (*Ausdruckswissenschaft*);
- from his research into the use of language, he developed the 'study of character' (*Charakterkunde*);
- by combining his observations in the study of expression with metaphysical reflections, he sketched a new theory of the will.

Over and above these specific areas, Klages's thinking began to take at least three new directions, to which we shall have to return to discuss them in further detail:

- he discovers the intellectual potential in two overlooked thinkers, discovering them or recovering them, and making them (through new critical editions) available to his contemporaries: the German doctor, painter, and *Naturphilosoph*, Carl Gustav Carus (1789–1869), and the Swiss anthropologist and legal historian, Johann Jakob Bachofen (1815–1887);
- he becomes a cultural critic who, through understanding the 'process of civilization', developed an urgent critique of the modern world, and pioneered the cause of environmentalism;
- he engages with the thought of the Hungarian philosopher, Menyhért (in German: Melchior) Palágyi (1859–1924),[16] whom he had met at the third International Congress for Philosophy in Heidelberg in 1908; and
- he acquired a philosophical vocabulary that enabled him to develop his own metaphysical system.

10   *Life*

Klages's career as a popular speaker, as a researcher, and as a thinker who was increasingly moving away from graphology to broader metaphysical questions was interrupted, as was so much else, by the outbreak in August 1914 of the First World War.

In tandem with his development from graphologist to characterologist, however, Klages became involved with one of the most important and influential figures in turn-of-the-century Munich, the Symbolist poet Stefan George (1868–1933), and the circle around him.[17] For Klages had moved to Munich precisely at the time when, in the famous phrase of Thomas Mann, the city was beginning to shine – *München leuchtet*.

Since the 1890s a group of followers (or more precisely, disciples) had been forming around Stefan George and the journal, the *Blätter für die Kunst*, which he edited between 1892 and 1919. George, who stylized himself as the 'Master' and exerted a powerful influence over his close friends that can only be described as charismatic, gathered around himself an assortment of brilliant, dedicated (and, in his eyes, beautiful) young minds. (The beauty of their bodies was, it seems, also a factor in determing membership of his Circle.) Over the years the members of the Circle included the literary historian, Friedrich Gundolf (1880–1931, otherwise known as Friedrich Leopold Gundelfinger); the historian, Friedrich Wolters (1876–1930); the industrialist, Robert Boehringer (1884–1974); the military officer, Claus von Stauffenberg (1904–1944), and his older brothers, Alexander (1905–1964) and Berthold (1905–1944); the economist, Edgar Salin (1892–1974); and the intellectual historian, Ernst Bertram (1884–1957).

One of the earliest members of the George Circle had been the poet and translator, Karl Wolfskehl (1869–1948). He acted as a point of contact between the George Circle and another, smaller group of likeminded friends, called the Cosmic Circle or the *Kosmiker*.[18] These thinkers and writers tried to practice in their work and their lives the injunction found in Nietzsche's unpublished fragments from 1881:

> *Stop feeling oneself to be such a fantasized ego!* Learn step by step to *throw away one's supposed individuality!* Discover the errors of the ego! Gain insight into *egoism as an error!* Understand that its opposite is not altruism! That would mean showing love towards *other apparent* individuals! No! Go **beyond** 'you' and 'me'! **Experience cosmically!**[19]

(Having said that, the members of the Cosmic Circle did seem to have quite large egos...) One might think of the *Kosmiker* as a kind of subset of the *George-Kreis*, although their interests transcended the literary and aesthetic ambitions of George and his followers. George himself can at one stage be identified as a member of the *Kosmiker*, as can the Dutch poet, Albert Verwey (1865–1937), associated with the group known as the *Tachtigers* or the 'Movement of the [Eighteen-]Eighties'; the college teacher and poet, Ludwig Derleth (1870–1948); the popular writer, Oscar A. H. Schmitz (1873–1931); the graphic

Schwabing years 11

artist, Melchior Lechter (1865–1937); and the pair who arguably formed the kernel of this group, Klages and the puzzling, perplexing figure of **Alfred Schuler** (1865–1923).

We already have enough on our hands in our attempt to recover the lost world of Ludwig Klages, so purely for reasons of space, there is no room here to say as much as we would like about the enigmatic figure of Schuler. In recent years, Schuler's entire œuvre has been republished;[20] although, because his written output is exceptionally small, other issues – centering on his accusations concerning his political outlook – have hindered his reception. Schuler was born in 1865 in Mainz, the son of lawyer who became a judge at the District Court. After living for several years in Zweibrücken, where he attended the local *Gymnasium*, Schuler began studying Law and Archaeology at Munich. But he soon abandoned his studies, dismissing archaeologists as no better than fraudulent graverobbers.

Instead, Schuler claimed to be able to discover things about the ancient world, not by digging it up on archaeological sites, but in a somewhat direct, quasi-Gnostic way. In fact, he claimed to be a reincarnation of a Roman citizen who had been born in the latter ages of the Roman Empire, and the critic Franz Wegener has described Schuler as 'the last of the German Cathars', thereby assimilating him to the heretical sect, the Cathars (from *katharoi*, the 'pure ones'), which flourished in southern France and northern Italy in the twelfth, thirteenth, and fourteenth centuries.[21] It is more likely, however, that Schuler's outlook would have been derived from the Spanish-born French occultist, Gérard Encausse (1865–1816), known as Henri Papus, the co-founder with Augustin Chaboseau (1868–1946) of the Traditional Martinist Order, itself a revival of the masonic organization founded by Martinez de Pasqually (*c.*1727–1774) in 1765, and subsequently propagated by his followers, Louis Claude de Saint-Martin (1743–1803) and Jean-Baptiste Willermoz (1730–1824).

From 1899 onwards, Schuler was in correspondence with Papus, and he read the *Green Books* (*Grüne Hefte*), a collection of occult documents, sent to him by Papus or someone else. When one learns that the material relating to these documents in Schuler's *Nachlass* includes extracts from the *Secret Doctrine* (1888) by the occultist and Theosophist, Helena (known as Madame) Blavatsky (1831–1891); a Gnostic-style treatise about an all-knowing master in the form of a serpent with references to the biblical exegesis of the sect known as the Ophites or Ophians (from *ophis*, 'snake'); and references to such occultists and/ or Theosophists as Eliphas Lévi (1810–1875), Franz Hartmann (1838–1912), and Carl Kiesewetter (1854–1895), one might well raise an eyebrow.

Yet this says as much about us as it does about Schuler. For Schuler's interest in occultism reflects a general revival of occultism at the end of the nineteenth century, and his engagement with Gnostic themes can be seen as part of a larger nineteenth-century revival of interest in Gnosticism, especially in the German-speaking world: in 1818, the theologian and Church historian, Johann August Neander (1789–1850), published his study, *Genetic Development of the Most Important Gnostic Systems*; in 1853, the theologian and founder of the Tübingen

12   *Life*

School of theology, Ferdinand Christian Baur (1792–1860), published a study entitled *Christianity and the Christian Church in its First Three Centuries*; in 1860, the theologian Richard Adelbert Lipsius (1830–1892) published a study entitled *Gnosticism, its Nature, Origin, and Development*; in 1881, Georg Koffmane published his study in in the form of twelve theses, *Gnosis according to its Tendency and Organisation*; in 1884, the theologian Adolf Hilgenfeld (1823–1907) published *The History of Heretics in Early Christianity*; and in 1899, the theologian and Church historian, Adolf von Harnack (1851–1930), dedicated a section to Gnosticism in his *Textbook of the History of Dogmatics*, vol. 1 (1886; [2]1888). Meanwhile, in Britain the Theosophist and private scholar, G. R. S. Mead (1863–1933), published *Fragments of a Faith Forgotten* (1900), a study of Gnosticism, and in 1906 he began to publish a series of short monographs under the title *Echoes from the Gnosis*. In Germany, the twentieth century saw a continuation in scholarly interest in Gnosticism: in 1904, the classicist and historian of religions, Richard Reizenstein (1861–1931), published his volume, *Poimandres: Studies in Graeco-Egyptian and Early Christian Literature*; in 1907, the theologian Wilhelm Bousset (1865–1920) published a study entitled *Main Problems of Gnosis*; in 1910, the classical scholar Wolfgang Schultz (1881–1936) published a collection of texts for the prestigious Eugen Diederichs publishing-house in Jena under the title, *Documents of Gnosis*. In other words, there is a strong current of scholarly interest in Gnosticism present in European thought in the late nineteenth and early twentieth centuries, right up to the work by Hans Jonas (1903–1993) on Gnosis, published in two volumes in 1954 and in 1993,[22] and it would be entirely appropriate to read the work of Schuler – and *a fortiori* Klages, who touches on Gnostic themes in *The Spirit as Adversary of the Soul*, and whose work has been described as embracing a 'pagan Gnosis'[23] – in this context.

Indeed, seen in this light, Schuler's interests appear far less eccentric than they might otherwise strike us as being, even if it seems that Schuler enjoyed playing up his eccentricities to the delight of the gallery. When he met Schuler in Munich in 1915, the German poet Rainer Maria Rilke (1875–1926) recorded his impressions in a letter to Marie von Thurn und Taxis:

> Imagine if a human being, from an intuitive insight into ancient imperial Rome, undertook to give an explanation of the world which presented the dead as the ones who really exist, the realm of the dead as one single enormous existence, but our small span of life as an exception: this all supported by an immeasurable learnedness and by such a degree of inner conviction and experience that the meaning of myths from time immemorial, released, seemed to rush into this bed of words, carrying the sense and idiosyncracy of this peculiar odd person on its great stream.[24]

And nearly two decades earlier, Stefan George had, in a dedicatory poem entitled 'A.S.' in *The Year of the Soul* (*Das Jahr der Seele*) (1897), paid tribute to Schuler as a member of the Cosmic Circle in these words:

Schwabing years 13

And was there really ever such a circle? Torches
Lit up the pallor of our faces, vapours mounted
From braziers for the godlike youth, and words you uttered
Uplifted for us to loud vermilion words of frenzy,
So that for days we were bewildered, and our senses
Reeled as if poisoned by too lush a banquet,
So that our brows still burned with roses, and we suffered
For spying at the wealth behind the screen of heaven.[25]

In 1940, Klages recalled his own first impressions of Schuler, recollecting how his own surprise and bemusement transformed into respect and even wonder:

> Returning in 1893 after the holidays to Munich, where I was dutifully studing Chemistry, I found late in the evening a written note from two friends, a budding psychiatrist and Hans Busse (the lyric poet and sculptor, now unjustly forgotten), asking me to come to a tavern which was popular at that time, where I would meet a third person, a strange individual whose acquaintance it was worth making. In the impression I got from this third person (it was, of course, Schuler) there was a mixture which at first I could not sort out: profoundly significant intellectual substance, a development from within that could never be changed from without, a combination of the most delicate sensitivity and inner inadequacy, a puzzling sense of being from completely different, and – even if only dimly intuited – an inability to come out of himself in the society of his contemporaries. Behind the gestures of obligation, the carefully chosen phrases testifying to great learning, lurked a secret vehemence; and where was it looking, that wide-eyed gaze under those bushy eyebrows, a gaze that missed no form, no colour, no motion round about him, no expression and no gesture of his interlocutors, and which seemed nevertheless to see images rising out of the depths of the soul as well as those sensorily present? Here is a miracle, or so I thought, but between the miracle and everyone who meets this person in the form of a one-and-a half millennium old *Roman*, there is a gaping ravine, which cannot be spanned by any bridge or gangway, on which one would cross over to him or on which he would come across to us, into an insane present age with its wicked thoughts. – The attempt nevertheless to form a bridge was later to form the main task of my struggles at midlife, and it took years before it succeeded.[26]

As for Schuler's quasi-mystical, quasi-metaphysical outlook and his highly mannered style of communicating it, the following text from his *Cosmogoniae Fragmenta* tells us all we need to know about both:

> Round / perfect and sterile is everything Cosmic. Self-sufficient in their own charms, the urns of antiquity float / and each one of its vessels bears the imprint of the primal urn.[27]

14 *Life*

Here the Plotinian One, the source of the Good and the Beautiful, has become a self-pleasuring vessel, turned in on itself rather than overflowing into the universe.

Yet it would be wrong to emphasize the *faux* solemnity, the hocus-pocus, the striking of decadent poses and, if you like, the sheer pretentiousness of the circles in which Klages moved in Munich. After all, in her recollections of Ludwig Klages, one of his female friends, Marie Römermann (known as Mieze), emphasizes the good humour and, above all, the *laughter* that characterized Klages's life in Munich:

> With whom else have I laughed so often and so heartily as with the people around Klages? Especially of course with Helene [i.e. Ludwig Klages's sister]. What she wrote as a teenage girl in my album has always been true: 'Always cheerful! – Helene Klages.' – That was a basic character trait of her being, being happy, affirming life, enjoying the moment. In the earlier 'good old days', when we were together – in particular I can remember Biedersteinerstraße, where Helene lived with Heidi [i.e. Ludwig Klages's niece] from 1904 to 1914 –, it sometimes happened that all four of us – Ludwig, Helene, Heidi, and I – literally fell to the floor with laughter. If someone had said something humorous, or something else happened that was hilariously funny, we were not slow to laugh. Perhaps it was [Max] Pallenberg [1877–1934, the Austrian singer and comedian] or [Karl] Valentin [1882–1948, the Bavarian comedian and cabaret performer] whom we were imitating, or [Hanns von] Gumppenberg's [1866–1928, German critic and cabarettist] *Das teutsche Dichterroß* or events in Schwabing, or perhaps almost nothing at all, we were happy, thank goodness, there was always our dear laughter.
>
> (*Erinnerungen*, 21)

The laughter was not to go on for ever, though, and as we know from world history, the trajectory of political developments after the turn of the century was slowly but surely making its way to a time when the laughter, even for Klages and his friends, would stop. For, after the assassination of Archduke Franz Ferdinand of Austria in Sarajevo on 28 June 1914, Austria-Hungary declared war on Serbia on 28 July, the German Empire began to mobilize on 30 July, then declared war on Russia on 1 August, and Great Britain declared war on Germany on 4 August. The First World War had begun, and it would last another four years. And after it, nothing in Europe would ever be the same again.

Perhaps it is instructive to compare Klages's reaction to news of the war with those of, say, Franz Kafka (1883–1924), Thomas Mann (1875–1955), or Carl Gustav Jung (1875–1961). In his famous diary entry of 2 August 1914, Kafka recorded events as follows: 'Germany has declared war on Russia. – In the afternoon, swimming lessons';[28] in his letter to his brother, Heinrich, on 3 August 1914, when France had declared war on Germany, Thomas Mann wrote 'that one should be happy to be allowed to experience such great things', and

Schwabing years 15

promptly penned his *Thoughts during War* (*Gedanken im Kriege*) (1913): 'War! What we experienced was purification, liberation, and a terrible hope';[29] while Jung's response was a decidedly odd one. When he read in the newspapers that war had broken out, 'nobody' (he recalled) 'was happier than I',[30] but only because it now became clear to him that the startling sequence of apocalyptic visions and dreams that he had been experiencing in the autumn of 1913 through to the spring and summer of 1914, had in fact been prophetic, and that he was *not* threatened, as he had feared, by schizophrenia or psychosis.

Nor were Kafka, Mann, and Jung alone in their responses, for similarly ecstatic reactions came from such other leading academics and intellectuals as Max Weber, Werner Sombart, Georg Simmel, Ernst Toller, Hermann Bahr, Ernst Troeltsch, Friedrich Meinecke, and Friedrich Naumann.[31] (And lest one suspect it was the Germans alone who were bellicose, in France the enthusiasm for the First World War of the philosopher Henri Bergson displays a very similar contour.) Klages, by contrast, was shocked, dismayed, and horrified.

His comments in his letters testify to his complete rejection of the outbreak of war, which he described as 'like the outbreak of insanity on the part of humankind'.[32] To another correspondent, he wrote: 'If only I could see the greatness that, whether we are victorious or defeated, could blossom from these bloodbaths'.[33] And in response to a poem embracing the war by the Austrian writer, Erwin Guido Kolbenheyer (1878–1962), Klages declared: 'No "gods" are present in *this* war, and never before have "gods" drunk blood in such a way'.[34]

In practical terms, Klages's response to the First World War was a twofold one. With the outbreak of the conflict, all his speaking engagements had obviously been cancelled, and because so many of its adherents had been called up for service, volunteered for duty, or were now otherwise occupied, his Psychodiagnostic Seminar in Munich had to close. This left Klages without a source of income, but of course, many others were experiencing the same difficulties. So Klages founded a Wartime Support Centre for Intellectuals (*Kriegshilfsstelle für geistige Berufe*), a project that aimed to provide free meals, cheap accommodation, and other forms of financial support for writers and artists who found that the war had taken their living away.

The support centre in Munich also offered a forum for the continuation of the intellectual life as well. Far away from the unfolding chaos on the frontline, could the artists and intellectuals left at home make a different kind of contribution to the war-effort – or to helping bring the war to an end? Among the lectures organized by the *Hilfsstelle* was a famous talk given in February 1915 by Norbert von Hellingrath on the Romantic poet, Friedrich Hölderlin (1770–1843), the significance of whose works was in the process of being (re)discovered;[35] as well as a series of talks on the Roman Empire by the individual who had begun to play such an important role in the development of Klages's ideas, Alfred Schuler.[36]

Despite his engagement in the work of the *Hilfsstelle*, Klages found the horror of war – even if experienced only at second-hand – increasingly difficult to bear. By August 1915 he found the situation in Germany had become unbearable, and

16   *Life*

on 25 August 1915 Klages left Munich and headed for Switzerland. Crossing the border, he made first for Zurich, and then for Winterthur, where he stayed with the Ninck family. After a month at the Brühlhof, Klages moved to Rüschlikon, a small town on the shore of Lake Zurich, where the landscape painter Hermann Gattiker (1865–1951) had had a studio built for him in the large garden of his house. Although plans were made for Klages to stay permanently with Gattiker, and in February 1916 Schuler visited Klages in Rüschlikon, when Gattiker fell ill in April 1916, the search for somewhere to stay resumed.

In Switzerland Klages soon found a new circle of friends. Among them was a carpet importer in Winterthur, Hermann Müller-Guex (1881–1935), a businessman with a keen interest in culture and history. Klages offered him private classes, training him in the theory and practice of graphology, as well as another of other (and more conventional) subjects. Klages wrote a small introduction to the 'Early History of Greek Thought' for Müller-Guex, and by giving such private classes, Klages was able to earn some income. He also pioneered a kind of 'distance learning', writing instructional letters (*Lehrbriefe*) for those unable to visit him in person; these documents sometimes formed the basis for Klages's later published works.

For instance: another of Klages's friends was Gertrude Hunziker, whom he had first met in 1909 in Munich, and with whom he renewed contact at a lecture he gave in Aarau in 1917. Subsequently she embarked on an informal 'distance learning' programme with him, and from their correspondence subsequently emerged his essay, 'Remarks on the Limitations of the Goethean Human Being' (*Bemerkungen über die Schranken des Goetheschen Menschen*); a short text entitled, 'Why Does It Bring Ruin If One Lifts the Veil of Isis?' (*Warum bringt es Verderben, den Schleier des Isis-Bildes zu heben?*), included as an appendix to *Of Cosmogonic Eros*; and another essayistic text, his 'Letter on Ethics' (*Brief über Ethik*). Other letters are said to have provided draft material for book 5 of his major work, *The Spirit as Adversary of the Soul*.

Then again, in the summer of 1918 Klages gave an extended lecture in private to three Swiss friends – Christoph Bernoulli (1897–1981), a Swiss antiquities dealer, Jakob Eugster, and Emanuel La Roche (died 1920). The subject of this lecture was the conditions under which human consciousness had developed. In this way, Klages returned to some of the themes with which he had been occupied before the outbreak of the war, and at the request of the participants he wrote up the material in the form of a short study, which Ackerknecht later encouraged him to publish as a book under the title *On the Essence of Consciousness (Über das Wesen des Bewußtseins)* (1921).

But where was Klages going to live? After leaving Gattiker in April 1916, he lived in a number of provisional locations until, in February 1920, he moved into the house in Kilchberg that had belonged to the historical novelist and poet, Conrad Ferdinand Meyer (1825–1898), and which was now occupied by the writer's daughter, Camilla Meyer. Her father had brought the house in 1877 and built an extension onto it. In the first floor of this extension were the two rooms into which Klages now moved. He was still in exile, but at least he had found somewhere permanent to stay.

The 'main business'

While he was working on the second part of his monumental dramatic poem, *Faust*, Goethe used, half-jokingly, half-seriously, to refer to this work as his 'main business'. This expression has been used by Hans Eggert Schröder (1905–1985) to refer to the project on which Klages now worked in his rooms in the Conrad-Ferdinand-Meyer house in the years – in fact, over a decade – following the end of the First World War. Yet progress was frequently interrupted: sometimes by financial worries, sometimes by commitments to other philosophical projects. Did, one wonders, Klages sometimes feel like Nietzsche who, in *Ecce Homo*, looked back on his life and saw 'the temporary sidepaths and wrong turnings, the delays, the "modesties", the seriousness squandered on tasks which lie outside *the* task'? Or did he, as Nietzsche also did, come to understand that, from the point of view of *becoming who one is*, even 'the *blunders* of life [...] have their own meaning and value'?[37]

The major work on which Klages now embarked was published in three volumes between 1929 and 1932, under a title (in German, *Der Geist als Widersacher der Seele*) which can be translated in various ways: more conventionally as *The Spirit as Adversary of the Soul*, more loosely (but concisely) as *Mind as Opponent of Psyche*. Elsewhere, as part of our 'toolkit', we shall examine some of the central ideas of this work more closely, but for now, let us concentrate on the role played by this work in relation to the development of Klages's thought.

The first book opens with a series of definitions of some fundamental philosophical concepts: being and reality, time and duration, object (*Gegenstand*) and person (*Person*), as well as the master categories, soul (*Seele*) and spirit (*Geist*). (Characteristically for Klages, the second book launches into a critique of a series of 'errors': the 'logistical' error, the 'Kantian' error, and the 'sensualist' error, before defining the difference between a thing (*Ding*) and an image (*Bild*) – for Klages, polemicizing and philosophizing were closely related activities.)

In approaching his topic with a set of terminological clarifications – or what the French poet, Paul Valéry (1871–1945), would have called *un nettoyage de la situation verbale* – Klages was doing what he often did when beginning to expound an argument. For instance, in two short pieces published in the *Graphologische Monatshefte* in 1912 under the title 'Conceptual Critique' (*Begriffskritik*), Klages had offered a clarification of the distinction, widely used (in graphological textbooks), between 'intuitive' and 'discursive', and of the various meanings accruing to the notion of 'fantasy'.[38] Then again, in a series of articles published in *Deutsche Psychologie* between 1917 and 1919, Klages expounded in detail two central categories of his thought, 'spirit' (*Geist*) and 'soul' (*Seele*).[39] Or finally in 1922, in his first major work, *On Cosmogonic Eros*, Klages dedicates its first chapter to what he calls a 'Preliminary Conceptual Reflection'.

All these early works can be seen as an attempt on Klages's part (as he later wrote to the publisher, Johann Ambrosius Barth) to 'provide a new *foundation for psychology* on a *biological* basis'.[40] When he first approached the publisher in 1917, Klages estimated that a book-length edition of *Spirit and Soul (Geist*

18   *Life*

und Seele) would amount to some 700 typescript pages. Given the fact that Germany was engaged in a war, it was planned that the work would be made available as a series to subscribers. Already by the autumn of 1917 Klages assured Barth that he had found 100 such subscribers, and Klages planned to have completed the work by the beginning of 1919. But the problem of finding accommodation in Switzerland interrupted the work, and financial difficulties intervened.

After the War, the galloping inflation ate away at Klages's savings, so that by 1923 his savings had disappeared, and he was faced with a large debt in Swiss Franks. Although he worked hard to pay off these debts, some days putting in 14, even 17 hours of work, he was unable to pay off the amount he owed. In the end, Klages was rescued from financial ruin by the generous support of a sponsor from Winterthur, Georg Reinhart (1877–1955), who gave him 300 Franks a month to cover costs. And so Klages was able to return to his 'main business', which continued to expand as he worked on it.

Finally, between 1929 and 1932, Klages was able to present his ideas in a fully worked-out, systematic – and correspondingly lengthy – form: as *The Spirit as Adversary of the Soul*, whose first volume was published in 1929 under the title *Life and Thinking Faculty*, whose second appeared in the same year as *The Doctrine of the Will*, and whose third was finally published in two parts in 1932 under the title of *The Doctrine of the Reality of Images* and *The World-View of the Pelasgians*.

When Camilla Meyer became severely ill in 1928, Klages decided to leave the house where he was staying in Kilchberg, but he stayed in the town. Living now in a house in the Rigistraße, Klages was assisted in the final years of his work on his philosophical masterpiece by his secretary, Hilde Althaus. When the lake froze over in the cold winter of 1929, Klages and Hilde Althaus took to their skates, and if the noise in the house when Klages was now living became too great, she provided him with a space to work and to complete the *Spirit as Adversary* in her own flat in Zurich.

Some of the interruptions to Klages's work on the *Spirit as Adversary* came from the need, sometimes as much financial as intellectual, to complete other publication commitments. And in these years Klages was, as a published writer, extraordinarily active and productive. In the run-up to the appearance of the first volume of *Spirit as Adversary*, for instance, he published *On the Essence of Consciousness* (1921), *Of Cosmogonic Eros* (1922), his *Introduction to the Psychology of Handwriting* (1924), *The Psychological Achievements of Nietzsche* (1926), and an extended edition of *The Foundations of the Study of Character* (1928).

At the same time, Klages was extending his circle of intellectual influence through a new set of friendships: in 1919 with the theologian and writer, Carl Albrecht Bernoulli (1868–1937); and in 1920 with the Hamburg bookseller, Kurt Saucke (1895–1970) and his wife, Alice Saucke, as well as with the psychiatrist and art historian, Hans Prinzhorn (1886–1933); in 1924 with the freelance writer and adult educationalist, Hans Kern (1902–1947); and in 1925 with Niels Kampmann (1873–1956) and his wife, Martina Kampmann. Among the visitors Klages

The 'main business' 19

entertained in Kilchberg were Rudolf von Larisch (1856–1934), Melchior Palágyi, Alfred Kubin (1877–1959), Rudolf Bode, and Werner Deubel (1894–1949), as well as Hans Prinzhorn and Niels Kampmann.

Thus there grew up around Klages a network of friends and supporters, contributing in different ways to his work. Carl Albrecht Bernoulli was a fifth-generation member of the famous Swiss patrician family of merchants and scholars, whose father Carl Johann Bernoulli had been a famous lawyer in Basel. As the editor of the literary remains of the Church historian and theologian Franz Overbeck (1837–1905), who had been a close friend of the philosopher Friedrich Nietzsche, Bernoulli became a critical opponent of the editorial policies pursued by the Nietzsche Archive in Weimar, directed by Nietzsche's anti-Semitic sister, Elisabeth Förster-Nietzsche. For legal reasons, Bernoulli was obliged to redact a number of passages in his two-volume study, *Friedrich Nietzsche and Franz Overbeck: A Friendship* (1908). Bernoulli also edited a compilation of passages from Overbeck's *Nachlass*, published under the title *Christianity and Culture* (1919).

Together Bernoulli and Klages were responsible for bringing the work of Bachofen to the attention of the reading public, in part through the publication in 1924 of Bernoulli's study, *Johann Jakob Bachofen and the Natural Symbol* (1924), a work written by Bernoulli in close collaboration with Klages.[41] (Bernoulli's study received a positive review from Walter Benjamin.)[42] In the following year, 1925, Bernoulli and Klages presented a second edition of Bachofen's *Essay on the Tomb Symbolism of the Ancients* (1859), to which Bernoulli contributed a foreword and Klages a tribute to Bachofen.[43] The reading of Bachofen offered by Bernoulli and Klages – one which emphasized his theory of the symbol and hence his *mythical* dimension – was directed against that proposed by the philosopher Alfred Baeumler (1887–1968), which foregrounded the political and hence the *historical* implications of Bachofen's work.

Then again, the relationship between Klages and Alfred Kubin highlights the reception accorded to the philosopher's theories within literary and artistic circles. In 1924, Kubin travelled through Switzerland, and visited Klages in Kilchberg. Kubin already knew Klages, along with Schuler and Friedrich Huch (1873–1913), from his time in Munich, and described the philosopher as 'a fascinating phenomenon, a researcher of the highest rank, [...] one of the most significant psychological experts of our times'.[44]

In his role as a bookseller, Kurt Saucke became an important suppporter of Klages's work, and Alice Saucke prepared the index to *Spirit as Adversary*. She also helped with the correction of proofs of his works, and accompanied him as an assistant on some of his lecture tours. Of the other figures who formed an intellectual circle around Klages, two of the most important, in terms of publicizing and developing his ideas, were Werner Deubel and Hans Kern.

While he had been a student in Munich, Deubel had first met Klages in Munich in the summer semester of 1914, and the two men quickly became friends. At the beginning of the 1920s the connection between the two men grew ever closer, and in numerous publications Deubel began to expound key aspects

20 *Life*

of Klages's philosophical thinking. In a series of articles, Deubel sought to expound and explicate Klages's system, frequently clarifying and explaining the terminology of his intellectual master. (In 1931, Deubel published a collection of essays under the title *German Cultural Revolution* [*Deutsche Kulturrevolution*], containing contributions by himself, Hans Kern, the journalist and writer Jorg Lampe (1897–1982), the graphologist Heinrich Döhmann (1893–1974), the surgeon and gynaecologist Wilhelm Schöppe (b. 1891), the graphologist Kurt Seesemann (1894–1965), the Germanist Hans-Friedrich Rosenfeld (1899–1993), and the doctor and psychiatrist Julius Deussen (1905–1975).)[45] Aside from personal conversations and Deubel's visits to Kilchberg, their intellectual relationship was conducted in large part through an extensive correspondence, which continued until Deubel's death in 1949.

For his part, Hans Kern had got to know Klages in the summer semester of 1924, when Kern had written to the philosopher for ask for advice on his dissertation on the figure of the German Romantic thinker, Carl Gustav Carus. Once again, the ensuing correspondence laid the grounds for a longlasting friendship, until Kern's death in 1945. Following the completion of his dissertation, Kern planned to write his *Habilitation* on the German physician and naturalist, Gotthilf Heinrich von Schubert (1780–1860), but in 1926 he abandoned plans for an academic career in favour of freelance writing and adult education. Along with Ackerknecht, Prinzhorn, and Deubel, Kern was able, through numerous publications around the theme of German Romanticism and *Naturphilosophie*, to bring Klagesian ideas to a wider public.

Thanks to a visit to Klages in Kilchberg, Kern met Christoph Bernoulli, and jointly they edited in 1926 a selection of extracts from the tradition of German *Naturphilosophie*, published by Eugen Diederichs, a leading publisher of philosophical (sometimes mystical, sometimes right-wing) works; even today, their *Romantische Naturphilosophie* remains a useful compendium of this line of German thought.[46] Furthermore, Kern also shared with Klages an interest in developing a psychological interpretation of the influential German philosophical figure of Friedrich Nietzsche. At this point, we should turn to a consideration of Klages's monograph, *The Psychological Achievements of Nietzsche* (1926), but first, let us ask ourselves: why Nietzsche?

Klages and Nietzsche

In some ways, the figure of Nietzsche has become so much part of our mental furniture that it would be easy to underestimate the impact of his thought at the time when Klages was writing his monograph on Nietzsche and psychology. Indeed, to say that Nietzsche's influence was enormous across the entire range of the arts and humanities is an understatement. In the field of music, for instance, one could mention Gustav Mahler (1860–1911), whose Third Symphony (1893–1896) includes as its fourth movement a setting of the 'Midnight Song' ('Mitternachtslied') from *Zarathustra*; or Richard Strauss (1864–1949), whose tone-poem *Also sprach Zarathustra* (1896) offers a musical synthesis of

Nietzsche's central work; or Frederick Delius (1862–1934), whose *A Mass of Life* (1904–1905) is based on a sequence of passages from *Zarathustra*. In the field of the visual arts, one could mention such *Jugendstil* artists as Max Klinger (1857–1920) or Henry van de Velde (1863–1957), or such Expressionist artists as Max Beckmann (1884–1950), Franz Marc (1880–1916), or Otto Dix (1891–1969), in whose works Nietzschean themes, both implicit and explicit, can be found. One could note Nietzsche's remarkable importance, both acknowledged and unacknowledged, for psychoanalysis: disavowed in suspiciously explicit terms by Freud, but significant as a source for the analysis of the inferiority complex proposed by Alfred Adler (1870–1937), and as a major starting-point for the analytical psychology developed by Carl Gustav Jung. Incidentally, it was around the same time that Nietzsche became an important figure for Rudolf Steiner, the founder of anthroposophy (who was, for a short time, part of the editorial team chosen by Elisabeth Förster-Nietzsche to work on her brother's *Nachlass*).

On the literary side, one of the greatest readers of Nietzsche was the novelist Thomas Mann. In a lecture given to the PEN Club in Stockholm in 1947, Mann drew attention to the continuity between, on the one hand, Schiller's *On Naïve and Sentimental Poetry* (1795) and the fragments of Novalis, and, on the other, *The Birth of Tragedy* (1872) and Nietzsche's critique of morality.[47] Mann proclaimed his admiration for Nietzsche as a writer and thinker – as

> an experience of immense fullness and complexity encompassing the whole of European culture, which absorbed much of the past and recalled or repeated it with greater or less conscious imitation and emulation, making it actual again in a mythic way.[48]

One should definitely mention the role played by Nietzsche in the intellectual life of the highly influential circle around Stefan George which was no less immense,[49] one fruit of which was the major study by Ernst Bertram published in 1918.[50]

And one could certainly mention the vast philosophical reception of Nietzsche, beginning with Wilhelm Dilthey (1833–1911), for whom Nietzsche's apparent lack of systematicity placed him in the tradition of such thinkers as Marcus Aurelius, Montaigne, Carlyle, Emerson, Ruskin, Tolstoy, and Maeterlinck,[51] or Georg Simmel (1858–1918), for whom Nietzsche's thought offered nothing less than a new vision of life itself:

> Nietzsche's attempt is to remove the meaning-giving goal of life from its illusory position outside of life and to put that goal back into life itself. There is no more radical way to do this than through a vision of life in which self-directed augmentation is but the realization of what life provides as potential, including means and values. Every stage of human existence now finds its meaning not in something absolute and definite, but in something higher that succeeds it in which everything antecedent, having been

22　*Life*

only potential and germinal, wakes up to greater efficiency and expansion. Life as such has become fuller and richer: there is an increase in life.[52]

Later, his philosophical reception included the large monograph by Karl Jaspers,[53] and the seminars given by Martin Heidegger between 1936 and 1946.[54] And this was just his reception in the German-speaking world.[55] There is the immense influence of Nietzsche on the literature and culture of America,[56] Russia,[57] Spain,[58] and above all France[59] to take into account as well.

In short, the Expressionist writer Gottfried Benn (1885–1956) was by no means exaggerating when he remarked that everything that his generation 'had discussed, had thought out inside itself, one might say: suffered, one might also say: done to death – all that had already been expressed and exhausted in Nietzsche, had found definitive formulation; all the rest was mere exegesis'.[60] And to the members of Benn's Nietzsche-influenced generation one should also reckon Klages, for his reception of Nietzsche marks him out as a member, along with such other figures as Rudolf Pannwitz (1881–1969), Schuler, and Derleth, as well as Alfred Mombert (1872–1942), Theodor Däubler (1876–1934), and Christian Morgenstern (1871–1914), to the 'lost generation' of German writers who have, with good reason, been described as 'Zarathustra's children'.[61]

Yet Klages's reception of Nietzsche was a complex and, in some ways, highly ambivalent one.[62] We can see this complexity and this ambivalence in the very title of Klages's monograph of 1926, *Die psychologischen Errungenschaften Nietzsches* – the 'achievements' of Nietzsche were pre-eminently 'psychological' ones (i.e. not 'philosophical' ones). As one reads the rest of the book, one of Klages's first philosophical publications, one cannot help noticing the combination of his admiration for Nietzsche with an implicit critique. It was not just ironic, so Klages believed, it was a 'devastating self-contradiction' that 'the same thinker who, like no-one else, reveals the crimes perpetrated against life by the will-to-power, should try to understand life itself as precisely this will-to-power'.[63] In fact, the structure of Klages's study underscores this clear trajectory from appreciation to critique.

The first three chapters are placed under the subtitle of Nietzsche's research goal and methods, highlighting his own understanding of his philosophical one: after all, in *Beyond Good and Evil* (§23), Nietzsche had demanded that 'psychology shall be recognized again at the queen of the sciences, for whose service and preparation the other sciences exist' – 'for psychology is now again the path to the fundamental problems'.[64] By psychology, Klages explains, Nietzsche meant both an understanding of the Other and an exploration of the self. As well as noting Nietzsche's acknowledgement of his intellectual debt to such previous thinkers as the French Renaissance philosopher, Michel de Montaigne (1533–1592), the French Catholic theologian and philosopher, Pierre Charron (1541–1603), or the French fashioner of maxims, La Rochefoucauld (1613–1680), Klages emphasizes the links between Nietzsche and the Greek school of Sophism, the chief of the schools whose influence Plato had sought to combat.[65]

In the *Theaetetus*, the view is ascribed by Socrates to Protagoras (152a–c; 161c–e; 169d–170b) that although one cannot distinguish between true and false, because it is right for each person to believe what he or she believes to be true, there are nevertheless better opinions and worse opinions, and the wise person should try to convert the unwise person, by means of persuasive rhetoric, to replace his or her own worse opinion with the better opinion of the wise person.[66] If, Klages argues, one replaces the values of 'better' and 'worse' with 'stronger' and 'weaker', then one can begin to see a connection to two core ideas of Nietzsche: first, that there are degrees of error and degrees of approaching the truth; and second, that the stronger personality reveals itself in an ability to *withstand* the less deceptive truth.[67] (Compare with Nietzsche's remark in *Beyond Good and Evil*, §39: 'the strength of a spirit should be measured according to how much of the "truth" one could still barely endure'.[68]) Pointing to the speech of Callicles in the *Gorgias* –

> Those who framed the laws are the weaker folk, the majority. And accordingly they frame the laws for themselves and their own advantage, and so too with their approval and censure, and to prevent the stronger who are able to overreach them from gaining the advantage over them, they frighten them by saying that to overreach others is shameful and evil, and injustice consists in seeking the advantage over others. For they are satisfied, I suppose, if being inferior they enjoy equality of status.
>
> (483c)[69]

– and to the speeches of Thrasymachus in book 1 of the *Republic* (338c–342e), Klages draws a link between them and Nietzsche's notion of 'master' morality and 'slave' morality, and even Nietzsche's concept of *ressentiment*. In other words, the Sophistic approach begins to formulate the chief Nietzschean task: to answer the question of how it was possible that vitally weak values should gain dominance over vitally strong values.[70] In the course of this task, which involves the notion of the will-to-power (see below), Nietzsche embarks on the project of uncovering deception and self-deception in general and ends up investigating the history of this process: in other words, Nietzsche is 'a developmental theorist of the value-character of general concepts'.[71]

In part two, which examines the 'applications and results' of this investigative methodology, Klages examines in turn a number of key ideas and motifs in Nietzsche's philosophy. These ideas and motifs are the motif of the 'nearest things';[72] a phenomenon which Klages dubs the persuasive power of success;[73] the desire to be (seen to be) the best, or the complicated relationship between striving for excellence and a need to be recognized;[74] so-called 'love for one's neighbour' (or, as Zarathustra puts it, 'In truth, I have often laughed at weaklings who think themselves good because their claws are blunt!');[75] self-overcoming (or, as Nietzsche puts it, 'In every ascetic morality man worships a part of himself as God and for that he needs to diabolize the other part');[76] the envy of life (or, to use Nietzsche's key term, *ressentiment*, which lies at the root of every

24   *Life*

other kind of envy – not surprisingly, perhaps, this is the longest chapter in Klages's book...); and the psychology of Christianity, the roots of which Nietzsche sees (and Klages, perhaps rather too enthusiastically, agrees) as lying in Judaism.

Last but very much not least, Klages highlights the theme in Nietzsche of the relationship between consciousness and life. This chapter takes Klages deep into some of the most difficult and problematic aspects of Nietzsche's thought: its Dionysian, ecstatic, orgiastic discourse, and after a series of quotations from *Thus Spoke Zarathustra* Klages concludes that 'these are the intellectual fruits of Nietzsche's orgiastic thinking, and it is the *blood* of his spirit'.

> Confronted with such trumpet blasts of vitalistic excess, the prison walls of a thousand doctrines of the millennia sink around us; but from the *world of images* behind them only flickers break through, and the voice of the prophet, whenever he wants to display it to us, breaks in a cry or loses itself in a confused mumbling,

– he declares, adding:

> However, this was not because the inner stream would not have been broad enough or deep enough, but because it was smashed on the rocks of Christianity. We do not know how better to convince of this anyone still able to perceive the tone and message of language other than by pointing to the final fragment (§696) of *The Will to Power*,

– and Klages quotes at length from the fragment that begins: 'And do you know what "the world" is to me...?'.[77]

And this brings us to the third and final part of Klages's study – his concluding critique. Already we can tell what the central charge against Nietzsche is: that, for him, the world is the will-to-power, whereas, for Klages, the world is a world of images. Yet Klages has another complaint about Nietzsche, too. Chief of this is what he calls Nietzsche's 'Socratism', by which Klages means – in this respect, anticipating Heidegger's later critique in his Nietzsche lectures[78] – that Nietzsche failed to escape the discursive space of Platonic (i.e. metaphysical) thought as found in the dialogues attributed to Socrates. Klages summarizes the case as follows: first, inasmuch as Nietzsche was a true sceptic, he must have been one from Socratic convictions; second, Socratism and scepticism are both statements of nihilism that differ in terms of rationality merely in form; and third, 'science' as a belief in the autocracy of the understanding is nihilism.

The second of these charges is substantiated (or so Klages would have us believe) by the following (contradictory) statements, all of which he claims to be able – and in this respect he anticipates Karl Jaspers's critique[79] – to derive from various writings by Nietzsche. (Jaspers's words have sometimes been used to justify an intellectually lazy approach to Nietzsche, and to short-circuit engagement with his thought by reducing it all to 'mere literature'. Such an approach entirely misses the point that Jaspers, and – in his own way – Klages, are making.)[80] First, the truth is undeniably desirable, even if it is dangerous; second, the truth is *not* desirable, but rather it should be decisively rejected; and third, complete scepticism. In an impassioned paragraph, Klages summarizes his argument against Nietzsche:

> If Nietzsche's entire work, as everyone can sense, is nothing other than a massive, and also massively successful, battle again errors inimical to life, then it must appear to us as a kind of absurdity if the creator of this work *also* pays homage to the view that *life* requires in order to survive and to flourish – error, and correspondingly considers his own philosophy from time to time unquestionably to be 'a kind of vampyrism'.[81] From the true and life-affirming sentence: consciousness is a disruption of life, there emerges in no time at all the ultra-erroneous and life-deriding sentence: life is *based on false judgements*. The reader will have long since realized how this all fits together. After Nietzsche was able to convince us like no-one else that the *will* actually needs errors – crude, subtle, and deliberately cunning – in order to implant itself into life and to take charge, then we *would have* to believe all that about *life*, if we, like he, had fallen prey to the daimon that inspired him to retract his unmasking of the will with the blasphemous claims that life itself is – this will.[82]

On this account, it is clear that Nietzsche got close to the truth, but not as close as Klages did. Or as he summarizes the paradox (as he sees of it) of Nietzsche, 'We can no longer doubt: something in Nietzsche is struggling passionately for the truth, and something in Nietzsche is in full flight away from – the truth'.[83]

Klages's dissatisfaction with Nietzsche for being – well, for being Nietzsche and not Klages – grows in the next chapter, which examines the theme of overcoming. Again, Klages detects something he considers fundamentally contradictory at the core of Nietzsche's argumentation. First, he argues that because Nietzsche cannot distinguish between a drive-impulse (*Triebantrieb*) and a volitional impulse (*Willensantrieb*) – a key distinction in Klages's taxonomy of instincts and drives, but obviously completely unknown to Nietzsche –, nor could he distinguish between the conditions of both; or, put more briefly, between drives and interests, and therefore he ought to have abolished either the drive or the will.[84]

Second, Klages invites us to consider Nietzsche's philosophy of the orgy and 'his rhetorically powerful praise of the love that gives';[85] we shall discover, Klages says, that it was this philosophy that enabled him to unmask the lust for power in the most highly prized social characteristics of human beings, but that it was his belief in the all-embracing power of the will that prevented him from investigating the qualities of the soul that are exposed to the infection of the will.[86] And third: for Klages, a sentence such as this: 'Love – in its methods war, in its foundation the mortal hatred of the sexes',[87] is not so much pulling a grimace as expressing an irresponsible limitation.[88] Deep down inside Nietzsche, so Klages believes, lies something disturbingly problematic:

26 *Life*

> Churning and straining away in the depths from the very outset, here and there revealing itself in spasmic upheavals and throes, the ascetic belief breaks out like a jet of flame in *Zarathustra*, setting the *whole* of Nietzsche on fire and covering him as it were with consuming fire. The fire was reduced again but never really extinguished, and its return which was definitely to be expected would certainly have even meant his physical demise. Yet *Zarathustra* itself contains a series of Dionysian passages which we ourselves can use as evidence, it contains insertions of songs and successfully continues the critique of the modernity of what is considered to be true and willing. If, however, one thinks, as Nietzsche did, that he [i.e. Zarathustra] is the true Dionysian witness (instead of *The Birth of Tragedy*, which really is), then such a confusion shows only that the Christianity of the reader has made the judgement and has been liberal in bestowing praise in the sense of commendation on his – most Christian work, which falls (and this is no coincidence) back into the language of the Luther Bible and into the tone of the preacher which must have previously so impressed the mind of the child (perhaps due to an inherited sensitivity to it).[89]

This focus on the person, rather than the philosophy, of Nietzsche prepares us for the devastating critique of the final chapter, entitled 'On Nietzsche's Self-Destruction'. True: Nietzsche's mental demise following his collapse on Turin in 1889 makes it hard to present him as a figure of uncompromising robustness. Yet Klages goes much further, using the opening of 'Of the Priests' as the occasion for the following analysis:

> One should read, after the discourse on the poets, another entitled 'Of the Priests', and if anyone could then still doubt where Nietzsche belongs, it would impossible even with a thousand reasons to teach him or her anything better. [...] In this way all doubt would be removed about the wording that should be used to describe his being: he was the site of conflict between the orgiast, as he depicted him to us, and the ascetic priest, as he uncovered him to us, or – in the abbreviating language of myth – the site of the conflict between *Dionysos* and *Jehovah*. We know no other 'world-historical' example for it! It was not and it is not unusual to find the conflict: Dionysos–Jehovah, even less unusual is the conflict: Socrates–Jehovah; but that one and the same personality should belong at the same time to Dionysos *and* to Jehovah is the rarest and most terrible case. From the standpoint of the Jehovist he represents a fallen priest, from the standpoint of the Bacchic an orgiast who has been condemned to 'dance in chains',[90] from the standpoint of life unavoidable self-destruction, from the standpoint of knowledge, however, a tragic lucky strike of the highest order: for it is precisely to the high voltage of this opposition that we owe the luminosity of Nietzsche's thought, which correspondingly reveals not so much his personality as its inexorable destruction.[91]

Klages and Nietzsche 27

For Klages, this insight – if this is what it is – has enormous explanatory value:

> If one has this key, then puzzle upon puzzle easily dissolves, many more than can be touched upon here; and, of course, one can hardly resist the conclusion that Nietzsche knew this: after all, he passionately sympathized with all those who have been tortured (e.g. with Pascal, e.g. with the Indian at the stake [*Dawn*, §135]), he described himself as a 'self-executioner',[92] and in *Zarathustra* he solemnly proclaimed: 'We all bleed at secret sacrificial tables, we all burn and roast to the honour of ancient idols',[93] and from his mouth there repeatedly came the shrieking cry for *redemption* (e.g. *On the Genealogy of Morals*, II, §24), even if, theoretically, he raged against nothing more angrily than against the Christian concept of redemption.[94]

And what about the doctrine of eternal recurrence? As far as Klages was concerned, this nonsensical idea was one of Nietzsche's biggest mistakes. In Klages's eyes, it was conceptually flawed through and through:

> Think about it: a Heraclitean as convinced as Nietzsche was knows no things, therefore no similarity of things, therefore no *repetition* of any kind. Similar things can recur, identical things never. Conversely, the assumption of repetitions constitutes the defining characteristic of mechanistic thought, irrespective of whether one is thinking of the numbers of plates that are manufactured from one and the same factory model, or the rotations of a wheel at a certain speed, *or* for that matter a *cosmic* wheel, whose each and every rotation requires billion upon billions of years. So much is evident. Simply unceasing repetition, the symbol of all mechanistic thought and the most unconditional counterexpression of life, is affirmed by Nietzsche the Heraclitean and in *The Will to Power*, where he tries to cover up the contradiction by separating the *infinity* of the repetitions from merely *finite* world machine of mechanistic through an emphasis on its terrible prospect: the most extreme exaggeration of a baroque ideal called perpetuum mobile![95]

In the final two paragraphs of his study, Klages reveals his sense of affinity with Nietzsche, as well as the immense gulf between both men:

> Place yourself in the mood of a thinker who turns to increasingly invocatory expressions to prove his *affirmation* of life in opposition to the despair which, from the unholy certitude that, within him, one part of him belongs to the *haters* of life, threatens him with suicide, and one can understand why he had to end up with the doctrine of recurrence, even though it is despair once again. With the declaration: this very same life, wrung a thousand times from the will to self-destruction, I shall live *again* thousands and thousands of times, he has achieved the most extreme form of what can be thought, not in terms of affirmation of life, but rather in terms of *negation of*

28 *Life*

negation. It is the defensive expression of the most inflexible self-assertion in opposition to the tendency to self-destruction.

Nietzsche burned; but in the glow of this fire two daimons, engaged in a fight to the death with each other, forged his Janus-faced work, which as befits such a genesis both in its truth as in its errors marks the furthest point to which until now reflection turned upon itself has ever reached.[96]

Klages could write this because he, too, understood all too well the power of the daimon: but whereas he, Klages, had been able to come to terms with his daimons, Nietzsche, for his part, had struggled – and ultimately succumbed.

Klages's monograph was widely reviewed – in *Der Bücherwurm* (by Hans Schmeer); in *Revue germanique* (by Henri Lichtenberger [1864–1941], a French Germanist who worked on Heine, Novalis, Wagner, and Nietzsche, and a translator of the whole of Goethe's *Faust*); and in the *Münchener Neueste Nachrichten* (by Hans Prinzhorn [1886–1933], a psychiatrist and art historian, who founded the famous Prinzhorn Collection in Heidelberg). In the *Schweizer Monatshefte für Politik und Kultur*, the Swiss philologist Martin Ninck (1895–1954) wrote an article on the 'turn' in psychology brought about by Nietzsche and by Klages, and the German philosopher Karl Löwith (1897–1973) published a lengthy article in *Reichls Philosophischer Almanach* entitled 'Nietzsche in Light of the Philosophy of Ludwig Klages'. And Klages's psychological approach to Nietzsche can be seen as one of the impulses behind Prinzhorn's *Nietzsche and the Twentieth Century* (1928), containing two lectures on Nietzsche's contribution to the development of psychological ideas.[97]

Celebrity ... and catastrophe

In 1932 Klages celebrated his sixtieth birthday, shortly after the publication of the second and third volumes of his main work, *The Spirit as Adversary of the Soul*. It is a measure of the celebrity that Klages had gained that this anniversary was an occasion for numerous acts of recognition and honour, including the award of the Goethe Medal for Art and Science, presented to him by the Reichspresident, Paul von Hindenburg. In the German press, numerous newspapers published articles congratulating him and presenting overviews of his philosophy. Nor was it just the press of his native city, Hanover, and his chosen native city, Munich; nor simply the press of Basel and Stettin, where his lectures had brought him a certain degree of fame; but the press across the whole of Germany, from Hamburg, Bremen, Lübeck, and Kiel in the north-east to Leipzig, Halle, Breslau in the east, from Königsberg and Danzig in the north-west to Stuttgart and Saarbrücken in the west, as well as all fifteen of Berlin's daily papers.

Klages's sixtieth birthday was also the occasion for a major academic tribute in the form of a *Festschrift*, a collection of writings presented to a scholar in his honour. Edited by Hans Prinzhorn, this volume was entitled *Science at the Crossroads between Life and Spirit* (*Die Wissenschaft am Scheidewege von*

Leben und Geist) (1932), and it contained some thirty academic essays by writers more or less associated with the intellectual circle around Klages. In his foreword to this *Festschrift*, Prinzhorn paid tribute to Klages and summarized his intellectual goals:

> In the life of Klages there is but *one* unrelenting task: to give shape to a bio-centric worldview that early on was experienced and intuited with tremendous force. Before such a task, all else had to recede that otherwise lends excitement and security and warmth in one's private life. The singer of praise to life became an ascetic dedicated to his work. A man who was full of respect for all true form and all creative growth became the most merciless unmasker of occidental errors – long before there appeared in the collapse of Europe what his Cassandra cries had announced. This combatant against his age could not be lured by any of its temptations. This lends his critique its powerful strike power, compared with which the efforts of smaller minds to combat those aspects of the age to which they themselves remained enslaved became irrelevant.[98]

More lyrically, Christoph Bernoulli contibuted the following poem in honour of Klages:

> Anyone who has seen him will never forget him.
> He possesses charm and, because of this, something of eternal youth.
> He possesses the healthy senses of a primordial vitality.
> He is full of intensity.
> He makes blue even bluer, red even redder.
> He cannot be diverted by anything from his path.
> His tyrannical devotion is directed to his work and *only* this.
> He is thorough.
> He is uncompromising in his attitude, original in his judgement.
> Unspoiled, this is how his sense of beauty is.
> His understanding is enormous. Whatever he ignites with the light of his mind, there everything resolves itself in clarity.
> He is a piece of nature, he is just as unsentimental as she is.
> He loves animals and they love him.
> He enriches, because he is in possession of the 'gift-giving virtue'.
> To experience *with* him means to experience *more*.
> A few hours in his presence can mean joy for a year.
> [...]
> He is no proselyte, he is no founder of a sect, he does not want to save the 'unredeemed'.
> He knows no 'ideals', he has no ethical goals. This is a reason for his tragic solitude.
> 'No longer to be able to will, this is the sign of regaining one's sight'.[99]
> He strives for truth, but he loves reality.

30   *Life*

He is eternally bound to the mystery. He knows that mysteries are not
puzzles.
And so he understands the world of symbols, differently from how Schuler
does, but no less profoundly.
The element of his intuitive power is fire.
He is a turning-point, far more than we, his contemporaries, can know.
He knows more than he says.[100]

As this poem suggests, Klages was a remarkably charismatic figure, and this
charisma clearly emerges from some contemporary accounts.

Here, for instance, is a recollection by Marie Römermann of what it was like
to attend a lecture by Klages in Munich:

Klages is giving a lecture in the Auditorium Maximum in Munich. The hall
is full to bursting. Ludwig comes in – loud trampling of feet; he stands at
the podium, commences his lecture; suddenly glances at the lecture theatre,
right up to the gallery, says: 'As Schiller (or was it Goethe) says...', and
gets stuck! Carries on without awkwardness, 'yes – the quotation escapes
me, I'll say it later', carries on, gets going, suddenly: '... and now I've got
the quotation!' – the listeners laugh and are amused and the lecture goes on.
I was flabbergasted that something like this could happen to Ludwig. He
explained to me later that he had looked at the hall again, seen that, even up
in the gallery, every seat was taken and noticed that he had not been speaking loudly enough, and so he had lost the thread.

(*Erinnerungen*, 20)

Elsewhere, Gustav Freytag (1816–1895) recalls Klages's power as an orator:

Perhaps I could say something about the specifically oratorical aspect of his
lectures. In a normal room or before a small gathering Klages was at his
best and most captivating. A larger lecture theatre poses certain challenges
to a speaker which not every one is equal to. What often comes across as
charming in a small space loses its effect in a larger room, and certain conditions have to be met in both visual and acoustic respects. Of course, Klages
usually had it easy right from the beginning, because he aleady knew a large
part of his audience personally or through their writings, and thus was
assured of the warmest of receptions. Even his appearance as a tall grown
man with an intellectual-looking head made him seem very congenial. Even
his voice was warm and pleasant-sounding. As a speaker he seemed digni-
fied and composed. His expositions were clear, always comprehensible even
to the uninitiated, expressed in a warm tone of voice, thereby – whether consciously or unconsciously – courting the listener's goodwill. Slight hints of
a Lower Saxon dialectic (despite long residence in Munich he never
acquired a Bavarian accent) had a hardly detrimental effect. What disturbed
more was his habit of letting his voice drop at the end of sentences, so that

at least those sitting further away could miss quite a bit, especially since, in German, the verb at the end of the sentence often offers the key to understanding the entire sentence. He was an autodidact without any proper training as a speaker. But his entire personality had such a strong effect that his talks always turned into a complete, often resounding success.

(Erinnerungen, 40–41)

And Freytag's account is confirmed by the one given by Wolfgang Olshausen (1911–1969), a wing commander of the general staff, of Klages's activity as a guest lecturer in Berlin in the 1930s:

Ludwig Klages's guest lectureship [at Berlin University, see above] was extended for the winter semester of 1933/1934, and his lecture bore the title: 'Spirit and soul!'. In the life of the German people there is a primordial German cultural stream, if I could simplistically call it that here, that usually flows on mostly unnoticed or even not recognized, only very rarely welling up and revealing itself in the full extent of the German landscape – the German youth and German researchers were as one in their participation in this clandestine primordial current!

What happened in that winter within this lecture hall was an incineration; namely, of three-millennia-old errors, and it was a day of reckoning with forces and powers which for the most part were consciously driving humankind and its planet toward the destruction of its soul.

The inaugural lecture of the semester seemed to be a solemn overture. This time every seat in the room was taken from the beginning. The first excitement erupted in signalling academic approval by stamping with one's feet, at first nervous and hesitant, then growing gradually more and more powerful until sustained, when Klages, who had begun by giving an overview of the structure and methodology of his lecture, said by way of guidance that he wanted to get into his topic using an historical approach: 'There have been,' he said, 'many different philosophical convictions and systems that have, one after the other right up to the present day and sometimes fiercely at loggerheads, speculated about and made statements on the relation between soul, body, and spirit; together we shall consider these systems in their essential claims and I shall then tell you what is right and what is wrong about them'.

This kind of talk was something that had never been heard at this highly modern university of Western thought in this century. Until now a sceptical relativism, which believed everything to be possible and tenable, yet nothing to be provable, and in the end was the ice-cold, fanatic apostle of a calculating and arbitrary use of power, had had its sinecure and secure stronghold: and now, in the midst of the phantoms of this temple of the Holy Spirit, a single man stood and touched the idols with his free, well-thought-out words, overturned them, and, breaking them, unmasked their hollowness.

32   *Life*

> Joyfully spurring on, the call to new and yet old shores rang out, and –
> Janus-headed as life itself – the angry genius of the German showed itself, a
> terrible sight to its opponents! [...]
>
> (Erinnerungen, 78–80)

At this point in our overview of Klages's life and works, we must turn to the
most difficult part of his intellectual career: his stance during the Third Reich.
Difficult, because one of the most commonly heard charges made against Klages
is that he sympathized with the National Socialists. As we shall see, however,
nothing could be further from the truth.

In an essay on Stefan George published in the Hamburg weekly magazine
Der Lotse in 1901, Klages had warned that the dream of a 'third Reich' would
forever remain 'metaphysically impossible'.[101] Yet in the 1920s and 1930s in
Germany, events around him seemed to prove that it was *politically* possible.
Founded on 24 February 1920, the National Socialist German Workers' Party
was led by Adolf Hitler from 1921 onwards, and came to power in Germany in
1933 when President Paul von Hindenburg appointed Hitler Chancellor. Now
the notion of a 'Third Reich' had its roots in the so-called Conservative Revolution movement of the 1920s, when the German cultural historian, Arthur Moeller
van den Bruck (1876–1925), used the term to describe an ideological position
synthesizing Right and Left, or nationalism and socialism.[102] Oswald Spengler's
notion of a 'Prussian Socialism' went in much the same direction.[103] But a chief
part of the National Socialist programme was its racist ideology, and in particular its anti-Semitism. In a footnote in one of his earliest works, *The Problems
of Graphology* (1910), Klages had analysed the psychological basis of anti-
Semitism:

> It is among the naiveties of widely-held 'anti-Semitism' to blame the Jews
> for what is their strength: a talent for business. Thanks to their instinctive
> sense of certainty in exchanging goods and changing money, over time they
> were able to make themselves indispensable to every Western culture. The
> complexification of the network of business relations is a task to which only
> the Jew can bring 'natural talent', while in this respect the Arian has to play
> the role of the apprentice, who is only able clumsily to imitate the knack of
> the master. To wish the Jews out of the business world is to replace what is
> subtle with something cruder, is to replace cleverness with limitedness:
> which in no way serves the purposes of society, but actually does damage to
> it in more than one way.[104]

The kind of language Klages uses here makes us uncomfortable today, and with
good reason. Yet the discourse about 'Jews' and 'Aryans' was, in fact, nothing
unusual at the beginning of the twentieth century; the ideologies that grew up in
the twentieth century around the nineteenth-century concept of 'race' regarded
themselves as scientific, and – as hard to believe as it may seem now – eugenics
was considered to be a serious discipline in the US and most European countries,

Celebrity ... and catastrophe 33

not just Germany. (Today we would baulk at ranking different nations or races, but in the UK and the US it is common to publish rankings of such institutions as hospitals, schools, colleges and universities, etc.). Even and especially the growing field of psychoanalysis seemed, at times, deeply invested in the notion of race;[105] after all, as Freud wrote to his 'best pupil', the psychoanalyst Karl Abraham (1877–1925), on 3 May 1908, 'You are closer to my intellectual constitution because of racial kinship', while adding that C. G. Jung,

> as a Christian and as a pastor's son, found his way to me only against great inner resistances. His association with us is the more valuable for that. I nearly said that it was only by his appearance on the scene that psychoanalysis escaped the danger of becoming a Jewish national affair.[106]

Klages's mistake, in this regard, is unthinkingly to have accepted the categories of the discourse of his day.

Chronologically, Klages's hectic lecture activities took place at the same time as the rise to power of the National Socialists; to posit a causal or ideological link between them is to misunderstand the reception of Klages in the 1930s and 1940s in Germany. For the political leadership of the National Socialist dictatorship soon realized there was a huge discrepancy between its own political goals and the critical stance towards modernity proposed by Klages. In 1934, Hans Eggert Schröder became the director of the Working-Group for Biocentric Research (*Arbeitskreis für biozentrische Forschung*), a group of scholars and researchers seeking to spread Klagesian ideas. On his account, in 1936 Schröder received a letter from the State Secret Police, ordering him to close down the Working-Group; and in 1938, he was warned by the Reich's Department for the Support of German Writing, an office under the control of one of the chief Nazi ideologues, Alfred Rosenberg (1892/93–1946), to desist from publishing articles about Klages.

It is true that, in the Third Reich, Klages continued to enjoy a considerable degree of support. In 1937, Klages celebrated his sixty-fifth birthday; in his honour, a journal called *Rhythm* (*Rhythmus: Monatsschrift für deutsche Kultur*), edited by Rudolf Bode, published a special edition with congratulations from no fewer than forty-six publicly-known wellwishers from across Europe. And in 1938, the journal of the National Socialist youth organization, *Will and Power* (*Wille und Macht*), published a remarkable article with the title, 'We Stand By Ludwig Klages'. Yet these individual voices need to be weighed against the much larger and much stronger public campaign organized against Klages.

For as well as individual acts of censorship and repression, Rosenberg issued a direct challenge and very public reproach to Klages in a lecture or speech, entitled 'Form and Life', held on the occasion of the beginning of the summer semester at the University of Halle in April 1938. In this public address, Rosenberg very clearly distances the National Socialist programme from the philosophy of Klages:

34 *Life*

The 'spirit' has precisely not, as Klages says, broken in as an extra-temporal-spatial cosmic power into a paradisiacal idyll, but it is a decisive component in our, and I repeat, our entire life. Will, reason, understanding – they have different functions in the process of this existence and stand in a relation of specific tension to what we call the body and what we call the soul. An abstract, destructive spirit only arises where a population, which is already racially divided, no longer possesses the full extent of its capacity for judgement, that is, where there is longer a healthy functioning of the body and the soul.

We cannot permit that this totality of our existence is destroyed by a fantasy based on prehistorical assumptions.

In order to save life, and to save *our* life, the will-o'-the-wisp-like will of a declining age was once again given a goal by the National Socialist *Weltanschauung*, directed not at business purposes, but at the preservation of vital energies.

[...]

Life is always a sculptural form; the expresssion of inner and outer form is the work; the work is concentrated deed; the deed, irrespective of whether it is artistic, philosophical, or political, is, if it is organic, always the total expression of soul, body, will, and reason. This is our innermost conviction. This overall attitude has, whether instinctively or consciously, supported our entire movement. This attitude was, we can now safely say, the precondition for the great German rebirth, for the rescue of German life. At the same time it was a turning-point in the fates, threatened by dangers, of the European peoples, and the future will show that the National Socialist *Weltanschauung* represents the revolutionary, life-giving turning-point for all the cultures of Europe.[107]

At this point, it is worthwhile summarizing some of the differences between National Socialist (NS) ideology and Klagesian philosophy, listed in Table 1.1.

Rosenberg's speech in Halle was widely reported in the National Socialist press, and reprinted in full in the cultural organ of the NSDAP, the *National Socialist Monthly* (*Nationalsozialistische Monatshefte*), before being published separately as a pamphlet-length book. As a follow-up to his lecture, Rosenberg organized a training week for his staff in the summer of 1938. The purpose of this training was to help them to combat different forms of what National Socialism described as 'sectarian' thought. Under this rubric fell various intellectual tendencies deemed incompatible with National Socialist ideology, including Oswald Spengler, the members of the circle around Stefan George, and Ludwig Klages and his followers. In a 'Parliamentary Expert's Report of the Rosenberg Department', we find the following declaration:

The official appointed by the Führer to be responsible for the entire intellectual and ideological education of the NSDAP has, through its timely intervention, prevented universalism from contaminating National Socialism; he

Table 1.1 Differences between National Socialist (NS) ideology and Klagesian philosophy

• NS interested in German paganism	• Klages interested in all forms of paganism
• NS in favour of modern technology	• Klages opposed to modern technology
• NS wrongly sees Nietzsche as forerunner of National Socialism	• Klages rightly sees Nietzsche a father of psychology
• NS sees war as a political option for political ends	• Klages understands war (*polemos*) in Heraclitean, metaphysical sense
• NS abuses Nature in its political programme	• Klages urges care and nurturing of the environment
• NS advocates racial anti-semitic policies, leading to the Holocaust	• Klages voices a cultural critique of Judeo-Christianity
• NS emphasizes instrumental reason	• Klages offers critique of instrumental reason
• NS looks to the future, trying to create a 'thousand-year *Reich*'	• Klages orientates the present around its continuity with the past
• NS is a political and military project	• Klages's philosophy is a metaphysical (and arguably aesthetic) project

is equally determined to avoid any kind of mingling of the 'biocentric' world-view with National Socialism.[108]

So where does the charge against Klages that he was, in some way or another, associated with National Socialism, come from? And why does his stance during the Third Reich in Germany remain a matter of controversy?[109] In part, it is due to the presence in Klages's writings of a discourse of race, although this discourse is neither central to his philosophical project, nor is he by any means alone in using it during this period. In part, it is due to a strategic blunder on Klages's part – perhaps in order to curry favour with the National Socialist authorities, or perhaps not – when in 1940 Klages published an edition of the *Nachlass* of his former *Kosmiker* colleague, Alfred Schuler, to which he added a foreword which include evidently, and inexcusably, anti-Semitic remarks. (This raises the difficult question: which is worse – to use the discourse of anti-Semitism, even if one does not believe it, or to use the discourse of anti-Semitism, because one really *is* a convinced anti-Semite?) And in part, the charge has stuck, because of intellectual laziness in academic circles and because it is politically convenient to let it stick. After all, if Klages can be written off as an anti-Semite, then one is spared the effort of dealing with his complex and – to be frank – linguistically and conceptually challenging works. Despite or even because of the recent work that has been done in this area by Nitzan Lebovic, all the evidence, internal and external, points to the fact that Klages's status during the 1930s and 1940s, both geographically and ideologically, was that of an outsider.

And he was an outsider in another sense, too. For in the 1930s, Klages did not just hide himself away in Switzerland, but he undertook a number of journeys within Europe that took him to many different countries in order to give his

36 *Life*

lectures. In 1935, for example, he visited the Netherlands, Denmark, Norway, and Sweden, as well as Finland, the Baltic States, and Danzig. And in 1937, he undertook a lecture tour to Italy, Greece, Bulgaria, Yugoslavia, and Albania.

Klages was by no means a stranger to the south of Europe, especially Italy. This was a country he had visited before, both in reality and in his imagination. In 1912, for instance, Klages had accepted an invitation issued by Richard Voss (1851–1918), a German dramatist and novelist who lived in Frascati, near Rome, to visit Italy and – in the footsteps of Goethe and virtually every other vistor of the seventeenth, eighteenth, and nineteenth centuries on the Grand Tour – had travelled to Verona, Bologna, Florence, Capri, Pompeii, Naples, and Rome. Writing to Rose Plehn (1865–1945) – a painter who owned an estate at Lubochin (then in western Prussia, now called Lubocheń), where Klages, who held her in great affection, regularly stayed between 1903 and 1913[110] – on 24 May 1912 from Capri, Klages had proclaimed:

> Florence is a city where I could *live*. To the element of the south is added an intimate element that reminds me of home – even the populace displays an unmistakeably northern streak. Nothing in the overall image of the city disturbs the wonderful unity, measured by which what is painful about *our* urban dwellings is all too alarmingly obvious. *This* is how one once could build entire cities, and today we can no longer put together even a single street without dissonance. The harmony with the landscape is perfect, and it is not easy to fit together a picture of where everything more perfectly agrees than Florence seen from the tower of the Palazzo Vecchio, from the square of Michel Angelo, or from the terrace of the wonderfully beautiful Fiesole. Now at least I have had an insight into the *real* Renaissance, which is not only Italian in origin but also Italian in spirit, and evidently could only be implanted in the north in an artificial way: it flourished there as little as figs, olives, and lemons would flourish. Palazzo Pitti and Strozzi show how much *authentic*, in particular Roman spirit they have absorbed and to what extent talking about a "rebirth" was not *entirely* a delusion.[111]

At the same time, Klages felt he was able to plunge back into the ancient past of Rome by using his intuitive imagination. In the early fragments he edited and published as *Rhythms and Runes* (*Rhythmen und Runen*), we find the following reflection on the splendour that was once ancient Rome:

> With more than two thousand temples this Rome was resplendent; and what has remained of them! The desert of rubble of the Forum, the even more alarming desert of the Palatine, the Pantheon which has been plundered bare, the ruins of the Colosseum and a few of the giant Baths. Who could still doubt that a curse is lashing down on humankind and, like an insatiable moloch, swallowing humankind's images of itself, the gifts of its most divine hours! As I was trying in vain to get over such sentiments, with their help I saw more brightly the germ of the disaster already in the blood and

the origins of the eternal city: it had always been an incomparably impressive, but pathological phenomenon. Next to the noble perfection of the Doric pillar, a Roman composite order looks like false pomp and decorative play. Inclined more to smallness than greatness in his formal expression, the Roman still insisted, full of morbid craving for power, on what was massive, gigantic, colossal. Measured by extent and width, his pillars and entablature would have required the antemundane lines of the Egyptian to achieve a perfection free of contradiction, yet they lose their way in humanly ambitious flamboyance. Not by chance, it seems to me, is it there that the Renaissance died from the creative hatred of Michelangelo, and it was true Roman soil, even if ploughed by a bad race, on which a St Peter's, on which the formal bombast of a Bernini, and all the exaggerated pomp of the hierarchical baroque, arose. What the latter in its theatrical excessiveness shows us is what clings to the essence of the Roman: the conflict between the smallness of form and boundlessness of absolute dimension; and it becomes apparent that one cannot strive unpunished to leave the limits of humankind, once one has ceased to be a god.

(*RR*, p. 528)

In 1937 Klages returned to Pompeii, a site which had long exercised his imagination, as this extract from *Rhythms and Runes* shows:

It is difficult, if not in prose impossible, to describe the images of this most remarkable of all ruined sites. Indeed, even the word ruin no longer fits. We think when we hear it of rubble, surrounded and overgrown by blossoming dense undergrowth, sinking back into the realm of nature and as it were towering only with lost battlements over the river of time that separates all things again. Here, however, it is different. You are entering a city whose houses and temples are missing their roofs, where only a few single pillars stand in the magnificent buildings of the forum; what did not simply break or was carried off still stands, not essentially different from how it did two thousand years ago, despite its incredible age hardly any less new than it was and exactly as if the inhabitants had only just left in their haste to flee. You enter into narrow streets, most of them criss-crossing at right angles, above the clear sky of the south, to the right and to the left the hot, low house-walls with beautiful doors and small windows; here, at the crossroads, a carved fountain, which no longer spouts any water; there, on the wall, an inscription which announces a tavern, on the other wall a colourful painting: two men carrying a large grape, the coat-of-arms of the cellarman or the wine-seller; deeply buried in the hard travertine road surface the wheel tracks of ancient carts.

And what a world opens up in a frightening presence when you cross the threshold of a house whose mosaics humorously or seriously proclaim the particular outlook of the owner! The cool atrium receives us with the impluvium in the middle and further back the delightful peristyle where, between

38   *Life*

the surrounding pillars, the statuettes of the house-gods still stand, of the silenes, erotes, nymphs, bacchantes, and where a spring fountain that has come to life again sprays a moist breath over the tender grasses. We enter the bathing rooms, the chambers for sleeping and making love, on whose walls there glow, in unchangingly luminous colours, images of sweet figures and an ever-streaming passion for life. As if by themselves the quilts and rugs arise again for the inner sense again; a mysterious twilight surrounds us, in which one rediscovers what has been stolen away into museums: the vases, flasks, lamps, dishes, tripods with cauldrons, ornate mirrors, clasps, pins; and how little does it take, in the place of stone and colour, for the delicate, noble figures from the past themselves to appear, from whose darkly gleaming pupils glows the mystery, lost for ever, of *the life of the senses*!

(*RR*, pp. 525–526)

This sense of the persistence of the past, wonderfully evoked in his rhythmic prose, is one of the chief characteristics of Klages's philosophy.

In 1938, Klages travelled to Paris, and on his return he allowed himself to be persuaded by Gustav Freytag to begin work on the *Nachlass* or literary remains of Alfred Schuler. In sifting through these handwritten documents, Klages received much-needed assistance from Martin Ninck, and Schuler's *Fragments and Lectures* (*Fragmente und Vorträge*) was published by J. A. Barth in 1940. Schuler's small but intense – and intensely startling – *œuvre* required a good deal of commentary in order to understood, and Klages supplied a lengthy introduction of over 100 pages to bring the reader into Schuler's extraordinary world.[112]

Having published Schuler's *Nachlass*, Klages turned to his own. At the time of the outbreak of the First World War, Klages had begun with sifting and sorting out his own literary *Nachlass*; now, at the height of the Second World War, Klages saw this project through to publication – it appeared, published by J. A. Barth, in 1944 under the evocative title *Rhythms and Runes*.

A year later, and the war was over. And in 1947, Klages turned seventy-five years old. As earlier, when he had turned sixty, a *Festschrift* to celebrate the occasion was prepared. Edited by Herbert Hönel, and with some twenty contributions, *Ludwig Klages – Explorer and Herald of Life* (1947) showed a researcher at the height of his reputation, as did the flood of invitations from Europe and overseas to participate in philosophical and psychological conferences. Or did they?

Because once notices that, after the Second World War, the name of Klages begins to be mentioned less and less often. He continued his philosophical work, as we shall see, but why did Klages disappear from the European intellectual scene? There are a number of reasons for this. First, Klages was never a big player within the academy. He did not have an academic post, and his audiences were composed of interested listeners outside the university scene. After the Second World War, this generation of listeners – and, in fact, an entire culture of

Celebrity ... and catastrophe 39

popular education – never recovered from the blow it had been dealt during the years of the Third Reich.

Second, Klages had never been a 'public intellectual' in the conventional sense. Although he spoke on the theme of environmentalism, he did not directly address political (or party political issues). Given the political challenges of the post-War environment – the economic reconstruction of Germany, the division of Europe into East and West through the 'Iron Curtain', the proliferation of nuclear weapons –, Klages seemed to many to have become less relevant. Third, there was the problem of the unavailability of his works in the bookshops (see below). Fourth, the sheer complexity of Klages's philosophical discourse and the uncompromising tone of its rhetoric no longer played as well with listeners and readers. The level of knowledge required to understand Klages's texts began to act as a barrier to their reception; he was simply too 'difficult' to engage a new generation of readers.

Fifth, Klages's philosophical system lacks the kind of jargon that one finds with, for example, existentialism in general and Heidegger in particular. One of the key members of the Frankfurt School, Theodor W. Adorno (1903–1969), accused Heidegger of using the 'jargon of authenticity'; at the same time, the Frankfurt School was highly elitist and exclusivist in its philosophical discourse (not least in its pick-and-mix combination of terminology from psychoanalysis and from Marxism). But such key Klagesian terms as 'spirit' and 'soul' proved to lack the necessary critical punch; and over time this became a big problem. 'Under the pavement lies the beach', for instance, one of the great slogans of the 1968 revolution, proved to have an appeal that 'spirit as adversary of soul' did not. Of course, by this time Klages had long been dead (he passed away in 1956), and this leads to the sixth and penultimate reason for his disppearance.

Klagesian philosophy was always something of one-man-show. True, there had been such prolific followers as Hans Kern, Werner Deubel, and Hans Eggert Schröder, not to mention Julius Deussen, Erwin Ackerknecht, and Hans Prinzhorn; and there had been an attempt to create a Klagesian school in the form of the Working-Group for Biocentric Research. But by and large Klages had not created a school on the same scale that phenomenology or existentialism had done, and as structuralism and post-structuralism would do. Finally, it was academic-politically and intellectual-strategically opportune for too many to allow Klages simply to fade away of his own accord. For he was simply too radical, too utterly opposed to modernity, and too consistent in his critique, to be a successful figure in the post-War environment.

Yet we have already overtaken ourselves at this point. For even in his old age Klages continued his work, right up to his death. Already in the 1930s, Klages had begun to explore a specific area in which to apply his biocentric insights: rhythm. In *On the Essence of Rhythm* (*Vom Wesen des Rhythmus*) (1934), he offered an extended meditation on how rhythm demonstrated the fundamental Klagesian antithesis between 'spirit' and 'soul'. As he put it, 'the beat repeats, but rhythm renews',[113] thus illustrating once again the conflict between a mechanical (and, in his view, ultimately morbid) view of the world and an approach

40   *Life*

that emphasizes and appreciates warmth, liveliness, spontaneity: the rythmic (because never quite exact) pulse of life! And when, in this work, Klages derives the real meaning of 'rhythm' from its etymology of *rheein*, i.e. 'to flow', he points the way forward to the major development in his thought in the late 1940s.

For with *Language as the Source of Psychology* (*Die Sprache als Quell der Seelenkunde*) (1948), Klages shows himself to be in line with at least one of the major trends of philosophy in the twentieth century, and undertakes his own version of the 'linguistic turn'. Although the shift towards considering the relationship between philosophy and language is largely associated with Wittgenstein and his *Tractatus Logico-Philosophicus* (1921) and his *Philosophical Investigations* (1953), as well as with the structuralism of Ferdinand de Saussure (1857–1913) and the poststructuralism of Jacques Derrida (1930–2004), Michel Foucault (1926–1984), and French feminist thought, a concern with language had already been evident in the German tradition in the thought of Johann Georg Hamann (1730–1788) and Wilhelm von Humboldt (1767–1835). Yet Klages's approach to language is, in keeping with the rest of his philosophy, an eminently *symbolic* one. What, he asked, does language tell us about the way we 'see' – and, in this sense, construct – the world? So Klages investigates the symbolism of sounds, names, conceptions of space, use of past tenses, and the like, for two of the most important principles of the Klagesian theory of expression are, first, that language is an excellent guide to psychology; and, second, that from words used in an everyday context one can make important psychological deductions.[114] His study demonstrates the fecundity of his philosophical approach, and *Language as the Source of Psychology* remains one of the great unread philosophical treatises of the twentieth century.

In 1952, Klages celebrated his eightieth birthday. The occasion was marked by a congratulatory letter from the West German Bundespräsident, Theodor Heuss (1884–1963); by the republication of his treatise, *On Dream Consciousness*; and by the decision of three publishers, Annemarie Meiner, Wolfgang Meiner, and Herbert Grundmann, to republish Klages's major work, *The Spirit as Adversary of the Soul*, in a new edition. The background to this decision was the fact that, in the years following the end of the Second World War, Klages's works had nearly all disappeared from the bookshops and become unavailable. His previous publisher, the Leipzig-based publishing house of Johann Ambrosius Barth, was now in the Soviet-controlled occupation zone that was to become the German Democratic Republic, and Klages's work was not the political flavour of the month. So no new editions were going to be published in Leipzig. With the help of Arthur Meiner, Klages began the task of reclaiming the rights to his works and gaining licences for other publishers, initially in Switzerland, to republish them. The new edition of *The Spirit as Adversary of the Soul*, reprinting the original three parts in one volume, appeared in 1954, published by Bouvier Verlag in Bonn.

Its owner, Herbert Grundmann, also agreed to the publication of Klages's complete works (*Sämtliche Werke*), a project which saw ten volumes, including

Celebrity ... and catastrophe 41

an index volume, published between 1964 and 1982. (This edition is not quite complete: his study of Stefan George; the *Nachlass* work, *Rhythms and Runes*; and his foreword to his edition of Schuler, for instance, were to be an included in a volume dedicated to Klages's literary output which, however, never appeared.) In a supplement of three volumes, Hans Eggert Schröder offered a biography of Klages, drawing on the extensive materials in the Ludwig-Klages-Archiv in the Deutsches Literaturarchiv in Marbach am Neckar; work on the third volume was completed by Franz Tenigl.[115]

In an article which appeared in the German weekly paper, *Die Zeit*, in 1952, Rudolf Ibel summed up Klages's achievements in the following words:

> The creator of this universal work of a lifetime, whose ideas and influences cannot be overlooked, lives today in Kilchberg outside Zurich, exposed to the poverty of everyday life. He has never had titles, awards, honours, or prizes, and it seems that official praise will continue to overlook him. Yet he nevertheless believes he is able to stake a claim to being 'the most plundered [unnamed!] author of the present age'.

Ibel continues:

> One might wish to ridicule his almost monomaniacal glorification of the primordial epoch and the Pelasgians as being mere spleen, and regret the way he overlooks what Christianity has done for us, one might consider him to be a Romantic seducer whose cultural pessimism for minds requiring faith and comfort is dangerous, and deny that he appreciates what our century has achieved (after the turn of the century he does not recognize any literature as being great): the monumental size of his work cannot be disputed, even by the most vehement opponent; and that he has many of these is honour enough.[116]

If having opponents is a sign of honour, then Klages is not only the most pillaged and plundered, but also one of the most honoured of the thinkers of our time!

A photograph taken in 1952 shows the eighty-year-old Klages at work, sitting behind his desk in his study in the Conrad Ferdinand Meyer House in Kilchberg. Behind him is a bookcase full of books; on the wall to the right, two pictures. To the left, a reproduction of a steatite rhyton in the shape of a bull's head from the Little Palace of Knossos. On display in the Heraklion Archaeological Museum, the original has horns that are gilded, eyes made of rock crystal, and its muzzle is made of mother-of-pearl. Created around 1500 to 1450 BCE, it is an iconic image of Minoan art and a powerful symbol of the life force. And to the right, there is a Chinese landscape, a New Year's gift to him by the art historian Otto Fischer (1886–1948).[117] In 1921, Fischer published a study of Chinese landscape painting (*Chinesische Landschaftsmalerei*, 1921), and this picture displays an entirely different kind of aesthetic from the one exemplified by the Knossos bull.

Figure 3 Klages at work in his study.

These two pictures from entirely different cultures, both removed in time and space from the Germanic cultural sphere, illustrate well the range of sensibilities that fascinated Klages.

Sitting at his desk, the philosopher is at work. Bent over some papers, it looks as if he might be correcting a manuscript draft. On his desk, a lamp, a potted plant, a teapot, a large mug, and what looks like a spoon in a bowl. Has he just been enjoying his lunch or his breakfast? The expression on Klages's face is one of concentrated dedication, as he works on the papers in front of him. The atmosphere is one of calm, of tranquillity, in which any excitement and tension are purely cerebral; perhaps somewhat isolated, or maybe – who knows? – even lonely; yet this is no fusty academic's study, there is also very much a sense of intellectual passion in evidence. And a passion for life – something which, from its beginning to its end, defined Klages's life as a graphologist, a characterologist, a psychologist, a metaphysical philosopher – and as a human being.

Notes

1 To date, the only full-length biography of Klages is in German; see H. E. Schröder, *Ludwig Klages: Die Geschichte seines Lebens*, vol. 1, *Die Jugend*; vol. 2/i, *Das Werk (1905–1920)*, vol. 2/ii, ed. F. Tenigl, *Das Werk (1920–1956)*, Bonn: Bouvier, 1966–1982. A new biography, again in German, is currently being prepared by Heinz-Siegfried Strelow.
2 Klages, letter to William Mackenzie of 13 December 1918; in *CAK*, p. 21.

Notes 43

3 Letter to Martin Ninck of 26 January 1945; in *CAK*, p. 23.
4 E.-V. Kotowski, *Feindliche Dioskuren: Theodor Lessing und Ludwig Klages: Das Scheitern einer Jugendfreundschaft (1885–1899)*, Berlin: Jüdische Verlagsanstalt, 2000.
5 Lessing, letter of 30 August 1933 to Carl von Hacht; in Kotowski, *Feindliche Dioskuren*, pp. 8–9.
6 L. Tieck, 'Novalis' Lebensumstände' (1815), in Novalis, *Briefe und Dokumente* [*Werke; Briefe; Dokumente*, ed. E. Wasmuth, vol. 4], Heidelberg: Schneider, 1954, pp. 7–25 (p. 12).
7 F. zu Reventlow, *Sämtliche Werke, Briefe und Tagebücher*, ed. M. Schardt *et al.*, 5 vols, Oldenburg: Igel, 2004. For further discussion, see C. Gianni Ardic, *La Fuga degli dèi: Mito, matriarcato e immagine in Ludwig Klages*, Milan: Jouvence, 2016.
8 See 'Hans H. Busse: Ein vergessener Pionier der Graphologie'. Available www. fvdg.graphologie-online.com/n1/busse.html. Accessed 6 January 2017.
9 E. Axel [L. Klages], 'Zum Goethebildnis', *Graphologische Monatshefte* 6, 1902, 103–104 (p. 104); in *CAK*, pp. 38–39.
10 'Urworte. Orphisch' ('Primal Word. Orphic'), in J. W. von Goethe, *Selected Poems* [Goethe Edition, vol. 1], ed. C. Middleton, Boston: Suhrkamp/Insel, 1983, pp. 230–233.
11 For further discussion of the historico-intellectual contest to Bode's 'expressive gymnastics' (*Ausdrucksgymnastik*), see O. Hanse, *À l'école du rythme...: Utopies communautaires allemandes autour de 1900*, Saint-Etienne: Presses de l'université de Saint-Etienne, 2010; O. Hanse, 'Rudolf Bode entre pessimisme culturel et engagement politique', in M. Cluet and C. Repussard (eds), *"Lebenreform": Die soziale Dynamik der politischen Ohnmacht; La dynamique sociale de l'impuissance politique*, Tübingen: Francke, 2013, pp. 183–208; and P. Crespi, 'Rhythmanalysis in Gymnastics and Dance: Rudolf Bode and Rudolf Laban', *Body and Society* 20, nos 3 and 4 (2014), 30–50.
12 Is Herta Wedekind the same person as Erika Wedekind, described by Theodor Lessing (in *Einmal und nie wieder*, chapter 17) as a relative of the writer Frank Wedekind?
13 In Musil's novel *The Mann without Qualities*, the figure of Dr Meingast is based on Ludwig Klages. For further discussion, see T. Schneider, 'Robert Musil – Gustav Donath – Ludwig Klages: Marginalien zur Meingast-Episode im *Mann ohne Eigenschaften*', *Musil-Forum* 25–26, 1999–2000, 239–252; and H.-P. Preußer, 'Die Masken des Ludwig Klages: Figurenkonstellation als Kritik und Adaption befremdlicher Ideen in Robert Musils Roman *Der Mann ohne Eigenschaften*', *Musil-Forum* 31, 2009–2010, 224–253.
14 A record of Klages's paper at the Viennese Psychoanalytic Society, given on 25 October 1911, is comtained in its published *Protocolls*. For further discussion of Klages and Freud, see W. Martynkewicz, 'Ludwig Klages und Sigmund Freud: Ein Seitenstück zur "Jung-Krise"', literaturkritik.de, Nr. 1, January 2006. Available www.literaturkritik.de/public/rezension.php?rez_id=8985. Accessed 6 January 2017.
15 Ninck was the author of *Jesus als Charakter: Eine psychologische Untersuchung seiner Persönlichkeit* (1925), republished Hamburg: SEVERUS Verlag, 2013.
16 Of Jewish descent, Palágyi's original name was Silberstein; born in Plaks in Hungary, he lived (and died) in Darmstadt, where he is buried. The relation between Klages's philosophy and Palágyi's physics is addressed in B. Müller, *Kosmik: Prozeßontologie und temporale Poetik bei Ludwig Klages und Alfred Schuler: Zur Philosophie und Dichtung der Schwabinger Kosmischen Runde*, Munich: Telesma, 2007, pp. 69–77. For an overview of Palágyi's thought, see W. R. Boyce Gibson, 'The Philosophy of Melchior Palágyi: (I) Space-Time and the Criticism of Relativity' and '(II) The Theory of Life and Mind', *Journal of Philosophical Studies* 3, no. 9, January 1928, 15–28 and no. 10, April 1928, 158–172.

44 *Life*

17 For further discussion of Stefan George, see R. E. Norton, *Secret Germany: Stefan George and his Circle*, Ithaca and London: Cornell University Press, 2002.

18 For further discussion, see P. Bishop, 'Stefan George and the Munich Cosmologists', in J. Rieckmann (ed.), *A Companion to the Works of Stefan George*, Rochester, NY: Camden House, 2005, pp. 161–187.

19 F. Nietzsche, *Kritische Studienausgabe*, ed. G. Colli and M. Montinari, Munich/ Berlin and New York: dtv; de Gruyter, 1988, vol. 9, 11[7], p. 443. This sense of the cosmic was explored at the beginning of the twentieth century by the Canadian psychiatrist Richard Maurice Bucke (1837–1902) in his study, initiated by his own mystical experience in London in 1872, of such experiences in such historical figures as Gautama Buddha, Jesus Christ, St Paul of Tarsus, Plotinus, the prophet Mohammed, Dante, Bartolomé de Las Casas, St John of the Cross, Francis Bacon, Jakob Böhme, William Blake, Honoré de Balzac, Walt Whitman, and Edward Carpenter (see *Cosmic Consciousness: A Study in the Evolution of the Human Mind*, Philadelphia: Innes, 1901). Bucke distinguished between the perceptual mind (sense impressions), the receptual mind (simple consciousness), the conceptual mind (self consciousness), and the intuitional mind (a mind in which 'sensation, simple consciousness and self consciousness are supplemented and crowned with cosmic consciousness') (p. 13). In fact, Bucke derived the term 'cosmic consciousness' from the thought of his friend, Edward Carpenter, who in *Civilization: Its Cause and Cure* (1889; 1920), argued in an almost proto-Klagesian manner that civilization is a kind of disease through which human societies pass.

20 See A. Schuler, *Cosmogonische Augen: Gesammelte Schriften*, ed. B. Müller, Paderborn: Igel, 1997; and *Gesammelte Werke*, ed. B. Müller, Munich: Telesma, 2007.

21 F. Wegener, *Alfred Schuler, der letzte deutsche Katharer: Gnosis, Nationalsozialismus und mystische Blutleuchte*, Gladbeck, KFVR – Kulturförderverein Ruhrgebiet e.V., 2003.

22 H. Jonas, *Gnosis und spätantiker Geist*, vol. 1, *Die mythologische Gnosis*, Göttingen: Vandenhoeck & Ruprecht, 1954; vol. 2, *Von der Mythologie zur mystischen Philosophie*, Göttingen: Vandenhoeck & Ruprecht, 1993; in English as *The Gnostic Religion: The Message of the Alien God and the Beginnings of Christianity*, Boston: Beacon Press, 1958.

23 M. Pauen, *Dithyrambiker des Untergangs: Gnostizismus in Ästhetik und Philosophie der Moderne*, Berlin: Akademie Verlag, 1993, pp. 135–198, 'Ludwig Klages: Heidnische Gnosis'.

24 Rilke to Marie von Thurn und Taxis of 18 March 1915; in *CAK*, p. 131.

25 S. George, 'A. S.', in *The Works of Stefan George rendered into English*, tr. O. Marx and E. Morwitz, Chapel Hill, NC: University of North Carolina, 1949, p. 104.

26 Klages, 'Editor's Introduction', in A. Schuler, *Fragmente und Vorträge: Aus dem Nachlaß*, ed. L. Klages, Leipzig: J. A. Barth, 1940, pp. 29–30; in *CAK*, pp. 200–201.

27 Schuler, *Cosmogoniae Fragmenta*, 'Lucernae dispersae: Tabula tertia', §11; in Schuler, *Gesammelte Werke*, ed. Müller, p. 94.

28 See T. Anz, 'Kafka, der Krieg und das größte Theater der Welt', in U. Schneider and A. Schumann (eds), *"Krieg der Geister": Erster Weltkrieg und literarische Moderne*, Würzburg: Königshausen & Neumann, 2000, pp. 247–262.

29 See J. Eder, 'Die Geburt des "Zauberbergs" aus dem Geiste der Verwirrung: Thomas Mann und der erste Weltkrieg', in Schneider and Schumann (eds), *"Krieg der Geister"*, pp. 171–187.

30 W. McGuire and R. F. C. Hull (eds), *C. G. Jung Speaking: Interviews and Encounters*, Princeton, NJ: Princeton University Press, 1977, p. 234.

31 See H.-U. Wehler, *Deutsche Gesellschaftsgeschichte, 1914–1949*, vol. 4, Munich: Beck, 2003, pp. 14–15.

32 Letter of 1 October 1914; cited in *CAK*, p. 67.

33 Letter of 2 September 1914; cited in *CAK*, p. 67.

Notes 45

34 Letter of 11 January 1915; cited in *CAK*, p. 68.

35 Norbert von Hellingrath, 'Hölderlin und die Deutschen'.

36 A. Schuler, 'Über die biologischen Voraussetzungen des Imperium Romanum'.

37 Nietzsche, *Ecce Homo*, 'Why I Am so Clever', §9; in *Ecce Homo*, tr. R. J. Hollingdale, Harmondsworth: Penguin, 1992, p. 34.

38 Klages, 'Begriffskritik', *Graphologische Monatshefte* 12, 1908, 19–20 and 59–60; in *SW*, vol. 3, pp. 610–613.

39 Klages, 'Geist und Seele: Psychologische Grundbegriffe', *Deutsche Psychologie* 1, 1917, no. 3/4, 281–314, no. 5, 361–397; 2, 1919, no. 5, 245–270, no. 6, 171–196; in *SW*, vol. 3, pp. 1–154.

40 Klages, letter of 8 September 1917 to Johann Ambrosius Barth; cited in *SW*, vol. 3, p. 750.

41 C. A. Bernoulli, *Johann Jakob Bachofen und das Natursymbol: Ein Würdigungsversuch*, Basel: Schwabe, 1924.

42 See W. Benjamin, 'Review of Bernoulli's Bachofen', in *Selected Writings*, ed. M. Bullock and M. W. Jennings, Cambridge, MA: Harvard University Press, 2004, vol. 1, *1913–1926*, pp. 426–427.

43 J. J. Bachofen, *Versuch über die Gräbersymbolik der Alten*, 2nd edn [mit einem Vorwort von C. A. Bernoulli und einer Würdigung von L. Klages], Basel: Helbing & Lichtenhahn, 1925.

44 A. Kubin, *Dämonen und Nachtgesichte*, Dresden: Reissner, 1926; in *CAK*, p. 82.

45 W. Deubel (ed.), *Deutsche Kulturrevolution: Weltbild der Jugend*, Berlin: Junker & Dünnhaupt, 1931. For an anthology of some of Deubel's most important articles, see W. Deubel, *Im Kampf um die Seele: Wider den Geist der Zeit: Essays und Aufsätze, Aphorismen und Gedichte*, ed. F. Deubel, Bonn: Bouvier, 1997.

46 C. Bernoulli and L. Klages (eds), *Romantische Naturphilosophe*, Jena: Diederichs, 1926. See I. Heidler, *Der Verleger Eugen Diederichs und seine Welt (1896–1930)*, Wiesbaden: Harrassowitz, 1998, pp. 347–350.

47 T. Mann, 'Nietzsche's Philosophie in Lichte unserer Erfahrung', in *Gesammelte Werke*, 13 vols, Frankfurt am Main: Fischer, 1974, vol. 9, pp. 675–712. For further discussion, see P. Bishop, 'The Intellectual World of Thomas Mann', in R. Robertson (ed.), *The Cambridge Companion to Thomas Mann*, Cambridge: Cambridge University Press, 2002, pp. 22–42.

48 T. Mann, 'Nietzsche's Philosophy in the Light of our Experience' (1947), in *Gesammelte Werke*, vol. 13, pp. 675–712 (p. 675).

49 See H. Raschel, *Das Nietzsche-Bild im George-Kreis: Ein Beitrag zur Geschichte der deutschen Mythologeme*, Berlin and New York: de Gruyter, 1984.

50 E. Bertram, *Nietzsche: Versuch einer Mythologie*, Bonn: Bouvier, 1918 (10th edn, 1989); *Nietzsche: Attempt at a Mythology*, tr. R. E. Norton, Urbana and Chicago: University of Illinois Press, 2009.

51 W. Dilthey, *Das Wesen der Philosophie* [1907], ed. M. Riedel, Stuttgart: Reclam, 1984, tr. S. A. and W. T. Emery as *The Essence of Philosophy*, Chapel Hill, NC: University of North Carolina Press, 1954, pp. 31 and 72.

52 G. Simmel, *Schopenhauer und Nietzsche: Ein Vortragszyklus*, Leipzig: Duncker & Humblot, 1907, p. 6; tr. H. Loiskandl, D. Weinstein, and M. Weinstein as *Schopenhauer and Nietzsche*, Urbana and Chicago: University of Illinois Press, 1991, pp. 6–7.

53 K. Jaspers, *Nietzsche: An Introduction to the Understanding of his Philosophical Activity*, tr. C. F. Wallraff and F. J. Schmitz, Tucson: University of Arizona Press, 1965.

54 M. Heidegger, *Nietzsche*, ed. D. F. Krell, tr. D. F. Krell *et al.*, 4 vols, San Francisco: Harper & Row, 1979–1987. For further discussion, see L. P. Blond, *Heidegger and Nietzsche: Overcoming Metaphysics*, London and New York: Continuum, 2010.

46 *Life*

55 See S. E. Aschheim, *The Nietzsche Legacy in Germany 1890–1990*, Berkeley: University of California Press, 1994.
56 See M. Pütz (ed.), *Nietzsche in American Literature and Thought*, Columbia, SC: Camden House, 1995.
57 See B. G. Rosenthal (ed.), *Nietzsche in Russia*, Princeton, NJ: Princeton University Press, 1986.
58 P. Ilie, 'Nietzsche in Spain: 1890–1910', *Publication of the Modern Language Association* 79, no. 1, March 1964, 80–96.
59 For a discussion of early French Nietzsche reception, see C. E. Forth, *Zarathustra in Paris: The Nietzsche Vogue in France 1891–1918*, Dekalb, IL: Northern Illinois University Press, 2001.
60 G. Benn, 'Nietzsche – nach fünfzig Jahren' [1950], in *Gesammelte Werke*, ed. D. Wellershoff, 8 vols, Wiesbaden: Limes, 1968, vol. 4, pp. 1046–1057 (p. 1046).
61 R. Furness, *Zarathustra's Children: A Study of a Lost Generation of German Writers*, Rochester, NY: Camden House, 2000.
62 For further discussion, see P. Bishop, 'Ludwig Klages's Early Reception of Friedrich Nietzsche', *Oxford German Studies* 31, 2002, 129–160; and 'Ein Kind Zarathustras und eine nicht-metaphysische Auslegung der ewigen Wiederkehr', *Hestia: Jahrbuch des Klages-Gesellschaft* 21, 2002/2003, 15–37.
63 L. Klages, *Die psychologischen Errungenschaften Nietzsches*, Leipzig: Barth, 1926, p. 180; in *SW*, vol. 5, pp. 179–180. For a more recent, and more positive, appreciation of Nietzsche's contribution to psychology as an understanding of the self, see G. Parkes, *Composing the Soul: Reaches of Nietzsche's Psychology*, Chicago and London: Chicago University Press, 1994.
64 F. Nietzsche, *Basic Writings*, ed. and tr. W. Kaufmann, New York: Modern Library, 1968, p. 222.
65 For an introduction to Sophistic thought, see W. K. C. Guthrie, *The Sophists*, Cambridge: Cambridge University Press, 1971.
66 Klages, *Errungenschaften Nietzsches*, p. 56; in *SW*, vol. 5, p. 57.
67 Klages, *Errungenschaften Nietzsches*, p. 56; in *SW*, vol. 5, p. 57.
68 Nietzsche, *Basic Writings*, p. 239; cf. *Beyond Good and Evil*, §270 (*Basic Writings*, pp. 410–411).
69 Plato, *Collected Dialogues*, ed. E. Hamilton and H. Cairns, Princeton, NJ: Princeton University Press, 1989, p. 266. As Callicles goes on to state, 'But in my view nature itself makes it plain that it is right for the better to have the advantage over the worse, the more able over the less' (483c–d): a highly proto-Nietzschean standpoint!
70 Klages, *Errungenschaften Nietzsches*, pp. 56–57; in *SW*, vol. 5, p. 57.
71 Klages, *Errungenschaften Nietzsches*, p. 57; in *SW*, vol. 5, p. 58.

72 There exists a feigned contempt for all the things which men in fact take most seriously, *for all the things nearest to them*. One says, for example, 'one eats only in order to live' – which is a damned *lie*, as is that which speaks of the begetting of children as the real objective of all voluptuousness. Conversely, the high esteem in which the 'most serious things' are held is almost never quite genuine: the priests and metaphysicians, to be sure, have in these domains altogether accustomed us to a feignedly exaggerated *linguistic usage*, but they have not converted the feeling which refuses to take these most serious things as seriously as those despised nearest things.
(*Human, All-Too-Human*, vol. 2, 'The Wanderer and his Shadow', §5; Nietzsche, *Human, All Too Human*, tr. R. J. Hollingdale, Cambridge: Cambridge University Press, 1986, p. 303)

We must again become *good neighbours to the nearest things* and cease from gazing so contemptuously past them at clouds and monsters of the night. In forests

Notes 47

and caves, in swampy regions and under cloudy skies – this is where man has lived all too long, and lived poorly, as on the cultural steps of whole millennia. There he has *learned to despise* the present and nearness and life and himself – and we, who dwell in the *brighter* fields of nature and the spirit, we too have inherited in our blood something of this poison and contempt for what is nearest.

('The Wanderer and his Shadow', §16; *Human, All Too Human*, p. 309)

Also compare the dialogue between the Wanderer and the Shadow at the end of this book, where the Shadow says: 'Of all you have said nothing has pleased me *more* than a promise you have made: you want again to become a good neighbour to the things nearest to you' (p. 394). Nietzsche returns to this theme in *Ecce Homo* when he argues that 'these little things', such as diet, location, climate, recreation, 'the entire casuistry of selfishness', are, in fact, 'inconceivably more important than everything hitherto considered of importance' (*Ecce Homo*, 'Why I am so Clever', §10; trans. Hollingdale, p. 36).

73 Cf. 'Success has always been the greatest liar' (*Beyond Good and Evil*, §269; *Basic Writings*, p. 408).
74 Cf.:

The Greek artists, the tragedians for example, poetized in order to conquer; their whole art cannot be thought of apart from contest: Hesiod's good Eris, ambition, gave their genius its wings. [...] To aspire to honour here means: 'to make oneself superior and to wish this superiority to be publicly acknowledged'. If the former is lacking and the latter nonethelesss still demanded, one speaks of *vanity*. If the latter is lacking and its absence not regretted, one speaks of *pride*.

(*Human, All To Human*, vol. 1, §170; tr. Hollingdale, p. 90)

75 'Of the Sublime Men', in Nietzsche, *Thus Spoke Zarathustra*, tr. R. J. Hollingdale, Harmondsworth: Penguin, 1969, p. 141.
76 Nietzsche, *Human, All Too Human*, vol. 1, §137; tr. Hollingdale, p. 74.
77 Klages, *Errungenschaften Nietzsches*, p. 174; in *SW*, vol. 5, pp. 173–174. Cf. *Will to Power*, §1067, in Nietzsche, *The Will to Power*, ed. W. Kaufmann, tr. R. J. Hollingdale and W. Kaufmann, New York: Vintage, 1968, pp. 549–550.

78 In the thought of will to power, Nietzsche anticipates the metaphysical ground of the consummation of the modern age. In the thought of will to power, metaphysical thinking itself completes itself in advance. Nietzsche, the thinker of the thought of will to power, is the *last metaphysician* of the West. The age whose consummation unfolds in his thought, the modern age, is the final age.

(M. Heidegger, *Nietzsche: Volumes 3 and 4*, vol. 3, *The Will to Power as Knowledge and as Metaphysics*, ed. D. F. Krell, tr. J. Stambaugh, D. F. Krell, F. A. Capuzzi, New York: HarperCollins, 1991, Part One, chapter 1, p. 8)

79 All statements seem to be annulled by other statements. *Self-contradiction* is the fundamental ingredient in Nietzsche's thought. For nearly every single one of Nietzsche's judgments, one can also find an opposite. He gives the impression of having two opinions about everything. Consequently it is possible to quote Nietzsche at will in support of anything one happens to have in mind.

(Jaspers, *Nietzsche: An Introduction to the Understanding of his Philosophical Activity*, p. 10)

80 To those 'many' who have 'concluded' that 'Nietzsche is full of confusion, is never in earnest, abandons himself to his own whim, and that it does not pay to take his inconsequential chatter seriously', Jaspers responds:

But it could also be that we have here to do with contradictions that are necessary and inescapable. Perhaps the contradictories, presented as alternatives and appearing

48 *Life*

reasonable and familiar to the reader when considered singly, actually are misleading simplifications of being.

(Jaspers, *Nietzsche*, p. 10)

81 See *The Gay Science*, §372, entitled 'Why we are no idealists'. Here Nietzsche writes: 'These old philosophers were heartless; philosophizing was always a kind of vampirism. Looking at these figures, even Spinoza, don't you have the sense of something profoundly enigmatic and uncanny?' (Nietzsche, *The Gay Science*, tr. W. Kaufmann, New York: Vintage, 1974, p. 333).

82 Klages, *Errungenschaften Nietzsches*, pp. 190–191; in *SW*, vol. 5, pp. 190–191.

83 Klages, *Errungenschaften Nietzsches*, p. 195; in *SW*, vol. 5, p. 195.

84 Klages, *Errungenschaften Nietzsches*, p. 198; in *SW*, vol. 5, p. 198.

85 Cf. 'Of the Bestowing Virtue', in *Thus Spoke Zarathustra*, tr. Hollingdale, pp. 99–104: 'The highest virtue is a bestowing virtue. [...] May your bestowing love and your knowledge serve towards the meaning of the earth!' (pp. 100 and 102).

86 Klages, *Errungenschaften Nietzsches*, p. 198; in *SW*, vol. 5, p. 198.

87 Nietzsche, *Ecce Homo*, 'Why I Write Such Excellent Books', §5; trans. Hollingdale, p. 76.

88 Klages, *Errungenschaften Nietzsches*, p. 199; in *SW*, vol. 5, p. 199.

89 Klages, *Errungenschaften Nietzsches*, pp. 203–204; in *SW*, vol. 5, p. 203.

90 Cf. aphorism §140 of *Human, All Too Human*, vol. 2, part 2, *The Wanderer and his Shadow*, entitled 'Dancing in chains', where Nietzsche writes:

With every Greek artist, poet and writer one has to ask: what is the *new constraint* he has imposed upon himself and through which he charms his contemporaries (so that he finds imitators)? For that which we call 'invention' (in metrics, for example) is always such a self-imposed fetter. 'Dancing in chains', making things difficult for oneself and then spreading over it the illusion of ease and facility – that is the artifice they want to demonstrate to us.

(Nietzsche, *Human, All Too Human*, trans. Hollingdale, p. 343)

In so writing, Nietzsche is echoing Voltaire's letter to Deodati de Tovazzi of 24 January 1761, where he writes, 'you are dancing in liberty and we are dancing in our chains' (*vous dansez en liberté et nous dansons avec nos chaînes*) (Voltaire, *Lettres choisies*, ed. Louis Moland, 2 vols, Paris: Garnier, 1876, vol. 1, p. 426; in his copy of this work, Nietzsche marks this passage and underlines the word *chaînes* (G. Colli and M. Montinari, *Kommentar zu den Bänden 1–13* [*KSA*, vol. 14], Munich; Berlin and New York: dtv; de Gruyter, 1988, pp. 192–193)). For further discussion of the centrality of this idea to Locke, Hegel, and especially Nietzsche, see J. F. Dienstag, *'Dancing in Chains': Narrative and Memory in Political Theory*, Stanford, CA: Stanford University Press, 1997, esp. chapters 3 and 4, 'The Reveries of the Solitary' and 'The Future of Pain', pp. 77–139.

91 Klages, *Errungenschaften Nietzsches*, p. 210; in *SW*, vol. 5, p. 209.

92 '*Self-hangman!*'; see the poem 'Amid Birds of Prey', in Nietzsche, *Dithyrambs of Dionysus: Bilingual Edition*, tr. R. J. Hollingdale, London: Anvil Press Poetry, 1984, p. 43.

93 'Of Old and New Law-Tables', §6; *Thus Spoke Zarathustra*, tr. Hollingdale, p. 217.

94 Klages, *Errungenschaften Nietzsches*, p. 210; in *SW*, vol. 5, p. 209.

95 Klages, *Errungenschaften Nietzsches*, pp. 215–216; in *SW*, vol. 5, p. 214. The problem of how to interpret the doctrine of the eternal recurrence is addressed by, for example, Gilles Deleuze (1925–1995) in *Difference and Repetition* [1968], tr. P. Patton, New York: Columbia University Press, 1994; London: Continuum, 2004.

96 Klages, *Errungenschaften Nietzsches*, p. 216; in *SW*, vol. 5, p. 216.

97 H. Prinzhorn, *Nietzsche und das 20. Jahrhundert*, Heidelberg: Kampmann, 1928. For further discussion, see H. Barth, *Truth and Ideology*, tr. F. Lilge, Berkeley, Los

Notes 49

Angeles, London: University of California Press, 1976, pp. 136–178, 'Nietzsche's Philosophy as the "Art of Mistrust"'.

98 H. Prinzhorn, 'Vorwort', in H. Prinzhorn (ed.), *Die Wissenschaft am Schweidewege von Leben und Geist: Festschrift Ludwig Klages zum 60. Geburtstag, 10. Dezember 1932*, Leipzig: Barth, 1932, pp. iv–v.

99 Cf. *On the Essence of Consciousness*, end of chapter 7; in *SW*, vol. 3, p. 299.

100 C. Bernoulli, 'On Ludwig Klages', in *Die Wissenschaft am Scheidewege von Leben und Geist*, pp. 251–252.

101 L. Klages, 'Stefan George', *Der Lotse*, 2, no. 11, 1901, 336–342; in *CAK*, p. 103.

102 A. Moeller van den Bruck, *Das Dritte Reich* (1923). For further discussion, see F. Stern, *The Politics of Cultural Despair: A Study in the Rise of the Germanic Ideology*, Berkeley, Los Angeles, London: University of California Press, 1974.

103 O. Spengler, *Preußentum und Sozialismus*, Munich: Beck, 1919.

104 Klages, *Die Probleme der Graphologie: Entwurf einer Psychodiagnostik* (1910); in *SW*, vol. 7, pp. 93–94, fn. 41.

105 For further discussion, see S. L. Gilman, *Freud, Race, and Gender*, Princeton, NJ: Princeton University Press, 1993.

106 Freud to Abraham, 3 May 1908, in H. C. Abraham and E. L. Freud (eds), *A Psycho-Analytic Dialogue: The Letters of Sigmund Freud and Karl Abraham, 1907–1926*, tr. B. Marsh and H. C. Abraham, London: Hogarth Press, 1965, p. 34.

107 Rosenberg, 'Gestalt und Leben', *Nationalsozialistische Monatshefte*, 98 (May, 1938); in *CAK*, p. 110. See A. Rosenberg, *Gestalt und Leben*, Halle/Saale: Niemeyer, 1938.

108 *Völkischer Beobachter*, Nr. 158, 7 June 1938; in *CAK*, p. 115.

109 T. Schneider, 'Ideologische Grabenkämpfe: Der Philosoph Ludwig Klages und der Nationalsozialismus 1933–1938', *Vierteljahrshefte für Zeitgeschichte* 49, no. 2 (April 2001), 275–294; T. Schneider, 'Sektierer oder Kampfgenossen? Der Klages-Kreis im Spannungsfeld der NS-Kulturpolitik', in W. Schmitz and C. Vollenhals (eds), *Völkische Bewegung – Konservative Revolution – Nationalsozialismus: Aspekte einer politisierten Kultur*, Dresden: Thelem, 2005, pp. 299–323; and, most recently, the work of Nitzan Lebovic (see above, p. xxv, note 32).

110 For further discussion of Rose Plehn, see *CAK*, p. 229. See also the notes in R. Huch, *"Du, mein Dämon, meine Schlange ...": Briefe an Richard Huch 1887–1897*, ed. A. Gabrisch, Göttingen: Wallstein, 1998, p. 788; and R. Aitken and E. Rosenhaft, *Black Germany: The Making and Unmaking of a Diaspora Community, 1884–1960*, Cambridge: Cambridge University Press, 2013, p. 179.

111 Letter of Ludwig Klages to Rose Plehn of 24 May 1912; in *CAK*, p. 120.

112 Schuler, *Fragmente und Vorträge*, ed. Klages, 'Einführung des Herausgebers', pp. 1–119. This edition superseded the earlier and privately printed selection of fragments edited by Elsa Bruckmann, Gustav W. Freytag, and Ludwig Klages, published as A. Schuler, *Dichtungen: Aus dem Nachlaß*, Hamburg: Saucke, 1930.

113 Klages, *SW*, vol. 3, p. 526.

114 Wertham, 'The Significance of Klages' System for Psychotherapy', p. 382.

115 See note 1 above.

116 R. Ibel, 'Der meistgeplünderte Autor der Gegenwart: Zum 80. Geburtstag des Kulturphilosophen Ludwig Klages', *Die Zeit*, 11 December 1952.

117 At one point in his study of Chinese landscape painting, Fischer draws on Klages's theory of the dream in order to appreciate the art of Chinese landscape art:

> For a psychological explanation of a feeling of space and a vision of space such as is expressed in images [*verbildlicht*] in Chinese painting, a decisive intervention is in Ludwig Klages's profound study, *Of Dream Consciousness* [*Vom Traumbewußtsein*], *Zeitschrift für Pathopsychologie*, III.4). For him, dreaming is a condition of pure vision – in contrast to sensation – the sense of distance is a simply

visionary sense, what is felt [*empfunden*] is physical presence, but what is envisioned [*geschaut*] is the never tarrying flowing image, the virtual image, which we envision [*schauen*] in *locationless space* of the mirror. 'One enters the sphere of dreams and magic only at the price of losing a bodiliness capable of feeling [*empfindungsfähige Leibhaftigkeit*]; one gains the removal of the limits of location at the cost of renouncing a physically present proximity [*eine leibhaft gegenwärtige Nähe*]' [cf. *SW*, vol. 3, p. 237]. If for Klages the sensible colour tone becomes the symbol of sensory quality itself, then the almost total renunciation of colour in the Chinese landscape acquires a new and profound explanation.

(O. Fischer, *Chinesische Landschaftsmalerei*, Munich: Wolff, 1921, pp. 167–168)

2 Works and key ideas

So much for the life of Ludwig Klages, offering a fascinating glimpse of and insight into the intellectual history of the late nineteenth-century and early twentieth-century Germany. But isn't this, some readers might ask, all very antiquated? What does any of this have to do with us today? Does Klages still have anything to say to us?

This book calls itself a toolkit, which presupposes that there is some way in which Klages's ideas can be used. Indeed there is, for Klages is, despite what his detractors (and there are many of them) say, a thinker of immense *practical* as well as *theoretical* relevance to the present world. True, his language is (a) German, which fewer and fewer people outside German-speaking countries can speak or read; (b) very difficult German, so that it is not always clear exactly what point he is trying to make; and (c) often highly philosophical in terminology and tone. Nevertheless, precisely these difficulties should give us pause for thought; and, most likely, the reader will find, they do. And, in other respects, Klages was a gifted poet, capable of producing a prose whose energy and intensity can still produce an effect an entire century after it was written.

So the task here in this section of the toolkit is to try and unpick the central ideas of Klages and explain their relevance; to share with the reader some of the most important and exciting passages of Klages's extensive works; and then, in the third and final section of the toolkit, the task will be to approach Klages, as the Germans might say, *aus seinem Kontext heraus*, that is to say, to understand his ideas in relation to the background against which he presented them and then to apply them to our contemporary situation. The reward of such an approach is that it makes available the immense philosophical resource of Klagesian thinking for our own lives, and invites us to think of his philosophy, not simply as an intellectual system, but as one that has enormous implications for the way in which we lead our lives as well.

Conceptual tool #1: science of 'expression'

What do we mean by 'expression'? Etymologically, the word derives from the Latin *ex + pressare* or *exprimere*: literally, to 'press something out'. (This idea is very clearly present in the German word, *Aus-druck*, something 'pressed out'.)

52 Works and key ideas

An expression is associated with the life of the emotions: we express our feelings by smiling, laughing, or crying, and we know what other people are thinking and feeling (or we think and feel we know what they are thinking and feeling) by observing their gestures and reactions. Even (and perhaps especially) in an era of high technology, we resort to emoticons to convey something that, it seems, language on its own (or at least a certain kind of language) cannot. The absence of expression is expressive, too: a grumpy face, for instance, is sometimes grumpy because it fails to move into a smile. The child looks up at the face of the parents, wanting reassurance; and in our professional and personal lives alike, we anxiously scan the faces of those around us, seeking approval, or looking for agreement, or trying to predict what on earth they are going to do next.

Emotional – and, in particular, facial – expression is something universal and, as far as we can tell, it has been part of humanity as long as it has been in existence. The study of expression, however, intensified and was codified in the eighteenth century; for instance, in the theories of the Swiss poet, physiognomist, and theologian, Johann Kaspar Lavater (1741–1801). His observations and ideas can be found in his massive four-volume work, *Physiognomic Fragments towards the Enhancement of Knowledge and Love of Humankind* (1775–1778). Lavater's fame has survived, perhaps because he was closely acquainted for a number of years with Goethe, although the two men later fell out with each other. In Lavater's view, there is a strict correspondence between the physical appearance of an individual and his or her character. One could summarize Lavater's views as follows: *what you see is what you get*.[1]

But the 'science of expression' as it is proposed by Klages rejects precisely this kind of simplistic equation. In an article entitled 'Principle Issues in Lavater' (1901; 1926), written by Klages but originally published in the journal *Graphological Monthly* (*Graphologische Monatshefte*) under the pseudonym Erwin Axel, he explained his objection to Lavater's theories as follows:

> That some correspondences of this kind *must* exist is, in principle, a correct consideration; but it brings us not a step closer to *knowledge* of it. Indeed, one could say that we *really know* nothing about relations between the characteristics of, say, the nerves or the blood and those of the soul – and even less between characteristics of the external structure of the body and the soul. No way lies here to get us out of generalities.
>
> More relevant and closer to modern thinking are those statements by Lavater that move more in the pathognomonic realm [i.e. a realm where there is a characteristic sign for a particular disease]. – All human beings engaged in activity have their own tone of movement, which – unbeknown to them – makes their inner being visible. This is true not only of temporary, more emotional conditions, but just as much for what is permanent about a character. This is the basis for the comprehensibility of all acting and the plastic arts, inasmuch as they relate to human beings.

(SW 6, 6)

What interests Klages, for example, about handwriting, is not any kind of *static* correspondence between its own characteristics and those of the person whose handwriting it is. Rather, what interests him is the prospect that it captures something of the *movement* that produces the handwriting, which in turn might reveal something about the person whose writing we have before us. In 1924, Klages published an *Introduction to the Psychology of Handwriting* (reprinted in 1927 and issued in a second edition in 1928). In its first chapter he explained the aim of graphology as he saw it:

> Because humans have, since prehistoric times, created images – sometimes as drawings, sometimes as sculpture – of their own shape, their tendency (comprehensible from the way the mind proceeds) to forget the dynamic of the world in the physical statics of the world misleads them entirely into the belief that the living organism of the human being is a shaped body; whereas it really is: a *system of movement* that never comes to a rest. Let us put to one side the question of what sort of magic of giving form it is through which the artist succeeds in making us experience the solid block of marble which signifies the Demeter of Knidos[2] as if it were a being alive with soul; it is enough that he has transposed into a language of mere forms something which, in the living body, is an entire language of its movements! The body of the living human being is irreconcilably separated from every kind of copy by a turbulence that never pauses, even for a second. This is even true of someone sleeping, whose chest rises and falls and whose cheeks reveal the play of blood; how much more true is it of someone awake!
>
> [...]
>
> Just as in the same way, however, that the living body is so much more a system of movement than a bodily shape in space, so we can most precisely call the life that invests it with soul a never-resting *process*; and we are now no longer in the field of supposition, but in that of axiomatic certainty, if we add that there is no emotional turmoil in the soul that does not appear in some sort of bodily processes. If we pick out from these movements in particular and especially those that can be immediately noticed, then we have in these that *expression* of the life of the soul that enables us immediately to understand both someone else's personality as well as that person's conditions, moods, emotional turmoil. If certain changes in posture of every person express a change in the state of his or her soul, so the distinguishing particularity of the posture expresses the individual character; which is why it is not difficult to read 'from the face' such qualities as courage or timidity, greed or generosity, softness or hardness, on the condition that the gaze has sufficiently attuned itself to pay attention to the soul at all. After all, no one really doubts that the *way* in which a human moves cannot be mistaken for that of anyone else! Whoever lives next to a stairwell and *hears* on a daily basis how numerous people climb up it, will immediately be able to recognize a particular person who regularly visits from their sound of his or her steps. For each person's way of walking is always so different from

54   *Works and key ideas*

> everyone else's way of walking that the speed and the tone of the echo will
> betray that person, just from the way the sole of the foot is placed on the
> steps of a staircase!
>
> (*SW* 7, 550–551)

Far from reducing the characteristics of individuals to a predetermined schema, Klages is interested in what makes each individual precisely that – i.e. *individual*. His example of the sound of feet on a staircase is one that proves his point, for it is surely one whose truth which will be instantly recognizable to anyone who has ever lived in a block of flats....

Far from playing down the difficulties that will be encountered by any study that is seeking to describe itself as a 'science' (or, in German, a *Wissenschaft*, a 'discipline' of scholarly 'knowledge') and, as such, based on something as swiftly fleeting as a sequence of movements, Klages tackles these problems head-on. These difficulties can, he thinks, be mitigated – by taking handwriting as an object of analysis:

> There is a circumstance that banishes such undertakings into the narrow
> boundaries of the attainable and – in view of the real goal, the *physiogno-*
> *mics* of movements – once more condemns them to end up in a dead-end.
> If we ignore the 'pathognomonic' traces of frequently occurring expres-
> sive manifestations, they are all without exception movements and con-
> sequently fleeting; they have hardly begun, and they are gone again. Way
> of walking, play of features, hand gestures, tone of voice and rhythm of
> speaking, body posture: each of these changes from moment to moment;
> and anyone who would seek to found on them a science of the characters
> would find himself or herself reliant on memory, and thus exposed to the
> danger of innumerable acts of erroneous recollection. He or she would
> have to renounce the indispensable precondition of any strictly binding
> investigation of facts, i.e. that the object of research is either permanently
> present or can be recalled as required for the purposes of investigation. On
> the other hand there is one, and only one, movement of a human being that
> is fixed in the moment it comes into being for years and even for centuries
> – it is handwriting.
>
> (*SW* 7, 553–554)

Handwriting thus captures a moment of movement and hence offers a picture of the individual's character.

As becomes clear from these passages, Klages's interest in graphology soon turned into an engagement with a more profound set of questions. He began to investigate how the economy of human movement could be separated into two kinds of movements:

- expressive ones
- voluntary ones

and on this basis he began to lay the foundation for what he regarded as an entirely new discipline – *the science of expression*. In other words, graphology was but a step on the road to developing a new study of expression. Consequently, Klages himself came to regard his work published in 1910, *The Problems of Graphology*, not so much as a textbook of graphology as an attempt to lay the foundations for a science of expression.

Some of the essential theses about the relation between *expression* and *character* can be found in the collection of essays he published in 1926 under the title *On the Study of Expression and the Study of Character*:

> *Every process in the soul,* insofar as counterforces do not thwart it, *is accompanied by a movement analogous to it*: this is the basic law of expressive movement and the interpretation of movement [...];

> (*SW* 6, 14)

> *The motion of the body increases in proportion to the motion of the soul* [...];

> (*SW* 6, 16)

> *The expressive movement is a likeness of the deed* [...].

> (*SW* 6, 21)

This fundamental law of the expressiveness of movement, first formulated in a paper entitled 'The Basic Law of Expression' published in the *Graphological Monthly* in 1905, was something to which Klages returned in order to explore further in his book, *Expresssive Movement and Formative Power* (1913). This work contains two further fundamental laws of the science of expression:

> *The bodily expression of every condition of life is such that its image can recall it again*;

> (*SW* 6, 162)

> Every expressive bodily movement carries out the impulse-experience [*Antriebserlebnis*] of the feeling that is expressed in this movement.

> (*SW* 6, 169)

By 1936, Klages had sufficiently revised and refined his ideas to present in his work entitled *Foundation of the Science of Expression*, the fifth and substantially revised edition of *Expressive Movement and Formative Power*, a complete account of how he proposed to interpret human movement. Up until now, he had distinguished between expressive movements and voluntary ones, arguing that the expressiveness of each had to be interpreted differently. Here, Klages set out a new taxonomy of different kinds of movement, now distinguishing between

56   *Works and key ideas*

- expressive movement
- voluntary movement
- impulse movement
- reflex movement
- automatic movement

and defining these different kinds of movement as follows.[3] An expressive movement (for example, a smile) is precisely that, an impulse movement that tells us something about the person who is making the movement; a voluntary movement (for example, throwing a stone) is an impulse movement subordinated to the will; an impulse movement is the most basic kind of movement, something that occurs without the mediation of reflection or the will; a reflex movement (for example, blinking one's eyes when emerging into bright sunlight) is an impulse movement that can be part of an expressive movement; and an automatic movement (for example, swimming or typing a message on the keyboard of a laptop) is a mechanical kind of movement, an impulse movement that has become habitual.[4]

By taking into account the full range of different kinds of movement, Klages wanted his work to present a phenomenological account of all the process of life – offering a parallel to the field of biology, as he explained in the foreword to *Foundation of the Science of Expression*:

> If we call every process that allows us either to perceive or to detect the living quality of its carrier its 'expressive manifestation', then the study of expression extends as far as does the science of life (biology) and develops from it an aspect that has hitherto been insufficiently appreciated. If, furthermore, the individual soul outside the organism's life is not known, then nor is the study of the soul (psychology) possible without the science of expression. And if, finally, the part of life endowed with soul [*beseelt*] as well as the part endowed with mind [*begeistet*] is knowable *only* from processes that *signify* it, then research into expression demands a precise investigation of the signs by means of which a significant [*bedeutungsinhaltig*] event is unmistakably distinguished from a mechanical one, and to this extent it coincides with the study of appearances (phenomenology).[5] If this name were already sufficiently familiar to the learned consciousness of the present day, then we would have without hesitation called our book 'the foundation of the science of appearance'.
>
> (*SW* 6, 317)

Just as Klages critically engaged in his science of expression with the teachings of physiognomics, so he undertook a critical investigation of the tenets of psychology in his construction of a study of character.

Conceptual tool #2: study of 'character'

According to the OED, the word 'character' – for once, very close to its related German term, *Charakter* – derives its etymological meaning from the Greek word *kharaktēr*, meaning an instrument for marking, and is related to the word *kharassein*, 'to engrave'. One's character, in other words, is something engraved in one's being, and on an intuitive level we all know what character means. Or what it means to be a character. 'He's a real character!' Or we use it about something fine to drink: 'This is a beautiful red wine, it has real character'.

But what actually *is* character? It is this question, at once a highly theoretical and an eminently practical one, that Klages tries to answer in his study of character (*Charakterkunde*). In a series of works, *Principles of Characterology* (1910), *The Foundations of the Study of Character* (1926), and *Primer of the Study of Character* (1937), Klages developed his increasingly subtle and ever more nuanced understanding of character. In his *Primer*, which first appeared in a series edited by the psychiatrist and art historian Hans Prinzhorn (1886–1933) called *Das Weltbild* under the title *Personality* in 1937 and was reissued in a revised version in 1937, Klages provided in an appendix entitled 'From the History of the Doctrine of Character' a short account of the intellectual-historical sources of his own approach:

> What until recently in an academic context was understood in an exclusive sense as 'psychology' (which is how it is still largely understood today) had its beginnings in ancient Greece at the latest with Protagoras and had formed a sub-category of philosophy since Aristotle, among whose works there is one famously dedicated to psychology, entitled *On the Soul*.[6] [...] Hardly any less older than 'psychology', however, is the doctrine of character; in fact, it is considerably older, if one includes what thinking individuals without characterological intention had declared about human nature. [...] For the researcher into character there are two kinds of material: unformed and formed. The unformed consists of human beings themselves along with everything they have deliberately produced since the earliest times: their customs and traditions, rituals and ceremonies, symbols and legends, their languages and writing systems, worldviews and arts, handiwork and inventions, their political constitutions and social institutions, their forms of dress, codes of behaviour, and finally their historical deeds. By contrast, formed material consists of the innumerable statements about human nature made by *wise men* and *poets*. If one were to compile everything wise and insightful about the human being that can be found in the written remains (to cite just a few names in the Western tradition) of Homer, Solon, Aesop, Theogonis, Epicharmus,[7] Aeschylus, Sophocles, Euripides, Democritus, Aristophanes, Plato, Plautus, Cicero, Virgil, Horace, Ovid, Martial, Petronius, Juvenal, Lucian, Apuleius, Boccaccio, Macchiavelli, Rabelais, Luther, Hutten, Cervantes, Shakespeare, Hobbes, Milton, Pascal, Voltaire, Lessing, Hamann, Schubart, Herder, Pestalozzi, Heinse, Goethe, Schiller, Jean Paul, Arndt, Hölderlin, Novalis, Tieck, Görres, Kleist, Eichendorff, Byron, Gotthelf, Heine, Balzac, Gogol, Dickens, Hebbel, Tolstoy, Keller, Dostoevsky, etc., then one would doubtless gain the impression of an inexhaustible richness comparable to that of humankind itself and that there will

58 *Works and key ideas*

remain enough 'subject matter' for an effort to come to terms with it scientifically for long to come. At this point we must leave this question to one side apart from a few exceptions […]. But we must also name two groups in particular.

First the great historians, of which one should mention from antiquity: Thucydides, Caesar, Sallust, Livy, Plutarch, Tacitus; from the interim period, Gregory of Tours; from the Middle Ages, Ekkehard of Aura, Marcus of Lindau; from the modern age, for example, Johannes von Müller, Carlyle, Ranke, Giesebrecht, Freytag, Mommsen, Gregorovius, Friedländer, Burkhardt, Scherr.[8] Then there are the great autobiographical writers, beginning with Augustine (the *Confessions*) via Thomas and Felix Platter, Götz von Berlichingen, Schärtlin, Schweinichen, and above all someone who should be mentioned here, Grimmelshausen (*Simplicissimus*) to the (in characterological terms) exceptionally insightful writers of the eighteenth century, such as Haupt, Sethe, Trenck, Laukhard, etc.[9] No researcher into characterology should leave the following unread: Rousseau's *Confessions*, Goethe's *Poetry and Truth*, Jung-Stilling's *Life Story*, and Moritz's *Anton Reiser*. It is only for reasons of space that we limited ourselves to listing German writers. For the same reason we must leave unmentioned the numerous extremely significant correspondences also bequeathed to us by the eighteenth century, perhaps most versatile century of humanity to date.

(*SW* 4, 485–486)

As well as providing a reading list for the rest of one's entire life (and at the same time displaying a remarkable erudition, even for the early twentieth century), these paragraphs indicate the extent to which Klages saw his work as belonging to a core strand of thinking and writing in the Western tradition. That Klages's approach to the concept of 'character' is anything other than reductive is clear from a lecture published in 1947, which gives us a sense of exactly what it is that, with his notion of 'character', Klages was trying to get at:

Where does one derive the *material* for the study of character? To this end one would have to know the Chinese as thoroughly as the Spanish, among every people would have to know the top bankers, leading industrialists, the middle class, the craftsman, farmers, industrial workers, but also the monks and nuns of a Cistercian monastery or the entire criminal world, whether in Shanghai or London or Chicago. One would have to be able to give a scientific explanation of character-related preconditions for the Catilinarian conspiracy,[10] a dance-orgy of African negroes, the grounds of the behaviour of a catankerous housewife, and so on.[11] No single person is in a position to gather this enormous amount of material through experience and observation. – Yet it is all available, as an inventory of instinctively acquired insights, in human *language*.

The wise men of all ages […] have provided us with profound glimpses into the essence of the human being. They would not have been able to

Study of 'character' 59

declare them without language; but without language they would not have been able to discover them. If Schiller is right to say:

> When you manage to write, in learned tongue, a verse,
> That writes and thinks *for* you, do you think you're a poet already?[12]

then we can add that this applies without exception to everyone, whether writing creatively, or contemplating, or simply doing some everyday task. But with one difference: that the wise man and the poets are aware of their dependence on language, while the others are not. All thought takes place on the basis of and with the help of the language one inherits.[13]

As we shall see, the importance he attaches to language as a source of uncovering how we really think and feel is a recurring motif in the philosophy of Klages, and closely related to his interest in aesthetics, especially poetry.

In 1910, Klages published in book form a series of lectures first given between 1905 and 1910, collected under the title *Principles of Characterology*, and issued as a fourth edition in 1926 as *The Foundations of the Doctrine of Character*. At the beginning of its first chapter, Klages sets out his ambition in this work in the following terms:

> If someone wanted to learn from psychology something to which one might justifiably expect it to offer a key, such as: what sort of changes mind has undergone since antiquity; in what respect the 'natural human being' differs from the 'civilized' one; which aspects of the interior life are revealed by the major world religions, which by class, race, and ethnic identities; which rules govern envy, greed, selfishness, etc.; how one can identify amid the changing actions of the human being his or her enduring character, or behind the mask of politeness someone's real motives; – if someone wanted to ask similar questions, then he or she would not only be disappointed by current trends in this field: but would actually have to conclude that he or she had turned to entirely the wrong person. For instead he or she would hear about sensations, perceptions, representations, judgments, tendencies, willed acts, feelings, i.e. about the most generalized indicators of mental life, or even about the physically quite amazing qualities of our sensory organs. Such a person would learn about how one arrives at conclusions, remembers something, constructs concepts and would take away for a study of history, of law, of religious consciousness, of forms of mental illness or for a knowledge of practical life not essentially more than someone who loves flowers would take away for botany through being told that plants are spatial bodies, located in a place, capable of growth, requiring certain nutrients, and dependent on light.
>
> (*SW* 4, 103)

Just as, for Klages, the science of expression represents a challenge to old-fashioned conceptions of physiognomy as a discipline, so the doctrine of character

60   *Works and key ideas*

represents a challenge to conventional psychology. Not the least of the innovations proposed by Klages was an emphasis on the significance of language, in particular the way in which human language reveals a dimension of meaning inherent in all experience.

Translated into English from the fifth and sixth editions in 1929, the study of character proposed by Klages in *The Science of Character* is, as one of its early commentators noted, 'exceedingly difficult'.[14] Nevertheless, Frederic Wertham managed to extract some of the chief elements of his study of character, the whole psychological system of which is based, as he rightly notes, on Klages's metaphysical ideas. And as Wertham also observes, it reveals Klages's indebtedness to Nietzsche and the common ground he shares with the Hungarian philosopher, Melchior Palágyi (1859–1924).[15] Wertham suggests that the term 'character' as used by Klages could be replaced by 'personality', and he highlights the originality of Klages's division of character or personality into three zones or spheres.

First, there is the 'material' of the character or personality, a specific set of resources or capacities to receive, assimilate, and process mental contents. (The 'material' includes both intellectual capacities and other 'character' traits, such as affective or emotional qualities.) Second, this 'material' is arranged in a particular way that constitutes the 'structure' of the character. This structure determines the ease or otherwise of interpersonal relations, depending on the capacity for stimulating feelings (i.e. affectivity), the capacity for stimulating will (i.e. volitional tendencies), the impulse toward and capacity for expression, and the fundamental attitude toward life or *Lebensgrundstimmung*. This 'existential mood', as one might also translate it, moves along a scale, at one end of which is a high key of 'expansiveness', and at the other end of which is a low key of *pathos* or passivity. Central to Klages's thinking here is the relation between urge and inhibition (or resistance), which determines the form of a reaction. For instance: one can react in a sanguine way because of a strong impulse, or because of a weak inhibitory response.

Third, the final zone of the character or personality is its 'quality', that is to say, the particular direction in which the two other zones, the 'material' and the 'structure', are realized in the context of the individual's specific impulses, urges, and instincts. This 'quality' results in a 'system of driving forces' which relates most closely to the narrow sense in which we usually talk about someone's 'character'. As Klages is well aware, however, character or personality is something essentially dynamic, either on the level of a dynamic internal to the individual or on the level of one's interpersonal relations. Thus there is a relation between the capacity for stimulating feelings (C) and the increasing or decreasing liveliness of those feelings (L or D), a relation which Klages expresses in the form of an equation, $C = L / D$.

At the same time, the difference between different personalities or characters is understood by Klages in terms of the difference between 'substances', that is, between the driving forces of self-assertion and those of self-devotion. (For Klages, these principles can be identified as the spirit and the soul, indexed

Study of 'character' 61

respectively to the masculine and the feminine, if for no other reason than the philological one that, in Greek, spirit or ὁ νοῦς is masculine while soul or ἡ ψυχή is feminine). Whereas the principle of self-assertion tends to bind vital forces together, the principle of self-devotion tends to 'unbind', release or dissipate them; and the relation between these two forces is, as so often in Klages, a polaristic one. Or as Klages puts it:

> If I am dominated by an assertive interest, then it dominates, among other things, a possible tendency to devotion, and accordingly every stimulus to devotion is felt as an irritant serving to intensify the assertive interest. If, conversely, I am dominated by a tendency toward devotion, then it also dominates my assertive interest and my strongest reluctance will be turned against assertive desires; the assertive functions of my will (which, of course, are indispensable) serve merely the realization of such ends as satisfy desires of devotion.[16]

Correspondingly, Klages derives the following 'system of driving forces' (or interests), set out in a sequence of tables which can be synthesized as shown in Table 2.1.

Within this overarching schema of spiritual (*geistig*), personal, and sensuous driving forces, Klages is able to incorporate a wide variety of specific tendences, including benevolence, fidelity, patience, suspicion, hypocrisy, love of intrigue, intolerance, etc., some under the category of releasing, some under the category of binding driving forces. In other words, Klages is proposing an entire typological system, akin to Jung's distinction in *Psychological Types* (1921) between the attitude of extraversion and introversion, and the psychic functions of thinking, feeling, sensation, and intuition.[17]

Table 2.1 Klages's system of driving forces

Releases [lösende Antriebe] *(Release of vital force)*	*Bonds* [bindende Antriebe] *(Binding of vital force)*
Self-devotion	Self-assertion
Capacity for enthusiasm	Reason
Depth of feeling (capacity for passion)	Egoism (selfishness)
Fundamental note of life:	Fundamental note of life:
passivity, belief in the past, reverence	activity, belief in the future, will to seize (utilitarianism)
Opposing poles of mood:	Opposing poles of mood:
melancholia – serenity	pleasure from success (euphoria) – displeasure from failure (dejection)
Opposing poles of self-estimation:	Opposing poles of self-estimation:
pride – humility	self-esteem – self-doubt
Fundamental conviction:	Fundamental conviction:
a world of animate phenomena (which happen and cannot be possessed)	a world of facts (which can be seized and held)

62　*Works and key ideas*

At the same time, the Klagesian approach to the personality is almost diametrically opposed to that of Freudian psychoanalysis, as an early British reviewer noted. According to the British psychologist Walter John Herbert Sprott, known as 'Sebastian' or as Jack Sprott (1897–1971), the difference between Klagesian psychology and psychoanalysis lies above all in their approach to language. Whereas the psychoanalyst, despite 'his play with etymology', says that 'by the very nature of the case the speech of everyday life can throw but little light on what is really there' and teaches us to 'become familiar', not with 'ordinary expressions', but with 'language which, to those who are ignorant of the subject, sounds indecent and ridiculous' (!), by contrast Klages 'takes human beings as we know them and not as they are interpreted for us, and he analyses their surfaces'; he 'takes such notions of everyday life as "ambition", "love of children", "contradictoriness", "probity", "sense of duty", etc., seriously and not as the unimportant masks of more important forces'; and he 'says that where you have a notion in current use, which everyone understands, there must be something behind it, and a branch of psychology must deal with the organization of that which has given rise to such notions'.[18]

As far as the third zone of the character or personality, its 'quality', is concerned, it is important to emphasize the distinction between its instincts and its conscious will, as Klages does in a conference paper given in 1928, 'The Drives and the Will', which he subsequently revised and included in a shorter form as Chapter 17 of *Language as the Source of Psychology* (1948), and in another conference paper called 'On the Theory and Symptomatology of the Will'.[19] As we shall see in the following section on our next conceptual tool, while the life of the instincts corresponds to self-devotion, to enthusiasm, and to passion, the will corresponds to self-assertion, to reason, and to egoism. So whereas instinctive tendencies involve such characteristics as passivity, *laissez faire*, or *laissez aller*, willing or volition involves activity, self-assertion, or consciousness, and in such a way that it can oppose the entire first zone, the 'material', of the character or personality. Yet, unusually, Klages argues that the will does not cause movement, but inhibits it; to will is not to cause something to happen, but to stop it from happening, albeit to the end of achieving a particular goal. As a consequence, the will can direct the character or personality, but, crucially, it cannot change it in any fundamental way.

Conceptual tool #3: theory of the will

We all think we know what the will is; but do we really know? The notion of the will and, in particular, the idea that it is in some way 'free' (i.e. autonomous), belong to some of the oldest philosophical discussions in the Western tradition, from Plato in antiquity via St Augustine in the Middle Ages to the latest neuroscientific discussions of our own time. For Klages, too, the questions of the status and nature of the will were central to his project, and on the basis of his research into the science of expression he suggested that the activity of the will was involved, not so much with individual actions, as with 'a tendency to *regulate*' all our

Theory of the will   63

sequences of movements. So on this account, *that* our movements will take place is not something for us to decide, but *how* we carry them out *does* fall within the province of the will. This position constitutes Klages's particular contribution to the debate over free will and determinism.

In a text written in 1905, an aphorism entitled 'Development of Personalism', Klages links the change in our conception of the will to some of the major developments in Western culture as follows:

> We can see today in every area of 'civilization' something happening, which had already similarly taken place in Hellas [i.e. ancient Greece]: the becoming-a-person of the sense-of-self. Egoism has left behind it the phase of criminal excess and has acquired 'style'. A coldness of the heart has become a completely accepted part of 'being educated' [*Bildung*]. Creative pathos lost its object: it lost its grip on all distance. The human being has attained omniscience (the telephone), omnipresence (the car), omnipotence (dynamite).[20] The spiritually dry atmosphere has been thoroughly 'cleansed' from what bubbles up from the primordial world [*Urwelt*], and instead emerging from the womb as a filthy infant the future human being will step out of the retort as a homunculus.[21]
>
> The preliminary stages of the goal of this development are the following. In prehistorical times, the fight of the patriarchal spirit with the daimons. Always only ever a partial success of the father and repeated relapses into 'sin', lust, and night. The hesitant play of antiquity. Rome's puzzled ambiguous role.
>
> Into the already profound breakdown rushes the Judaic masked hordes. Rome becomes a global spider.[22] – A Nordic counterwave shatters on the higher 'style' of the South.
>
> Church militant: the disciplining will manifests itself in violent self-chastisement, asceticism, turning the drive inward – all embraced by the dungeon ironwork of the monastic orders and cloisters. The hard-pressed element seeks release in visionary eruptions, the heart 'is transfigured'. The spirit as the anti-person.
>
> Renaissance: the conclusion of the process, victory attained by the spirit, but premature becoming of personhood. The 'world' keeps breaking through when discipline is relaxed in individual minds. – The final and most deadly counterstroke: Protestantism. *Ratio* becomes a private matter, discipline an aspect of instinct. The understanding has 'freedom of thought', while the will lies in the strictest moral imprisonment. The ecstatic wave in the *blood* made harmless by giving it the *brain* as an unrestricted playground! Thus the far more benign Credo of Catholicism is reversed, which allows the blood freedom on the condition that one assents to a certain abstention of thought, and in its place steps forward the inviolability of that categorical imperative that tolerates no exception: *Thou shalt*, whatever you nevertheless choose to *believe*.
>
> The present: the final release of the person. Partly as a reaction to it, partly as a result of a cosmic storm-wave, in the Nineties [i.e. the 1890s] a

64   *Works and key ideas*

primordial fire [*Urfeuer*] flames up and casts uniting sparks from a few individual spirits into the past lying aeons ago. Constellations burst forth and are swiftly extinguished. The wave of spirits subsides – the essence drains away.

The person begins to stylize itself. The atmosphere has become empty and cold and bright. The end of the religious age of humankind is imminent.

(*RR*, 341–342)

As Klages suggests in this highly compressed passage, the main instrument that is used to discipline the will is something we call 'ethics' or 'moral customs'; as he remarks, 'the making moral and the spiritualization of humankind takes place at the cost of an unforeseeable repression of expression' (*SW* 6, 128). Or as he put it in his short treatise 'On the Characterology of the Criminal' (1912; 1926), 'all ethical systems of humankind demand the mastery, that is to say, the repression of the expressive feeling-drives and thus lead at least unintentionally to a denial of life' (*SW* 4, 518).

As far as Klages is concerned, we misunderstand the will if we think of it as a force that sustains all our movements or even lies at the source of them; instead it is, he argues, rather a force that inhibits, limits, or otherwise regulates the movements we make. In *Expressive Movement and Formative Power: Foundations of the Science of Expression* (1921), a second and extensively revised edition of an article called 'Expressive Movement and its Diagnostic Evaluation', subsequently published in book form (1913), Klages explains how, according to this conception, the will functions:

We have seen that the distinctive function of willing is to aim at something predetermined, and with the example of the marksman who takes aim we have shown that each act of taking-aim does not at all command, for instance, movements, but commands rather that they are not completely avoided. Anyone who judges the aim at the goal the most exactly, shoots with the weapon the most accurately; and if, to do this, he or she needs to make an extremely perceptible effort, it also means that he or she must constantly master anew a gentle but constant trembling of the limbs! How one takes aim with the body is exactly analogous to how one takes aim with the mind in the experience of willing. Just as the act of judgement adjusts our vital intuition, so the act of willing adjusts a vital action to a specific object; and herein lies the exertion of the *will*, that we *contain* the ceaselessly onflowing vital wave in the purposive aim as if between the sides of a canal, by preventing it from dissipating away into adjunct channels through the constant application of ever renewed barriers! It is one of the oldest heresies of humankind that the will sets into motion, that the will even creates, whereas in reality it does precisely the opposite, retarding the unbroken vibration of vital movement. We are willing beings precisely insofar as we *repress* impulsive stimuli. Whoever elevates the act of will to the completion and end of an emotion, has stood the truth on its head in the most

Theory of the will 65

complete way that could possibly be imagined. Feelings and will stand to each other in a relationship of exclusive opposites, in such a way that, understood in analogy to the drives, the will should be considered as a *universal retarding motivational force* [*universelle Hemmtriebfeder*].

[...]

What is, in respect of the vital processes, a limitation of their expression becomes, in respect of the activity of the mind, the *regulation* of expression. The will itself would bring every movement to a complete stop; a will associated with the drives has to content itself with regulating the way movements are manifested.

(SW 6, 216 and 221)

In his conference papers, 'The Drives and the Will' and 'On the Theory and Symptomatology of the Will', Klages insists that to will is not to cause movement, but rather to inhibit it; for him, the will does not mean something should happen, but rather that something – or anything that might distract from the achievement of a specific goal – should *not* happen. Can, then, the will bring about a transformation of the character or personality? In Klages's eyes, it cannot, and throughout his philosophical career, Klages continues to meditate on the question of what the will really is. His discussion of the will in two later texts – his major work, *The Spirit as the Adversary of the Soul*, the second volume of which was published in 1929, and one of his last treatises, *Language as a Source of the Study of the Soul* (1948) – demonstrates something of the way in which he elaborated his concept of the will.

Book 4 of volume 2 of *The Spirit as Adversary of the Soul* is subdivided into three sections, entitled respectively 'Law and Intentionality', 'Drive and Will', and 'Deed and Reality'; the motto placed by Klages at the beginning of book 4, 'What could not be a miracle wants to become a work; what could become a work, becomes a deed' *(GWS=SW* 1, p. 513), anticipates the title of this section, the 53rd chapter of which is called 'Will and States of Consciousness'. Here Klages explains some of the historical sources of the modern (and, indeed, postmodern) world:

The will to deeds which has ruthlessly broken out from the beginning of the so-called modern age – enslaving the powers of nature, devastating the face of the planet, pumping out humankind itself into ever more relentless wars of 'competition' – was actually 'prepared' in the disciplines of the medieval monasticism through a *disciplinary regulation of the blood* that lasted for over a thousand years. Anyone who wants to know the intermediate stages that the will had to go through in order to force life completely into obedience to the spirit should study the terrible history of Christian 'mysticism', as Görres[23] has offered it to us on the basis of a comprehensive study of the sources in his five-volume work, *On Christian Mysticism* which, for magnificence and profundity, could be placed next only to the poetry of Dante among the entire literature of Catholicism. Then one will understand that

66   *Works and key ideas*

the supposed 'freedom', the 'enlightenment', and the idolizing of the under-standing in the modern age were all merely the opening-up of a way that leads *out*, after the will had finished its cruel work on the human *soul*, and it will no longer appear surprising, even if it leads to odd conclusions, that the Middle Ages came to an end with two inventions – the invention of printing and the invention of firearms.

If it is the case – as our book has tried, page by page, to show – that the spirit as it is implanted into life is will, but that will is the unrelenting adver-sary of life, then, from the perspective of what is still rooted in life but has capitulated to spirit, the shift towards spirit must appear to be a shift away from life and, in respect of the personhood of the carrier of life overcome by spirit, to be self-overcoming, self-dispossession, and finally self-destruction, and the road leading to this as a gradually increasing training in self-*torture* and self-*denial*. Now Christianity, as long as it was still fighting, was in praxis as in doctrine a struggle with the 'temptations of the flesh' that was turned into a system, and the 'triumph' to which it aspired, the complete subjugation of life, is to be, in human beings, under the authority of the 'Lord', i.e. the will. Pater *vult*, filius *facit*, spiritus *perficit*! [The Father wills, the Son performs, the Spirit perfects].[24] Its highest rule of practice is accordingly *obedience*, because of all the ways to exercise the will the most powerful is practising obedience without any contradiction.

(*GWS=SW* 1, 757–758)

And in chapter 17 of *Language as the Source of Psychology*, entitled 'On the Theory of the Will', Klages offered a concise recapitulation of his theory of the will. The following extracts can help explain what Klages was getting at when he described the spirit (or, in German, *der Geist*) as the 'adversary' or 'opponent' of the soul (in German, *die Seele*).

For what he means is that the will, separated from the vital impulses, is not simply an individual decision of the will on the part of its carrier, but a power which, in its very essence, is *opposed* to life. In other words, Klages is develop-ing a critique of the dreadful state of affairs brought about by the world-historical enthusiasm for deeds, as part of which the will directs its singular effort at 'increasing the power of humankind, which is unthinkingly confused with increasing its value'. Klages's theory of the will is thus part and parcel of his larger critique of civilization as a whole:

The will is not a motivating force or anything similar, but it is a unique *inhibiting measure*, and willing, whatever the purpose of the person who wills, aims at the *control* of a vital process and really does control it to the extent that it is available to be controlled. To use an image: if the vital process corresponds to the sailing boat *together with* the wind that blows it along, then willing is the helm together with whomever is manning it. Without the wind, the boat would not get anywhere despite having a helm; without the helmsman, it would not in general be able to go in the desired

Theory of the will   67

direction; and our image is faithful to the facts of the matter in this further respect, since one cannot steer the boat in a direction in which the wind does not *also* want to direct it. How to respond to an objection which immediately suggests itself and is logically entirely justified – if to will [*das Wollen*] is to steer, then the will [*der Wille*] is obviously like an opposing force, willing [*die Wollung*] itself is like an opposing impulse [*Gegentrieb*], and is not at all fundamentally different from the vital impulses [*Antrieben*] – is something into which we unfortunately cannot go within a *sketch* of this matter, but it makes it all the more necessary to explain, even if only briefly, in what way *that* inhibiting force we call the will is different from all vital inhibiting forces.

Drive-impulses [*Triebantriebe*] can disrupt each other and consequently can inhibit. For example, when I hold out the nutritious grains in my hand to a blackbird, the desire in it to eat begins to struggle with the fear of human hands, and so for the time being the act of pecking them up will not occur. There are many such conflicts of drives in the animal realm, and there are truly innumerable conflicts of interest in the human sphere. *That* inhibition, however, that derives from the controlling force of the will is, irrespective of the particular goal of the person who is willing, always one and the same, and it ought therefore to be distinguished from the collected drive-impulses, even if, whether for logical reasons or because it is easier to do so, one tried to subordinate it to the general concept 'impulse' [*Antrieb*] or 'inhibiting impulse' [*Hemmantrieb*]. Inhibiting and *only* inhibiting constitutes its essence. If on one occasion fear *inhibits* the bird from the movements of flying along and pecking, on another occasion it can *cause* the movements of taking flight. By contrast, the will can never produce movements, but only control otherwise occurring movements. If we were to transpose vital emotions into the communicative form of judgments, then fear, for instance, would sometimes be expressed as declining something, e.g. with 'Let's not go!', sometimes as giving consent, e.g. with 'Let's get out of here!', but the will would speak its one and only, 'No!'. The origin and meaning of this No is something to which we should now turn. Let us remember here the linguistic usage according to which drives are spoken of in the plural, but the will in the singular. The German language does not even allow it a grammatical plural, other languages are less strict in this respect. But when Augustine, one of the greatest theoreticians of the will, announces: Omnes nihil aliud quam voluntates sunt [everyone is nothing other than a will],[25] then he has in mind, as one might expect, the plurality that follows from the plurality of the *carriers* of the will.

And so we come to the decisive point. Anyone who senses a drive-impulse [*Triebantrieb*] [...] feels himself or herself as the driven person; anyone (let us continue) who, by contrast, takes a decision, feels himself or herself as the producer, namely: of the decision of his or her will, and in relation to one's performance this means the control of all available movements towards the goal that is no longer intrinsic to the process as a whole

68 *Works and key ideas*

but is 'predetermined'. The controlling power is, according to the evidence of immediate self-reflection, the *ego*. Let us call the vitality, and in particular that aspect of it by means of which it becomes the point of origin of the drives (and in order to profile its opposition to the *ego*), the *id*, and then the following sentences may serve as a doctrinal exposition of the facts of the matter:

1. Drive-impulses [*Triebantriebe*] of the most varied kinds originate in the id.
2. The ego is, in comparison with them, the passive part.
3. Insofar as the ego is able to resist the driving force of the id, we call it a willing ego or, more briefly, the will.
4. As every carrier of life is a single individual, so its ego is only one ego and consequently so is its own will.
5. The *performance* of the will, i.e. the effect of the resistance of the ego against the drive impulses on this, consists in the control of the impulse, and in the direction of a *predetermined* goal.

With the distinction between the ego and the id, the opposition of both *those* parties, whose duel combat and alternating victory constitute the meaning of the person and hence of 'world history', is indicated in relation to the scope of their effect in the individual being. If we want to give them a name, we have to oppose *life* to *spirit*. From what is in each case a characteristic mixed relation of them both, sometimes in the form of a violent dispute or a permanent tension, sometimes in an attempt at a balance, sometimes in their tearing each other apart, indeed in their disintegration, one can derive every system of the motivating forces and ultimately the entire make-up of every personality. – Let us come back to the problem of the will by posing the question of the *deeper* reasons for which the will was considered to be a cause of movement and its nature as a powerful inhibiting measure was so completely misunderstood. The answer is: because all willing, bearing witness to the activity of the ego, is a wanting-*to-do*, and because with regard to external activities we think of doing as the execution of movements. [...]

Think first of all: if something can be meaningfully willed, it can also be *not* willed, or: if something can be meaningfully willed, its opposite can also be meaningfully willed. Just as I can take the decision to go for a walk, I can also decide to stay at home; or, just as I can decide to speak, I can also make the decision to remain silent. The same is also true of the reverse: anything that *cannot* be meaningfully willed, the opposite of it can also not be willed. Just as I cannot increase my heart beat by a mere decision, so I cannot reduce my heart beat by a mere decision. – If we call any positive deed a deliberate action, and negative action a deliberate omission, then we can see for ourselves, secondly, that deliberate omissions involve basically the same exertion of will as deliberate actions, indeed often require a greater one. If I have decided to remain silent when a particular topic arises in social

Theory of the will 69

conversation, then I really have to exert myself not to be unfaithful to my decision as soon as I am condemned to hear the most awful stupidities; and when, according to the legend, Wilhelm Tell refuses to show respect to Gessler's hat, this required a power of decision and a strength of will a hundred times greater than taking a detour.[26]

If a deliberate omission, or not doing something, can also be included in the category of doing, then we can also be sure, third, that there are *also* no deliberate actions without the assistance of a particular category of deliberate omissions, namely: those whose constitutional precondition is usually described as a 'power of resistance against distracting stimuli' or more simply as an 'ability to master oneself'. Indeed, here and here alone lies the deliberateness of an action – that any deviation in question from the direction of the goal is *not* permitted to a process that is carried out of its own accord. If the wind blows the sailing boat forwards in exactly the right direction, then steering it is unnecessary; and, similarly, the steering 'intention' is superfluous, if the vital process is reaching its goal anyway. Just as steering the ship prevents any deviation from the direction towards a spatial goal, so the will prevents any deviation from the direction towards attaining a purpose, irrespective of whether the action consists of acting or omitting to act. To will is to will action, *to will action, however, is to will not to allow something to happen.* Here we get to the core of action and are given not just one, but the single key to the doctrine of the will.

[…]

In the paragraph above we spoke about the drive-impulse [*Triebantrieb*] as the vehicle of willing and tried to express how the impulse [*Antrieb*] is something in motion and, in relation to the body, something that does the moving, and the will something that controls the movement. Insofar as the will steers, it is the master of the journey; insofar, however, as the bodily or the soul-related pole of vitality has determined the goal of the journey, the helmsman of the vehicle stands in the service of life, entrusted with the task of hindering, if he can, every deviation from the direction towards goals he has not chosen and which, if it were left up to him, he would avoid. The starting-point of *his* effective agency [*Wirken*] in the person of someone who wills is the ego. If the ego were to become more and more independent and if its tool, the will, were to make itself more and more free from the attractive force of the goals of the bodily and the soul-related poles alike, then this would go hand-in-hand with a *negation* of caring for life, extending life, enriching life, and its place would be taken by acting in the cause of increasing the power of the ego. The will that emancipates itself from life and imperiously enslaves it brings forth evil (the despicable, the satanic), and the hunger for power that accompanies such a formation of the will in the personal ego – before the will has extinguished the life of its carrier and thereby, of course, itself – is the mask, grown into the flesh of the personality and deceiving it, the mask of a hatred that aims ultimately at the destruction of the world.

(*SW* 5, 616–617; 618–619; 625)

70   *Works and key ideas*

Or to summarize this argument in Klages's own words, taken from the concluding retrsopective chapter in *The Spirit as Adversary of the Soul*, 'our work locates the key to the essence of the spirit [*Geist*] *not* in the intellect, but in the *will*' (*GWS=SW* 2, 1420). Another aspect of the spirit, similarly opposed (as is the will, on Klages's account) to life, is consciousness.

Conceptual tool #4: genesis of consciousness

On one level, we all know what consciousness is. We know we are reading this book (consciousness); and we know that we know we are reading this book (self-consciousness). On another level, consciousness remains a huge mystery. What *is* it exactly? What does it mean to be conscious? How did consciousness originate? And how do I know that other people are conscious in the same way as I am?

These are fundamental questions, and ones that Klages did not shy away from tackling and on his own terms. In fact, his major work, *The Spirit as Adversary of the Soul*, devotes the entirety of its third book and most of its fourth to the issue of consciousness. Now Klages approaches consciousness through the conceptual tool we have just been examining, for he writes that 'the doctrine of the will is a major part of the doctrine of the conditions under which the consciousness arises' (*GWS=SW* 1, 515). (In fact, Klages had already worked out his theory of the will by 1912, the year when he began to turn his attention to the problem of the origin of consciousness.)

In 1915 Klages published an essay in the *Allgemeine Zeitung* with the title 'Consciousness and Life'. Subsequently he included it in a collection of essays (possibly the work that has in recent times come the closest to being a best-seller), first published in 1920 under the title *Humankind and Earth*. In this essay Klages tells us:

> The elements of the construction of life, in plants and in animals alike, are, as is well known, cells. Life always clings to the cell body; but as such it is completely and forever closed to consciousness. Yet in each and every one of us individual beings, ephemeral in our millions of deaths and births, the life of the cell reaches without the smallest interruption back to the first protoplasmic clump of the planetary primal sea;[27] whereas, by contrast, our conscious remembering does not preserve even the embryonal life of our body in the womb, let alone the experience of our ancestors. While life in us is only the frontline at a particular moment of a stream, inexorably pushing ahead, that goes back in an unbroken line at least to the carbon age of the earth, consciousness finds itself limited to what is in comparison the literally disappearing time-span of an individual human lifetime. How could one believe it is possible that life and consciousness have nevertheless been confused?
>
> (*SW* 3, 648–649)

Genesis of consciousness 71

It is not the stream of experience that is consciousness, but it arises insofar as this stream is struck by the lightning of being registered. And just as consciousness is not already life, so life is just as little already consciousness.

(cf. *SW* 3, 648)

This wonderfully concise essay on 'Consciousness and Life' can be profitably read alongside another seminal work, first published in two parts in 1914 and 1919 in the *Journal for Pathopsychology* (*Zeitschrift für Pathopsychologie*), called 'Of Dream Consciousness'. The aim of this treatise is summarized by Klages at its outset in the following terms:

We would like to show that the view in antiquity, which originally accorded a significance that was more than merely subjective to dreams as such, and later at least to certain dreams, came closer to the truth than the view of the present-day which disagrees with this. And in this way we would like to make a contribution not so much to the understanding of dreams as to the theory of consciousness, the wakefulness of which cannot be understood without insight into the nature of dreaming.

(*SW* 3, 158)

For his theory of consciousness Klages was indebted to the work that had been done by the philosopher, Melchior Palágyi, a Hungarian thinker of Jewish descent who, in 1901, had produced a new theory of space and time. In *A New Theory of Space and Time: The Fundamental Concepts of a Metageometry* (1901), Palágyi proposed a phenomenological conception of space-time relativity, rather than the physical relativity proposed shortly later by Albert Einstein in 1905 and 1916 (in his special and general theories of relativity). The importance of Palágyi for Klages's thinking justifies the inclusion at this point of an extract from Palágyi's work, *Natural Philosophical Lectures: On the Fundamental Problems of Consciousness and of Life* (second edn, 1924):

We ought never confuse the activity of our consciousness with our vital process. The process of life can influence the activity of our waking consciousness in a beneficial way, yet it can, however, also inhibit and, despite the greatest efforts, can bring our will in a mysterious way to a standstill, or lead it into the dream state. Already this well-known fact includes a completely sufficient reason to consider (and rightly so) the activity of our consciousness and the course of our process of life as two entirely separate concepts from each other. It is something quite different merely to *live* and then again something different to live with *consciousness*, namely with waking consciousness.

[...]

The entirety of everything that might happen in the universe can be divided for the knowing human mind into three classes of events: into (a) acts of consciousness; (b) vital processes; and (c) mechanical occurrences. Each of

72   *Works and key ideas*

these three classes of events has its own specific character to such an extent that one of them can never be 'attributed to' another. Rather it is the task of human research to fathom the incomparable particularity of these three realms as far as possible; I say 'as far as possible', because it is not in the gift of the human mind ever completely to exhaust what is particular to mental activity, to the process of life, or even to mechanical occurrences.

(pp. 35 and 45 = *CAK*, 189)

From this stage in his intellectual development we can find a summary of Klages's thinking to this date in the form of a private lecture he gave to three of his friends – Jakob Eugster, Christoph Bernoulli, and Emanuel La Roche – in the summer of 1918. Klages gave this lecture the title 'On the Doctrine of Life', and although in the end it was never published,[28] the contents of this lecture have been summarized by Hans Eggert Schröder as follows, providing an overview of how Klages saw the role of consciousness in relation to the larger problem (as he regarded it) of life:

The doctrine of life states: The universe is alive; the earth is alive; the creatures of the earth – plants, animals, human beings – are alive; correspondingly there are cosmic, planetary and organismic (individual) life forms, life [*Leben*] means to experience life [*erleben*]. For the carrier of organismic life, experiencing life consists in the reciprocal exchange with the organismic, planetary, cosmic life-processes of its environment; from them it continually receives influences, on them it continually exercises influences. The life process is a polar process; its poles are called bodily and soul-related events. (Poles are different sides of a single, inseparable process!) The result of, on the one hand, the reciprocal relation of the individual and its environment, and of, on the other, the polarity of its own life processes, are the four basic forms of the course of life: on the receptive side of experiencing life, sensation [*Empfindung*] as the intensity-related experience of bodiliness and intuitive vision [*Schauung*] as the quality-related experience of the appearance of the surrounding world; on the emotional side, the drive-impulse [*Triebantrieb*] as the urge to enter into contact with the surrounding world of bodies, and the impulse to formation [*Gestaltungstrieb*] as the urge to intervene creatively in the phenomenal image [*Erscheinungsbild*] of the environment.

The analysis of the basic forms of the course of life leads to the genesis of consciousness with the help of the distinction between vegetative, animal, and human life-processes. The life of plants (and of every vegetative life process in animals and humans) runs its course in a way comparable to the state of sleep. The life of animals (and of every animal-like process in human beings) represents, by contrast, an awakening of the bodily processes, but only these (moving of one's own accord; predominance of the life of the drives; blindness towards differentiated distinctions in quality), and is similarly not capable of becoming conscious. The human life form

The doctrine of 'the reality of images' 73

distinguishes itself from the animal through the awakening of soul-related experience of life (meaningful formation of life instead of blind life of the drives) and thereby creates the precondition for the capacity for consciousnessness of experiencing life.

For this to happen, the body-and soul-related experience of life in the state of soul-related wakefulness must be surrendered to the intervention of acts of the spirit. Dreaming in sleep is soul-related waking experience of life during the bodily state of sleep. Dream consciousness is the one single experiential paradigm for the life process of predominant vision and confronts us with the unlimited world of images. The waking consciousness – by means of the act of taking-in, which refashions flowing images into fixed facts – creates the precondition for the intervention of the act of will, which can only be executed on fixed facts.

(CAK, 189–190)

As becomes clear from the summary of this lecture, the key to understanding Klages's account of the origin or genesis of consciousness lies in grasping his notion of the 'unlimited world of images', as he calls it in the final paragraph of this text. So the next conceptual tool to which we shall turn our attention in this Klagesian toolkit is the doctrine he called 'the reality of images'.

Conceptual tool #5: the doctrine of 'the reality of images'

If the theory of the will is one of the two core themes of Klages's philosophy, then the second is the doctrine of what Klages calls the 'reality of images'. This apparently mysterious idea crops up time and again in his writings, and understanding it will enable us to appreciate those passages where he offers wonderful descriptions of what it means to contemplate the natural world. Yet the concept of the image or *Bild*, so central to Klages's thought, remains one of his most difficult to grasp or understand. Various commentators on Klages have emphasized different aspects of this notion.

For instance, Hans Kasdorff glosses Klages's concept of the image (*Bild*) as follows:

The word 'image' should not be restricted here to the optical image, such as that in physics nor, for that matter, of the visual arts. Rather it refers to the invisible formative powers, which, for example, are at work in the fertilized nucleus of the maternal organism, and transmit the image of the species to which this organism belongs, so that it renews itself in a similar form.[29]

Kasdorff identifies the term *Bilder* with 'intuitive images' (*Anschauungsbilder*) and 'imagistic appearances' (*Bilderscheinungen*), adding that these, too, should not be confused with 'mere optical, visibly apprehended images, however often intuitive images may be *seen*'.[30] Likewise, Hans Eggert Schröder emphasizes that the Klagesian *Bild* is not simply visual but is rather 'a formative power'

74   *Works and key ideas*

(*eine bildende Macht*), playing on the etymological relation between *Bild* (image) and *bilden* (to construct, to form).[31] Kasdorff cites the following passage from Klages's essay 'On the Concept of Personality' (1916) which describes the power of the image in sensation (*Erlebnis*) as opposed to judgement and experience (*Erfahrung*):

> In the sensation the image of the world grips, lures, seduces, enraptures, overpowers; in judgement the comprehending spirit seizes hold of it, reifies it, and locks it up in the vault of experience.[32]

And according to Michael Großheim, 'the expression "image" [*Bild*] stands [...] for the irreducible and vital unities of original experience, vivid impressions, saturated with moving atmospheres, which is surely right.[33]

The development of the concept of the image or *Bild* can be traced through Klages's published writings. In an essay first published under the title 'On Sympathy' in the *Graphological Monthly* (*Graphologische Monatshefte*) (vol. 3, no. 1) in 1899 and reprinted under the title 'On the Source of Immediate Feelings of Affection' in the *Journal for Anthropology* (*Zeitschrift für Menschenkunde*) (vol. 1, no. 5) in 1926 – an indication of the continuity between Klages's early work on graphology and his later writings – we can gain an insight into how the doctrine of the 'reality of images' is anchored in concrete human experience:

> It is not his or her greatness that makes us like someone, but this: that we become greater through him or her.
>
> *Every presence of a fellow human being has a specifically transforming effect on the character of a human being.* The one and the same character *is* indeed another, depending on the viewer across from whom he or she is.
>
> We are not talking here about someone consciously acting a role. Rather it is a question of the transformations of an individual being that take place in the depths of the individual's mind and soul furthest removed from intentionality and with such a domineering force that, *if* we become conscious of them, the will nevertheless remains completely incapable of preventing them.
>
> The behaviour imposed unintentionally on us merely by how the nature of an individual appears can fill us with joy, displeasure, or strong resistance.
>
> In truth the natural elective affinity of minds and souls can never be produced by moral agreement nor reduced or cancelled out by the strongest oppositions in ethical behaviour.
>
> [...] A change that immediately takes place within us is the occasion for and the cause of our affections.
>
> *The primary and essential result is joy or displeasure about a change that we ourselves undergo.*

The doctrine of 'the reality of images' 75

The harmony of inner minds and souls is felt by each individual as an inner *enrichment* and *increase*.

The growth and development of not a few characters [...] depends exclusively on whether they encounter in those decisive years those minds and souls which, one is tempted to say, can redeem them.

(*SW* 4, 16–18)

The inner transformation of which Klages speaks here is brought out in an immediate (i.e. unmediated) way through the *appearance*, through the *image* of another human being who is present.

In Klages's words (from 'On the Theory of Writing Pressure', 1902/1903), 'the bodily expression of every condition of the soul is such that it for its part can elicit this condition again' (*SW* 8, 99), an idea which he reformulated later in 'The Expressive Movement and its Diagnostic Exploitation' (1913) and in 'Expressive Movement and Formative Power' (1913, 1921, 1923) as 'the bodily expression of every condition of consciousness' – or 'condition of life' – 'is such that its image can elicit this condition again' (*SW* 6, 70 and 162). Klages believes this to be true, not just of every movement in the emotional heart of being (our heart, mind and soul), but equally for every emotional disposition of a fellow human being. What might be called the inner eye, something that perceives the image and its transformative effect, is (as Hans Eggert Schröder explains) a visionary power of the soul that, in the animal, is subordinated to the life of the drives, but in the human being is awoken as part of his or her spontaneous development.

In chapter 7 of *The Foundations of the Study of Character*, Klages has this to say about the reality of images:

According to our doctrine of the *reality of images* [...] we must understand the rule of the images in living material as vital processes that *can* produce phantasms [*Phantasmen*] but in no wise *have* to, and least of all may they be confused with the mental [*geistigen*] activity of making present that some people term 'to represent'. In response to the justified question as to whether there are those sorts of processess and what would give us cause to see images manifesting themselves in them, we can best reply with some examples.

If we reflect that, following fertilization in the germ-cell of the maternal organism, the drive [*Trieb*] or the impulse [*Drang*] is aroused to join cell to cell, through millions and millions of repetitions, until a new organism, related in shape to the maternal one, has grown, then we could hardly better describe the growth process than with the observation that, in the fertilized cell, the *image* of the developing body works as a material-shaping power! Anyone to whom it seems it is too bold to argue that this – to be sure, deeply unconscious – growth and ripening occur through the power of images which only begin to manifest themselves thanks to the former, will no longer fail to recognize this power and its unconscious rule when glancing

76 *Works and key ideas*

at the *relations* of the finished organism to the surrounding world. After all, the essence of the so-called instincts mentioned above of the animal lies in the fact that, thanks to them, it can make a selection from the images of the world, searching for what it is essential to its life and fleeing from what is detrimental and hostile to it!

A vital magnetic attraction binds together a thirsty horse and the sight of water, a hungry cow with the impression of grass, an eagle out hunting with the appearance of chickens, goat kids, hares, and equally each of these and *that* side of the images and *that* segment of the world which it has the gift unconsciously to recognize as nourishment and as habitation! A duckling that has just learned to walk plunges into the pond, while the hen from which it has hatched warns it in alarm; it has recognized in water its element, not from the slightest conscious reflection, but rather as a result of the quite specific prompting to which the impression of the water has made its soul receptive. The impression *is* not this prompting, but merely awakens it. An animal in need of food *looks for* its food when it is not present, looks for its habitation, its element, when it is lacking them, and the flocks of migratory birds that set off in autumn are separated by thousands of kilometres from *those* impressions – the atmospheric gases, the climate, the places of habitation – toward which, as if attracted to them by some vital magnetism, they strive as a sleepwalker would.

People talk about drives, rightly emphasizing the drive's aspect of need, its lack.[34] But merely a glance at any random example is sufficient for one to recognize that a need could never lead to a satisfaction of a need without the unconscious presence of the attractive power of the image that promises satisfaction. We can analyse the sensation of thirst physiologically, we can analyse it psychologically, but we shall never find in it even the remotest similarity with the phenomenon [*Erscheinung*] of water (irrespective of whichever sense organs detects it), and we shall forever remain unable to make even a single statement about the experience of thirst, until we decided to call it – with Aristoteles – a drive toward union with what is liquid;[35] in which case we would have imported into the need of thirst the *image* of liquid as an unconscious attractive force.

The distinction [...] between the aspect of impulse [*Antriebsseite*] and the aspect of mood [*Stimmungsseite*] in feeling also applies, of course, to animal feelings. Just as motivating forces [*Triebfedern*] are *only* observed in human feelings, so *drives* [*Triebe*] are in animal feelings. Drives are vital causes of movement, and vital movement is, in contrast to merely mechanical movement, always directed toward a *goal* which can be categorically defined. What is manifested in the strength of the drive-impulse [*Triebantrieb*] is the greatness of the need, of the lack; in its direction, what is manifested is the attractive power of the image, as we have just discussed. It is this which, even on the animal level of the various drives of hunger, thirst, migration, play, the striving for sexual union, care, attack, defence, flight, lends to each of them its peculiar quality, and it is at least involved in the

The doctrine of 'the reality of images'   77

mood aspect of all human feelings. If, accordingly, the mood aspect of feeling testifies to (and also requires) the connection – sometimes tighter, sometimes looser – of the soul with the reality of the images, then we may with good reason speak of an *image content in the feelings* [*Bildgehalt der Gefühle*], and we must then call those feelings in which the mood aspect becomes considerably less important than the impulse aspect, image-*weak* feelings, and by contrast feelings with a decidedly predominant mood aspect, image-*strong*. [Klages's footnote: It might appear as if euphoric states were thereby disadvantaged vis-à-vis depressive ones, especially since the latter are usually considered as '*bad moods*'; but any such appearance would be deceptive. As its name indicates, usual despondency, just like moroseness or grumpiness, is characterized primarily by a general inhibition of the impulse and sheer listlessness, and not at all by sombre-coloured mood tones. Compared with this, the youthful sadness of one's adolescent years, the melancholy of the poet, wistful nostalgia, deep resignation, the mourning of love, etc., are quite different! These are moods saturated with images, compared with which the inhibitions of the impulse associated with them have little significance.] With this insight we hold in our hands the key to understanding the fact that images can be experienced and that they guide vital processes without the *necessary* addition of phantasms, let alone consciousness of them.

Primordial humankind escaped from the animal state by means of a change in the weight of the poles, when the hitherto dominant vital process of sensing (of one's own body as well as others' bodies) became dependent on the hitherto subordinated vital process of vision (of images), and hence the bodily or emotional side of feeling became dependent on the soul's mood; accordingly, from now on fantasy or the gift of day-dreaming was able to liberate one from the shackles of the here and now. What had previously been realized only in the change of bodily states, the attractive force of the images, now came to light as an autonomous force, determining the body henceforth in a different way and in an activity which was different from what the mere drive-impulse [*Triebantrieb*] had been able to determine. If a thirsting stag is forced to look for water and is lacking it until it finds water, so a thirsting human being has the ability to dream, waking, about water and drinking, to *picture* water and drinking, and finally to make their image objectively present in matter, or more generally: the images which until now had acted as if without eyes in the direction-setting attraction of the drives *awaken* in the human being, and there also awaken, leaving behind and overcoming animal emotions, innumerable new urges, as innumerable as the possible images *of those* elements that gave birth to the human being, and so the world awakens and is revealed as what it is: a reality itself of *images*, in relation to which all vital processes now appear as the means and the pathways to the *vision* of reality. Here lies the deepest root of myth, symbol, and art, here too lies the deepest root of all magic.

(*SW* 4, 322–325)

78 *Works and key ideas*

In Klages's main philosophical work, *The Spirit as Adversary of the Soul*, its entire fifth book (constituting the third and final volume published in 1932) is placed under the title, *The Reality of the Images*. The conceptual and rhetorical complexity and sophistication of these pages, from chapter 55 to chapter 75, should leave the reader in no doubt about the seriousness, depth, and richness of Klages's philosophical project.

The phrase 'reality of images' is first used in this work in chapter 29, where Klages clarifies the way in which he wishes to separate himself from the existing metaphysical tradition, indexed to its Greek and German forms:

> Neither Schopenhauer nor Plato (who is, of course, much stricter) ever attained to the *reality of images*; rather both of them, each in his own way, devalue the phenomena and teach the 'higher' reality of a being-related, noumenal, conceptual world. But what already lends the 'Ideas' of Plato, and the complete backwardly view of Schopenhauer in its entirety, an ambiguously shimmering colour, is this wish of their promulgators, which cannot be placated, to present what they regard as 'a priori' objectivity at the same time as something visible, recollected, phantasmatic, in short, as *mirroring* reality. In this respect, a fundamental experience expresses itself, revealing to us its nature of a particular proximity to the spirit, something they share and something which both of them overlook: the experience no longer of having a vision [*Schauen*], but of looking [*Hinblicken*] at something that once was part of a vision [*Geschautes*]. In the process of life, not flowing images [*Bilder*] but static copies [*Abbilder*] lie at the root of ideal things, whether thought of as internal or external. The vital movement has to be neutralized at the point where it reverses direction and the flow of images has to be present in the reflection, so that the spirit is able to bind what is eternally passing away into the object, something certainly unchanging, because it is precisely outside time.
>
> (*GWS=SW* 1, 287)

When he returns, in part 1 of book 5 entitled 'The Doctrine', to the notion of the 'reality of images', Klages begins by recapitulating some of the main arguments of his work as a whole.

The fundamental antithesis of his thought, the oppositon of 'spirit' (*Geist*) to 'soul' (*Seele*), is explored (in section 1) in relation to the distinction between 'waking' and 'sleeping', and in turn to the distinction between 'visionary' and 'conceptualizing' wakefulness. In a fascinating chapter (the fifty-seventh), Klages offers a 'prehistory' (or *Vorgeschichte*) of the discovery of this idea of the images, beginning with the ancient Greeks. After discussing Heraclitus, Protagoras, and Plato, Klages then turns to Aristoteles, Plotinus, and Plutarch. On all of these thinkers, Klages has something fresh and original to say. A short sub-section on medieval philosophy leads to a lengthy sub-section on the mysticism of the Renaissance, followed by another sub-section on Romanticism, especially German Romanticism. (This tradition is represented for Klages not so

The doctrine of 'the reality of images' 79

much by Jean Paul, Hölderlin, Kleist, Novalis, Tieck, Arnim, E. T. A. Hoffmann, and Eichendorff, as it is by C. G. Carus, J. D. Passavant [1787–1861], Gotthilf Heinrich von Schubert [1780–1860], C. W. F. Hufeland [1762–1836], Heinrich Bruno Schindler [1797–1859], Franz von Baader [1765–1841], Johann Joseph von Görres [1776–1848], and Lorenz Oken [1779–1851] – i.e. not so much by poets and novelists as by philosophers, psychologists, and historians). These pages contain some of Klages's finest writing on the history of philosophy. A penultimate sub-section on Klages's contemporaries, especially J. J. Bachofen, is placed under the title 'Dithyrambicians of Decline', before, in a concluding reflection, Klages names as particularly important these two thinkers: Friedrich Nietzsche and Alfred Schuler, whose significance we discussed in the first chapter of this toolkit.

But Klages is not simply concerned with the history of this doctrine, but with its current applicability! So he returns (in section 2) to a more fundamental level, discussing the oppositon between the 'soul' and the 'body', explored in relation to the 'here-and-now'; to 'body' and 'thing'; to 'matter' and the 'phenomenal world'; and finally the question of 'being' itself. In sections 3 and 4, Klages concerns himself with the relation between closeness and distance, and then with the question of how the images are able to have an effect (i.e. their context and relation). In chapter 67, part of this fourth and final section in part 1 of book 5, Klages investigates the essence of reality itself. Significantly, the starting-point of these reflections is the phenomenon of language:

> *Reality as a singulare tantum* [i.e. having only a singular form]. We can devise an odd objection [i.e. to the argumentation of *The Spirit as Adversary of the Soul*], but one which might appear to many readers as perhaps not so odd at all. If reality itself should come to audible depiction in the transmission of similar rhythms in linguistic sounds, how then could thousands of different languages arise? How can the same linguistic sound in *one* language have entirely different meanings? How, finally, would translations be possible, if the new sounds were no longer to depict the same images?
>
> We could make things easy for ourselves by recalling how this capacity for depiction was claimed to be only a pre-rational stage of linguistic-creative processes. Although such processes had, even later, not completely stopped, they became a minority in comparison with the imagistic motivations from levels of lingustic feeling already saturated with spirit. We could further recall that the soul, always individual, of the linguistic creator belongs to reality, a creator whose linguistic sound would, in the case of the greatest phenomenal adequacy of its contact with world, have to deviate from that of another soul because, in both, the image characters themselves would be different from each other. Such considerations have force, but they would hardly be of any use to us. For immediately the question would arise of the standard according to which, under such circumstances, the reality content of the linguistic sound could be judged. We have to go back to the drawing-board and dig deeper.

80   *Works and key ideas*

Not just the objection, but also what has been brought forward as an attempt to counter it, take their stand on the belief in a reality of objects and know nothing of any reality of images. If we were to place both expressions, 'reality of objects' and 'reality of images', side by side, measuring the meaning of the one against the meaning of the other, then the thought, which would of course immediately arise, of the difference between things and [intuitive] images [*Anschauungsbilder*][36] would in no way be sufficient to open up the meaning of the second expression, until we had also thought through the difference in what recurs, on both occasions under the same name, under the name of 'reality'. So we can hardly do anything other than also to apply 'reality' to at least the things of perception, because those concepts of being, by means of which we relate to their being real, are *im*mediately caused by appearances and distinguish themselves so sharply from objects that are nothing-other-than-objects-of-thought [*Nichts-als-Denkgegenständen*], whose relation to what is real is mediated by a row, often a long one, of intermediaries; but to equate the things of perception with reality would mean confusing the product of one of the two conditions of its production, i.e. the vital [*vital*] one, and completely suppressing the second and as at least important one, i.e. the spirit-related [*geistig*] one.

(*GWS* = *SW* 2, 1176–1177)

And then Klages goes on to give one of those anecdotal case-studies in the phenomenology of the everyday that reveals how his thought, however abstract in conception and complex in expression, is rooted in a keen analytic sense of concrete experience:[37]

Because the appearance of the wood to which one draws closer from a distance is continually changing slightly and becomes completely different when one enters it, it is easy to distinguish and to understand why the wood as a thing [*dinglicher Wald*] and the appearance of the wood [*Erscheinung des Waldes*] are two different things. Only someone for whom the appearing wood and the material wood fall into separate categories has crossed the threshold of understanding the doctrine of the 'reality of images', or more precisely: someone for whom the realities that come to appearance in the images of what is called 'this wood here' and the one and the same thing which – is also called this, fall into separate categories. For it is first of all one kind of something *real* that appears as applicable to 'this wood here' from a distance, and another kind that appears as applicable to it from close up. 'The wood here' as one and the same from a distance and from close up is perceived, 'the wood here' as a transformation of uncountable realities between distance and closeness is on the occasion of its perception experienced, suffered, envisioned; the former involves the relation of the carrier of the perception, the latter stands or, better expressed, its changing realities stand in a relation to the carrier of the vision [*Träger des Schauens*].

The doctrine of 'the reality of images'   81

Of course, perception [*die Wahrnehmung*] also presupposes a relation [*ein Zusammenhängen*] for a few fractions of a second; but this falls prey, even before it could become memorable experience, to the divisive act of the spirit and it finds itself, having hardly arisen, already replaced by differentiating relatedness [*unterscheidendes Bezogensein*]; and such a process of division and separation is identical to the one which tears away the inner linguistic sounds, and hence thought, from the magical area of action of the soul, in this way changing the carrier of the vision [*Träger des Schauens*] into a carrier of *consciousness* [*Träger eines Bewußtseins*] that tries to seize the world of perception, which it is now driven to want to 'grasp' conceptually, through violent *intervention* [*Eingriff*]. It is not a question of a multiplicity of phenomena [*Erscheinungen*], but of a multiplicity of *realities* [*Wirklichkeiten*] which appear in them: and this is what is meant by the 'reality of images' ["*Wirklichkeit der Bilder*"].

(*GWS=SW* 2, 1177–1178)

Despite being anchored in concrete experience, Klages's doctrine is, at first blush, not an easy one for us to grasp, because it goes entirely against our conventional understanding of perception – and hence against our conventional understanding of reality. In a way, the difficulty we have in understanding Klages's argumentation might even be seen to confirm his thesis: we are so saturated with *Geist* that we can no longer hear what the *Seele* is telling us.

The following three passages sum up the essence of Klages's teaching about 'the reality of images'. First, a short saying found in *Rhythms and Runes*, and again in a later essay, *On the Nature of Consciousness* (1921):

The image that falls into the senses
It and nothing else is the sense of the world.

(*RR*, 280; *SW* 3, 279)

Second, a passage from *The Spirit as Adversary of the Soul*, in one of his most beautiful chapters, entitled 'The Elementary Souls', Klages declares:

What in a moment of grace touches a chord in us from nature or from the works of the spring-spirits with a daimonic force is not something intellectually devised and constructed in the imagination, rather it is – *born*.

(*GWS=SW* 2, 1132)

Third, Klages explains what he means by the 'reality of images' in reference to a painting as a kind of objective correlative; in this case, a wonderful work by the Swiss Symbolist painter Arnold Böcklin (1827–1901) entitled *Playing in the Waves* (*Im Spiel der Wellen*) (1883). This painting, usually on display in the Neue Pinakothek in Munich, shows us centaurs and mermaids at play among the waves of the ocean, but what it also *shows* us, as Klages suggests, is something else:

82 *Works and key ideas*

Figure 4 Arnold Böcklin, *In the Play of the Waves* (1883).

The elements of the ancients are universal thoughts, and the symbols that have proceeded from them have, like all symbolic names, at least general meanings; with their help, the spirit is related to the general characteristics of images, rather than of things, and originally it had encountered these characteristics in unique appearances. What the arts have bequeathed to us gives us the opportunity to explain those material souls by means of examples. – Böcklin comes to mind. For, whatever his artistry may lack, as a poet who uses colour he remains one of the rare primordial spirits through whom planetary powers make themselves audible with unheard-of force.

To the unmistakable traces that the Baroque – on this occasion, thanks to its hidden Romanticism! – has left in the art of painting belongs a depiction of the qualities of material elements in a way never found before. Neither the Quattrocento nor the classical period has, irrespective of whether through over-emphasized formal clarity or through revelling in the richest colours, tried to capture in copies so passionately: the misty, cloudy, dripping, smoky, fiery, glowing, the stony, metallic, wooden, the wet, dry, brittle, springy, the dense and the spacious copse forest, the cracked quality of bark, the gentle swelling of foliage, the flesh colour of meat, the hirsute character of hair, the rough softness of animal skins, the texture of clothing materials, the folds in clothes that sometimes fall in flows, sometimes billow

The doctrine of 'the reality of images' 83

out heavily, sometimes crisply crinkle, the qualities of velvetiness, silkiness, brocade, atlas, carpets, veils, and so forth. On a degenerative path this leads one out of the world of image-appearances into the world of *only* bodily appearances, and finally to that style of depiction called 'Realism' which, wherever it emerges in a distinctive way, it would be better to call 'Theatricalism'; reaching its conclusion, however, it leads to the banishment of the image souls that are at the same time and above souls of *material elements*.

We cannot explore here (although as we go on it will be suggested) to what extent the shivers and shudders of the depths and distances of Böcklinian space are related to what we are inclined to see as his main characteristic feature: the revelation of the essence of material elements; it is sufficient that this is never missed in any of his most important paintings. No one else has opened up the ground of his extrahuman soul to the primordial world of the reeds, the storm-entangled nature of the tree, the cracks and holes of ageing walls. However, what is most characteristic about him can be more precisely defined: he is the discoverer of the *soul of water*. Granted, not just Böcklin alone! Not only had the Dutch preceded him, but such artists as Corot, Daubigny, Dupré, Rousseau, Stäbli, and Schleich have achieved immortal things in the depiction of the liquid element.[38] But however diverse the forms in which they allow the essence of water to appear, it is still either in some way *useful* water, as it is presented to our eyes as drinkable water, as navigable water, as water that tempts one to bathe, as garden ornamentation and a fountain, as a fish-bowl, etc., or it lends its soul as a mirror for feelings – sometimes light, sometimes dark – of the human soul. From the wondrous showers of rain in Stäbli's works the unnameable melancholy of one's youthful years sings forth! With Böcklin all this is stripped away. To him, *only* the element speaks: the element, as it was before humankind came into being, and unconcerned about it, but the birthplace of all individual life on earth.

Among his most successful paintings there is none from which something of such magic moistness does not waft, rejuvenating and transforming, even if no actual water is to be seen; it comes through most powerfully on those occasions when, sparkling from ponds, brooding from swamps, flowing from the mouth of the spring, rushing from the brook, rolling in waves, crashing as surf, disappearing as spray, water appears; no, is bodily conjured up in its elementary primordiality from the night of becoming. The roots of the soul of most people today can no longer reach down into these waters; and so it can only be communicated to those who are willing and capable of drawing from such a spring.

But then one needs only to reflect quickly on oneself to realize: what is human in us *also* responds alternately with yearning, melancholy, passion, flames of love, resignation; as if we were children dancing on a meadow still bathed in sunlight in front of a wood already growing dark, behind the tree-tops of which, towering like the Himalayas, a dark blue thunderstorm is rising up. And just as, under the approaching shadows, the dance disperses

84 *Works and key ideas*

and the children flee from the gusts of the wind, so those human, now all-too-human feelings grow anxious; but, as they become paler and paler until they dissolve, we are filled by something more than human passion and human pain, the life – which can only be sung, no longer spoken – of the elements: measured against humans, a compulsion that is blindly raging and devouring, because all renewing, an *eternal drunkenness* from its own self. And because what we have been trying to analyse can in reality be only rarely, if ever, completely distinguished, so our melancholy, our yearning, our passion instead acquired the dimension of a depth, to which what we usually call yearning, passion, melancholy are just as little related as a little boat out on the ocean is to the abyss beneath him by which he is borne.[39]

The most authentic works of this master are not lacking in a rising, bursting, indeed overflowing passion for life, but they are entirely lacking in a so-called warmth of feeling, unless one includes a sublime melancholy which is at least a characteristic of many. But precisely thereby testimony is borne in the midst of these feelings to the dependence of what is human about the world on the *fate* that overpoweringly holds sway in it. Through sexual lust and sensuality, indeed through humour and dancing and high spirits, we sense the stirring of an activity that builds as it destroys, and that is already shattering what it was building. – We have touched on the *cosmic content* of Böcklin's poems in colour; but he, too, is fed by the soul of the telluric water, to which we now wish to approach as closely as we can without weakening our power of vision.

The popular work, 'Play of the Waves', can doubtless be enjoyed for its humorous touch. Indeed, if one took this away, the painting would no longer be what it is. And if somone should notice in it a touch of 'genre painting' and see at least in the two nudes on the righthand side of the painting no more than two sprightly female swimmers, not without characteristics typical of the time (let us say nothing about lapses that have been reprimanded elsewhere), we should have to agree; but those would be at worst tiny artistic slips in the irresistibly compelling content of the painting: the soul of water appearing as a wave of the sea [*die Wasserseele als Meereswoge erscheinend*]. And precisely because the painting is entirely lacking in pathos, abstains (not entirely, but almost) from making things appear at a distance, and parades the good-natured, crude aspect of the powerful element, it provides an *im*mediate proof that the essence of water has hitherto revealed itself so profoundly to no other artist.

There is one thing we no longer have to defend, because it has escaped no understanding observer: namely, that the huge, ungainly water centaur, the mermaid in the foreground, the lascivious merman next to her, the person plunging to the depths of the sea behind her, are not least essentially *one and the same* as the water from which they emerge. Even if they are partially making swimming movements, they do not need to swim; they can just as little sink in the sea as the rolling wave can, and they can disappear just as quickly again as the wave disappears, whether in the smooth surface

The doctrine of 'the reality of images'   85

of the water, or in the tongues of foam that seep away on the shore. We have certainly met poets, rather than painters, who, like Böcklin, offer us an insight into the ground of becoming of the daimonic mythical figures of antiquity, in such a way as, in effect, to 'place before our eyes' two truths: in contrast to the spiritualized 'gods' of the later Olympus, the daimons largely derive from the Poseidonic element; and, in contrast to the only *human* beauty of those 'gods', they display with their human half-bodies *not* the personification of nature, but the taking-back of humankind itself into the fluid action.

If we now look for a moment at the water, then another truth will make itself clear to us: to capture the *soul* of water in the painting means to make present the *phenomenal appearance* of water [*Wasserscheinung*] with a clarity and a perfection in such a way that the most precise observation of water as a *thing* [*Wasserding*] could never succeed in doing; and because that soul is the soul of matter, so its appearance is the appearance of a substance. Not that Böcklin has painted what Impressionism would call 'appearance' and what is usually mere surface appearance, but the appearance of the soul of the material element. For this reason his sea is no less than the surface of the sea; for this reason our gaze is drawn into the *depths* of the water, and we become aware with amazement that the wave rises and lifts up from *within*, even if the wind, its paramour, awakens it; we see its *skin*, wavering and in motion like it is, adorned with jewellery of foam and silvery crests; we sense in the revealed secret of transparency of the material element, too, the ground of the connection between *hyle* and the aether;[40] we begin to understand that, in the world of matter, around all nakedness a veil is woven which, without having to conceal, preserves: the veil of the transforming, because self-transforming, moisture (it forms the magic of Greek reliefs);[41] and we have, along with all this, glimpsed in the image of the close and approaching wave, whose pounding we hear, whose surge we sense, whose salty coolness we think we can taste, the most authentic, the elementary *water of life*. – But enough of a much maligned, much praised master who, it seems to us, has not been sufficiently appreciated, and who became 'a knowing one' because it was granted to him to enter into dialogue with daimons.[42]

(*GWS=SW* 2, 1127–1131)

Finally, the relation between the doctrine of the 'reality of images' and the dimension of existence that one might describe as *the aesthetic* clearly emerges from the following passages in Klages's works. First, the beginning of the passage about the wood from *The Foundations of the Study of Character*, cited above; second, this passage from *Handwriting and Character*:

A beech-nut falls from a beech-tree and grows on the forest floor into a new tree. Does the maternal beech-tree still live on in the offspring beech-tree? Certainly not! The former we can fell and burn, the latter will happily carry

86   *Works and key ideas*

on growing. Or is there something of the material element from the old in the rejuvenated beech-tree? Equally, there is not! For the fully-grown young tree no longer contains even a single atom of the material element of the fruit from which it grew! If, however, in the new individual neither the old individual nor its matter remains, *what* is it actually that uninterruptedly *persists* through thousands and thousands of generations? The answer is: an *image*. The image of the oak, the image of the pine-tree, the image of the fish, the image of the dog, the image of the human being recurs in every single individual carrier of the species. 'Reproduction' means the physically eternally inaccessible process of the handing-on of the primordial image of the species from place to place and from time to time. The nomadic image is a *self-transforming* image, and our capacity for recognizing the genus in each individual carrier together with the ability to name it accordingly, is found in turn in the experience of *similarity*. The youth is not the same as, but similar to, the man; the child is not the same as, but similar to, its parents; every genus is not the same as, but similar to, the kind of phylum from which it derives, for the species arise and disappear no less than do their individual carriers, only over much longer periods of time. 'No one remains', says Plutarch, 'no one is a single case, but we become many, as matter only gathers around a *single image* and then slips away again'.[43] Reproduction is a recurrence of *similar* images within *similar* spans of time; whereby the proof is concluded that rhythm is the primordial appearance of life.

(*SW* 7, 332; cf. *SW* 3, 286 and *SW* 6, 264)

Klages's doctrine of the reality of images sits, then, at the curious (yet fascinating) intersection of biology and aesthetics. According to Hans Eggert Schröder, water is for human beings no longer only, as it is for the animal, the drive-complement to thirst or to the drive to swim, triggering movements; instead, it additionally serves to depict innumerable symbolic appearances, which 'reveal to [us] ever new characteristics of the world' (*CAK*, 196).

As Schröder explains, in the animal realm of the life of the drives the image is to be understood as an impulse that triggers movements. Every natural movement-impulse is goal-oriented toward the image that has triggered it. What we usually call instinct is nothing other than the process of the image-control of the life of movement. It is only thanks to the suppression of the life of the drives that our individual receptivity to images (visionary power) becomes blind, and the drive-impulses become available to the goal-setting of the will as imageless energies. It is here, in the splitting of the drive-impulse from the image goal, that the basis of the negative character of the performance of the will lies. Its effect is to give rise to that kind of life-threatening lack of instinct that one might call 'narrow-mindedness' (*CAK*, 197). And so, once again, what begins as an apparently para-metaphysical argument in Klages ends up as a shrewd observation which is all too readily confirmed by one's experiences from everyday life.

The doctrine of 'the reality of images'   87

Tucked away in a footnote to chapter 53 of *The Spirit as Adversary of the Soul* is an extraordinary meditation, taking its cue from a distichon by Schiller, on stupidity:

Schiller's line, 'Against stupidity even the gods themselves fight in vain',[44] has profound meaning, for it draws attention to the absolute incurability, because complete blindness, of stupidity. 'Stupid' [*dumm*] is related to 'dumb' [*stumm*]; but '*tump*' also has in Middle High German the meaning of 'deaf', which many linguistic researchers, following the rule that 'words for the functions of a sense perception can easily be transferred to those corresponding to another' (Kluge),[45] equate with the Greek *tuphlos*=blind. In any case the basic meaning of '*dumm*' is 'insensitive, vacant' or as it were 'dumb and blind'. If we remember this, then we can see the close relation of meaning with the term, even harsher nowadays, of 'narrow-mindedness' [*Borniertheit*]. To narrow means to limit. Just as deafness and blindness narrow the field of sense experiences, so narrow-mindedness means the limitation of the soul itself and, as a result, of inherited boundaries which are placed around vitality in accordance with our decisions through the activity of the will. Narrow-mindedness is the organic *effect* of 'ill will' and hence so much worse than this. Ill will can in principle be intimidated or broken and, at least in individual cases, can be won round from time to time; but *unconscious* ill will, called narrow-mindedness, can just as little be broken or won round as one could transform the blood of its carrier. – Meanwhile, the essential connection between them both, narrow-mindedness and ill will, has much deeper roots. For [...] the 'instinct' has to have been already blinded in some respect, so that it can provide the intensity of the drive as 'energy' to the will; hence the following process ends up as a vicious circle: out of the blindness *or* blinding of vision the will grows, the will narrows vitality, and the blind will of narrow-mindedness is the hardest possible hammer in the hand of the will that, as it were, sees (just as, according to one version of the myth, the blind Hodur unwittingly serves the intentions of Loki when he throws the twig of mistletoe that kills Baldur).[46] It has always been the case that initiatory whim has been victorious with the help of fanaticized masses!

(*GWS=SW* 1, 799–800)

So what is it that nevertheless makes any kind of creative use of impulses of the will possible at all? The answer is supplied by Klages in the two following extracts, where an essentially *aesthetic* dimension to his theory again emerges. In the first, a passage from *The Foundations of the Study of Character*, Klages draws on the rich philosophical tradition of using sculpture to explain the creative force of *form*:[47]

When a great artist carves the statue of a god using hammer and chisel from a block of marble, it is certainly not his will that has inspired in him the outline of the divine image, but his capacity for vision, which is blessed by

88 *Works and key ideas*

life, and the willed act of carving is related to this capacity exactly like the chisel, which can never do anything except shatter the stone. The example shows with perfect clarity why the destructive nature of willing does not exclude the use of willing in the service of affirmative stirrings and creative impulses to give form, but also that the act of willing itself consists in a series of simply destructive acts, and that the will is an entirely negatory power. It requires little to picture to oneself the terrible consequences that would arise if the will became autocratic, because it had become detached from the supportive force of vitality that determines its direction, transforming its still available strength into blind energies, as if it were the murderous intent of an indiscriminately pulverizing tool.

(*SW* 4, 350)

This second extract comes from *On the Nature of Consciousness*, and it reveals the cultural-critical potential that is bound up with the Klagesian doctrine of the 'reality of images':

Insistent on the 'freedom of the will', *we* have become the slaves of mechanicism. As a proof that, by contrast, the entirety of antiquity was fundamentally *pathic* in its disposition,[48] let it suffice to recall those powers to which all people closest to the source believed the birth and death of human beings, and even their gods to be subject: the Moirai of the Greeks; the Fortunes, Fates, and Parcae of the Romans; Belisama and the fairies of the Celts; Wala and the Norns of the Germans. In all these is mirrored among other things the belief, rooted in the depths of life, in the mysterious, incalculable rule of a destiny, which not even divine, let alone human, caprice would never be able to resist or escape. And anyone who could recognize this can no longer 'will' (unless it is his or her 'work'!) and can only look with horror on the insanity of those who do deeds. And because he or she now no longer stands free of the spirit *in* life – in other words, in permanent ecstasy, where there is no longer any searching, questioning, striving, judging, willing –, he or she will have to become a deed-avoiding *observer* of life. To have to will is the distinguishing feature of blindness, *no longer* to be able to will is the distinguishing feature of setting blindness aside.[49] And if someone were to ask this person: what should we do, what should we cease doing; then he or she could only reply as follows: be ready for and worthy of the moment of conception; and even if it should never come, then at least you did the only thing you could, in order – to save your *soul*!

(*SW* 3, 299)

In short: whereas the spirit works in the logical realm of 'dead' logical concepts, the soul is receptive to the reality of images: and this is one of many significant differences for Klages between 'spirit' and 'soul'.

Conceptual tool # 6: the opposition of 'spirit' and 'soul'

It may seem strange that we have waited until the sixth conceptual tool in our toolkit to address the fundamental thesis of Klages's thinking, and the aspect of his thought for which he is known (if he is known at all). Yet it should now be easier to understand the opposition of 'spirit' (*Geist*) and 'soul' (*Seele*) in the light of the previous conceptual tools we have adduced and the passages from his writings we have already considered.

For his notion of spirit or *Geist*, Klages is profoundly indebted to Aristotle who, in his treatise *On the Generation of Animals*, advanced the view that, in conception, the female contributes the matter of the future composite, while the male contributes the soul. The intellect, however, enters the individual at another point: it is, in Aristotle's phrase, an 'intellect from without' (*nous thurathen*).[50] Klages himself specifically mentions this doctrine on two occasions in *The Spirit as Adversary of the Soul*, referring to it as 'the doctrine that the spirit is added to life from outside (=*thurathen*, according to Aristotle's expression)' (*GWS=SW* 1, 369; cf. *GWS=SW* 2, 868); and see his comments in 'Truth and Reality' (*SW* 3, 736). Thus the model with which Klages operates is not the Cartesian dualism of body and soul to which, in modern times, we have become accustomed, nor is it the more general dualism of matter and mind, but rather it is the more ancient (and Aristotelian) tripartite division of *nous – psyche – soma*, of spirit, soul, and body (see 'Spirit and Life'; in *SW* 3, 562–563; cf. *GWS=SW* 1, 6).

What follows are some of the classic statements of his core thesis, first from *Of Cosmogonic Eros* (1922; [2]1926) – the treatise which so impressed Walter Benjamin –, in which Klages declared:

> The cosmos is alive, and all life is polarized into soul (*psychae*) and body (*soma*). Wherever there is living body, there is soul; wherever soul, there is living body. The soul is the sense of the body, the image of the body is the appearance of the soul. Whatever appears, that has a sense; and every sense reveals itself as it appears. Sense [*der Sinn*] is experienced internally, appearance [*die Erscheinung*] externally. The former must become image if it is to be communicated, and the image must become internal again, for it to have an effect. Those are, expressed without metaphor, the poles of reality.
>
> (*SW* 3, 390)

As Klages goes on to suggest, the world seen from outside exhibits 'the Pelasgian trinity' (see below) of two poles distinguished within the overarching and unifying totality of the whole. Although Klages frequently expresses his ideas in a dualistic way, this dialectical moment of distinction-within-union is, as the following passage makes clear, central to his thought:

> If we grasp and think the world from outside, it will exhibit everywhere the Pelasgian trinity of the poles that are separated out in the unity of the

90 *Works and key ideas*

whole. Space is the body of time, time is the soul of space. The soul and sense of the night is the day, the womb of light is the night. Winter and summer, sleeping and waking, dying and arising form a series. The feminine is the body and soul of the soul, the masculine is the revealed and revealing sense of the womb of the mother. Blood and nerve, solar plexus and brain, 'heart' and 'head', mouth and eye, left and right stand in the same relation. If one separates one of these limbs from the other, the world is destroyed.

(*SW* 3, 390)

What Klages presents us here in 'cosmic' terms – a dialectical interrelation between dynamic opposites, a union born of an energic tension – is, he thinks, also observable in world history (a theme which we shall shortly explore in more detail):

The history of humanity shows us in humankind and *only* in humankind the war 'to the knife' between all-embracing life and a power *outside space and time*, which wants to sever the poles and thereby destroy them, to 'de-soul' the body, disembody the soul: it is called spirit [*Geist*] (Logos, Pneuma, Nus).

(*SW* 3, 390)

Around ten years later, in *The Spirit as Adversary of the Soul*, Klages stated in his 'Introduction' that, for around three decades, all his research had led him to the following conclusion:

Body and soul are *poles* of the life-cell which belong inseparably together, into which from *outside* the spirit, like a wedge, inserts itself, in the endeavour to split them apart, to 'de-soul' the body, to disembody the soul, and in this way finally to kill all the life it can reach.

(*GWS*=*SW* 1, 7)

In book 1, part 3, chapter 9, entitled 'The Opposition of Soul and Spirit', Klages reiterates this thesis:

The soul is the transience of the body. [...] As souls we are inescapably intertwined in what is essentially a fleeting reality, but as spirits we are based literally outside this reality, unable, even for the briefest moment, to merge with it!

(*GWS*=*SW* 1, 71)

(This claim is woven around a classical reference: a quotation from Plutarch's essay 'On the Inscription "E" on the Temple at Delphi', to the effect that no one ever stays the same but is continually changing).[51] Finally, in book 4, part 3, chapter 54, Klages offers the following remarkable image to describe his thesis:

The spirit resembles a wedge driven into the life-cell, a wedge whose goal is to tear it in half or, less metaphorically expressed, to deprive the body of soul, to deprive the soul of body, and in this way to kill life itself.

(*GWS=SW* 1, 755)

So it would be fair to say that Klages's central thesis is admirably summed up in the title of his major work: for he is opposed, not just to the spirit of the age (or the *Zeitgeist*), to spirit in a theological sense (as *der Heilige Geist*), or to spirit as Hegel (in his *Phenomenology of Spirit* [1807]) uses the term, but to *Geist* in its broadest possible sense. For him, *Geist* is the enemy of *Seele*, or (more usually) 'the spirit is the adversary of the soul', or (less conventionally) 'mind is the opponent of psyche'. Klages would have us believe that the rational mind has split us apart from the passionate-intuitive part of our selves, so that our (instrumental) consciousness is purchased at the price of alienation from the emotional and affective component of our identity.

He uses a variety of images to describe this catastrophic state of affairs. For example, there are the passages cited above, or this one:

Spirit and Life – thus a gorgon's head takes ever firmer shape – are two realities, forever in hostile opposition: the extra-spatio-temporal power, whose deed shoots timelessly into the cosmos and shatters reality into atoms of being; and the spatio-temporal ocean of happening, from whose ceaselessly quivering mirror bursts forth the dancing reflection of the furthest stars

(*GWS=SW* 1, 253)

– or in an earlier formulation:

The awakening of self-consciousness is the declaration of war of a god inimical to all against life.

(*RR*, 423)[52]

On what level does the struggle between spirit (or mind) and soul (or psyche) take place? On the one hand, it takes place on the ontogenetic or individual level, for Klages describes this conflict between *Seele* and *Geist*, between pathic feeling and objectivizing intellect, as internal to each individual human being:

As souls we are inescapably intertwined in what is essentially a fleeting reality, but as spirits we are based literally outside this reality, unable, even for the briefest moment, to merge with it.

(*GWS=SW* 1, 71)

On the other hand, there is a phylogenetic, or historical, dimension to this argument, too. As a thinker, Klages is a dedicated apocalyptist; yet, in the case of Klages, the apocalypse has already taken place, and the world we inhabit is a post-apocalyptic one.[53] For Klages, it is (always) (already) too late.

92   *Works and key ideas*

Yet this fact of our lateness does not prevent Klages from pondering the history of humankind. In one of his *Nachlass* fragments, Klages speaks of the dual reality of, on the one hand, everyday consciousness and, on the other, the soul, in terms of the intellectual expression of the fissure of inner being that first entered the world of life deep in the past, and became especially problematic with Plato and then with Christ. As Klages writes at one point, 'no cultural expressions have been found in which the spirit had not in some way played a part [...]. The initial entrance of the spirit therefore took place when the earliest cultural monuments were created' (*GWS=SW* 2, 1239; cf. *RR*, 475). In other words, Klages offers, in addition to a theory of consciousness, a theory of history as well.

At the beginning of his account of history stand the Pelasgians, that legendary and ancient people of the Neolithic and Bronze Ages of Homer, Thucydides, and Herodotus, characterized by a 'pathic consciousness', which 'thinks in symbols' (*GWS=SW* 2, 1258).[54] More generally, the 'Pelasgians' is used today to refer (in the words of the OED) to the pre-Hellenic people inhabiting the coasts and islands of the eastern Mediterranean Ocean and Aegean Sea regions. In the nineteenth century, the term Pelasgian was used by scholars, including Bachofen, to refer to the pre-Indo-European population of Greece, a counterpart to the pre-Aryan *dasyu* and *dāsa*, the native inhabitants of India.[55] So while Klages is by no means alone in the postulating the historical existence of this ancient people,[56] his account contains a characteristic inflection in the symbolic consciousness he attributes to them.

Then comes the Promethean age, which coincides with the rise of Platonism, classical Athens, then Christianity, down through to the Renaissance (*GWS=SW* 1, 750–751); Prometheus symbolizes the emergence of consciousness, the faculty of knowledge, for he 'made men masters of their minds', as the bound god in Aeschylus's tragedy puts it.[57] Finally, there is the Heraclean age – our own – in which, like the Greek hero, Hercules, in the legend (whose significance Klages inverts!) related by the Sophist philosopher, Prodicos of Ceos, we choose the world of work and purposiveness rather than the pleasure of the moment (*GWS=SW* 1, 752).[58] (In the fable related by Prodicos and subsequently others, Hercules is confronted by two allegorical figures, namely: Virtue and Vice, and challenged to choose between them; Hercules chooses a difficult but noble life over an easy but ignoble life, and the rest is history ... or mythology ...).

And so, in 'Humankind and Earth', an address written to commemorate the Freideutscher Jugendtag held on the Hoher Meißner in October 1913, Klages attacks 'progress', lambasts 'capitalism', laments the disappearance of the chthonic gods, draws attention to the destruction of the environment, and comments gloomily on the bleakness and greyness of the workaday world.[59] It is with a description of this post-Enlightenment, post-Romantic world of the 1890s that Klages brings his account of the 'prehistory' of the discovery of the images to a close (in a passage which, incidentally, caught the attention of the Marxist philosopher, Ernst Bloch [1885–1977]):[60]

The opposition of 'spirit' and 'soul' 93

This wave [from 1770 to 1900, encompassing *Sturm und Drang*, Romanticism, and *fin-de-siècle*] was the last one, because along with it the essence [of life][61] *left* the planet. Never perhaps have human beings experienced and suffered more ardent shudders than they did then. The horizons flamed in the sunset of a departure, that in the language of humans was a departure for ever, and – 'all those who take their leave speak like drunkards and like to behave festively'.[62] [...] What we have offered as motives and facts for the advance of unrestrainable disaster is verifiable, the source of our inner certainties is not. Of them one can convince only those who share the same fate; and for this reason these words have been given space, so that the reader may know why we have described the last bearers of earth's essence as dithyrambic panegyrists of decline [*Dithyrambiker des Unterganges*]. They were surrounded by lemurs and vampires,[63] who meanwhile have almost completed their work.[64] The earth gives off smoke as never before from the blood of the slain, and all that is apelike struts with the spoils plundered from the shattered temple of life.

(GWS=SW 2, 923)

What are we to make of this apocalyptic scenario? To cast his argument in the framework of an institutional parallel: in the world as Klages conceives it, the administrators have seized control and, howling with glee, brutally suppress the pleasure of learning and the sheer joy of the exchange of ideas between those who love their subject.... On this account, judgment and common sense have been replaced by a blind and counterproductive trust in implementing policies and procedures; the individual is no longer a human being, he or she has become a customer, a client, a number....[65]

Indeed, much of Klages can be read today as an extended metaphor for the growth of bureaucracy; and there is evidence that Klages's indictment of 'instrumental rationality' was an influence on the Frankfurt School's more well-known critique of 'the totally administered society'.[66] Walter Benjamin, in particular, was a devotee of Klages, until ordered to drop his interest by Theodor W. Adorno.[67]

In fact, the influence of Klages was widespread, and among the philosophers who – some despite, others because of, his rhetoric of apocalypse – responded (and/or reacted) to his works are Martin Heidegger (1889–1976), Max Scheler (1874–1928), Ernst Cassirer (1874–1945), and Otto F. Bollnow (1903–1991), as well as such vitalist or philosophico-anthropological psychologists as Wolfgang Metzger (1899–1979), Philipp Lersch (1898–1972), Albert Wellek (1904–1972), Viktor von Weizsäcker (1886–1957), and F. J. J. Buytendijk (1887–1974); such philologists and ethnologists as the author of *The Homeric Gods* (1929), Walter F. Otto (1874–1958); the author of a major study of the Nordic God Wotan, Martin Ninck (1895–1953); a pioneer of 'cultural morphology', Adolf Ellegard Jensen (1899–1965); and the great scholar of Native American culture, Werner Müller (1907–1990); not to mention the novelist Friedrich Georg Jünger (1898–1977) and the artist Alfred Kubin.[68] And, thanks to Klages's editorial work, the matriarchal

94 *Works and key ideas*

thought of J. J. Bachofen and the Romantic aesthetics of Carl Gustav Carus were made available to the twentieth century.[69]

So it is not entirely without justification that Klages once described himself (in his 'Foreword to Contemporaries' written in 1929) as 'the most plundered author of the age' (*SW* 2, 1535). Ultimately, Klages can be seen to be addressing one of the key questions – if not *the* key question – of modern times, posed by one of the characters in a play by the Enlightenment writer and thinker, Gotthold Ephraim Lessing (1729–1781): 'How reasonable is your reason?'

Conceptual tool #7: '*Schablonisierung*'

One of the most useful concepts one finds in the work of Klages is the notion of *Schablonisierung*, the problem in the modern world of 'becoming stereotyped'. In the later chapter of his treatise, *The Foundations of the Doctrine of Character* (4th edn, 1926; 10th edn, 1947), entitled 'Sketch of a System of Motives' (i.e. *Triebfeder*), Klages propounds the following typological distinction between:

- pathos = the basic vital mood of a human being who is primarily relaxed
- activity = the basic vital mood of a human being who is primarily bound up

According to Klages, each of the fundamental moods has its typical poles, in between which it moves:

- pathos = between horror and bliss, or in weaker forms between being happy (cheerful) and being sad (depressed)
- activity = desire for success and fear of failure

And each of the moods has a characteristic set of poles, between which a sense of (ego-bound) identity moves:

- pathos = between pride and modesty
- activity = between admiring the self and doubting the self

Klages emphasizes the polarity internal to each of these 'basic life attitudes' (*Lebensgrundstimmungen*) or characterological categories as well as the polarity between them; similarly, in his psychological typology, C. G. Jung (1875–1961) distinguishes between intraverted and extroverted types, but then complicates matters by introducing four different psychological functions (thinking, feeling, sensation, and intuition), such that any individual possesses these functions in an introverted and an extraverted mode.[70]

Jung's typology forms the basis of the Myers–Brigg Type Indicator® test, still used in business and management today; Klages's typology, by contrast, has not (yet) been exploited in this fashion. And perhaps it never will, for it is clear from Klages's discussion that, on balance, he favours the pathic type. Moreover, he

Schablonisierung 95

suggests models or historical exemplars for each of these different characterological types as well:

> Just as it is certain that the light pole can never exist without the dark pole and vice versa, so it is certain that extremely large differences of character emerge according to whether the light or the dark pole is predominant; and so we have, then, on the relaxed side the gloomy, indeed the dark carriers of metaphysical horror (e.g. Lenau or Nietzsche), and the shining carriers of metaphysical bliss (e.g. Mozart and, to a certain extent, Goethe), on the bound-up-side, however, the always annoying, always complaining carriers of personal discontent, called depressives, and the always pleased, indeed sometimes even comical carriers of personal content, called euphorics. – 'Lifted up into consciousness', the world-view of the pathic type would express itself in the conviction that reality is a world of the ceaseless coming-and-going of primordial images endowed with soul [*beseelter Urbilder*], and that of the active type would express itself in the conviction that the world is a fundamentally locatable, conquerable, possessable world of facts. The former is turned toward transience as it is to the past, as the maternal ground of his or her life, to which he or she will return; the latter – virile and inimically opposed to the past – is turned to the future, in which he or she hopes to continue to exist, whether it be through offspring, be it through deeds and achievements, by means of which to influence what is to come. The work of the pathic person are, like the pyramids, memorials, and commemorations of the dead, those of the activist person are creations of utility, like machines.
>
> (*SW* 4, 406–407)

As Klages has explained in the previous chapter in this work, the difference between pathos and activity is analogous to the fundamental distinction between those ages which are 'life-dependent' or 'turned away from the spirit' and those which are 'spirit-dependent' or 'turned away from life' (chapter 8).[71] What enables these fundamental tendencies to bring about 'that confusing and colourful play of personal characters' is said by Klages to be a reciprocal interplay of life and spirit, 'the turning of spirit to life, of life to spirit, and as it were the struggle between both of them' (*SW* 4, 407). However, there are long-term consequences to this struggle:

> If this struggle were not interrupted by long pauses thanks to incalculable changes in the depths of life, during which life can recover from its efforts, then it would unfailingly sink into complete exhaustion and, before totally expiring, it would sink into a perhaps much longer lasting general process of stereotyping [*Schablonisierung*]. Nobody can mistake the fact that 'civilized' humankind and, with it, humankind itself is moving at a rapid pace toward such stereotyping.
>
> (*SW* 4, 407)

96   *Works and key ideas*

At this point, Klages explains what, on an everyday level, happens in the case of such *Schablonisierung*:

> Already today it is those who think differently on whom one may rely for any kind of independent judgment. The great masses, who have never, as long as there have been human beings, been more susceptible to suggestion than they are today, have become a plaything of that 'public opinion' which is *made* by the daily newspapers, obviously in the service of the dominant world of finance. Whatever is printed this morning in the pages of papers with the widest readership becomes this evening the opinion of nine-tenths of their readers. America, in whose rapid 'progress' the immediate future becomes from day to day more evident, is well ahead us in the stereotypization of thought, of work, of leisure activities, etc. It conducted the war against Germany with genuine indignation, because it was written in its papers that Prussian 'militarism' wanted to conquer the world and was revelling in devilish crimes, and that sort of thing was written in the papers because a handful of high dignitaries of mammon expected extremely lucrative business for themselves from America's participation in the war. The average American fought with good faith for such beautiful phrases as freedom and justice, whereas in reality he was fighting to enrich the contents of the bank-safes. [Editorial footnote in *SW*: This refers to the World War of 1914.] These 'free citizens' are in truth puppets who imagine themselves to be free, and just a glance at the American world of work, no less than at the American world of leisure, is sufficient to allow us to realize that 'l'homme machine' is no longer merely standing at the door, but has already become a reality.
>
> (*SW* 4, 408)

The object of Klages's rhetoric and invective in this passage is what he describes as the *mechanization* of humankind; or, in other words, our transformation into *l'homme machine* (to use an expression originally associated with eighteenth-century French materialist thought in general and with Julien Offray de La Mettrie [1709–1751] in particular):[72]

> Nobody can foresee whether a completely mechanized humankind will last for decades or for centuries, and what interests us is this mechanization itself. The further it extends, the more the *personality* has played its last card. – It is the tragic fate of knowledge, by which we mean real knowledge and not what usually passes for knowledge, which constitutes nothing more than the intellectual equipment for technicians and mechanics, that it also provides, as it were, the funeral music accompanying the departure of a vital essence [*Lebensessenz*], if not actually its burial. We only *know* what we no longer *are*. Somnium narrare vigilantis est (Seneca).[73] Similar to writing history, only going incomparably deeper and revealing the secret source of the events of the day and the directing forces behind the 'history of the world', it is a kind of *chronicle of what has come and gone*. And so, if we

are not mistaken, the foundation of the doctrine of character means the beginning of – its end, and those who succeed us had better hurry up; otherwise they shall be dealing, not with a world of human characters, but with the quickly fading memories of it.

(*SW* 4, 408–409)

In this passage, Klages quotes Seneca, citing a passage which was interest to the great essayist of the French Renaissance, Michel de Montaigne (1533–1592) and to the Danish existentialist philosopher, Søren Kierkegaard (1813–1855) (cf. *Journal NB17*) alike.[74] The elegaic flavour and melancholy tone of Klages's thinking are unmistakable; the idea behind the quotation from Seneca chimes, surprisingly enough, remarkably well with Hegel's well-known dictum in the preface to his lectures on the *Philosophy of Right* (1820) about the owl of Minerva. Here Hegel makes his famous declaration:

A further word on the subject of *issuing instructions* on how the world ought to be: philosophy, at any rate, always comes too late to perform this function. As the *thought* of the world, it appears only at a time when actuality has gone through its formative process and attained its completed state. This lesson of the concept is necessarily also apparent from history, namely that it is only when actuality has reached maturity that the ideal appears opposite the real and reconstructs this real world, which it has grasped in substance, in the shape of an intellectual realm. When philosophy paints its grey in grey, a shape of life has grown old, and it cannot be rejuvenated, but only recognized, by the grey in grey of philosophy; the owl of Minerva begins its flight only with the onset of dusk.[75]

In almost every other respect, however, Klages is a most un-Hegelian, if not actually anti-Hegelian, thinker. It would, for instance, be unimaginable to find Klages agreeing with any the following statements made by Hegel:[76]

- The sole thought which philosophy brings to the treatment of history of the simple concept of *Reason*: that Reason is the law of the world and that, therefore, in world history, things have come about rationally. (p. 11)
- The time has finally come to understand also the rich product of creative Reason which is world history. (p. 18)
- Spirit, on the stage on which we observe it, that of world history, is in its most concrete reality. (p. 22)
- World history is the progress of the consciousness of freedom – a progress whose necessity we have to investigate. […] Freedom in itself its own object of attainment and the sole purpose of Spirit. It is the ultimate purpose toward which all world history has continually aimed. (p. 25)
- World history is the manifestation of the Divine, the absolute process of Spirit in its highest form. It is this development wherein it achieves its truth and the consciousness of itself. (p. 67)

98 *Works and key ideas*

- World history only shows how the World Spirit gradually attains the consciousness and willing of truth. Dawn arises in the Spirit; it discovers focal points; and finally, it attains full consciousness. (p. 67)

By contrast, Klages would argue throughout the course of his writings that:

- The un-reason of Reason is the law of the world.
- In world history things have come about irrationally.
- The time has finally come to understand world history as the catastrophic product of deleterious Reason.
- World history is the progress of the enslavement to consciousness, and hence the spirit (*Geist*).
- World history, far from being a manifestation of the divine, is a manifestation of an almost devilish spirit (*Geist*).
- World history shows the gradual dominance of the spirit over the soul, until it extinguishes all life.

Nevertheless, there remains something curiously quasi-Hegelian about Klages's account of how, in world history and in the individual human being alike, the 'powers at work' (*wirkende Mächte*) are 'the spirit and life':

According to the ideological account of history, a change of thinking or at least its articulation *brings about* physical transformations; according to the materialistic, these are derived from restructuring in the economy. Yet both ideas and economic facts, including finance and technology, are only present for humankind to the extent that they 'come to consciousness' here or there. Anyone who, together with the author of this work [i.e. Klages] has become converted to the view that all consciousness is something that has been brought about, but is never something that brings something about [*etwas Bewirktes, aber nie etwas Wirkendes*], must reject both of these positions. The powers *at work* – in human beings – are the spirit and life. The latter exhibits an interval period of increasingly shorter rhythms and, furthermore, telluric changes; the former, whose goal is the destruction of life, has to adapt itself to these fluctuations and responds especially to every telluric change with a violent reaction. What, in the waves of the soul and the intellectual battles which we have listed [i.e. the intellectual battles and subsequent military conflicts of the sixteenth century, the anti-social movement of the 'Sturm und Drang' in literature and the subsequent French Revolution in the eighteenth century, the ideas of the period 1890–1900 and the subsequent decline in the twentieth century], is *manifested* in – for humankind – transformations of the life of the earth, and each of these is followed every time by an outbreak of action, because the spirit finds itself afterward in a humankind whose soul has changed and in this way must overcome its victim with new means. Thus both of them, the changing of minds and the resultant political or social crises, are caused by one and the same event in the spirit-bound vital space and are related to each other as action and reaction.

(*GWS=SW* 2, 917)

So while Klages, like Hegel, thinks in dialectical terms, he places a key Hegelian category – *Geist* or spirit – under a negative sign; and Klages produces, not so much (as does Hegel) a theodicy (or, in other words, a justification of God and an explanation of the world as the best of all possible worlds), as a theory of catastrophe.

What marks Klages out as a truly great thinker is the extent of his wide-ranging philosophical focus. Klages is alert to the many and varied dimensions of catastrophe, in its etymological sense of an 'overturning' or 'sudden turn' (cata + *strephein*, 'turn'), as the following passage from *The Spirit as Adversary of the Soul*, chapter 40, suggests:

> The carefully cultivated plant in the clay jug blossoms and gives off a lovely scent, while the other next to it, which someone forgot to water, withers and fades; the cat on the prowl experiences a surge of joy when it rips apart the small bird perishing in its claws; the same building accommodates the ageing hypochondriac and the young lad flowering into life whose singing makes the former grow bitter; the exploiter who enjoys feasting and the young working woman who goes hungry for her children and starves; the exchange rates rise and the stock market jobbers celebrate, when a poison-gas war against a people armed with spears in exotic parts of the world ends 'happily' and the golden sandy location of the now smoking villages become accessible to 'civilization': in such examples, which could be multi-plied any number of times, it becomes shockingly clear that, in individuals, life has separated itself from life to the point of the agonzing end of one life as a result of the lust for power of the other. In the end, death leaves its impression on the loneliness of us all.

(*GWS=SW* 1, 471)

For Klages, world history can also be understood as a catastrophe, because he rejects the Hegelian conception of *Geist* as Reason. Or rather, he regards Reason as something inherently irrational, inimical to the soul, and destructive of life. As he puts it in his concluding restrospective at the end of his magisterial work, *The Spirit as Adversary of the Soul*, 'our work finds the key to the essence of spirit, *not* in the intellect, but in *the will*' (*GWS=SW* 2, 1420). If this is so, what are the consequences for each of us in our everyday lives?

Conceptual tool #8: images are elementary souls

'Inasmuch as we sleep, we live; as soon as we awaken, we begin to die': this remarkable statement is drawn from the work of Karl Fortlage (1806–1881), a philosopher whose outlook would have been congenial to Klages for a number

100 *Works and key ideas*

of reasons. First, while originally an adherent of Hegel's philosophy, he turned to the German Idealist philosopher, Johann Gottlieb Fichte (1762–1814), and thence to the psychologist, Friedrich Eduard Beneke (1798–1854), who viewed psychology as the basis of philosophy.[77] Second, Fortlage gives a pre-eminent place in his psychology to impulse, as a process that combines consciousness (or representation) and pleasure (or feeling) – in other words, as an essentially vital process. And third, because this statement can stand for an entire outlook on life that spans from the Presocratics to the German Romantics.

In his first lecture, 'On the Nature of the Soul', of his *Eight Psychological Lectures (Acht Psychologische Vorträge)* (1872), Fortlage makes the remarkable claim: 'Inasmuch as we sleep, we live; as soon as we awaken, we begin to die' (*Nur insofern wir schlafen, leben wir; sobald wir erwachen, fangen wir an zu sterben*).[78] In so writing, however, Fortlage – and, after him, Klages – are rearticulating an idea found in the Presocratic philosopher Heraclitus (*c.*540–*c.*475 BCE), a mysterious thinker known even to the ancient world as 'the Riddler' and 'the Obscure'. (Indeed, if Martin Heidegger [1889–1945] considered Hölderlin, Hegel, and Nietzsche to be three Heraclitean thinkers, we might well add to this list Klages as a fourth ...).[79] As early as 1902,[80] Klages had recognized in Heraclitus an 'ecstatic', a 'dithyrambic writer', a kindred spirit who, like himself, saw life in terms of ceaseless flux:[81] everything is one (*panta einai*),[82] and everything flows (*panta rhei*).[83]

In *The Spirit as the Adversary of the Soul* Klages cites the following fragment of Heraclitus: 'death is what we see when awake' (*Tod ist, was wir im Wachen sehen*) (*GWS*, 814).[84] Now the text of this fragment is corrupt, and its meaning is in dispute;[85] so here I shall follow the reading provided by Miroslav Marcovich: 'What we see when awake is death, and what we see when asleep is life (reality)'.[86] This reading corresponds closely to Klages's use of the passage, which is reflected in his later citation from Fortlage's lectures on psychology, 'inasmuch as we sleep, we live; as soon as we awaken, we begin to die' (*GWS*, 814). What, however, does this principle actually mean?

According to Klages, in our sleep, and specifically in our dreams, we have access to images (in German, *Bilder*) which are, he claims, ontologically prior to bodily sensations.[87] These images should not, as we have seen, be thought of as purely visual; they are rather, as we have also seen, *Anschauungsbilder*, or more precisely *Urbilder*, archetypes, which are not optically perceived but rather are experienced (*erlebt*). In other words, it is important to note that Klages distinguishes two modes of experience: first, 'the sensuous experience of the bodiliness of [...] images'; second, and more important, 'the intuitive experience of a reality of images' (*GWS*, 811). Consequently, as a disciple of Heraclitus, Klages regards the sleeping state as more important than the waking one.[88] In fact, there is an important sense in which Klages regards the dream world as more 'real' than the waking world.[89]

It is essential to grasp this Klagesian distinction between 'sensing experience' (*empfindendes Erleben*) and 'visionary experience' (*schauendes Erleben*), or more simply between sensation (*Empfinden*) and visionary intuition (*Schauen*),

Images are elementary souls 101

the first mode of perception having as its object the sensuous, bodily world, and the second 'the reality of images' (*die Wirklichkeit der Bilder*), the reality of 'intuitive images' (*Anschauungsblder*) or 'primordial images' (*Urbilder*). For Klages – to the consternation of such critics as the Marxist philosopher Ernst Bloch,[90] to whose own messianic and utopian 'Not-Yet' (*Noch-Nicht*) Klages resolutely opposes a defiantly dystopian 'No-Longer' (*Nicht-Mehr*) – also calls these images the 'elementary souls' (*Elementarseelen*), the perception of which constitutes a third dimension of perception – *Schauung*.[91] Of this mode of perception Klages writes that it constitutes 'the inner equivalent of the *reality of images* which consists of constant transformation', and that it is thus 'a sequential and completely inactive process' (*GWS=SW* 1, 159). Hence, within Klagesian epistemology, perception (*Wahrnehmung*) corresponds to the dimension of the object, and intuition (*Anschauung*) to the dimension of the image (*Bild*), but *Schauung* is a *visionary experience* that reveals the dimension, not of spirit, but of soul – or souls (*GWS=SW* 1, 182 and 285).

Within this scheme, the 'elementary souls' (or *Elementarseelen*) belong, not to the temporal-spatial world of the spirit, but to the sphere of life. In *The Spirit as Adversary of the Soul*, Klages writes that 'phenomenology' – or he calls it, *Erscheinungswissenschaft* – is the science of essences [*Wesenswissenschaft*]', but he adds that 'the science of essences becomes the knowledge of the elementary souls' or *das Wissen von Elementarseelen* (*GWS=SW* 2, 1138).[92] What are these elementary souls? To begin with, we should set aside any religious preconceptions when we hear this phrase. For Klages speaks of 'the *souls* of the images of light and darkness, warmth and cold, storm and calm, of cliff and tree, river and sea, wood and desert, of sunlight and moonlight, starry sky and daylit heaven, gorge and peak'; in this respect, drawing again on Heraclitus,[93] and – potentially, more problematically – he adds:

> Assuming that something of the elementary souls became known to us, we could follow them right into the individual beings and in the end right into the human being, thus establishing the *essences* on which in humankind the differences of the characters of individual people, the characters of nations, races, epochs depended.
>
> (*GWS=SW* 2, 1138)

On this particular point, we should not misunderstand Klages: the emphasis is not on *nation*, it is on *character*; not on *race* but on *character*; not on *peoples and epochs*, but on *character*.

Further on, Klages speaks of the 'images' as *daimons*,[94] or a kind of spirit which he identifies with the *genius loci*, the protective 'spirit of a place' in classical Roman thinking:[95]

> The preliminary form and root of the knowledge of the reality of the images is polydaimonism. [...] The true daimon is the daimon of a place, of an area, of an element, changing with their appearances, accepting the sacrifices of

102   *Works and key ideas*

its devotees, whose daily, monthly, or yearly rhythm is founded in the forms of its revelations, and is at work in those events or tasks which the spirit was driven to accept as powerfully effective by means of their pathically intuited images [*pathisch erschaute Bilder*].

(*GWS=SW* 2, 1264)

Elsewhere, however, Klages speaks outright of 'the gods', commenting that the (Platonic) world of 'immobile "ideas" offered to a certain extent the shadow-image of the reality of previous living gods'.[96] As a consequence, he argues for a plurality of such gods:

There are gods of water and gods even of particular stretches of water, gods of the plant kingdom as well as of a particular tree, gods of the hearth as well as of the hearth of a particular house, but also gods of the night, of the day, of the dawn, of the light, of the darkness, of the thunderstorm, of the rainstorm, of lightning, furthermore of love, friendship, revenge, reconciliation, of anger, furthermore of death, of sickness, of fertility, finally of prayer, sacrifice, exchange, healing, making war, swearing, warding off evil and so on into infinity.

(*GWS=SW* 1, 202)

From this perspective, we might well call Klages the most significant restorer of polytheism since Julian, the Roman Emperor known as 'the Apostate', because of his anti-Christian policies, his attempt to revive traditional Roman religion, and his promotion of Neoplatonic paganism![97]

On one level, it is possible to see in Klages a call for a return to polytheism or pantheism, inasmuch there are significant affinities between his outlook and the cosmogony of the ancient Greeks, who saw each individual part of the world in pantheist and pagan terms. Within a pantheist view of the world, there is no god separate from the world; instead of god(s) nowhere, we have god(s) everywhere. Corresponding to every energy or force, associated with a cross-roads, or a house, or the world, there is a god; and so every place has its *genius loci* or tutelary deity. For example, Hecate is the goddess of the cross-roads, and we should leave anything we come across there as a sacrifice to her.[98]

From his earlier work, *Of Cosmogonic Eros*, we know that Klages regarded 'the gods' as the ancestral souls (*Ahnenseelen*), and he claimed that 'the souls of the past that appear' are the 'primordial images' (*Urbilder*) (*SW* 3, 452 and 470). So we might well see in Klages a thinker in the same mould as such others as the philologist Ulrich von Wilamowitz-Moellendorf (1848–1931), for whom 'the gods exist';[99] or the philologist and philosopher Walter F. Otto (1874–1958), who spoke about 'the reality of the gods';[100] or even perhaps Heidegger who, in his seminar on Heraclitus organized with Eugen Fink (1905–1975) in the winter semester of 1966–1967 in Freiburg, recalled a particular moment on a Greek island: 'I remember an afternoon during my journey in Aegina. Suddenly I saw a single bolt of lightning, after which no more followed. My thought was: Zeus'.[101]

Specific happiness   103

For all of these thinkers seem to have believed that the Olympian gods do in some sense actually exist.

On another level, however, we should note that, most of the time, Klages chooses to talk about *Bilder*, 'images', with its panoply of echoes and resonances in the aesthetic and visionary traditions, including the notion as the primordial image or *Urbild*, as one finds it in the writings of Goethe.[102] So could it be that art is, as Michael Pauen has suggested, the secret paradigm of Klages's thought?[103] Is what Klages is offering us in the pages of his *Collected Works* best understood as a description of the structures of experience and consciousness, or as a study of the purality of divinities, or as a theory of art? In short, is Klages's philosophy a phenomenology, a (poly)theology, or an aesthetics? For the purposes of this toolkit, this must remain an open question.

Conceptual tool #9: specific happiness

Some of the early writings reproduced in *Rhythms and Runes* point us in a particular direction in relation to the aesthetic dimension of Klages's thought. In a fragment from 1901 Klages wrote that 'deep art is the bridge between *nus* [spirit] and *hyle* [matter], between *Helios* [the sun] and *Gaia* [the earth]' (*RR*, 258). And further on, in tones that are distinctly mage-like (or even messianic), Klages writes of the poet (or, in German, the *Dichter*):

> Although the poet remains an individual, he still remains an aspect of the cosmic flux: he is animal, star, sea, plant; he is the eye of the elements; he is matriarchal and earthly to the core. The praxis by which he expresses his inner vision is *magic*.
>
> (*RR*, 261)[104]

Finally, the following question, posed by Klages, gives substance to an attempt to go beyond the equation image (*Bild*) = soul (*Seele*) = primordial image (*Urbild*) and to re-think Klages in aesthetic terms, even terms that are specifically Goethean: 'Is the botanist', Klages asks, 'concerned about the beauty of the flower, whose nature he wishes to explore, and in particular does he think that its life is unrepeatable?' (*RR*, 276). Clearly, the implication of this question is that, while the botanist is not concerned about the beauty of the flower, the poet – revealing through language the world of essences, 'the reality of images' – is. Even more clearly, the implication is that we, too, should be concerned about the beauty of the flower and the unrepeatability of its life, too.

In fact, Michael Pauen has suggested that the Klagesian moment of ecstasy can be understood as an inversion of the kind of intuitive contemplation expounded and promoted by the Neoplatonist philosopher, Plotinus (*c.*205/205–270).[105] In one of his *Enneads* – so called, because his disciple, Porphyry of Tyre (*c.*234–*c.*305), divided Plotinus's writings into six groups of nine (in Greek, = *ennea*) texts – entitled 'The Good or the One', Plotinus tells us that 'awareness of the One comes to us neither by knowing nor by the pure

104 *Works and key ideas*

thought that discovers the other intelligible things, but by a presence transcending knowledge'.[106] Plotinus calls this 'contemplation': a 'vision beyond discourse', an 'awareness of that life that is beyond', 'a rapture within the soul like that of the lover come to rest in his love',[107] and he insists on the quasi-erotic nature of this experience:

> The soul, different from the divinity but sprung from it, must needs love. When it is in the realm above, its love is heavenly; here below, only commonplace. The heavenly Aphrodite dwells in the realm above; here below, the vulgar, harlot Aphrodite.[108]

(Compare the two allegorical figures of Virtue and Vice in Prodicos's fable about the choice of Hercules.)

In the contemplative experience, someone 'who obtains the vision becomes, as it were, another being', and 'ceases to be himself, retains nothing of himself'.[109] In the *Ennead* entitled 'On the Intelligible Beauty', Plotinus explains that the object of knowledge in contemplative experience are not concepts or 'propositions', but 'the Forms we speak about are beautiful images in that world [...] images not painted but real'.[110] For the chief category in Plotinus's thought – or rather, the category beyond all categories – is the One, because 'from Him beauty comes', and according to this conception the One is 'the divine, whence beauty springs and all that is akin to it'.[111] Given what we have suggested above, can we read this moment of intuitive vision (or *Schau*) in terms of Goethe's aesthetic apprehension of the moment: 'No past recalled, no future time to guess; / Only the present – Is our happiness' (*Nun schaut der Geist nicht vorwärts, nicht zurück, / Die Gegenwart allein – Ist unser Glück*) (*Faust II*, lines 9381–9382)?[112]

In Klages's thinking, the parallels with – and, even more important (as Pauen emphasizes), the inversions of – Plotinian thought are clear. First, common to Plotinus and Klages alike are the experiential dimensions of their thought. We find this in Klages in his constant rhetorical appeal: 'anyone who has felt...', 'anyone who has experienced...', 'anyone who has suffered...'; this structure can be found time and again in his writings, as the passages selected for inclusion in this toolkit demonstrate. As for Plotinus, his disciple Porphyry tells us that Plotinus achieved the goal of being 'united with and close to the god above all' at least four times, 'not virtually but in unspeakable actuality'.[113] At the beginning of the *Ennead* entitled 'On the Descent of the Souls into Bodies', Plotinus himself reports:

> Often I have woken up out of the body to my self and have entered into myself, going out from all other things; I have seen a beauty wonderfully great and felt assurance that then most of all I belonged to the better part; I have actually lived the best life and come to identity with the divine; and set firm in it I have come to that supreme actuality, setting myself above all else in the realm of Intellect.[114]

Second, the moment of inversion involves the erotic aspect in which Klages and Plotinus are interested. It is around this aspect that Klages's critique of Plotinus is focused. This critique is found, for instance, in Klages's remark in chapter 57 of *The Spirit as Adversary of the Soul*, 'From the Prehistory of the Discovery of Images', where he describes the thought of Plotinus as marking 'the highest cornice on the Babylonian Tower of life-denying detachment from the world which the mental confusion of paganism in its final burst could attain' (*GWS=SW* 2, 870). For there is much in Klages's writing, not least his fascination with the ancient Greek figure of the hetaira, a female companion renowned for her sophistication and learning as well as her sexual complaisance, to suggest an affinity with the earthly, as opposed to the heavenly, Aphrodite.[115] (The figure of the hetaira points the way to a vitalist feminism, as the work of such thinkers as Simone de Beauvoir (1908–1986) and Toni Wolff (1888–1953) suggests.)[116]

Yet – and third – there is an important aspect of Klages's understanding of the erotic that also has a certain affinity with that of Plotinus. While Klages can be read as a thinker who celebrates hedonistic pleasure, he also introduces the concept of the *Eros of distance*, an understanding of the erotic that finds its fulfilment in a union beyond sexuality, in a relationship that embodies the principle, 'you can look but you can't touch'. For Plotinus and Klages alike, what alerts us to the possibilities of another kind of consciousness – and another kind of being – is an awareness of beauty.

So it would be entirely wrong, as Klages is quick to insist, to read him as a reactionary, as a pessimist, as someone fixated on the past; in other words, as a hopeless nostalgic, especially in the etymological sense of the word (=*nostos*, 'homecoming', and *álgos*, 'pain' or 'ache'). While believing that there *was* a Golden Age, which he identifies above all as the age of the Pelasgians, he does not believe that we can ever go back to it. In his 'Retrospective' in *The Spirit as Adversary of the Soul*, he declares: 'Just as it is certain that there can be no going back, so there *could* be – a turning around' (*GWS=SW* 2, 1424). A turning around? An *Umkehr*? A *metanoia*? In other words, a conversion?

Klages gives us a clear sense of what this 'turning around' or conversion would look like when he tells us that a person who 'turns round' would have the following ambition, if it may be called an ambition: '*To do everything one does as perfectly as possible*' (*GWS=SW* 2, 1424). And this 'turn', in its turn, would bring us to 'the moments of great experience', and thereby to happiness, albeit a transitory happiness, inasmuch as a moment of happiness is the only kind of happiness we can know:

> The moments of great experience either come or do not come, and *if* they do come, then they also go again: no willing, not activity can compel them to come back. Only each single thing done *perfectly* grants the gift of a minute of happiness, that is not by a long way the highest or most profound happiness, but is nevertheless a pure happiness and, moreover, the only one that it is given to the human being to obtain.
>
> (*GWS=SW* 2, 1424–1425)

106 *Works and key ideas*

And this kind of happiness is what Klages goes on to describe as a 'specific happiness':

> Whilst in mechanistic thought objectivity and logic serve at best the task of establishing objective relations between objects of thought, metaphysical thought reserves the name of 'truth' exclusively for *insights into the characteristics of reality* and establishes *its* relations in regard to them.[117] Inasmuch as knowledge of this kind consists of indications, 'demonstrations', indeed recollections of 'primordial phenomena', it necessarily has at the same time the form of a way of looking at the world and, in respect of its content, resembles a *world-view* or even an epistemological *construction*. These are no more than analogies, but they express in a simple way why steeping oneself in such a 'system' or, put more generally, participation in a way of thinking about the *sense* of the world, means, for anyone who is willing and able to do so, a specific happiness and a lightning-like gleam that can, in principle, illuminate *every* path of life, inasmuch as it lights up depths of significance even in the supposed trivialities of everyday life at its gloomiest.
>
> (*GWS=SW* 2, 1429)

In taking this position, Klages reveals himself as not simply an anti-Hegelian thinker but also – for all his reservations expressed in his great monograph of 1926 – as a pro-Nietzschean one.

After all, in *The Gay Science*, §278, Nietzsche (in an aphorism surely written during one of his visits to Genoa) reflected:

> I derive a melancholy happiness from living in the midst of this confusion of streets, needs, voices: how much enjoyment, impatience, desire, how much thirsty life and drunkenness of life comes to the light of day every moment! And yet for all these noisy, living, life-thirsty people it will soon be so still and silent! How behind each of them stands his shadow, his dark companion! [...] It makes me happy to see that men are altogether disinclined to think the thought of death! I should like to do something to make the thought of life a hundred times *more worth thinking* for them.[118]

And in an earlier aphorism (§12) in this work, Nietzsche proposes that science might yet be found to be 'the *great dispenser of pain*', whose counterforce might at the same time be found, namely: 'its immense capacity for making new galaxies of joy flare up'.[119]

The thought of Ludwig Klages taps into the vitalist tradition that goes back to Nietzsche and, beyond him, to Carl Gustav Carus, Arthur Schopenhauer, and arguably as far back as to Friedrich Schlegel (1772–1829).[120] It engages with innumerable thinkers in the classical tradition, including Cicero, Plutarch, and Seneca, to say nothing of the Presocratics, Aristotles, and the Neoplatonists. And it draws (in ways that still urgently require further research) on some of the most

Figure 5 Klages in conversation.

important contemporary thinkers of its day, including Melchior Pálagyi, Hermann Lotze, and Theodor Lipps (some of whom have become almost as forgotten as Klages himself). Yet his thought is not simply an exercise in exploring some of the less-well-known by-ways of the German – indeed, European – philosophical tradition. It does something far more important of that; for it reminds us of the truth of Goethe's saying, 'the point of life is life itself'.[121]

Notes

1 For an historical (and critical) overview of physiognomic theories in Germany, beginning with Lavater, and including Goethe (pp. 139–151), Carl Gustav Carus (pp. 151–157), and Klages (pp. 157–163), up to their ethnological and racial applications in Nazi Germany, see R. T. Gray, *About Face: German Physiognomic Thought from Lavater to Auschwitz*, Detroit: Wayne State University Press, 2004.
2 The Demeter of Knidos is a life-size marble statue of the goddess, discovered in the port of Knidos in Turkey and on display in the British Museum, London.
3 For further discussion, see M. Streicher, *Reshaping Physical Education*, ed. B. E. Strutt, tr. C. R. M. Larner, Manchester: Manchester University Press, 1970, chapter 17, 'Expression and representation', pp. 128–144.

108　*Works and key ideas*

4　Some of these examples I have taken from H. Kasdorff, 'Die Ausdruckslehre von Ludwig Klages', in H. Kasdorff, *Ludwig Klages: Gesammelte Aufsätze und Vorträge zu seinem Werk*, Bonn: Bouvier Verlag Herbert Grundmann, 1984, pp. 135–147 (p. 137).

5　For further discussion of Klages in relation to the philosophical tradition of phenomenology (especially the thought of Martin Heidegger, Edmund Husserl, and Max Scheler), see Michael Großheim's study, *Ludwig Klages und die Phänomenologie*, Berlin: Akademie Verlag, 1994.

6　Protagoras was a pre-Socratic philosopher and a Sophist, associated with the phrase, 'Man is the measure of all things' (see Diogenes Laertius, *Lives and Opinions of Eminent Philosophers*, vol. 2, book 9, chapter 8). For a useful edition of Aristotle's work, see *De Anima (On the Soul)*, tr. H. Lawson-Tancred, Harmondsworth: Penguin, 1986.

7　Epicharmus of Kos was a Greek dramatist and philosopher, often regarded as one of the first comic writers; cf. Plato, *Theaetetus* (152e), and Aristotle, *Poetics* (1448a33 and 1449b5).

8　Of these modern names, some will be more well-known than others: Ekkehard of Aura (d. *c.*1126), medieval chronicler; Marcus (or Marquard) of Lindau (d. 1392), fourteenth-century historian and theologian; Johannes von Müller (1752–1809), Swiss historian; Thomas Carlyle (1795–1881), Scottish historian; Leopold von Ranke (1795–1886), German historian; Wilhelm von Giesebrecht (1814–1889), German historian; Gustav Freytag (1816–1895), German writer; Theodor Mommsen (1817–1903), German historian; Ferdinand Gregorovius (1821–1891), German cultural historian; Ludwig Friedländer (1824–1909), German classical philologist; Jacob Burckhardt (1818–1897), Swiss cultural historian; and Johannes Scherr (1817–1886), German writer and critic.

9　While St Augustine (354–430), the author of the *Confessions*, and Hans Jakob Christoffel von Grimmelshausen (1622–1676), the author of *Simplicissimus*, will be known to most readers, the rest will be less familiar: Felix Platter (1536–1614) and Thomas Platter the younger (1574–1628), two Swiss physicians and sons of the Swiss humanist, Thomas Platter (the Elder) (1499–1582) (Thomas the Elder wrote an autobiography, Thomas the Younger kept a journal, including a travel diary of his visit to London in 1599 with his brother); Götz von Berlichingen (1480–1562), known as Götz of the Iron Hand, whose autobiography served as a major source for Goethe's famous play about this Imperial Knight; Sebastian Schertlin von Burtenbach (1496–1577), a *Landsknecht* or mercenary soldier who wrote an account of his 'life and deeds' (*Leben und Thaten*); Hans von Schweinichen (1552–1616), a Schlesian knight who kept a detailed diary between 1568 and 1602 which was published by the academic folk historian Johann Gustav Gottlieb Büsching in 1820–1822. The identities of Haupt and Sethe as eighteenth-century autobiographers is not clear to me, but the other figures mentioned by Klages are Friedrich von der Trenck (1726–1794), a Prussian officer who wrote a three-volume autobiography; and Friedrich Christian Laukhard (1757–1822), a German writer who took part as a soldier in the War of the First Coalition (1792–1797) and wrote an account of it.

10　The Catilinarian conspiracy, sometimes known as the Catiline conspiracy, was a secret plot organized by a Roman senator, Catiline, to overthrow the Roman Republic. When the plan was revealed by Cicero before the Senate in the Temple of Jupiter Stator, Catiline fled Rome. Cicero's denunciation of Catiline is the first speech in the series of four *Catiline Orations*.

11　Klages's choice of examples and his style of introducing them reflect the cultural commonplaces of his time, not ours; they are not intrinsic to his argument.

12　Schiller's distich is entitled 'Dilettante', and is one of his *Votive Tablets* (*Votivtafeln*), included in his *Poems* (*Gedichte*) of 1804, and revised as *Tabulae Votivae*.

Notes 109

13 L. Klages, 'Key Concepts of the Doctrine of Character' (1947); in *CAK*, pp. 179–190.

14 F. Wertham, 'Progress in Psychiatry III: The Significance of Klages' System for Psychopathology', *Archives of Neurology and Psychiatry*, 24, no. 2 (1930), 381–388.

15 Wertham, 'The Significance of Klages's System for Psychotherapy', p. 382.

16 L. Klages, *The Science of Character*, trans. W. H. Johnston, London: Allen & Unwin, 1929, chapter 9, p. 235.

17 See C. G. Jung, *Psychological Types* [*Collected Works of C. G. Jung*, vol. 6], trans. H. G. Baynes and rev. R. F. C. Hull, London: Routledge & Kegan Paul, 1971.

18 W. J. H. Sprott, [review of] '*The Science of Character*. By Ludwig Klages. Translated by W. H. Johnston. [...]', *Mind* [NS] 38, no. 152, October 1929, 513–520 (p. 515).

19 Ludwig Klages, 'Die Triebe und der Wille', *Archiv für Psychiatrie und Nervenkrankheiten* 85, 1928, 478–479; cf. 'Die Triebe und der Wille', in *SW*, vol. 3, pp. 693–709 (and commentary on pp. 792–798); and 'Zur Theorie und Symptomatologie des Willens' (1914), in *SW*, vol. 3, pp. 637–641.

20 Evidently Klages's argument requires some updating: today we have omniscience in the form of the internet and mobile communications, omnipresence through high speed travel, and omnipotence through nuclear power.

21 Cf. the figure of Homunculus in Goethe's *Faust II*, the tiny mannikin being manufactured using alchemical techniques by Wagner in Act II. For further discussion, see A. Scholz, 'Goethe's Homunculus', *The German Quarterly*, 17, no. 1, January 1944, 23–27.

22 This language, however provocative, even offensive, derives from rhetoric found in Nietzsche's writings; compare his analysis of Judeo-Christianity in *On the Genealogy of Morals* and, in particular, *The Antichrist*.

23 Johann Joseph von Görres (1776–1848) was a German writer associated with the Romantic tradition. In *On Christian Mysticism* (*Christliche Mystik*), published in four volumes between 1836 and 1842, he presented a series of hagiographical portraits, together with an overview of Roman Catholic teaching on mysticism. This work has been reissued in a new edition edited by Ute Ranke-Heinemann (in six volumes, Frankfurt am Main: Eichborn, 1989).

24 A quotation from Johannes Scotus Eriugena (*c*.1813–1891), *De Divisione Naturae*, where Eriugena argues for the one creative energy of the divine Trinity. For further discussion, see H. Watkins-Jones, *The Holy Spirit in the Medieval Church: A Study of Christian Teaching concerning the Holy Spirit and His Place in the Trinity from the Post-Patristic Age to the Counter-Reformation*, London: Epworth Press, 1922, p. 65.

25 St Augustine, *The City of God* (*De civitate Dei*), book 14, chapter 6 (entitled 'The character of the human will determines the quality of the emotions'). The context of this remark is the following argument:

> What is important in a man is this: *which* is his will: for if it is perverse, he too will be perverse in his actions; if it is straight, not only will he not be guilty, but even praiseworthy. For in everyone the will is found or, better, everyone is nothing other than a will.
>
> (cf. J.-L. Marion, *In the Self's Place: The Approach of Saint Augustine*, tr. J. L. Kosley, Stanford, CA: Stanford University Press, 2012; p. 162)

26 In Schiller's drama *Wilhelm Tell* (1804), the huntsman Wilhelm Tell conspicuously fails to salute the cap of the tyrannical governor, Gessler, as it hangs outside a prison, and is promptly arrested by a guard. In the famous scene that follows, Gessler challenges Tell to prove his skill with his bow and shoot an apple – placed on the head of his young son.

110   *Works and key ideas*

27 Compare with the famous opening lines of the poem 'Songs' ('Gesänge') by the German Expressionist poet Gottfried Benn (1886–1956), which begins: 'O to be like our great-great-ancestors! / A little clump of slime in a warm marsh' (*O daß wir unsere Ururahnen wären / Ein Klümpchen Schleim in einem warmen Moor*) (G. Benn, *Selected Poems*, ed. F. W. Wodtke, Oxford: Oxford University Press, 1970, p. 53).

28 See Deutsches Literaturarchiv Marbach, 'Zur Lebenslehre. Aus einer Vorlesung (Sommer-Semester 1918)'; Sig. 61. 3798.

29 H. Kasdorff, *Ludwig Klages: Werk und Wirkung: Einführung und kommentierte Bibliographie*, 2 vols, Bonn: Bouvier, 1969, vol. 1, p. 46.

30 Kasdorff, *Ludwig Klages: Werk und Wirkung*, vol. 1, p. 81.

31 H. E. Schröder, 'Vom Sinn der Persönlichkeit: Ein Beitrag zum Menschenbild von Ludwig Klages', *Psychologische Rundschau* 8, 1957, 207–217 (p. 211).

32 Kasdorff, *Ludwig Klages: Werk und Wirkung*, vol. 1, p. 48; cf. L. Klages, *Mensch und Erde: Elf Abhandlungen*, Stuttgart: Kröner, 1973, p. 58.

33 M. Großheim, '"Die namenlose Dummheit, die das Resultat des Fortschritts ist" – Lebensphilosophische und dialektische Kritik der Moderne', *Logos: Zeitschrift für systematische Philosophie* 3, 1996, 97–133 (p. 114).

34 The relation between lack and drive might be compared to the relation (articulated in Plato's *Symposium*) between lack and desire which would later form a plank of the psychoanalytic system devised by Jacques Lacan (1901–1981).

35 See Aristotle, *On the Soul*, book 2, 414a 13–14. Here Aristotle defines thirst as 'a desire for what is cold and moist' (Aristotle, *The Complete Works*, ed. J. Barnes, 2 vols, Princeton, NJ: Princeton University Press, 1984, vol. 1, p. 660).

36 In German, the term *Anschauung* is used by Kant in the sense of 'empirical intuition' (*empirische Anschauung*) to talk about sensory perception, in contrast to 'pure forms of intuition' (*reine Formen der Anschauung*), i.e. time and space.

37 At the end of the second book of *The Spirit as Adversary of the Soul*, Klages describes 'the recovery of experienced contexts from the net-mesh, made up of dividing lines crossing them in thousands of different ways, that the power of relational judgement casts over them' as 'the most important goal of our research' (*GWS=SW*, vol. 1, p. 214).

38 I.e. the French landscape and portrait painter, Jean-Baptiste-Camille Corot (1796–1875); a painter of the Barbizon School of landscape painters and a precursor of Impressionism, Charles-François Daubigny (1817–1878); another member of the Barbizon School, Jules Dupré (1811–1889); yet another Barbizon School painter, Étienne Pierre Théodor Rousseau (1812–1867); a pioneer of the *Stimmungslandschaft* (or 'mood landscape') style of painting in Munich, Adolf Stäbli (1842–1901); and another exponent of *Stimmungslandschaft*, Eduard Schleich (the Elder) (1812–1874). For brief entries on these painters and their respective schools and stylistic directions, see G. Norman, *Nineteenth Century Painters and Painting: A Dictionary*, Berkeley and Los Angeles: University of California Press, 1977.

39 Klages's image is reminiscent of the description given by Schopenhauer in *The World as Will and Representation*, vol. 1, §63, of how individual human beings trust in the principle of individuation:

> Just as the boatman sits in his small boat, trusting his frail craft in a stormy sea that is boundless in every direction, rising and falling with the howling, mountainous waves, so in the midst of a world full of suffering and misery the individual man calmly sits, supported by and trusting the *principium individuationis*, or the way in which the individual knows things as phenomenon.
>
> (A. Schopenhauer, *The World as Will and Representation*, trans. E. F. J. Payne, 2 vols, New York: Dover, 1969, vol. 1, pp. 353–354)

Notes 111

Nietzsche, too, alludes to this passage to describe the principle of the Apollonian in *The Birth of Tragedy*, §1; *Basic Writings*, ed. and trans. Walter Kaufmann, New York: Modern Library, 1968, pp. 35–36.

40 The Greek word *hyle* (ὕλη) refers to matter or substance, while aether (αἰθήρ) refers to the air, the sky, or the atmosphere (sometimes personified as a deity, Aether). For further discussion of the problems of defining these elements in ancient Greek thought, see P. Kingsley, *Ancient Philosophy, Mystery, and Magic: Empedocles and Pythagorean Tradition*, Oxford: Clarendon Press, 1995, chapters 2 ('*Aither*') and 3 ('*Aer*'), pp. 15–35.

41 In a relief, a figure is cut in such a way that it appears elevated against the background plane; typically relief work was used to decorate the metopes of Greek temples, such as the Parthenon Frieze or the Elgin Marbles.

42 Klages plays here on the etymology of the word 'daimon', which may derive from a Greek root meaning 'to know', so that a daimon means 'a knowing one'. Similarly, Plato uses the term *daimonion* as signifying 'knowing' or 'wise'; see W. E. Vine, *Amplified Expository Dictionary of New Testament Words*, Iowa Falls, IA: World Bible Publishers, 1991, p. 203; and Marvin Vincent, *Word Studies in the New Testament*, Wilmington, DE: Associated Publishers & Authors, 1972, p. 92.

43 Plutarch, *Moralia*, 'On the Inscription "E" on the Temple at Delphi', §18; cited by Klages from the translation by J. F. S. Kaltwasser; see Plutarch, *Moralisch-philosophische Werke*, vol. 3, tr. J. F. S. Kaltwasser, Vienna and Prague: Haas, 1797, 'Ueber die Inschrift Ei im Tempel zu Delphi', pp. 162–189 (p. 184): 'Keiner bleibt, keiner ist ein einziger, sondern wir werden viele, indem nur die Materie sich um ein einziges Bild, um eine gemeinschaftliche Form herumtreibt, und wieder entschlüpft'. See Plutarch, *Moralia*, vol. 5, tr. F. C. Babbitt, Cambridge, MA, and London: Harvard University Press, 1936, 'The E at Delphi', pp. 193–253, p. 243: 'Nobody remains one person, nor is one person; but we become many persons, even as matter is drawn about some one semblance and common mould [cf. Plato, *Timaeus*, 50c] with imperceptible movement'. The passage from Plato to which Plutarch alludes reads as follows:

> [Universal nature] is the natural recipient of all impressions, and is stirred and informed by them, and appears different from time to time by reason of them. But the forms which enter into and go out of her are the likenesses of eternal realities modeled after their patterns in a wonderful and mysterious manner.
> (Plato, *Collected Dialogues*, ed. E. Hamilton and H. Cairns, Princeton, MA: Princeton University Press, 1989, p. 1177)

44 From Schiller's drama *The Maid of Orleans* (1801), Act 3, Scene 6.

45 The German linguist Friedrich Kluge (1856–1926); Klages is referring to Kluge's *Etymologisches Wörterbuch der deutschen Sprache* and the entry in it (p. 57) for 'dumm'.

46 Klages is referring here to the legend recounted in the Norse Poetic Edda.

47 For further discussion, see P. Bishop, *On the Blissful Islands: With Nietzsche and Jung in the Shadow of the Superman*, London: Routledge, 2017, pp. 115–119.

48 By 'pathic' – derived from the Greek *pathikos* and in turn from *pathos*, 'suffering', and associated by Klages (see 'Theory of Willing' [1915], in *SW*, vol. 3, pp. 642–645, esp. 643) with the Greek (i.e. Aristotelian) distinction between νοῦς ποιητιχός, *nous poietikos*, 'active mind' or 'active intellect', and νους παθητιχός, *nous pathetikos*, 'passive intellect') – Klages means a faculty for being receptive, i.e. for abandoning oneself to an object or an image and intuiting, viewing, experiencing, or 'suffering' it, without any autonomous activity of one's own (see H.-P. Preußer, *Pathische Ästhetik: Ludwig Klages und die Urgeschichte der Postmoderne*, Heidelberg: Winter, 2015, p. 1; cf. pp. 147–149). For this famous distinction between active and passive intellect, see *On the Soul*, book 3, chapter 5 (430a 10–25):

112 *Works and key ideas*

[I]n every class of things [...] we find two factors involved, a matter which is potentially all the particulars included in the class, a cause which is productive in the sense that it makes them all [...], these distinct elements must likewise be found within the soul. And in fact thought [...] is what it is by virtue of becoming all things, while there is another which is what it is by virtue of making all things [...].

(Aristotle, *Complete Works*, vol. 1, p. 684)

Other contemporary thinkers address themselves to this theme in Aristotle; see, for example, F. Brentano, *Die Psychologie des Aristoteles, insbesondere seine Lehre vom ΝΟΥΣ ΠΟΙΗΤΙΚΟΣ* [Mainz, 1867], Darmstadt: Wissenschaftliche Buchgesellschaft, 1967, and *Aristoteles' Lehre vom Ursprung des menschlichen Geistes*, Leipzig: Veit, 1911; and M. Heidegger, *Basic Concepts of Aristotelian Philosophy* [1924], tr. R. D. Metcalf and M. B. Tanzer, Bloomington and Indianapolis: Indiana University Press, 2009, pp. 220–221. For further discussion, see C. Jung, *Die doppelte Natur des menschlichen Intellekts bei Aristoteles*, Würzburg: Königshausen & Neumann, 2011; and the entry on '*intellectus*' by A. de Libera in B. Cassin (ed.), *Dictionary of Untranslatables: A Philosophical Lexicon* [2004], tr. S. Randall, C. Hubert, J. Mehlman, N. Stein, and M. Syrotinski, ed. E. Apter, J. Lezra, and M. Wood, Princeton and Oxford: Princeton University Press, 2014, pp. 492–501.

49 Cf. C. Bernoulli, 'On Ludwig Klages', in H. Prinzhorn (ed.), *Die Wissenschaft am Schweidewege von Leben und Geist: Festschrift Ludwig Klages zum 60. Geburtstag, 10. Dezember 1932*, Leipzig: Barth, 1932, pp. 251–252.

50 Aristotle, *De Anima (On the Soul)*, tr. Lawson-Tancred, 'Introduction', p. 95. See *De Generatione Animalium*, Book 2, 736 b 27 ('Reason alone enters in, as an additional factor, from outside') and 744 b 22 ('a mind, external to them') (Aristotle, *Generation of Animals*, tr. A. L. Peck, London; Cambridge, MA: Heinemann; Harvard University Press, 1943, pp. 170–171 and 230–231); cf. Aristotle, *'De Partibus Animalium' I and 'De Generatione Animalium' I (with passages from II.1–3)*, tr. D. N. Balme, Oxford: Clarendon Press, 1972, pp. 63–64 and 159–160. For further discussion, see F. Brentano, *The Psychology of Aristotle: In Particular His Doctrine of the Active Intellect*, ed. and tr. R. George, Berkeley, Los Angeles, London: University of California Press, 1977, pp. 134–135 and 253, n. 272; and H. Seidl, *Der Begriff des Intellekts (νους) bei Aristoteles im philosophischen Zusammenhang seiner Hauptschriften*, Meisenheim am Glan: Hain, 1971, pp. 127–128.

51 Plutarch, *Moralia*, 'On the Inscription "E" on the Temple at Delphi', §18:

The man in his prime passes away when the old man comes into existence, the young man passes away into the man in his prime, the child into the young man, and the babe into the child. Dead is the man of yesterday, for he is passed into the man of to-day; and the man of to-day is dying as he passes into the man of to-morrow.

(pp. 241–243)

This passage from Plutarch is also quoted by other writers and thinkers in a wide variety of contexts – by, for example, C. G. Carus, *Symbolik der menschlichen Gestalt: Ein Handbuch zur Menschenkenntnis* [2nd edn, 1858], Hildesheim: Olms, 1997, p. 8; and R. Steiner (1861–1925), *Christianity as Mystical Fact* [1902; 2nd edn, 1910], tr. A. Welburn, Hudson, NY: Anthroposophic Press, 1997, chapter 1, 'The Mysteries and Mysteriosophy', p. 12.

52 According to Klages, even the inscription above the temple of the oracle at Delphi – *know thyself* – was 'no harmless saying', but a 'saying that foretold the belief in a world beyond' (in *RR*, 423); after all, the entire inscription is said to have read: 'Know thyself, and thou shalt know the universe and the gods'. As Klages concludes, 'the life

Notes 113

of the Greeks allowed itself be to be guided by this saying, and the knowledge of the Pelasgians was shattered by it' (in *RR*, 423).

53 For an analysis of how, in Klages, 'the apocalyptic moment' unites 'the living primordial images and the opened soul, standing opposite each other, gazing spellbound into each other's eyes', see the work by the Swiss theologian H. U. von Balthasar (1905–1988), *Apokalypse der deutschen Seele: Studien zu einer Lehre von letzten Haltungen*, vol. 2, *Im Zeichen Nietzsches* [1939], Freiburg: Johannes, 1998, pp. 78–108 (p. 94).

54 See Homer, *Iliad*, Book 2, line 840; *Odyssey*, Book 19, lines 172–127; Thucydides, *The Peloponnesian War*, Book 1, §3; Herodotus, *The Histories*, Book 1, §56–58.

55 S. Arvidsson, *Aryan Idols: Indo-European Mythology as Ideology and Science*, tr. S. Wichmann, Chicago and London: University of Chicago Press, 2006, p. 100.

56 For further discussion, see J. L. Myres, 'A History of the Pelasgian Theory', *Journal of Hellenic Studies* 27, 1907, 170–225; J. A. R. Munro, 'Pelasgians and Ionians', *Journal of Hellenic Studies* 54, no. 2, 1934, 109–128; and A. Lang, *The World of Homer*, London: Longmans, Green, 1910. Klages would have agreed with Lang's assessment that 'Homeric civilisation, in all its details, was lived at a brief given period; [...] it was real' (p. 2), and applied it to the Pelasgians.

57 See Aeschylus, *Prometheus Bound*, line 442.

58 Compare with 'Consciousness and Life', in *SW*, vol. 3, pp. 646–655 (p. 650). For Xenophon's account of Prodicos's lost work, 'On Heracles', see his *Memorabilia* (or *Memories of Socrates*), book 2, chapter 1, §21–§34; cf. Xenophon, *Memorabilia; Oeconomicus; Symposium; Apology*, tr. E. C. Marchant and O. J. Todd, rev. J. Henderson, Cambridge, MA: Harvard University Press, 2013, pp. 692–695. A similar legend is told of a vision experienced by Scipio Africanus, in which Virtue and Pleasure contend for his allegiance; see Silius Italicus, *Punica*, Book 15, 18–128 and Raphael's painting 'An Allegory ("Vision of a Knight")' (*c.*1504) in the National Gallery, London. For further discussion, see E. Panofsky, *Hercules am Scheidewege und andere antike Bildstoffe in der neueren Kunst* [*Studien der Bibliothek Warburg*, vol. 18], Leipzig and Berlin: Teubner, 1930.

59 'Humankind and Earth' (in German, 'Mensch und Erde'), in *Freideutsche Jugend: Zur Jahrhundertfeier auf dem Hohen Meißner 1913*, Jena: Diederichs, 1913, S. 89–107; republished with slight modifications in L. Klages, *Mensch und Erde: Zehn Abhandlungen*, Stuttgart: Kröner, 1956, 1–25; reissued in *Mensch und Erde: Elf Abhandlungen*, 1–25; cf. in *SW*, vol. 3, pp. 614–630. Looking back on this text in 1929, Klages wrote that in this essay he had 'provided a terrible analysis of the rape of nature by humanity in the present day' and 'sought to prove that humankind, as the carrier of spirit [*Geist*], has torn itself apart just as it is tearing apart the planet to which we owe our birth' ('Foreword for Contemporaries', *SW*, vol. 2, p. 1537).

60 See E. Bloch, 'Imago as appearance from the "depths"', in *Heritage of Our Times*, tr. N. Plaice and S. Plaice, Cambridge: Polity Press, 1991, pp. 312–318 (pp. 315–316).

61 In German, the term Klages uses is *die Essenz*. For the notion of the 'essence of life', see *The Spirit as Adversary of the Soul*, chapter 40, 'The Research of Melchior Palágyi':

> Just as it is certain that life goes beyond individual life and thus beyond organic life, so it is certain that organic life is individual life and the experiences of each organic being are in the first instance only its own experiences, between which and the experiences of another organic being there is no *im*mediate connection. More profound investigation would tell us that the limitations inevitably imposed by every individuation are sometimes more relaxed, sometimes more stringent: more relaxed in the case of the experience of plants than in the case of the experience of animals, in another way more relaxed in the elementary experience of

114 *Works and key ideas*

primordial humankind than in the already spirit-governed [*geistig*] experience of the Promethean human being from the late ages of prehistory, but of unyielding severity – which death alone can break – in the Heraclean human being of 'world history', i.e. in the human being of will and of action. [...] [...] However inscrutable the puzzle of how life builds up may be: how beings are born and how they die, how they breathe and how they have to nourish themselves, testify to the fact that the *essence* of life was merely lent to its individual bearer, and for this reason can never be understood in relation to it. Without the feeling of life [*Lebensgefühl*] there is no feeling of the peculiarity of what is experienced, and without the feeling of individuality [*Eigengefühl*] there is no consciousness: in this order lies the reason for why we try in vain to throw light on the meaning of experience, so long as we believe we can find its criteria in the impossibility of documenting one's own experience from any other consciousness than one's own.

(*GWS=SW*, vol. 1, p. 471)

62 A line from Friedrich Hölderlin's novel, *Hyperion*, vol. 2; see the passage where Alabanda cries:

My soul seethes over of itself and will no longer be confined to the old circle. Soon the beautiful days of winter will be here, when the dark earth is but the foil to the shining heavens – that would be the right time, then the isles of light glimmer the more hospitably! – You are amazed by what I say? Dearest one! all who are departing talk like drunken men and delight to behave as at a feast. When the tree begins to wither, do not all its leaves bear the red of morning?

(F. Hölderlin, *"Hyperion" and Selected Poems*, ed. E. L. Santner, New York: Continuum, 1990, p. 116)

63 There are echoes here of the final scene of Goethe's dramatic poem, *Faust II*, with its references to 'ringed all about by perils' ('umrungen von Gefahr') (l. 11577) and to the ghastly creatures, the lemures, that dig Faust's grave; see J. W. von Goethe, *Faust: A Tragedy*, ed. C. Hamlin, tr. W. Arndt, 2nd edn, New York and London: Norton, 2001, p. 329.

64 At this point, a footnote (*GWS=SW*, vol. 2, p. 1447, n. 27) refers the reader 'who wishes to learn more' to Klages's essay 'The Case of Nietzsche and Wagner Examined Graphologically' ('Der Fall Nietzsche-Wagner in graphologischer Beleuchtung') [1904], in *SW*, vol. 8, pp. 565–589. Yet quite how this paper – which surveys Nietzsche's critique of Wagner, clarifies Klages's own position in relation to Wagner (as well as to Stefan George), and contains an important footnote on the physicality of Apollonian beauty – contributes to a better understanding of Klages's analysis of global decline remains unclear.

65 See D. Graeber, *The Utopia of Rules: On Technology, Stupidity, and the Secret Joys of Bureaucracy*, Brooklyn and London: Melville House, 2015. In the TV series *The Prisoner* (1967), Number 2 shouts: 'I am not a number. I am a free man!'

66 For further discussion, see A. Honneth, 'L'esprit et son objet: Parentés anthropologiques entre la "Dialectique de la raison" et la critique de la civilisation dans la philosophie de la vie', in G. Raulet (ed.), *Weimar ou l'explosion de la modernité*, Paris: Éditions Anthropos, 1984, pp. 97–112; G. Stauth, 'Critical Theory and Pre-Fascist Social Thought', *History of European Ideas* 18, 1994, 711–727; G. Stauth and B. S. Turner, 'Ludwig Klages (1872–1956) and the Origins of Critical Theory', *Theory, Culture and Society* 9, no. 3 (1992), 45–63; and A. Wellmer, *Zur Dialektik von Moderne und Postmoderne: Vernunftkritik nach Adorno*, Frankfurt am Main: Suhrkamp, 1985, pp. 72 and 77. When Klages writes in 'Humankind and Earth' that 'behind the effort at gaining knowledge there stands, demanding and directing it, the purposes of humankind, and only in the light of the latter can we understand the former' (*SW*, vol. 3, p. 625), he anticipates the central distinction of Jürgen

Notes 115

Habermas (b. 1929) in the title of his major work of 1968, *Knowledge and Human Interests*.

67 For further discussion of Benjamin's interest in Klages and his reception of Bachofen, see M. Großheim, 'Archaisches oder dialektisches Bild? Zum Kontext einer Debatte zwischen Adorno und Benjamin', in *Deutsche Vierteljahrsschrift für Literaturwissenschaft und Geistesgeschichte* 71, no. 3 (1997), 494–517; J. Mali, 'The Reconciliation of Myth: Benjamin's Homage to Bachofen', *Journal of the History of Ideas* 60, no. 1 (1999), 165–187; and R. Block, 'Selective Affinities: Walter Benjamin and Ludwig Klages', *Arcadia* 35, no. 1, 2000, 117–135.

68 See R. J. Kozljanič, *Lebensphilosophie: Eine Einführung*, Stuttgart: Kohlhammer, 2004, p. 188.

69 See L. Klages, 'Über Bachofen: Würdigung', in J. J. Bachofen, *Gräbersymbolik der Alten*, Basel: Helbing & Lichtenhahn, 1925, pp. ix–xiii; and C. G. Carus, *Psyche*, ed. L. Klages, Jena: Diederichs, 1926.

70 C. G. Jung, *Psychological Types* [*Collected Works*, vol. 6], ed. G. Adler, tr. R. F. C. Hull, Princeton, NJ: Princeton University Press, 1976.

71 Cf. *The Foundations of the Doctrine of Character*, chapter 5, §2: 'The vital and the spirit-related ways of perception', where Klages expounds this difference with relation to the classical German figures of Schiller and Goethe (*SW*, vol. 4, 277–279).

72 See J. O. de La Mettrie, *Man A Machine*, trans. G. C. Bussey, rev. M. W. Calkins, La Salle, IL: Open Court, 1912; and A. Vartanian (ed.), *La Mettrie's 'L'homme machine': A Study in the Origins of an Idea*, Princeton, NJ: Princeton University Press, 1960.

73 See Seneca, *Epistulae morales*, 53.8, where Seneca writes to Lucilius:

> For he whose sleep is light pursues visions during slumber, and sometimes, though asleep, is conscious that he is asleep; but sound slumber annihilates our very dreams and sinks the spirit down so deep that it has no perception of the self. Why will no man confess his faults? Because he is still in their grasp; only he who is awake can recount his dream [*somnium narrare vigilantis est*], and similarly a confession of sin is a proof of sound mind.
>
> (Seneca, *Ad Luciulium epistulae morales*, tr. R. M. Gummere, vol. 1, London; Heinemann; Cambridge, MA: Harvard University Press, 1967, p. 357)

74 N. W. Bruun, '*Disjecta membra* in Kierkegaard's Writings', in J. Stewart (ed.), *Kierkegaard and the Roman World* [*Kierkegaard Research: Sources, Reception and Resources*, vol. 3], Farnham and Burlington, VT: Ashgate, 2009, pp. 111–124 (pp. 119–120). For further discussion of Kierkegaard's outlook on history, see G. Patios, *Kierkegaard on the Philosophy of History*, New York: Palgrave Macmillan, 2014.

75 G. W. F. Hegel, *Elements of the Philosophy of Right*, ed. A. W. Wood, tr. H. B. Nisbet, Cambridge: Cambridge University Press, 1991, p. 23.

76 G. W. F. Hegel, *Reason in History: A General Introduction to the Philosophy of History*, tr. R. S. Hartmann, Indianapolis and New York: Bobbs-Merrill, 1953. Page references in parentheses are to this edition.

77 To what extent is Klages a philosopher or a psychologist? According to Kasdorff, Klages saw himself as both a psychologist and a metaphysician, inasmuch as he did not distinguish between these disciplines (H. Kasdorff, *Ludwig Klages: Werk und Wirkung: Einführung und kommentierte Bibliographie*, 2 vols, Bonn: Bouvier, 1969, vol. 1, p. 50).

78 C. Fortlage, *Acht Psychologische Vorträge*, Jena: Mauke, 1872, p. 35.

79 See M. Heidegger and E. Fink, *Heraclitus Seminar*, tr. C. H Seibert, Evanston, IL: Northwestern University Press, 1993, p. 115.

80 See the fragment entitled 'Heraclitus' ('Heraklit') in *Rhythmen und Runen*, p. 314. Later, in chapter 57 of *The Spirit as Adversary of the Soul*, 'From the Prehistory of

116 *Works and key ideas*

the Discovery of the Images', Klages acknowledged Heraclitus as his predecessor (*GWS=SW*, vol. 2, pp. 853 and 854–855). Above all, Heraclitus was, for Klages, a *symbolic* thinker, in the sense that he defined this term (*GWS=SW*, vol. 1, p. 857).

81 See the following aphorism from *Rhythms and Runes*,

> Life is flux, persistence is death. Life rigidifies and ends in the belief in the reality of things, the illusion of permanence. The universe has the reality of ceaseless process. Only in the repetition of powers that cling and powers that wander lies the pledge of life.
>
> (*RR*, 249)

In 'On Truth and Reality' (1931), Klages argues that: 'What happens to us is continuously changing; it is, as Heraclitus puts it, caught in eternal flux' (*SW*, vol. 3, p. 721).

82 See Heraclitus, fragment DK 22 B 50. The Presocratic thinkers are usually cited according to a system of reference originally devised by the German classical scholar, Hermann Alexander Diels (1848–1922), and revised in 1934–1937 by Walther Kranz (1884–1960), and hence known as a Diels-Kranz (or DK) number.

83 Although this second sentence cannot be found in this form in any of the surviving fragments of Heraclitus, it is traditionally ascribed to him and can be derived from two sources, Plato's *Cratylus* (402 a) and Aristotle's *Metaphysics* (see DK 65 A 3).

84 See Heraclitus, fragment DK 22 B 21.

85 See the discussion in T. M. Robinson, *Heraclitus: Fragments*, Toronto: University of Toronto Press, 1987, pp. 90–91.

86 M. Marcovich, *Heraclitus: Greek Text with a Short Commentary*, Merida, Venezuela: Los Andes University Press, 1967, p. 248. This reading is sustained by another fragment cited by Clement of Alexandria in his *Stromatae* (DK 22 B 26), and by the view attributed to Euripides in *Gorgias* (493 a) that the whole of waking life constitutes death; for these references and for further discussion, see the commentary in *Les Présocratiques*, ed. J.-P. Dumont, Paris: Gallimard, 1988, pp. 1235–1236.

87 See 'Consciousness and Life' (1915), in *SW*, vol. 3, pp. 649–650; and 'On the Relation of Education to the Essence of Humankind' (1935; 1956), in *SW*, vol. 3, pp. 723–730 (p. 724).

88
> The dream-state is the state of intuition and the dream a reality of *images*; the waking state is the state of sensation and what is sensed is *bodiliness*. In such a way we have also graphically demonstrated what every awakening consists in when the intuitive slumber is broken. What breaks up the dreaming stream of the soul like a wave is sensuous bodiliness; there would be no more 'silent rocks' of fate, provided that the intuitive soul no longer found itself trapped in the sensual-painful *location* of the transitory body.
>
> (*GWS=SW*, vol. 2, p. 811)

89 This is clearly a radical position, but surely no more radical than Socrates's argument in the *Gorgias* that maybe Euripedes was right when he said, 'Who knows, if life be death, and death be life?' (*Polyidus*, fragment 7), and his subsequent reflection that 'perhaps we are actually dead, for I once heard one of our wise man say that we are now dead, and that our body is a tomb' (*Gorgias*, 492e-493a; Plato, *Collected Dialogues*, p. 275).

90 E. Bloch, *Erbschaft dieser Zeit* [extended edition], Frankfurt am Main: Suhrkamp, 1985, pp. 330–331.

91 For further discussion, see R. J. Kozljanič, *Kunst und Mythos: Lebensphilosophische Untersuchungen zu Ernesto Grassis Begriff der Urwirklichkeit*, Oldenburg: Igel, 2001, pp. 63–73.

Notes   117

92 Cf. the following passage from *The Spirit as Adversary of the Soul*:

> That reality does not consist of things, does not need to be repeated; that it comes to appearance [*erscheint*], is certain; that there is something that comes to appearances in the appearances [*ein in den Erscheinungen Erscheinendes*], is no less certain; that there are vital powers [*lebendige Mächte*] that come to appearance cannot be dismissed in the case of plants, animals, and humans; then, however, there *must* also be vital powers that come to appearance in the suns, planets, moons.
>
> (*GWS=SW*, vol. 2, p. 1119)

93 'The behaviour [or character] of a human is his fate' – or his 'daimon' (*ethos anthropo daimon*) (DK 22 B 119). See the discussion of this passage by Heidegger in his *Letter on Humanism*, who translates it as 'the human is the habitation of the divine' (M. Heidegger, *Platons Lehre von der Wahrheit: Mit einem Brief über den 'Humanismus'* [1947], Berne and Munich: Francke, 1975, p. 109).

94 For discussion of the 'daimonic-mythological' world-view, particularly in relation to Goethe's conception of the daimonic, see K. Jaspers, *Psychologie der Weltanschauungen*, 5th edn, Berlin, Göttingen, Heidelberg: Springer-Verlag, 1960, pp. 191–203; W. M. Zucker, 'The Demonic: From Aeschylus to Tillich', *Theology Today* 26, no. 1, 1969, 34–50; H. B. Nisbet, '*Das Dämonische*: On the Logic of Goethe's Demonology', *Forum for Modern Language Studies* 7, 1971, 259–281; and A. Nicholls, *Goethe's Concept of the Daemonic: After the Ancients*, Rochester, NY: Camden House, 2006. For discussion in relation to Ernesto Grassi (1902–1991), Friedrich Nietzsche (1844–1900), and Arnold Böcklin (1827–1901) as well as to Klages himself, see R. J. Kozljanič, 'Böcklin und die daimonische Dimension der Natur', *Hestia: Jahrbuch der Klages-Gesellschaft* 19, 1998/1999, 104–128.

95 For further discussion, see Kozljanič, *Kunst und Mythos*, pp. 63–73.

96 In the *Symposium*, Socrates relates how Diotima had described the daimons to him as mediating between humankind and the gods:

> They are the envoys and interpreters that ply between heaven and earth, flying upward with our worship and our prayers, and descending with the heavenly answers and commandments, and since they are between the two estates they weld both sides together and merge them into one great whole.
>
> (202e)

One of these 'very powerful' spirits, 'halfway between god and man', is Eros (202d).

97 See R. Noll, *The Aryan Christ: The Secret Life of Carl Jung*, New York: Random House, 1997, p. xv, where this title is bestowed on the analytical psychologist, C. G. Jung.

98 See Plato, *The Laws*, Book 11, 914 b. For a discussion of the vexed question of the ancient Greek 'belief' in polytheism, see P. Veyne, *Les Grecs ont-ils cru à leurs mythes? Essai sur l'imagination constituante*, Paris: Seuil, 1983.

99 According to Wilamowitz-Moellendorff, 'the gods exist' (*Die Götter sind da*) (*Die Glaube der Hellen*, 2 vols, Darmstadt: Wissenschaftliche Buchgesellschaft, 1973, vol. 1, p. 17). For further discussion, see E. Flaig, 'Towards "*Rassenhygiene*": Wilamowitz and the German New Right', in I. Gildenhard and M. Ruehl (eds), *Out of Arcadia: Classics and Politics in Germany in the Age of Burckhardt, Nietzsche and Wilamowitz*, London: Institute of Classical Studies, 2003, pp. 105–127 (especially pp. 113 and 115–116).

100 See W. F. Otto, *Die Wirklichkeit der Götter: Von der Unzerstörbarkeit griechischer Weltsicht*, Reinbek bei Hamburg: Rowohlt, 1963, pp. 66 and 71.

101 M. Heidegger and E. Fink, *Heraclitus Seminar*, tr. C. H. Seibert, Evanston, IL: Northwestern University Press, 1993, p. 115. See also Heidegger's accounts of his

118　*Works and key ideas*

visits to Greece of 1962 and 1967, in Heidegger, *Zu Hölderlin; Griechenlandreisen* [*Gesamtausgabe*, vol. III, 75], ed. C. Ochwadt, Frankfurt am Main: Klostermann, 2000, pp. 211–273.

102 In fact, Klages's writings are steeped in references to Goethe; see, too, his essays 'Observations on the Limits of the Goethean Human Being' ('Bemerkungen über die Schranken des Goetheschen Menschen') (1917) (*Mensch und Erde*, pp. 62–75); and 'Goethe as Psychologist' ('Goethe als Seelenforscher') (1928) (*SW*, vol. 5, pp. 217–259; cf. *SW*, vol. 4, pp. 564–567). These studies should be contextualized and contrasted with contemporary psychoanalytic approaches to Goethe (too numerous to be listed here in detail), such as P. J. Möbius, *On the Pathological in Goethe* [1898], republished as *Über das Pathologische bei Goethe*, Munich: Matthes & Seitz, 1982; P. Sarasin, 'Goethes Mignon: Eine psychoanalytische Studie', *Imago: Zeitschrift für Anwendung der Psychoanalyse auf die Geisteswissenschaften* 15, 1929, 349–399; T. Reik, *Why Did Goethe Leave Friederike? A Psychoanalytic Monograph* (*Warum verließ Goethe Friederike? Eine psychoanalytische Monographie*, Vienna: Internationaler Psychoanalytischer Verlag, 1930). An investigation of the psychoanalytic approaches to Goethe in the late nineteenth and early twentieth centuries constitutes a major desideratum of scholarship on this central, if currently marginalized, figure of German culture.

103 See the chapter on Klages, entitled 'Pagan Gnosis', in M. Pauen, *Dithyrambiker des Untergangs: Gnostizismus in Ästhetik und Philosophie der Moderne*, Berlin: Akademie-Verlag, 1994, pp. 135–198 (esp. pp. 177–179).

104 *RR*, p. 261; compare with the following fragment from 1900: 'Poetry [*Dichten*] is a kind of ecstatic vivacity. The life of the poet is inner poeticizing [*inneres Dichten*]. Poetic experience [*Dichterisches Erlebnis*] is magical experience of language [*magisches Spracherlebnis*]' (*RR*, p. 243).

105 Pauen, *Dithyrambiker des Untergangs*, pp. 178–179. For further discussion, see P. Hadot, *Plotin ou la simplicité du regard*, Paris: Gallimard, 1997, pp. 48–69.

106 Plotinus, 'The Good or the One' (VI, 9 [9]), §4; in *The Essential Plotinus: Representative Treatises from the Enneads*, ed. and tr. E. O'Brien, Indianapolis, IN: Hackett, 1964, p. 78.

107 'The Good or the One', §4; *The Essential Plotinus*, p. 78.

108 'The Good or the One', §9; *The Essential Plotinus*, p. 85.

109 'The Good or the One', §10; *The Essential Plotinus*, p. 87.

110 Plotinus, 'On the Intelligible Beauty' (V, 8 [31]), §5; in Plotinus, *Ennead V*, tr. A. H. Armstrong, Cambridge, MA, and London: Harvard University Press, 1984, p. 255.

111 Plotinus, 'Beauty' (I, 6 [1]), §6; p. 251

112 For further discussion, see P. Hadot, ' "The Present Alone is our Joy": The Meaning of the Present Instant in Goethe and in Ancient Philosophy', *Diogenes* 133, 1986, 60–82.

113 Porphyry, *On the Life of Plotinus*, §23; in M. Edwards (tr.), *Neoplatonic Saints: The Lives of Plotinus and Proclus by their Students*, Liverpool: Liverpool University Press, 2000, p. 45.

114 Plotinus, 'On the Descent of the Soul into Bodies' (IV, 8 [6]), §1; in Plotinus, *Ennead IV*, tr. A. H. Armstrong, Cambridge, MA, and London: Harvard University Press, 1984, p. 397.

115 Compare with what Pausanias in Plato's *Symposium* says about the 'heavenly' Aphrodite (or Urania) and the 'earthly' Aphrodite (or Pandemos) (see *Symposium*, 180d-e; in *Collected Dialogues*, pp. 534-535).

116 See S. de Beauvoir, *The Second Sex* [1949], tr. H. M. Parshley, London: Vintage, 1997, pp. 107–122. In her famous paper, Toni Wolff (1888–1953) distinguishes between four types of the feminine, namely the Mother, the Medial Woman, the Amazon, and the Hetaira (T. Wolff, *Structural Forms of the Feminine Psyche* [1934; 1951], tr. P. Watzlawik, Zurich: Students Association, C. G. Jung Institute [privately

Notes 119

printed], 1956; also T. Wolff, 'Structural Forms of the Feminine Psyche' [tr. Gela Jacobson], *Psychological Perspectives: A Quarterly Journal of Jungian Thought*, 31, no. 1 (1995), 77–90.

117 Compare with Klages' distinction between *knowledge* and *recognition*, between truth and *veritas*. In 'Spirit and Life' (1934) Klages distinguishes between *knowing* (or *Erkennen*) in the sense of *intelligere, perspicere, percipere*, and *recognizing* (or *Wiedererkennen*) in the sense of *cognoscere, agnoscere*; and in regard to 'judgmental knowledge' (*urteilendes Erkennen*) or 'faculty of judgement' (*Urteilsvermögen*) he makes the following remark:

> Judgments are sometimes correct, sometimes wrong. Correct judgments are called truths, wrong ones errors. Aside from the logical use of 'truth' there is a poetic use, that derives from a past that thought in mythical terms. Of the numerous 'conceptual deities' of the Romans, it is, next to Justitia, especially Veritas that has remained alive.
>
> (*SW*, vol. 3, p. 568)

Or as he put it in *Of Cosmogonic Eros*, chapter 5: 'If conceptual language serves the communication of judgments, symbolic language serves the reawakening of intuitive vision [*Schauen*]; and if the concept forms the starting-point of scholarly or scientific research, the symbol forms the starting-point of myth' (*SW*, vol. 3, p. 428).

118 R. J. Hollingdale (ed. and tr.), *A Nietzsche Reader*, Harmondsworth: Penguin, 1977, pp. 266–267.

119 F. Nietzsche, *The Gay Science*, ed. and tr. Walter Kaufmann, New York: Vintage Books, 1974, p. 86.

120 See Kozljanič, *Lebensphilosophie*, chapters 2 (Friedrich Schlegel), 3 (Schopenhauer), 4 (C. G. Carus) and 5 (Nietzsche).

121 Or, in German, *Der Zweck des Lebens ist das Leben selbst* (Goethe, letter to Johann Heinrich Meyer of 8 February 1796; in Goethe, *Briefe*, ed. K. R. Mandelkow, 4 vols, Hamburg: Wegner, 1962–1967, vol. 3, p. 215).

3 For advanced readers – selections from Ludwig Klages

So far in our toolkit we have looked, in Chapter 1, at the life of Ludwig Klages and at the intellectual and cultural context to his work. Then, in Chapter 2, we looked at some of Klages's 'signature concepts', and considered some key passages from his writings where he presents them. Now, in Chapter 3, we offer a further selection of passages from Klages's works, based on a collection of excerpts made by Hans Kern, and expanded by Hans Kasdorff, originally published as *Vom Sinn des Lebens* (1940; 1943; revised 1982). The very title, *Of the Meaning of Life*, and even more its subtitle, *Worte des Wissens*='*Words of Wisdom*', may arouse some resistance among readers today. After all, how can one take seriously an idea which was used as the title for a Monty Python film?

Now it is true that Klages's literary style can sometimes seem almost Pythonesque in its baroque complexity and it often presents a problem for the modern reader. His syntax is usually convoluted, and his vocabulary is occasionally obscure to the point of incomprehensibility – to this extent, Klages serves as a reminder of the gulf between the levels of cultural knowledge and the sophistication of expression in nineteenth-century Germany and those of today. As one commentator has noted, Klages frequently uses philosophical words in a specific technical sense, without making it clear that this is what he is doing; and he is a great creator of neologisms.[1] Amid all this, something else should become clear: as well as operating on an abstract argumentational level, Klages's theories are informed by an experiential dimension which is just as important as their theoretical one.

In a way, the convolutions, oppositions, and other rhetorical strategies of Klages's writings re-enact on a textual the kind of vertiginous experiences which feeds his argumentation. And consequently, we should remain alert to the possibility that there is a concrete dimension of applicability of what Klages is trying to argue within our everyday life and experience. For this reason, we should regard the notion of 'wisdom' not just in its immediate contemporary cultural context for Klages – I am thinking, for example, of the so-called 'School of Wisdom', founded in Darmstadt in the 1920s by Count Hermann von Keyserling (1880–1946). Rather, we should think of wisdom in the same way as Klages himself does when, in his treatise on education, he lists important qualities for any educator: they are *truthfulness, courage, moderation, and wisdom*.[2] From the

Life 121

perspective of a vitalist ethics, which still remains to be fully worked out, if one is truthful, courageous, and moderate, then one is wise. And if one is all these things, then one is really alive. Or, in the words of Goethe, 'the point of life is life'. And it is with the topic of life that this collection of extracts begins.

Life: what could be more vital?

The category of life is obviously the most important for thinkers in the tradition of vitalism (or, in German, *Lebensphilosophie*). In this passage, Klages draws attention to the dimension of feeling (*Fühlen*) in our experience of what it means to be alive. In contrast to other philosophical traditions (such as the Platonic or the Cartesian) he highlights feeling as a primary in tool in understanding ourselves and the world. By 'feeling', Klages does not mean something simplistically irrational; rather, he means (as he explains in *Consciousness and Life*) a profound engagement with the world which draws on all our intellectual and physiological resources:

> Life is not perceived, but it is *felt* [*gefühlt*] with a strength that obscures everything. And we need only reflect on this feeling to become aware, with a certainty beyond which there can be none more certain, of the reality of being alive [*Lebendigseins*]. Whether we judge, think, will or wish, dream, phantasize, all of these are sustained and shot through by one and the same torrent of an elementary feeling of life [*Lebensgefühls*], which can be compared to nothing, traced back to nothing, that cannot be thought through and analysed, and also of course never 'understood'. And because we feel ourselves as being alive, what is vital meets us in the image of the world. Expressed in a short formula: we experience our own life and, in it, we also experience the other life [*das fremde Leben*]. From this it follows that we can know about life exactly only insofar as we, ourselves alive, submerge sufficiently deeply into it in order to preserve and secure a recollection [*Erinnerung*] of it for waking consciousness.
>
> (*SW* 3, 653)

Klages is not alone in emphasizing that consciousness and ego are two entirely separate concepts. For instance, Nietzsche tells us that

> a thought comes when 'it' wishes, and not when 'I' wish, so that it is a falsification of the facts of the case to say that the subject 'I' is the condition of the predicate 'think'. It thinks; but that this 'it' is precisely the famous old 'ego' is, to put it mildly, only a supposition, an assertion, and assuredly not an 'immediate certainty'.
>
> (*Beyond Good and Evil*, §17)

And before Nietzsche, Lichtenberg had argued against the same Cartesian proposition:

122 *Selections from Klages*

We become conscious of certain representations that are not dependent upon us; others believe that at least we are dependent upon ourselves; where is the border line? We know only the existence of our sensations, representations, and thoughts. One should say, *it thinks*, just as one says, *it lightens*. It is already saying too much to say *cogito*, as soon as one translates it as *I think*. To assume the *I*, to postulate it, is a practical requirement.[3]

Klages is certainly in line with this anti-Cartesian tradition when he argues:

Whenever we will or think, then we say: *I* think, I will, I do, and we emphasize the ego all the more categorically, the more emphatically we are thinking or willing. Yet whenever we experience something great in a feeling [*fühlend*] way, it strikes us as feeble and insubstantial to say: I felt the following; and instead we say: *it* has taken hold of me, shaken me, enthralled me, overpowered me, enraptured me! What is that enraptures us? Life! And what is enraptured? The ego!

(*SW* 3, 392)

In other words, the experience of life is a precognitive one. The means by which we are enchanted and enraptured by life is not the ego; rather, it is what Klages, as he explains in *Of Cosmogonic Eros*, calls the 'soul' (*Seele*):

To be alive [*Lebendigsein*] means to be able to experience, and to be able to experience demands an experiencing *soul*.

(*SW* 3, 273)

In this passage (from *Of Cosmogonic Eros*) Klages contrasts mere physical existence with a more intense quality of experience he calls life. Even if someone dies young (and throughout this toolkit, inclusive language is used to indicate both genders, unless this is expressly not the case), he or she is still able to participate in the quality of life that Klages describes the 'moment of eternity':

Some people are born old, and even if they *exist* for nearly ninety years, it may be that they have not *lived* for even two minutes. But anyone who dies young does not, on this account, lose the moment of eternity [*Ewigkeitsaugenblick*] to which he or she was divinely blessed to be privy!

(*SW* 3, 396)

The notion that the world is a living being is an ancient one, associated with the pre-Socratic philosopher Anaxagoras. In one of his maxims and reflections (Hecker, #134), Goethe refers to the view that 'the rational world is to be considered as a great immortal individual, that incessantly brings about the necessary and thereby masters even chance'. And in aphorism 109 of *The Gay Science*, Nietzsche warns his readers: 'Let us beware of thinking that the world

Life   123

is a living being'.[4] Even more radically than Goethe and Nietzsche before him, Klages argues that the question of whether the world is a living being is not even worth thinking about. (Getting our philosophical priorities straight is an important part of the project of vitalism.) Instead, in this passage (from *Humankind and Earth*), Klages paints a powerful picture of the totality of the universe as a natural harmony, in which everything natural – but also human culture – has its place:

> We do not need to decide whether life extends or not beyond the world of individual beings; whether the earth is, as the belief of the ancients maintained, a living being or instead (according to the view of the moderns) an unfeeling clump of 'dead matter'; for this much is sure: that terrain, cloud formations, stretches of water, the exteriors of plants, and the activity of animals together form out of every landscape a profoundly moving whole, which embraces the individual organism as if in an ark, weaving it into the great action of the universe. Like so many indispensable chords in the melodic storm of the planet there are the sublime desolateness of the desert, the solemnity of the Alps, the aching melancholy of broad heathland, the mysterious tapestry of the high forest, the pulsing of lightning-covered stretches of coast. In them are embedded or are fused as in a dream the primordial works of humankind. Whether we turn our gaze to the admonishing profundity of the pyramids, the rows of sphinxes, the lotus-topped pillars of Egypt, to the illusory delicacy of Chinese bell towers, the structured clarity of Greek temples, or to the warm domesticity of a North German farmhouse, the freedom of the steppes of a Tatar tent – each of them breathes and reveals the soul of the landscape from which they arose. Just as earlier peoples liked to describe themselves as having sprung from the earth, so everything they created has sprung from the earth in shape and colour, from their dwellings to their weapons and household utensils, their daggers, spears, arrows, axes, swords, their chains, clasps, and rings, their formally beautiful and richly decorated vessels, their pumpkin bowls and copper dishes, their thousandfold wickerwork and fabrics.
>
> (*SW* 3, 619)

How do we know about the universe? For Klages, human culture in its most profound forms talks only about life, although we have forgotten (as he tells us in *Humankind and Earth*) how to listen to the songs of the past:

> Weddings and funeral ceremonies, revenge, war, and downfall, the high-spiritedness of a drinker and the desire of a traveller, the boldness of a horseman, the instinct of a child, and the wish to be a mother – these breathed and flowed in inexhaustible songs, sometimes spurring listeners on to fierce deeds, sometimes lulling them into the slumber of forgetting. People wrote poetry and sang when dancing, when drinking deeply, when

124   *Selections from Klages*

taking leave and returning, in uttering words of consecration or magic spells, in the half-light of the weaving rooms, before a battle, at the bier of the fallen, people used to bestir themselves with satirical songs, fought out disputes in song contests, wove light and dark shades of poetry around mountains, springs and shrubs, domestic animals, wild animals and plants, the passing of clouds and downpours of rain. And – something which today it is almost impossible for us to understand – even work became a celebration. Not only when on the road and at festive banquets, people also used to sing at the winding-in of the anchor and to the rhythm of the oar strokes, when carrying heavy burdens and when towing ships upstream, when putting barrels together, to the measure of the ironsmith's hammer, when sowing seed, when reaping, threshing, and grinding corn, when breaking flax, weaving, and braiding.

(*SW* 3, 622)

Klages's vitalist approach does not begin with individual living organisms and work up or out to life in the universe as a whole. Rather, it posits a cosmic life – where else could individual life have come from? – as its starting-point, and it considers (here, in a passage from *Foundation of the Science of Expression*) the degree to which this vitality is maintained, dispersed or enhanced in each individual case:

If one knows that vital processes are experiential processes, then one also knows that living substance cannot originate from non-living substance, and one will no longer resist the only possible assumption that a vitality, albeit of its own kind, must be attributed to non-organic process-carriers [*Vorgangsträgern*]. If life as such were not cosmic life, there would be neither the living cell nor growth nor reproduction. If, in this way, the individual living being lives only as the transient carrier [*Träger*] of cosmic life, then the degree of its vital intensity is measured according to the degree of its mental capacity for *life itself* or, in other words, according to whether and to what extent it is, in the here and now, able to interpret what happens in the universe; or finally, expressed in relation to a possible lack of intensity, according to the respective degree of *individuation* of life. According to this universal gradation, unequal value accrues to different human beings (including their achievements), different animals, trees, crystals, landscapes, and so on.

(*SW* 3, 623)

The notion of the 'struggle for existence' is a key proposition of Darwin's theory of natural selection and a commonplace of our post-Darwinian world, but it is one that is rejected outright by Klages. Although the individual matters little in the cosmic economy of life, the wholesale extermination of species, such as those witnessed on our planet at the moment, is – in his view – something entirely unnatural. Here (in a passage from *Humankind and Earth*) as elsewhere, we see how closely for Klages ecological concerns and metaphysical speculation belong together:

> Nature knows no 'struggle for existence', but only the one arising from care for life. Such little weight is placed by Nature on survival that many insects die after the act of procreation, as long as the tide of life sweeps on in similar forms.[5] What makes one animal hunt and kill another is the need of hunger, not acquisitive desire, ambition, lust for power. Here lies a yawning abyss, which no logic of development will ever be able to bridge. Never have species been exterminated by others, for every excess on the side of one party is immediately followed by a set-back, as a larger removal of a prey means its enemy's food runs out; indeed, their alternation took place across giant stretches of time for planetary reasons and caused a constant increase of intermediate forms. The extermination of hundreds of species across a few human generations cannot be compared with the dying out, for example, of the dinosaurs or the mammoths. – The transference of human physical laws, such as those of the preservation of energy, onto questions of life is entirely bereft of intellect. Never yet has the retort brought forth a living cell and, if it were to do so, then it would not happen through a combination of 'powers', but because even chemical substances already harbour life. Life is a form capable of constant renewal; if, by exterminating a species, we extinguish that renewal, then the earth is for all time impoverished by this, notwithstanding the so-called preservation of energy.
> (*SW* 3, 624)

While rejecting the Anaxagorian notion that the world is a living organism, Klages argues that the entirety of the cosmos is, in fact, alive. Here (in *Of Cosmogonic Eros*) he introduces the idea of the Pelasgian trinity of two separate poles and the unity the form, the Pelasgians being the name used by ancient writers to refer to the population that constituted the ancestors of the ancient Greeks. Throughout Klages's writing we find this kind of triple formula consisting of the following triangle:

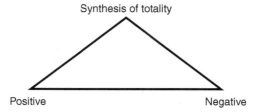

The cosmos is alive, and all life is polarized into soul (psychae) and body (soma). Wherever there is living body, there is soul; wherever soul, there is living body. The soul is the sense of the body, the image of the body is the appearance of the soul. Whatever appears, that has a sense; and every

126 *Selections from Klages*

sense reveals itself as it appears. Sense is experienced internally, appearance externally. The former must become image if it is to be communicated, and the image must become internal again, for it to be effective. Those are, expressed unmetaphorically, the poles of reality. – If we, judging and thinking, were to consider the world from outside, then it would everywhere display to us the Pelasgian trinity of the separated poles in the unity of the whole. Space is the body of time, time is the soul of space. The day is the soul and the sense of night, the night is the womb of light. Winter and summer, sleeping and waking, dying and coming into being form a line. The feminine is the body and mother of the soul, the masculine is the revealed and revealing sense of the womb of the mother. Blood and nerves, solar plexus and brain, 'heart' and 'head', mouth and eye, left and right stand in the same relation. If one separates each of these items from the other, then the world is destroyed.

(SW 3, 390)

Nevertheless, Klages's view of the universe as a harmonious whole – or, rather, as a whole in which even dissonance has its place – is no comfortable, complacent New Age fluff. Instead, Klages is a tragic thinker, and our human tragedies are as nothing compared to the tragedy which is the whole of reality, as he explains in *Humankind and Earth*:

Stronger, greater, deeper than all merely human tragedy is the tragedy of reality itself, according to which the following belong inseparably together: the perfection of *life* in the form of exuberant beauty, its flaming up in intoxicating bliss, its image-producing torrent and in the inexorable *fate* on which all life inevitably founders. After its pleasurable lusts have sounded their flute, there finally follows eternal silence.

(Mensch und Erde, 180)

Yet while Klages's thought is tragic, it is not defeatist; in fact, the ability to recognize the reality of the negative while committing oneself to the positive is what constitutes the core of tragedy. Here (in *The Spirit as Adversary of the Soul*) Klages cites a celebrated line by the German classical writer Friedrich Schiller, which reveals a metaphysical dimension to military activity. Yet Klages is patently not advocating war; what he is doing is trying to understand that most difficult of concepts, sacrifice:[6]

Let us turn [...] and consider the ecstatic exuberance of surrender, by thinking, for instance, of the blood sacrifice made by a soldier in a war, the preferred form of sacrifice of heroic peoples, as Schiller expresses it in the immortal lines from his 'Rider's Song', 'For if your own life you're not willing to stake, / That life will never be yours to make.'[7] Then it will become completely clear to us why all the greatness and depth and breadth of life would disappear along with the tragedy of life; and why fulfilment can only lie in

The symphony of the rhythms 127

defeat, and why the guarantee of their eternity lies in the death of the divine images.

(*SW* 2, 1410)

The symphony of the rhythms: living to the beat

One of the key differences in Klagesian thought is that between (mechanical) beat and (organic, vital) rhythm. Whereas the mechanical beat involves the notion of a repetition of the identical, rhythm involves something much more interesting – similarity.[8] In *Expressive Movement and Formative Power* Klages contrasts rhythm, as a vital phenomenal form, to a tact or a beat as a mathematical structuring of what happens, drawing on an image used by Nietzsche, which itself derives from Voltaire, to make his point:

> A perfect piece of prose has perfect rhythm, but certainly not a beat. Nietzsche on one occasion finds an image for this contrast with the brilliant remark, that to write poetry means 'to dance in chains':[9] here the dance would be the rhythm of linguistic movement, the chain the metre! Many a disciple of music as an art-form begins to sharpen his or her sense of a beat with the help of a metronome; but anything that is learned in this way he or she will later have to try to *un*learn to avoid his or her playing being 'mechanical', soulless, dead! Rhythmically, is how *life* expresses itself and appears; in a beat, by contrast, the *spirit* forces the rhythmic vital pulse into its own law. The spatial regulation of a construction derives from the same source as its temporal regulation, to which one usually restricts the concept of the beat. 'Tact', from *tangere*=to hit, refers to a beat that follows in time-periods that are always identical, which each time *interrupts* the rhythmical process and subordinates the inconstancy of a *series* to its constant rising and falling. Just as the sequence of beat measures forms a temporal series, so the sequence of, for instance, the measurement marks on a tape-measure forms a temporal row, and just as the latter serves the almost mathematically precise repetition of spatial distances, so the former serves the similarly precise repetition of periods of time.

(*SW* 6, 262)

Picking up on the contrast between rhythm and beat, so important for his thinking about vitalism and aesthetics, in this passage (from *The Spirit as Adversary of the Soul*) Klages uncovers the 'essential similarities' between all forms of life (mineral, vegetable, mineral) – and even between the individual and the cosmic:

> Anyone who investigates with thought the great symphony of rhythms will, sooner or later, find himself or herself obliged to consider organic and cosmic processes as polar opposite forms of a rhythmic whole which correspondingly *lives*, even if supra-organically. After all, at least our earth stands under the sign of continuous pulsing! Think of the rhythmical (never

128 *Selections from Klages*

regular!) periods of time when the snow melts, of the annual rhythm of the rising and falling of the rivers, of the daily rhythm of the quantities of water every hour which any spring provides, of the rhythmical return of the rainy season in the tropics, of the periodic fluctuations in the level of ground water, of the daily periods of air pressure, temperature, moisture, electric conductivity, of the daily, annual, and secular rhythms of magnetic declination and inclination, of the monthly, bi-annual, and annual periodicity of the Northern Lights, of the periodic fluctuating of the doldrums, and so on. If one investigates the rhythms of *forms*, it would be impossible to overlook that the rhythmic (never regular!) wave of water shapes as it were the mould for a large number of telluric formations. We recall the ossified waves of dunes and wandering dunes, the so-called crescentic or transverse dunes (barchans) in the middle of continental deserts, the wavelet-like ordered wispy or fleecy clouds, the wave-shaped forms finally even of hills and mountains. – The type of plant form returns in the structural layers of animals as well as in the face of the earth. Who has not noticed the similarity between the rhythmic branching of a tree and every larger river network or the tree-like ramification of human nerve fibres! After all, it is not by chance, but under the compulsion of elementary similarities, that one calls the bush-like structures at the edge of central ganglion cells, which serve to pass the neuronal stimuli to the neighbouring ganglion, 'dendrites' = little trees [cf. Greek, δένδρον, 'tree']!

(*SW* 2, 827)

This distinction between a rhythm and a beat is important in itself, but it also provides Klages with another basis for explaining one of most difficult notions, the idea of the image (*Bild*). As (in *Foundations of the Science of Expression*) he offers this explanation, however, we can also see the phenomenological precision which underlies, not just Klages's argumentation, but his view of the world:

Every song has its rhythm and its beat. Perhaps these two had first to be confused with each other in order for us then to learn to distinguish strictly between them. Although in verse and in song they appear to form an alliance like a pair of dancers, in terms of essence and origin they are opposites, which of all creatures only the human being has, not without violence, woven together. What is rhythmic is the beating of the wings of migrating birds as they set off, the trotting of as yet untamed horses, the wave-like gliding of fish; but to run, to fly, to swim in accordance with a beat is something animals can do just as little as we could manage to breathe in accordance with a beat. Steam engines, drop-hammers, pendulum clocks function to a beat, but not in a rhythm; a piece of perfect prose has a perfect rhythm, but certainly not a beat. Life expresses and manifests itself in rhythms; by contrast, in a beat the spirit compels the rhythmic life-pulse to submit to its own peculiar law. The spatial regulation of a picture derives from the same source as the temporal regulation to which one usually limits the concept of

The symphony of the rhythms 129

a beat. Just as a sequence of beat-measures forms a temporal series, so the sequence of, for instance, dividing lines on a measuring tape forms a spatial series, and just as the latter allows for an almost mathematically precise repetition of spatial distances, so the former allows for a similarly precise repetition of period of time. What could, on the other hand, rhythm actually be?

The name 'rhythm', from *rheein*=to flow, reveals to us first of all a constancy that can appear with particular beauty in a wave of water. Its incessant alternation of peak and trough takes place without break, leap, or gap from an indivisible, gradual change between two limiting states. And thus a second characteristic of rhythm becomes immediately apparent: to bring back in always similar periods of time something only ever similar. No wave of water has precisely the same shape and duration as the previous one, no breath and pulse exactly the same length as the following one, no left side of a leaf, an animal, or a human being exactly mirrors the right side. – Yet if, moreover, the inevitable involvement of vital processes in every human action excludes the creation of two measuring roles of mathematically precisely identical lengths or of two mathematically precisely synchronized clocks, this should not serve to blur the difference between mechanical and living objects. For the differences in size between mechanical copies can only be established with the aid of special tools and using scientific techniques of comparison, compared to which the differences in size in rhythmical recurrence are noticeable and are, as a result, a constituent of the immediate impression. This is what is characteristic about a rhythmic structure: that within a border area, beyond which the disruption of the rhythm would begin, the deviation from the rule is subject to a constant variation in size, which defies any attempt at calculation. The rhythmic superiority of ancient and medieval quarry stone constructions over those in the modern age resides not only in the higher perfection of so-called style but, as did not escape thoughtful architects, pre-eminently in the way one avoided building with stones of exactly the same size cut in a factory, and in this way brought the wall surfaces alive with a fascinating diversity of noticeably different joint lines.

In our enumeration of rhythmical characteristics of vital phenomena we have deliberately passed over the most important one: we are thinking of the so-called capacity for reproduction. Accordingly, each organism alive today is related to the very first protoplasma that came into being on the earth millions of years ago. But what constitutes the point of connection, since individual organisms live separated from one another and are alive for themselves? – A beech-nut falls from a beech-tree and grows on the forest floor into a new tree. Does the maternal beech-tree still live on in the offspring beech-tree? Certainly not! The former we can fell and burn, the latter will happily carry on growing. Or is there something of the material element from the old in the rejuvenated beech-tree? Equally, there is not! For the fully-grown young tree no longer contains even a single atom of the

130   *Selections from Klages*

material element of the fruit from which it grew! If, however, in the new individual neither the old individual nor its matter remains, then *what* is it actually that uninterruptedly *persists* through thousands and thousands of generations? The answer is: an *image*. The image of the oak, the image of the pinetree, the image of the fish, the image of the dog, the image of the human being recurs in every single individual carrier of the species. 'Reproduction' means the physically eternally inaccessible process of the handing-on of the primordial image of the species from place to place and from time to time. The nomadic image is a *self-transforming* image, and our capacity for recognizing the genus in each individual carrier together with the ability to name it accordingly, is found in turn in the experience of *similarity*. The youth is not the same as, but similar to, the man; the child is not the same as, but similar to, its parents; every genus is not the same as, but similar to, the kind of phylum from which it derives, for the species arise and disappear no less than do their individual carriers, only over much longer periods of time. Reproduction is a recurrence of *similar* images within *similar* spans of time; whereby the proof is concluded that rhythm is the primordial appearance of life.

(*SW* 6, 626–628)

Whereas a beat relies on the repetition of something identical, the case of a rhythm involves something more supple, more fluid, more difficult to determine. In fact, it is impossible to define the variation in measurable or conceptual terms, Klages maintains. In *On the Essence of Rhythm*, he assimilates this view to the outlook of the poets, mentioning one in particular: Wilhelm Jordan (1819–1904), one of Klages's favourite writers.

If rhythm consists in the alternation of coming and going, it cannot consist in duration, and if what is coming is supposed to be something renewed, it should not be a repetition of something that has already been! 'Repetition' means that something is or takes place once again which – just previously or at some other time – was or *has* taken place; as a result, insofar as we comprehend a temporal succession or a spatial arrangement as *being identical* in relation to its members, we precisely do *not* compehend the means by which the change would appear in the context of the rhythmical alternation. Thanks to the profundity of their experience, poets have always *known* this and frequently proclaimed it, for the most part unconcerned about the concept of what they know, but sometimes drawing on what they have already conceptualized. Whenever one of them paints for us the picture of the world in such a way – as does, for instance, *Jordan* in these lines, apparently simple yet wonderfully beautiful:

And so shows
This world
Only what rises
Or falls…[10]

The symphony of the rhythms 131

– it is a picture *not* of existence and duration, but one of the inexorable alternation of two Dioscuri-like, mutually bound ways of happening.[11]

(*SW* 3, 538)

In *The Spirit as Adversary of the Soul*, an example of how we live in a rhythmic, not a mechanical, way is provided for Klages by the ancient practice of dancing. In the dance, an individual loses herself or himself, yet paradoxically finds herself or himself through becoming unified and as one with the rhythm of the universe:

> We have only to reflect on the *dance* – understood in its widest meaning of rhythmic movements of the body that occur in accord with the beat either of a melody or even of just noises – to recognize that the essence of the profound pleasure in it – which, among primitive human beings, grows into a drunkenness of the soul – resides in the fact that the occasionally extremely changeable wealth of dynamic individual movements is, thanks to a powerful sense of emotional turmoil, ever increasingly carried away (and, in the final instance, entirely swallowed) by the (in its own turn) aimless pathic state of *being* moved or, as it were, by the passage of a wave rolling through the soul. So the more the dancer is granted the grace of becoming completely absorbed in the dance, the more it is not about movements, not about a change of locations and a measuring of line segments, but about the will-less, indeed almost impulse-less, *resonance* in the element of a wave-creating motion, which henceforth experiences and, *while* it is experiencing, at the same time is 'worked and woven'. In the rhythmically perfect dance something reaches its consummation as a primordial unique experience which, in the meantime, is experienced only at the sight of falling leaves, passing clouds, or the surge of ocean waves: the sense of being carried away by the *stream* of things in action, and this to such a degree that it even *takes into itself* the individual movement in a direction *away* from one location *toward* another; in this way tangibly revealing to us, in our own body, the dependency of the dynamic of 'working and weaving' among the elements.

(*SW* 2, 1054)

What rhythm reveals is a different quality of perception about a different dimension of existence, one that eludes the mechanistic-causal approach of materialistic science. Here, in an extract from *On the Essence of Rhythm*, and in the form of an allusion to the great German mystic theologian Jakob Böhme (1575–1624), Klages comes close to suggesting that this kind of philosophical apprehension is similar to mystical intuition:

> If reality is a reality of things happening, then the spatial dimension of phenomena does not escape unceasing transformation, and in the cosmos, which is said to be alive, the spatial pole of the images would be related to their temporal pole as the soul is to the body. The space of

132 *Selections from Klages*

reality would be the body of the time of reality, and time would be the soul of space. But if the soul appears in an unlimited way in rhythm, then the alternation of coming and going, which became for us the essential key to rhythm, would be characteristic of temporality, and, however mythological it might sound to the physicist, who knows only measuring equipment and the linearly sequential second, the deepest level of the meaning of rhythm would lie in the *pulsating passage of real time*. The individual soul, if it were to resonate in rhythm, would – even if only for the shortest moment – become one with what unites both poles of an event, with the *eternity* of dying and becoming. Perhaps the mystic had something similar in mind when he wrote these verses:

> For whom time is like eternity
> And eternity is like time,
> He is free
> Of all adversity.[12]

(SW 3, 551)

For Klages, life takes place in the play between two opposites: a play that is based on similarity (and hence rhythm) and not identity (like a mechanical beat). Yet there are two opposites which do not fit this schema, even as they define it – the opposites of being born and dying, which (in *The Spirit as the Adversary of the Soul*) he describes in a technical sense as 'catastrophes' (that is, 'overturnings' or 'sudden turns', as the etymological root of the word suggests):

Just as it is certain for us that 'eternity' can be 'like time', because every arriving moment is another and different from all those that have gone before, so it is certain that 'time' can be 'like eternity', because this moment is similar to those that have come and gone. For the sake of similarity, which appears together with difference, we experience coming and going in the fleeting nature of the images, and from the fullness of vision we *can* experience, in the alternation of both [coming and going], the eternity of the self-renewal of the world. However, *this* going and coming is a *cosmic* state of affairs, which may become tangible for us in the alternation of the seasons of the year, in the phases of the moon, in the starry firmament itself, in the alternation of night and day, of ebb and flood, in the periodic growth of vegetation and sometimes even of an individual plant, finally in many a periodic change in one's own body and in the alternation of one's own soul's moods. But although such a sinking and rising, declining and increasing, growing dark and growing light again, comparable to the image of the rhythmic breaking of waves, is in some sense *similar*, although extremely distant, it resolutely resists in other characteristics the alternation of dying and being born, resisting them all the more as the being which is subjected to this alternation

The symphony of the rhythms   133

carries within itself the centre of its vital existence. – For to the extent that this is the case, dying and being born are *catastrophes*, very different from the withering and germination of a plant, almost incomparably different from the waning and waxing of the moon. And there is more: dying is no longer the kind of ending that would be followed by a new beginning, but an ending of the very world itself without which the vital centre of a mortal being cannot or can never be experienced. Ancient songs lament this: spring will return again and along with it, in virginal freshness, an abundance of flowers that had disappeared in autumn, but a human being, when dead, never returns.

(*SW* 2, 1412)

Accordingly, in *The Spirit as Adversary of the Soul*, Klages discerns a 'natural law' in the reciprocal relation between birth and death, manifesting itself in the process of passing away and being renewed:

Not being born and not dying, not being alive and not being dead, but the reciprocal relationship that underlies them demands the assumption as a common third element of the necessity – as it were, a natural law –, according to which whatever is living in the present must forever return to the past, and what has previously been must forever be constantly renewed.

(*SW* 2, 1328)

As evidence of this natural law, Klages turns in the final pages of *The Spirit as Adversary of the Soul* to the great Mystery religions of antiquity and, in particular, to the Mysteries of Eleusis. In ancient times, corn was 'symbolic of Nature as a source of nutrition for plant, animal, and human life, nourishing all things from herself'.[13] In the case of the Eleusinan Mysteries, the ear of corn had a particular symbolic association: 'The Greater Mysteries ... were sacred to Ceres, the mother of Persephone, and represent her as wandering through the world in search of her daughter. Ceres carried two torches, intuition and reason, to aid her in the search for her lost child (the soul). At last she found Persephone not far from Eleusis, and out of gratitude taught the people there to cultivate corn, which is sacred to her. She also founded the Mysteries' (p. 70).

As the Neoplatonist commentator Thomas Taylor (1758–1835) remarked, while the Lesser Mysteries 'occultly signified the miseries of the soul while in subjection to body', by contrast the Greater Mysteries 'obscurely intimated, by mystic and splendid visions, the felicity of the soul' – i.e. the soul in a Neoplatonic, not a Klagesian, sense – 'both here and hereafter, when purified from the defilements of a material nature, and constantly elevated to the realities of intellectual [spiritual] vision' (pp. 70–71):[14]

The harvested ear of corn was the symbol of perfection among the Eleusinians. What can it have been that could be *revealed* to the illuminated sense

134 *Selections from Klages*

of the initiate in the moment of the completed consecration ceremony (irrespective of whether afterward his understanding interpreted it correctly or falsely)? Certainly it was not the immortality of 'his' body, of 'his' soul, or any thing or any other being that he would have been able to call 'his own'; for, by contrast, it would have become clear to him, if he had previously been in any doubt, that such things will without exception irrevocably disappear. For this ear of corn will definitely wilt and die; indeed, as grown *up* and gathered *in*, it *is* already doomed to decline: a painful emblem of that state of having been, back into which everything in the present is destined inexorably to sink. Yet out of the transitoriness of this ear of corn and, in fact, reaffirmed by it there arises, shining and *deathless*, the *primordial image* of the ear of corn; a symbol of the eternity of the living renewal of each vital form in the womb of the Mater!

(*SW* 2, 1412)

The reality of images: what's real is what works

Klages's philosophy has the reputation for being complex, and it is. Yet its essence is summarized by just two short lines, found in *On the Essence of Consciousness*, which are replete with all kinds of significance (metaphysical, existential, and aesthetic). It plays on two different meaings of the German word, *Sinn*: *die Sinne*, meaning 'the senses', and *der Sinn*, which means 'meaning', but also with the implication of mind (as in the famous poem by Heinrich Heine: 'Ich weiß nicht, was soll es bedeuten', which includes the line, 'Das kommt mir nicht aus dem Sinn', i.e. I can't get it out of my mind). The first line of this couplet by Klages was chosen by Hans Eggert Schröder as the title for his short book containing a collection of anecdotes about Ludwig Klages:

The image that falls into the senses,
That and nothing else is the sense of the world.

(*SW* 3, 279; cf. *RR*, p. 280)

For Klages, the effect of the image (*Bild*) is one of the most powerful experiences, if not the most powerful experience, one can have. This emphasis on the experiential dimension is crucial to understanding his thought, and it is telling that, once again, Klages seeks (in *The Spirit as Adversary of the Soul*) an analogue for what he is talking about in the ancient discourse of the Mysteries, specifically the experience of ecstasy (literally, being 'outside oneself'):[15]

Whether one thinks as a 'nature enthusiast' of the enigmatic 'mood' of lonely landscapes; or, as a daytime person, of a mortal danger, a conflagration, a shipwreck; or, as an art lover, of the decisive shudder with which one's favourite work of art bowled one over; or, as a spectator of life, of extinguished passions, hours of hopeless abandonment, the earliest playful instincts of childhood; or, as a 'mystic', of the most perplexing dream, whether it be full of cruel anxieties or full of melting bliss; or, as a scientific researcher, of intensive searching and liberating discovery; or, as a man of deeds, of the most audacious plans and despair in the moment of sudden failure: what turned each of these individual 'events' [*Erfahrung*] into a real 'experience' [*Erlebnis*], because into a passion [*Erleidnis*], of the soul, was the force of an image, and it was *not* the violence, but rather the *profundity*, of the feelings that corresponded in the closest possible way to the degree in which the image was able either to dissolve or to smash the *limit* of the soul which is called personal ego. If such a delimitation of the ego becomes complete destruction of the ego, then its carrier [*Träger*] has experienced what the ancients called ecstasy and in which they rightly saw the imme-diate precondition for perfection (*teletae*),[16] more precisely the *end* lying beyond not just 'pleasure' and 'pain', but even beyond horror and bliss, in comparison with which *feelings* are always only 'on the way'.

(*SW* 2, 1254)

For Klages, the experience of ecstasy – which one could gloss as 'rapture, beauty, adoration, wonder, awe, mystery, sense of the unknown, desire for the unknown'[17] – is a key philosophical moment (to this extent, Klages would disagree with E. M. Cioran's statement that an orgasm is never a philosophical event...):[18]

Whereas every non-human living being, even if separated and having its own interiority, pulses in the *rhythm* of cosmic life, the human being has been detached from this by the *law* of the spirit. Whatever appears to him or her as the carrier of ego-consciousness in the light of calculating thought's superi-ority over the world, will appear to the metaphysician, if he penetrates deeply enough into it, in the light of an enslavement of life under the yoke of con-cepts! To free life from it again, both in respect of the soul *and* of the body, is the secret inclination of all mystics and narcotists, whether they know it or fail to recognize it; and this inclination is fulfilled in ecstasy. [...] That only human beings possess an ego-consciousness and necessarily so from participarting in the spirit that is always one and the same, is something several eminent modern thinkers have advocated. [...] If ecstasy is removing the spirit from the soul, then it *must* also be: removing the self from the soul. This is com-pellingly confirmed for us by, among other things, language and, above all, the German language. Literally translated, ecstasy does not mean 'to be carried away', but 'to be outside oneself' (=outside the ego). Drunken or intoxicated individuals, whether through enthusiasm or as a consequence of narcotics, no longer 'feel right in themselves', but are 'out of it'; are in danger of 'forgetting themselves'; and, when sober, 'come to themselves again'.[...]

(*SW* 3, 391–392)

In *Of Cosmogonic Eros* Klages develops a subtle phenomenological analysis of ecstatic experience, differentiating its various aspects while emphasizing the visual, or even the aesthetic, aspect common to all manifestations of the ecstatic:

136   *Selections from Klages*

There are three characteristics which, for all the massive differences, always recur in the primordial experience of great ecstatics: the (apparent or real) transportation of the soul to distant places, or even to 'another world' – a lack of sensitivity to painful impressions, which is expressed as being immune to wounds – and a receptivity to life-determining revelations. Only the third is involved for us in answering the question of how the experience is constituted whose value of certainty overwhelms the persuasive power of all profane truths. [...] And we come across first of all in initiatory societies the following recurrent fact of the matter: mystical certainity derives from the experience of the 'epopteia', i.e. in the *visionary intuition*[19] – the visionary intuition relates to the *appearance of the deity* (epiphany, parousia) – and this in turn takes place on the occasion of the symbolic representation of his death with the subsequent rebirth out of a '*sacred marriage*'. To anticipate the final conclusion: the initiate experiences the consecration of the fulfilment as he, himself deified, is wed to a god (communion, *unio mystica, hierosgamos*),[20] and he unites himself with him as he sees him. [...] The initiatory rites are something regulated, something set down by a human founder, which is said to interlink the generations of many into a living community and to take from the rhythm of the universe the power to loosen once more the compulsory formations in which the spirit seeks to alienate those bound to it from life. However, the experience, the renewal of which aims to unburden them – primordial ecstasy – once supported *all* the works of humankind in the era of the Pelasgians, the fragments and ruins of which we collect together as 'primitive peoples' who are dying out, and even today it still supports (or it used to do so until very recently) true poetry and true art; which is why their content cannot be conveyed by mere statements. The expression commonly used for at least a group of arts-forms, the 'plastic arts' [*bildende Kunst*], reminds us that the formative activity serves to turn images [*Bilder*] into objects, and gives us reason to assume: the event that compels the spirit to imagistic endeavours is related to the shining of inner images. [...] For anyone who, in ecstasy, explodes the form of being a person, the world of facts in that very moment comes to an end, and before him or her there arises, with an all-suppressing power of reality, the *world of images*.

(*SW* 3, 414, 416, 417)

In *The Spirit as Adversary of the Soul* (SW 2, 286–287), Klages rejects the 'aesthetic' interpretation of the Platonic Ideas (in the specifically Schopenhauerian sense), and proposes instead that only exploding the *principium individuationis* in ecstatic vision gives access to the 'reality of images' (see below). In the following passage from his essay *On Dream Consciousness*,[21] Klages explores what exactly ecstasy tells us about ourselves – and about the world:

From the earliest times – beginning in the West with the Orphism of the ancient Greeks and concluding in the metaphysics of Platonism – there has

The reality of images 137

developed a misunderstanding of the process of ecstasy, which has resulted conceptually in colouring the entire history of higher thought. We encounter its original meaning in the literal sense of 'being-outside-oneself', which at first implies that a personal being has been *un-selfed* [*entselbstet*] and at the same time that the soul, freed from its captivating location, is 'in raptures' or 'swarming' *outside the ego*. Even in recent times this is confirmed by the words of true Dionysian knowledge from the mouth of one of the greatest disciples of the Sufi Order: in intoxication 'the *ego*, the dark despot, dies!'.[22] The thought of the mystical '*epopteia*' which recurs in many different forms also leaves us in no doubt about what sort of happiness is hoped for the soul released from the spirit and what would crown its wandering drunkenness with unforgettable fulfilment. Escaped from the compulsion of having to grasp things, it [=the soul] replaces the mechanistic reality of unfeelingly persistent *objects* with flowingly transformable vital *images*, or the short-term minor role of transitory *existence* with the divine participation in parturitive *vision*, which has 'eternity' because it is the star-like eye of what takes place and has an effect [*vom wirkenden Geschehen*]. To the earliest mystagogues this stepping-outside *appeared* in the very different light of liberating a higher principle from the bonds of *bodiliness*, and it leads someone ill-informed, who flees on his or her own from the tortures of the *sensory* world, into the doubtful 'freedom' of a world of disembodied '*vision*'. If in both these cases the unatmospheric brightness can seem like a shadowy pallor, very different from the resounding splendour of a real spring landscape, the joyfulness of the visionaries is as it were lacking the colourful shadows which lend depth and weight to every feeling. What serves as a basis for all this and finds a confirmation in it is a change in the essence of something which alone can explain to us the violence of the procedures that put such a seemingly pathological stamp on the 'ecstasies' of the Middle Ages. – Strengthening the sense of ego in the organism of the human being naturally brought with it a loosening of the cord between the body (as its vehicle) and the soul (as its antagonist), and at the same time there developed next to the original way of releasing the soul a second (and, we might say, an Asiatic) way. This places an emphasis on the *separation* of the powers opposed as enemies, and wants not so much to fuse the individual life freed from the spirit with the life of the universe as rather to 'redeem' an ego-shaped individual life from the 'mortal frame of the body'. Turning-away from the spirit became turning-away from its material carrier, and if the precondition of the former was either the periodic exhaustion of the senses or an elementary overflowing, this was sparked off by the corrosive ferocity of an excessively alert sensitivity.

(*SW* 3, 231–232)

What is the relation between an image and an object of a thing? In defining the image, Klages comes up with the following complex list of oppositions, which begins to allow us to understand the specificities of his concept of the image:

138   *Selections from Klages*

An image has presence only in the moment of being experienced; a thing is 'determined' once and for all – an image flows along with ever-flowing experience; a thing persists, remains, stands unmixed and inimical to life – an image is only there in the experience of the person who experiences; a thing, in any and all acts of perception of every person – while I can remember an image, I cannot make it present in a judgement; at any time I can relate in thought to a thing, because it is now the same thing it was previously, and through announcing my judgement relating to it I can turn it into the identical point of relation of everyone who hears it – an image, immersed in the stream of time, changes as everything changes, including the experiencing soul; the thing, because it is outside time, falls, measured in relation to it, prey to destruction – an image is received by the soul; a thing is achieved for the person receiving it through the spirit's act of judge-ment – an image has reality independent of consciousness; a thing is brought through thought into the world by consciousness and only exists *for* an interiority of *personal* beings.

(*SW* 3, 416–417)

In *The Foundations of the Doctrine of Character*, Klages gives us a concrete – or rather, a jewel-like – example of what it means to be 'gripped' by the power of an image in this evocative and memorable passage:

Suppose that someone is looking at a shining precious stone (in a shop display, for instance) and is 'seized' by the sight of it. Such a person is first of all aware of a feeling of himself or herself and the image of the stone. And now let something happen which, in its full force, is only per-mitted to few, although the beginning of it is, depending on the appropri-ate object (for instance, the sight of the setting sun or the shape of the beloved), in the end known to everyone: namely, that the person who is contemplating 'sinks' into what is being contemplated. At this point con-sciousness has become a mirror, in which the sparkle of this stone is the only thing still burning and, by the universal power of the image, the feeling of ego is extinguished. Someone enjoying a perfect vision is no longer aware of any 'existence', he or she has 'forgotten' himself or herself, and is nevertheless in a state of passion, compared with which the most sublime intellectual content is pale. Released from being an indi-vidual, he or she *becomes* the reflected content and, through it, becomes something of which it 'in itself' is not a part but a glimpse and a rune: the world, 'infinity', the universe.

(*SW* 4, 364)

Elsewhere (in *Expressive Movement and Formative Power*), Klages repeats his link between the ancient idea of a magic experience of rapture and the power of what he calls the image:

The reality of images 139

> Whoever forbids the soul to feel deeply moved has mistaken mere perception for the reception of images – in the consecration rituals of the ancients, authentic 'conception' – and the act of cognition itself for being enraptured.
>
> (*SW* 6, 253–254)

Just as passionately as he laments the historical development which has 'alienated' human beings from their connection to nature, Klages expresses dismay over our loss of an awareness of the symbolic dimension of life. The loss of this symbolic awareness is described by Klages (in *Expressive Movement and Formative Power*) as a 'logocentric' error:[23] an exclusive focus on rationality instead of a richer and more holistic approach to life. In other words, we have to realize that, as Klages puts it, reality is a reality of *images* (see below):

> If human beings, instead of separating themselves, full of power-hungry spirit, from reality, had investigated the sense of symbols, which even their vision intertwined with the world was able to find, then they would have avoided the logocentric aberration and truly understood something which, even today, everyone whose individual life extends deeply enough to be capable of conception still experiences: namely, that what appears in the images, and thus what is 'actually' real, is the *souls* of the images! The reality of images is a reality of appearance [*Erscheinung*], insofar as it is a reality of souls that appear or, since souls certainly live, a reality of incessantly self-transforming *life*. The comparison: real, more real, most real, means: vital, more vital, most vital; and the basis for all hierarchies of values compatible with the world lie in the degree of *vital plenitude*.
>
> (*SW* 6, 256–257)

Although 'vital plenitude' is the key benchmark by which the reality (or otherwise) of phenomena are to be judged, this does not mean that Klagesian vitalism is not interested in value. On the contrary, as he tells us in *The Spirit as Adversary of the Soul*:

> Far from the doctrine of the effective potency [*Wirkungsvermögen*] of images denying values and differences in values, one of its main concerns is rather to investigate the roots of those *values* right down into the life of the *elements*.
>
> (*SW* 2, 1237)

Correspondingly, Klages extends the meaning of life to objects conventionally regarded as being (in a telling phrase) 'inanimate', i.e. lacking in soul. For Klages, as he relates in *On the Essence of Consciousness*, nothing could be further from the truth:

> Phenomena [*Erscheinungen*] are without exception alive, things [*Dinge*] are without exception not alive. So understood in the sense of images to be

140   *Selections from Klages*

experienced, it is not only plants, animals, and human beings that are alive, but also rocks, clouds, water, wind, and flames; solar dust, bricks, writing-desks, the starry firmament, indeed space and time are alive. By contrast, understood in the sense of things to be cognized, even a human being is, like all other things, merely a collection of moving atoms. Perhaps we can make our view clear with the help of the incontrovertible distinction that exists between the life in the bodiliness of the dead and the living animal, or of the dead and the living plant. Yet, for us, what this difference repres-ents is this: in the wood of the living tree, the individual life of the tree appears; by contrast, the logs of the tree when cut down and sawn up are a partial expression of the *life of the earth*. Thus we distinguish the life of the macrocosm from the life of the microcosm, and our question about the so-called origin of life on earth is *not*: how did a living plasma emerge from dead material, but rather: how did the life of the earth become cellular life?

(*SW* 3, 284)

In fact, Klages wants to extend the category of soul beyond discrete objects to such aspects of them as warmth, colour, etc. Why? Because in our experience of life, it is these things that make reality 'real'. Because Klages also identifies these aspects of reality as 'souls', he draws (in *On the Essence of Consciousness*) the remarkable – but, given his definition of soul, entirely logical – conclusion that reality is really a reality of souls:

Colours, degrees of warmth, qualities of space, and so on are only useful for describing ensouled *personalities* because they themselves are *ensouled*. It would be impossible, and it could not even be attempted, to characterize souls with the help of the *appearance* of the world, if it were not precisely souls and exclusively souls which were 'appearing' in the world! Reality 'in itself' is a world of ensouled images or appearing souls; and, if it were otherwise, then no one would ever have announced what was moving his or her own soul, because there would have been no one whom the message would have been able to reach!

(*SW* 3, 253)

The following passage (from *On the Essence of Rhythm*) might help explain what Klages is trying to get at in this notion that reality is a reality of souls. It shows how he wants to say that the world is objective without reducing it to an object; and he wants to take seriously our phenomenal perceptions, without reifying them into material qualities. Do we invent the world? No. Rather we 'find' it (we discover it, or we come across it, or we encounter it); and it is liter-ally beyond our wildest dreams:

Let the reader forget for a moment all expert philosophical opinions and turn instead to the sight of a centuries-old lime-tree, seeing how in it the regularly spreading growth agrees with the gentle bend of the branches

The reality of images   141

and twigs and the beautiful swing of the lines of the leaf edges; or then again a centuries-old oak-tree, whose defiant gnarledness similarly extends to the serrated shapes of the leaves; and let the reader ask himself or herself whether it is his or her spirit that invented and created this always unified formation, or whether this spirit did not rather *find* something lime-tree-like and something oak-tree-like, in order to distinguish them henceforth according to what is most easy to grasp about them? The spherical shape of the apple returns in the round shape of the apple-tree, the bell-like shape of the pear in the oval shape of the pear-tree: but *we* have so little done it that our attention must first be alerted to it, in order for us to see it. Did human spirits devise the fantastic shapes of agaves, cacti, euphorbiaceae?[24] Does not the world of orchids and the even more species-rich one of asteraceae[25] exceed in richness of colours and shapes everything which human imagination could dream up over millennia? Which spirit would presume to create from itself such fragrances as those of woodruff, lilac, elderberries, wallflowers, honeysuckle, lily of the valley, thyme, lavender, or such tastes as those of raspberries, honey, hazel-nuts? And were bullocks and quartz and seagulls not there, before a human eye ever espied them? What sort of devilish arrogance has then whispered into the human ear that he or his spirit *fabricates* from an unshapen mass the world of perceptual images [*Anschauungsbilder*]?! The truth could not more shamefully be stood on its head: the phenomenal world (or, if one prefers the ambiguous loanword, nature), from its furthest clumps of luminous clouds and spiral nebulae of the universe to the microscopic bacterium or infusorium, is *always* an elaborately shaped image, which it was reserved to the human being to confuse, to disrupt, and sometimes even to transform into a 'chaos'!

(*SW* 3, 507)

Again, the passage above shows the patient attention to delicate detail that characterizes Klages's outlook and philosophical approach. Or, as he puts it in *The Foundations of the Doctrine of Character*: we do not bring any impressions into the world, or so he argues, except our capacity for interpreting impressions:

If the soul does not bring any impressions into the world, nevertheless it has aptitudes for the *interpretation* of impressions, and it is precisely these which one usually calls 'innate instincts'.

(*SW* 4, 254)

For evidence of the world-shaping power of the image, Klages turns (in *The Foundations of the Doctrine of Character*) to the realm of biology. In the development of an individual organism, he sees the power of the image at work, as well as in the 'vital magnetic' attraction between individual organisms and their environment. Always it is the drive, or the impulse, that reveals the vitality of life:

142   *Selections from Klages*

If we reflect that, following fertilization in the germ-cell of the maternal organism, the drive [*Trieb*] or the impulse [*Drang*] is aroused to join cell to cell, through millions and millions of repetitions, until a new organism, related in shape to the maternal one, has grown, then we could hardly better describe the growth process than with the observation that, in the fertilized cell, the *image* of the developing body works as a material-shaping power! Anyone to whom it seems it is too bold to argue that this – to be sure, deeply unconscious – growth and ripening occur through the power of images which only begin to manifest themselves thanks to the former, will no longer fail to recognize this power and its unconscious rule when glancing at the *relations* of the finished organism to the surrounding world. After all, the essence of the so-called instincts mentioned above of the animal lies in the fact that, thanks to them, it can make a selection from the images of the world, searching for what it is essential to its life and fleeing from what is detrimental and hostile to it!

A vital magnetic attraction binds together a thirsty horse and the sight of water, a hungry cow with the impression of grass, an eagle out hunting with the appearance of chickens, goat kids, hares, and equally each of these and *that* side of the images and *that* segment of the world which it has the gift unconsciously to recognize as nourishment and as habitation![26] A duckling that has just learned to walk plunges into the pond, while the hen from which it has hatched warns it in alarm; it has recognized in water its element, not from the slightest conscious reflection, but rather as a result of the quite specific prompting to which the impression of the water has made its soul receptive. The impression *is* not this prompting, but merely awakens it. An animal in need of food *looks for* its food when it is not present, looks for its habitation, its element, when it is lacking them, and the flocks of migratory birds that set off in autumn are separated by thousands of kilometres from *those* impressions – the atmospheric gases, the climate, the places of habitation – toward which, as if attracted to them by some vital magnetism, they strive as a sleepwalker would.

(*SW* 4, 322)

One could say that, for Klages, human beings are the result both of evolutionary development *and* imagistic development. The developmental power of images, he argues (in *The Foundation of the Doctrine of Character*), has made us what we are: and their power lies at the heart of our cultural achievements, by which he means the following – myth, symbol, art, and even magic:[27]

The primordial human being emerged from the animal state through a change in the weighting of the poles, as the vital process of sensation (both of other bodies and of one's own body), hitherto dominant, became dependent on the vital process of vision (of images), hitherto subordinate, and thus the bodily or impulsive side of feeling became dependent on the mood of the soul; accordingly, fantasy or the gift for waking dreams was

The reality of images 143

henceforth able to free itself from the shackles of the Here and Now. Something which had previously realized itself only in the change of bodily conditions, the attractive power of the images, now revealed itself as autonomous, from now on determining the body differently and to do different things compared with what the mere drive-impulse [*Trieb-Antrieb*] would ever have been able to. If the thirsty deer is compelled to search for water and does without it until it has found water, so the thirsty human being had, and has, the ability to dream in a waking state about water and about drinking, to *imagine* water as well as drinking, even to make the images of them objective in material form; or, to put it more generally: in him or her *awaken* the images which had previously been at work, as if blindly, in the directional promptings of the drives [*Triebe*], and at the same time, leaving behind and overcoming his or her animal impulsiveness, innumerable new drives awaken, as innumerable as the possible images of *those* elements which bore him; what awakens and is revealed is the world for what it is: a reality itself of *images*, in relation to which all vital processes now appear as the ways and means to the *vision* of reality. Here lies the deepest root of myth, symbol, and art, here too is the deepest root of all magic.

(*SW* 4, 324)

Klages was well aware of the fact that his thought was emerging from a vitalist tradition in German thought,[28] and he was keen to emphasize the links between, for example, Goethe's thought and his own. One of the places where he did so was in *The Spirit as Adversary of the Soul*. For Klages, there is a direct line of continuity between two traditions, usually seen as opposed: the classicism of the 'Apollonian' Goethe and the Romantic 'Dionysianism' of Eichendorff:

What is it, then, by which we are gripped [*ergriffen*] and not rarely *shaken* on account of a phenomenal world that is neither human nor animal, and of which at the very most the plants are part, whether it be called 'nature' or called 'art'? Let us stick for the time being with the former! Is there anyone who has *never*, even in his or her earliest youth, experienced its 'mysterious shimmer', in which 'we sometimes see again as in a dream unknown, strange places'; whom a 'gleaming distance' with ineffable promises has *never* enticed; whom a 'silence lurking with hostility' has *never* surrounded; who has never experienced 'the time of the predatory heat', which 'in the south overwhelms everything alive'; to whom twilight has never seemed 'confused', daybreak like an heroic awakening; to whom lightning has never appeared to 'stray', the sound of bells never to 'waft'? And if almost everyone must acknowledge having experienced such things, then what *is* it that has spoken from 'streams, trees, and mountains, as if with fragmented sounds' to the soul?! We have used some expressions taken from Eichendorff;[29] some may disparagingly call them 'Romantic' and perhaps even imagine thereby to have said something of consequence. So let us listen to the 'Apollonian' Goethe![30]

144 *Selections from Klages*

The artist, he says, 'may enter the workshop of the cobbler or a stable; he may look at the face of his beloved, his boots or the world of antiquity, everywhere he sees sacred vibrations, [...] with which nature joins together all things [...]. With every step he takes is revealed a *magic world*, which intimately and steadfastly surrounded all great masters, whose works will forever inspire reverence in the striving artist [...]. Every human being has felt several times in his or her life the force of this magic [...]. Who has never been overcome by a shudder when entering a sacred forest? Whom has all-embracing night never shaken with an uncanny horror? To whom has, in the presence of his lover, the entire world not appeared golden? [...] This is what [...] weaves its way through the soul of the artist, what presses forward in him [...] to the most understandable expression, without going through the power of cognition.'

Thus 'Romanticism' has only gone *further* along the path along which Goethe had gone, from the world-image [*Weltbild*] of the artist to the world-image of the poet, one is tempted to say, and so let us interweave again some sentences by Eichendorff, which at the same time assure us that such a 'further' leads to a vantage point that Goethe could *not* yet reach. 'With humility and joyfulness the poet, himself full of wonder, contemplates heaven and earth, and his heart rejoices in the overwhelming sight, and so he sings of the world: which, like Memnon's Statue full of silent meaning, only rings out fully when the dawn of a poetic disposition touches it with its similar rays.'[31]

What *is* it that takes hold of us in the propitious hour and *changes* at the sight of palaces, sparkling with water, in ancient India, the forest of pillars of the temple ruins at Karnak or Luxor, the pyramid of Cheops, the thermal baths of Caracalla, Roman aqueducts, the marvellous churches of Ravenna and Byzantium, the pillared courts of the Alhambra, Romanesque castles and crypts, northern Gothic, to say nothing of the effects, that still sometimes almost approach the magical, made by music and kinds of singing or even those remains left to posterity from the so-called Stone Age, Bronze Age, and Iron Age, with which the secret of which we are speaking *still* confronts us in an immediate and, so to speak, daimonic contemporaneity? ... Anyone who has been shot through and transformed, even if only *once*, by such wondrous works knows from thenceforth, with unalterable certainty, that its elementary content can be disturbed and restricted, sometimes gently, sometimes perceptibly, by personal feelings and intellectual inclinations which may have seeped into it from the voluntary or involuntary participation of the characteristics of its creator whom the *powers* had chosen to be their tool.

(*SW* 2, 1116)

What makes Klages's discourse so difficult to assess is his choice of examples from, on the one hand, the realm of aesthetics (see above) and, on the other, the 'pathological' dimension of ecstasy. What both reveal, however, is what Klages (here, in *Of Cosmogonic Eros*) dubs 'the reality of images' (see below):

The reality of images 145

For anyone who, in ecstasy, explodes the form of being a person, the world of facts in that very moment comes to an end, and before him or her there arises, with an all-suppressing power of reality, the *world of images*. The visionary soul is its interior pole, the envisioned reality is its exterior pole. The former is now related to the latter (=continuous *gamos*),[32] but it never coincides with the former to form a whole (=continuous vision). From the polar *contact* of inner and outer is incessantly born the image ensouled with itself (=continuous birth). The exterior procreates, the interior conceives, and from the sexual embrace of them both breaks forth the singing fiery stream of the images of the universe, the 'dancing star' of a chaos structured into a cosmos.[33] The prophetic sentence of Novalis, 'the exterior is an interior elevated into a *mysterious state*',[34] expresses with effortless grace the sense of ecstasy and the ground for all visionary certainty.

(*SW* 3, 417)

In this passage (taken from *The Spirit as Adversary of the Soul*), Klages investigates the power of the aesthetic, using a stanza by one of his favourite poets, Nikolaus Lenau (1802–1850), as an example. Klages reveals himself as one of the most subtle analysts of the power of language, and behind the aesthetic lies, as always, the power of the Klagesian 'image':

There has always been a group of human beings – and even today there are still remnants of it – who for the whole of their lives seek, with the help of a use of language which is at least similar to the use of language in primordial times, nothing other than not simply to communicate, but rather to represent, the soul-related content of what is experienced: they are called the poets. To the extent one admits that it testifies to the authenticity of a poetic work if it can somehow take hold of a listener who is linguistically receptive to it, and if one briefly surveys the poetry of all tribes and times (including popular songs), one will have to acknowledge that what enables it to take a hold is only and exclusively *images*, which become alive in the understanding listener when the words are heard. We have tried to explain *how* it happens that images clothe themselves in words; but even if the last and best of it were to remain a secret, then the admission *that* it happens would nevertheless be enough for us. To write poetry is to liberate the soul of the word through using words, and the word is endowed with soul and thus has, like everything endowed with soul, the power to bestow soul, insofar as it is the *sense-body of an image*. Of course, a poetic work always offers 'thoughts' as well and it is not uncommon for it to present itself bedecked in jewellery, often in fact in the all-too-rich jewellery of metaphors, comparisons, literary figures. Only what is strictly thought and is identically rethinkable about those 'thoughts' can just as well be said in even amateurish prose, and at any rate without the slightest loss in the completely different sounds of any given foreign language; what is poetic about the poetic work, by contrast – [...] can, as

146 *Selections from Klages*

something non-transferable, at best be adapted and even then never without loss. As far as metaphors are concerned, however, they are interwoven into the giving birth to the word to the extent that they are in the service of an *announcement of the image*!

> Silently and motionlessly enclosed within itself
> The deep sea rests, poured out,
> Sending no greeting to the shore;
> Its pulsing waves have subsided,
> Undetected gleam the evening rays,
> As if on the face of a corpse.[35]

The 'face of a corpse' is a metaphor, but chosen in a divinatory way with the aim of *sensualizing* the *image* of this sea, on whose shores this single stanza has compelled us to await, full of an anxious feeling of unease, an imminent disaster, if only we were able to open ourselves to the velvety shudder of these verses. What here appears before the inner eye in the name of the sea has the reality of an image, and only of an image; it has nothing of the reality of that identically named object in whose waters one goes fishing, whose depths one sounds, whose plants one can dry and put into one's collection. And it permits just as little of any comparison with the 'representation' of this object. We find the objective sea as always the same, always in the same place, in one and the same universe, and we can think it or imagine it on the basis of this identity. Never and nowhere shall we find the sea of the poet, apart from in the happy moment in his poem and *never a second time as one has before!* In vain does our spirit want to grasp it: for then, in order to become aware of it, we should have rather to renounce all activity to the point that we, bereft of spirit and full of devotion, are only those seized by it. The perceptible sea is detected and thought, Lenau's sea was experienced by the poet and envisioned; with the physical body of the former, the thing which is signified by sounds as it were puts on a mask, in the naming sound-body of the latter there *appears* the undetectable, but gripping, image. In the language of mysticism as expounded above: the sea of the poem has a 'sidereal body', which, 'when seen, becomes intangible',[36] and it comes for the listener into appearance according to the extent of his or her capacity and willingness to be carried away by the magic of words.[37]

As already we have indicated a number of times: the *thing* would not have been able to 'appear', and consequently would not have been detected and understood, without the *reality* of that image which only the poet and, from time to time, the seer succeed in releasing from its imprisonment in being a thing, and, even for them, only in those rarest moments of love transporting them beyond their senses. If it is unquestionably images which live in the word-body of poetry, and if through it something which can grip any one of us in the actually existing world becomes alive for us, then what stands opposite to the soul and seizes the spirit must be a reality of images and only of images!

(*SW* 2, 1254–1256)

As a passage from *Of Cosmogonic Eros* makes clear, however, this ego-stripping power of beauty is not restricted to the contemplation of works of art. Klages gives an example of the wood he could see from his window; until, on one occasion, he is stunned to see something completely different – and irrevocably unique:

Hundreds of times I must have looked out of the window and seen the wood without experiencing anything other than just a thing, the same thing which the botanist also sees; but on one occasion, while it was aflame in the gleam of the evening sun, the sight of it succeeded in tearing me away from my ego; and behold, my soul suddenly saw in a vision something I had never seen before, perhaps only for a minute, indeed perhaps only for a second; in the meantime, for however long or short a time, what was now seen in a vision was the primordial image of the wood, and *this* image will never return for me nor for anyone else.

(*SW* 3, 422)

One could even, as Klages says in *Of Cosmogonic Eros*, describe this moment in which one beholds the 'primordial image' as a moment of 'illumination' (or, in German, '*ein erhellter Augenblick*'):

The fate of the world stands in the moment of illumination as something present; right into the distances of space and into the distances of time, everything that has ever happened and is happening has its light and its sense from the image, however swiftly it may be scattered.

(*SW* 3, 427)

To describe the power of the image, Klages has recourse in *The Spirit as Adversary of the Soul* to a vocabulary of 'atmosphere',[38] comparing this modern idea to the ancient idea of a tutelary deity or daimon:

The ancients knew the *genius loci*, the nimbus, the aura, and we too still speak of the 'atmosphere' of a human being, a house, a location. Now this 'atmosphere', perceived by so-called sensitive natures, sensed by delicate ones, and unknown to more robust hearts and minds, is a reality that *has an effect*, giving and enriching or soaking up and weakening, embracing and warming or undermining and chilling, swiftening and stimulating or inhibiting and curbing, extending or restricting, inspiring or disabling, and its effect is essentially different from the contact between themselves of *bodies*.

(*SW* 2, 1103)

148 *Selections from Klages*

Following (while reversing the sense of) a distinction found in St Paul (and, later, in the Gnostic tradition), Klages distinguishes (in *On the Essence of Consciousness*) an ordinary and limited form of perception from an extraordinary and visionary one. Yet far from promoting a *gnosis* for the few, Klages is reminding us of a lost heritage of perception that belongs to us all:

> For a humanity in whom the understanding is triumphant and which consists almost only, to speak in the language of St Paul, of 'pneumatic individuals',[39] it is difficult to speak convincingly of matters which are only accessible to the 'psychic individual', but to him of course appear to be considerably 'more obvious' than *our* belief in the laws of mechanics! The whole of antiquity (just as, even today, every 'primitive people') did not only know human souls, but rather *daimonic* souls, and it has left us precise testimony about how they used appear to the visionary. Accordingly, the daimonically ensouled image stands in a 'nimbus',[40] which is as much to say as: in a cloud that illuminates and surrounds it; for which reason we still occasionally speak today about the 'nimbus' of a personality and, more clearly, about 'shining beauty'. If we translate what in those days was experienced with full visionary power into a form of expression more suited to people of today, using the example of Celtic oaks that were honoured as being divine,[41] then we might perhaps hope in so doing to put a stop once and for all to the tendency to confuse the living image with the lifeless reflection which the perceptual deed of the understanding retains in the 'visual thing'.
>
> If, in an inspiring moment, the 'psychic' individual is able, instead of perceiving the oak-tree (whether with, or without, 'aesthetics'), to envision its 'primordial image', then, by means of the same object which for us means a tree with such-and-such qualities, a daimonic soul has appeared to him, and this means: he has sensed as overpoweringly *real* the fluid *shudder* which mysteriously whispers down from the tree-top. That may roughly be true for the nimbus within the limits of forming a character, which at best still makes possible the recognition of a suprapersonal content from the depths of *feelings* that bubble up, feeling one's way and intuitively finding the way back to reflection on the experience of having the vision.
>
> On this account, the mechanical intervention in a non-mechanical reality more clearly takes place in the following way. Become blind in his soul to the nimbus, the 'pneumatic' individual still perceives the particular tree, including the accompanying atmospheric conditions of the moment, but as if *cut out* from the pantheon of life through spatially and temporally, qualitatively and generically outlined *borders*! In this way the 'primordial image' has become altered right at its very heart. So instead of a daimonically vital being, conversing with stars and with storms, there was now the unity snatched from the world of a thing determined by a specific class, whose supposedly individual life disintegrates in the obtrusively penetrating gaze of the understanding into a machine-like play of measurable 'energies'.

The reality of images   149

Nevertheless this mask is yet again the primordial image for a second time: although *bereft of its nimbus,* removed from its 'veil of Maya', stripped of its protective (because interwoven with everything) cover, become naked, disenchanted and from henceforth lacking the ability to make itself perceptible to a human *soul!* And for this reason the deed directed toward things will also do violence to the *image* of the world and because, blinded, it smashes the phenomenon, it will smash the phenomenal soul along with it.

(*SW* 3, 293)

The suggestive Klagesian notion of the nimbus as a kind of epiphanic moment is explored in this passage from *The Spirit as Adversary of the Soul*:

The ancients, who were blessed with visionary wakefulness more often, more profoundly and more abundantly than we are, called intuitive images that were capable of becoming entirely image, images in a 'nimbus'. The 'nimbus', not in the sense of a 'rain cloud', but understood as a candida et lucida nubes = "shining and gleaming cloud",[42] surrounded in principle the epiphanies of the gods, furthermore of most heroes, as well as sometimes of sacred animals, and finally human beings in moments of powerfully elated arousal. In such cases it easily turns into an aura surrounding the head. (Compare with the *Iliad*, book 18, ll. 203–227, and its magnificent description of how the fire which blazes around the head of the profoundly shaken Peleion strikes with terror the Trojans fighting over the corpse of Patroclus!).[43] But even without this the name already used earlier is sufficiently revealing for us. Surrounding with cloud the primordial image yet at the same time not separable from it, it symbolizes the cosmic space which – stretched between distance and distance – embraces the visionary soul, not in the sense of the relation of the whole to part of the whole, but in that of the embedding and protecting cradle or, put in a less figurative way, of the "fluidum", i.e. the vital humidity between the world foci: soul and image. Thanks to its nimbus every primordial image reaches as far as the universe (which is why every copy of the primordial image has its own!); thanks to this *gleaming veil* its contours are loosened, unbordered, incomprehensible and bring – undamaged by the perceptibility of its core – into appearance something which Romanticism mysteriously calls the "infinite" [*das "Unendliche"*]; thanks to the transformation of an aura, whose form and colour and brightness never tarry, the image *is transformed* as well: entirely appearance and entirely deed in one.

(*SW* 1, 844)

Against the charge of pure subjectivism, Klages defends himself (in *The Spirit as Adversary of the Soul*) by pointing to objective shapes found in the natural world as constituting expressions of what he called the 'planetary soul':

From the image of the heath landscapes in central latitudes one cannot separate pine-tree, birch-tree, juniper, oak-tree and the lilac-coloured

150 *Selections from Klages*

carpets of erica; nor, from the image of the Alps, beech-trees, spruce, and brushwood; nor from the image of tropical river branches, jungle-covered shores with palm-trees, bamboo, papyrus perennials, surrounded by snake-like roots and in the death-nets of profuse lianas ... The 'characters' of landscapes are character *traits* of the planetary soul; and it is especially to this and more richly than to itself that vegetative growth testifies, most visibly in the northern hemisphere, where it accompanies the dance of the seasons with budding, blossoming, flowering and leaf-fall, changing the location as it itself changes; and, in this respect, no less so in the tropics, where it mirrors the change of dry and rainy periods in manifold phenomena. But if water and plants are missing entirely, then the sublime desolateness of the deserts opens up, and the exaggeratedly telluric landscape is replaced instead by the exaggeratedly sidereal landscape or the earth in an exchange with the stars.

But this means that an individual plant, too, breathes the 'spirit' of the zones, climates, high-lying valleys, lowlands, swamps, prairies, where it is originally 'at home', and on the other hand, if forcibly replanted in intrinsically alien areas, it changes its overall appearance over the course of time. Compare the flowing leaves of a birch-tree with the leathery foliage of tropical shrubs or the rigid and brittle fans of palm-trees with the soft and flexible switches of a willow-tree, and one has next to each other at close quarters the soul of the warmer and cooler latitudes! This is equally true, of course, of animals and even of human beings, and it is true of all individual beings on the earth, but it is true of plants to a higher degree, and precisely in this respect we see an expression of the fact that their vital principle is much less than that of an individualized life.

For the human beings of prehistory, and for a long time for the human beings of antiquity, the individual being contained a treasury of the world-secret that was all the richer for appearing to be bound to the planetary soul. For this reason, the worship of human-shaped gods was preceded by the worship of animal-shaped gods, but both were preceded by the cult of the tree, which survived *alongside* these and has done into the age of modern civil society, indeed fleetingly into the present day.

(*SW* 2, 1114)

In a short and aphoristic sentence, found in *The Spirit as Adversary of the Soul*, Klages captures the essence of his doctrine of the 'reality of images':

What in a moment of grace comes from nature or from the works of the spring-spirits and touches a chord in us with a daimonic force is not something intellectually devised and constructed in the imagination, rather it is – *born*.

(*SW* 2, 1132)

Mineral, vegetable, human, cosmic: these are the dimensions of existence in which Klages (in *The Spirit as Adversary of the Soul* and in the rest of his works) is interested:

Distance and ancestral worship   151

Wandering and self-transforming images, but unborn ones, are the images of uninhabited planets and moons, which no telescope hitherto has been able to espy; essentially unborn are also the images of the plants *among themselves*, the images of the vegetative processes of all individual beings, including elementary processes which in turn provide the basis for them; what are essentially born are the images of reality, first of all, yet only partially, in the souls of animals, but entirely in the souls of visionaries.

(*SW* 2, 1224)

For Klages, the visionary is (as he argues in *The Spirit as Adversary of the Soul*) able to gain access to a dimension of reality that will forever elude his or her counterpart, the person of (blind) activism:

If *this* is the sense of cosmic activity, that it *appears*, then it reaches perfection first of all when it has an impact on visionary souls. It is only through being paired with the suffering of the soul-related pole that primordial images are born from the action of the active pole, whereas action itself would remain the primordially powerful, yet non-participatory, flaming blaze to which the ancients attached the easily misunderstood name 'chaotic'.[44] And it is in comparison with visual images and in relation to them that primordial images are visual images in the 'nimbus' or in the 'aura'[45] or in other words phenomena of distance.

(*SW* 2, 1207)

Distance and ancestral worship: how the past persists in the present

Two of the most important categories in Klagesian thought are proximity and distance, or the categories of what is near (at hand) and what is far (away). In this passage from *Of Cosmogonic Eros* he uses these terms in a spatial, but also in a temporal sense, and he explains that the relation between them is essentially polar:

The immediately convincing statement made by *Stendhal* to the effect that the beauty of the artistically perfect painting is a 'promise of happiness'[46] was perhaps supposed to mean in the mind of its inventor what Nietzsche reads into it in order to support his own view that art has the purpose of persuading the spectator to an affirmation of life at all costs.[47] Yet the expression in question teaches us something else, if we reflect that this promise, contained in the pain lamented in song, the love celebrated in poetry, the grace chiselled in stone, the storm portrayed on the canvas, the cosmic affinity immortalized in stone in, for instance, the Porta Nigra,[48] would never find fulfilment in the wakefulness of daytime existence. Anyone whose heart has, even if only once, begun to beat more quickly at the sight of the cloud-covered sea in the distance which Böcklin's paintbrush evoked

152   *Selections from Klages*

in the painful drunkenness of his triton's gaze,[49] how could he or she hope to see this more-than-human shudder of yearning die away in a satisfaction that brings it to an end! Anyone who has walked along the monuments of the Via Appia, spell-bound by the compelling brilliance of irretrievably dead millennia, how could he or she imagine that what cannot be possessed would belong to them if they were to return back to imperial Rome![50] Anyone who feels the pull of the nameless melancholy of the steppes in lost songs of the Volga,[51] how could he or she believe they could find on foot the place where that prompting would reach its goal! And how so much more true of the secret of life itself is what Stendhal's statement explains about a humanly communicated *expression* of life! To proximity belongs, as its counter-pole, the essentially never attainable distance. Each time we open our eyes, entrusting ourselves if only to the breadth of space, holds promise and entices us; only what it entices us towards is something we would never find, if we set out and made our way 'into the distance'; the horizon flees away from us, and no traveller has yet traversed the sunset.

(*SW* 3, 411)

In the passage quoted above (p. 145), Klages alludes to an aphorism by Novalis, and in this passage from *Of Cosmogonic Eros* Klages essays an explanation of what, in the context of his own doctrine of spatial and temporal distance and proximity, this aphorism might mean. As so often, Klages invites the reader to reflect on his or her own experience:

Imagine being at rest on a flat seashore, contemplating without any particular thoughts the farthest edge of the horizon, denoted by the dissipating cloud of smoke from a steamer that has already disappeared; and now compare in the mirror of recollection the accompanying feeling of the experienced depth of space and being immersed in the memory-images of irretrievable youth; and you will find them both similar to the point of confusion, if you have the gift of finding anything at all in the realm of the interior. What enables the distant fragrance of the horizon as something unattainable to fill the heart with a gnawing yearning, painfully arousing and sweetly soothing at once, is the reality of the past which can no *longer* be touched; and what, in the inner image, enables things long since gone to distinguish themselves from what has recently happened and what has recently been present, is the distant blue of the depth of space that cannot be compared to anything else in the world. Shifting like clouds across mountain firns and with the 'deceptively remote' shining stars,[52] the time of prehistory eternally passes by, eternally taking leave, before the gaze of anyone who is captivated by those images! Let us remember once more the mystical revelation: what is external is something internal raised to a mysterious condition.[53]

(*SW* 3, 46)

Distance and ancestral worship 153

For Klages (in another passage in *Of Cosmogonic Eros*), those thoughtful, even poignant, moments in one's life are a moment of insight into the nature of time:

> When the adult is overcome from time to time by a mysterious homesickness for his childhood, the dark memory resonates in him of the profundity and fullness of the vital shudder especially in his very earliest youth, together with the knowledge of its irretrievability. It is the mysterious gleam of an unbrokenly idiopathic bliss,[54] which separates especially the ecstasies of the boyish soul from the wave-peaks, nearly always emotionally burdened, of older age. That summer sky, knowing nothing of itself, of an entirely self-sufficing solitude, which not even the most delicate veil of intuition clouds with the painful tendency to togetherness, covers with its universal arch only the magic garden of childhood years.
>
> (*SW* 3, 402)

In this passage (from *The Spirit as Adversary of the Soul*), Klages offers an extended thought experiment, in which a traveller returns to his native village and has a vitalist experience of time. In its final sentence, Klages reprises an expression first used in his treatise *Of Cosmogonic Eros*:

> Imagine the scene: a traveller returning after forty years, perhaps unaware of where he is, to the village where he was born, catches sight of the lime-tree, the roofs with chimneys puffing smoke, the narrow lane, the spring, the moss-covered churchyard railings, and is *amazed*; what he sees is *not* these things, just the same as other things, but he sees – memorials of generations-old destinies, both of themselves and of the people who, in their shadows, by their banks, under their protection, blossomed and grew old, came and went, were noisy and were silent, hated and loved, found each other and separated; he sees what he remembers, covered up by the flow of those times which, while it was, roared past and, in roaring past, *transformed* it: who would dare to deny that he is about to be transported into the past! And if the sense of wonder overcame him with such force that it *transformed* him entirely in a trice, then the distance of time would be *awakened* in him, and what constitutes his present would not be these things, it would be the *reality of the images* which, linked by endless chains, reaches back into what has not beginning. 'Primordial images are appearing souls of the past'.[55]
>
> (*SW* 2, 846)

Klages is aware that the questions he is considering belong to some of the greatest that have ever been asked, but in his view (represented here in a passage from *Of Cosmogonic Eros*), none of his predecessors in the tradition of philosophy – not the Platonic, nor the Neoplatonic, nor the German Idealist – has understood properly the true relation between distance and proximity, between past and present:

154 *Selections from Klages*

In the mirror of the doctrine of essences what is near at hand is sober and sobering, only what is far away is intoxicating; the present is near, only the past is distant; and this latter is the evidently suprarational sense of the visionary condition: that it 'transports' into the 'realm never to be entered',[56] into the maternal world of what has been or, then again, *brings back* the 'spirits' of those who have long since passed away! No Plato, no Plotinus, no Schopenhauer has ever fathomed this!

(*SW* 3, 436)

So what is really real? For Klages, the answer (as given in *The Spirit as Adversary of the Soul*) is simple – the only reality is the present moment in its vitalist flux:

Reality only pertains to the present moment, which sometimes overflows with different pasts, sometimes is desolate as lacking any past; there the primordial images flare up in it, here it 'un-becomes' in the reflection of phantoms and ghosts.

(*SW* 3, 1232)

Here (in a passage from *Of Cosmogonic Eros*) Klages make clear the link between temporal past and spatial distance, both of which are different kinds of eros:

The eros of what once was is the eros of distance. Because it is ignited by bodiless images, however, the latter places the visionary in touch with the untouchable world of the stars, in such a way as to send pulses through the earthly life of those still present in the light, pulses in the rhythm of the universe; hence its carriers were literally 'cosmic' essences and in their highest consecrations what they were called was: sons of the sun.

(*SW* 3, 440)

Sometimes Klages uses the ancient language of the mystics to talk about the soul; here, as in this sentence from *The Spirit as Adversary of the Soul*, his definition of soul is as metaphysical as it is concise:

The soul is the transience of the body. (*Die Seele ist des Leibes Vergänglichkeit.*)

(*SW* 1, 71)

The essential thing about the phenomenal world, Klages argues (in *Of Cosmogonic Eros*), is that it is not at all essential, but rather constantly changing:

The cardiac nerve of visionary thought is the experiential certainty of the *transformability of the phenomenal world.*

(*SW* 3, 450)

Distance and ancestral worship 155

Although Klages is sometimes regarded as an 'irreligious' thinker, this passage (taken from *Of Cosmogonic Eros*) makes clear that, in fact, he had a strong spiritual sense; only his religion was one of life, and not·one morbidly focused on death:

> The spirit-based way of thinking, for which dying means the destruction of existence, was the first to produce a previously incomprehensible horror of death and, along with this, the passionate desire for immortality. By contrast, the primordial human being, for whom the merely existent world still hid itself like a shadow behind the vital images of the soul-world, knew neither of these. He or she was still not sufficiently a person for the thought of existence, even if only in relation to the individual ego, to have been able to muzzle him or her to anything like the extent it does a human being of today and to determine his or her customs. Just as it is certain that everything, whether a thing or whether a human being, 'existed' for him or her as if it were only secondarily, so it is certain that for him or her it was not just a human being that *lived*, but also the so-called dead thing, even the 'matter' of which it consisted, a word which, as one ought not to forget, derives from *mater*=mother;[57] in other words, the sense-image of the primordial source! Although dying was still a powerful event for the primordial human being, it was not destruction of existence, but transformation of life. In those days one did not 'die' in our sense, because there was still nothing that in our sense was essentially dead!
>
> In order to understand the relation that pertains between the visionary condition and the immortalization of life, one has first of all to have worked one's intellectual way into the unbridgeable gulf that separates the conception of death in the primordial age from the conception of death in the present. For this reason, we shall first present the latter in the context of the primordial age. – Every true adherent of the spiritual religion of Christianity believes in personal immortality. But if a Protestant or Catholic clergyman were to be approached by a farmer in his parish who told him that the grave of his grandfather is haunted and that his grandfather's soul is abroad, then the 'pastor' would tell him that the grandfatherly soul in question is in the 'beyond' or in 'heaven' and so it is impossible for it to be abroad anywhere. The belief in immortality points souls *away from the world* to such an extent that it turns 'powerful souls' into 'poor souls'[58] and devalues the entire opposing belief in souls to the level of a 'superstition'. In the rite of Extreme Unction,[59] the celebration of the Mass and the Feast of All Souls, the Catholic still preserves the remnants of the ancient custom of caring for the dead. For the Protestant, that is, for the perfected Christian, dust returns to dust, spirit to spirit, while the soul along with the Here only loses the There and finally the last foothold of being at home. Located neither on earth nor on one of the thousands upon thousands of stars, it does not reside in space at all, but in a Not-Here, a 'place beyond the heavens', in – the beyond. Hence what had stood right at the centre of the service of the soul in the prehistoric world becomes with

156 *Selections from Klages*

logical consistency a matter of caprice for a feeble 'piety': the care of the corpse, of the grave, of the ashes! The art and culture of the prehistoric world flourished in the soil of the funerary cult, because they know *no* immortality of the soul, but instead its *perpetual presence*; the whole of Christianity, with its belief in immortality, sees in the corpse no more than a cadaver, in the grave a location which after thirty or forty years can be ploughed over and returned to use, and in the ancestor who once existed a completely impotent, because deceased, being, who no longer intervenes in the conflict of different interests among the living. To displace the soul as immortal into the beyond means to rob it of its worldly home, to turn it into a 'departed' soul and in this way into a trivial soul!

(*SW* 3, 444)

In *Of Cosmogonic Eros*, Klages proposes a different sort of piety, one that could be described as a pagan (and is certainly anti-Christian), but one that is keenly motivated by aesthetic responses to the beauty (and the sublimity) of the natural world:

Everything which is spatially distant *can* [...] move forward into what is close at hand, with the unconditional exception of the stars! If our eye may, thanks to polished lenses, penetrate deeper by thousands of light years into the abysses of space, and in the darkroom of myriads of stars capture a likeness in places in the heavens which were previously spanned only by dark emptiness, if we may draw the ring-walls of the craters of the moon to the exact extent of their height, chemically analyse the material of suns and burning mists of other worlds: as before we still only have 'present' the *appearance* of the stars, never their (merely deduced) physicality! And this is because the stars, 'one does not hanker after them',[60] and their 'presence' – if we may permit ourselves a joke that illustrates what is paradoxical beyond all presumption about it – 'is conspicuous through its absence'! – But if, correspondingly, no more a convincing symbol of what is past can be thought of than the starry magnificence of the nocturnal firmament, then we can understand not only the sublime shudder that still runs at the sight of the shining firmament through every spectator open to the world, but we can also understand why, for the primordial way of thinking, the stars were sometimes souls of those who had once been, sometimes their places of residence, but always singing choirs, who had passed away from the earth and were now shining resplendent amid what abides, of a prehistory to which 'all earthly transformation' remained bound.[61]

(*SW* 3, 438)

As Klages makes clear in *Of Cosmogonic Eros*, there is an experiential as well as a conceptual dimension to his philosophy. The experience of ecstasy reminds us of the limitations that are, the rest of the time, imposed on the daimonic power of the soul:

Anyone who has been blessed with 'journeying', by means of ecstatic vision, into the untouchable distance, now experiences, once returned back to himself or herself, the eternal here-ness of the touchable body as a *shackle* of the soul. One's soul, having taken flight like a bird, was pulled back by invisible threads to a firmly binding place and into a limited proximity. If it were to tear those threads, then, instead of temporary freedom and reversible transformation, its lot would be a fate of newly-born wandering and unlimited transformability, promising a deeply problematic (because, so to speak, cosmic) vital fullness and threatening to lead it off the path and lure it astray. But these threads really do tear in death, for then without a doubt the soul leaves the corpse, surrendered to the endless possibility of reshaping itself in the universality of space. Herein primarily lies its daimonic power; but from it ... at the same time grows the danger of it becoming alienated, lost forever.

(*SW* 3, 450)

The relation between being alive and being dead is, in this passage from *Of Cosmogonic Eros*, redefined in terms of the status of the image:

The soul of what is presently alive is an image *bound up* with matter, the soul of the dead is an image *released* from matter. Entirely become image, the latter has the reality form of an appearance in a dream, it comes and disappears, unencumbered by material limitations.

(*SW* 3, 450)

In *Of Cosmogonic Eros*, Klages explains death in terms of the release of the material-bound soul into a different dimension of vitality:

Far from being snatched away from the world into the invisibility of the beyond, the soul of the dead is rather a daimonic-vital image, now of a star, stone, tree, or animal, now of a spring, a stream, of the breeze as it passes by, instead of the likeness again of its previously physical carrier. The belief of prehistory is not that there are invisible souls or even a personal continued existence, but it is: that the images of things are vital [*lebendig sind die Bilder der Dinge*], and something lives so much more unshackled, something took on so much more the character of the soul capable of magic transformations, as it became an image and nothing other than this!

(*SW* 3, 451)

What Klages tirelessly points to in *Of Cosmogonic Eros* is the continuity provided by eros:

Untorn, the web of eros is spun between the *images* of prehistory and the minds and souls of those in the present day.

(*SW* 3, 454)

158 *Selections from Klages*

Consequently, in *Of Cosmogonic Eros* Klages redefines, in a vitalist sense, the meaning of the concept of immortality, relating it to ancient customs of the veneration of the dead:

> Think through the following pair of opposites for a few minutes, and one will seize with both hands the fact that each denies the other: the wish for immortality and the immortalization of life. The care for the dead *preserves* something that has really been, the belief in immortality *promises* something that never exists; the former commits itself to the past, the latter is alienated even from the present, has completely collapsed with what has flowed by and sacrifices the only eternal thing there is, the moment blazing with life, to the future that can only be caught in a concept; the former, something physically alive and blossoming from love for the light and dark *images* of life, places its carrier in the swiftly changing 'circle of necessity', with the latter the selfish hybris of uprooted individuals flees from the horror of having to end and takes refuge in the credulous lie of a supra-temporal continuation of existence. Summarized and illuminated in a harsh light: the way of thinking associated with the cult of the dead asks: what has *become* of those who were, and how may their lot be made more beautiful; that associated with the belief in immortality asks: what will become *of me*, when I am no longer, and how can I gain a joyful, continued existence?
>
> (*SW* 3, 467)

The guarantee of immortality, which is nothing to do with 'eternal life' in a Platonic or a Christian metaphysical sense, but is everything to do with a vitalist sense, was known to the ancient culture of the Pelasgians, the (mythical?) ancient people to whom, in *Of Cosmogonic Eros*, Klages refers at some length (book 5, part 2, 'The Pelasgian World-View'):

> So the world of images lights up only in the *visionary eros of those experiencing it*. So-called continued existence – in fact, however, the vital present which the Pelasgian demands for the souls of his departed – strips, moment by moment, the blossoms from the elementary-erotic connection of those who have been with the physically living. The soul-image dies, when it dies in the souls of those who remember it!
>
> (*SW* 3, 469)

All-embracing love: 'this kiss for the whole world'

In *The Foundations of the Doctrine of Character*, Klages uncovers the 'erotic' – in a Klagesian sense – dimension of everyday life and practice:

> Even when among primitive peoples, to whom *our* conception of property is so strange, the great warrior is lain in his grave along with his bow, his spear, and his battle-horse, then the deepest reason for doing this lies as

All-embracing love   159

little in an egotistical will to possess as it was an egotistical will to possess that could have motivated someone fascinated by precious stones to take a gem; rather, it lies in eros. There *is* an eros for one's homeland, for the soil, for the settlement, for one's domestic animal, for a memory, for a tool that one has made or with which one has formed a bond through long use, for the tree one has planted and tended, etc., and accordingly there *can* be an eros in principle for every object of perception that becomes for us a symbol of a period, now happy, now sad, of our pilgrimage through life; for which reason the devotions that arise from this fact have as much to do with egotisms as does a mother's milk, namely: nothing! If one wants to call them attachments, then they are erotic attachments, or in other words not attachments on the part of the ego, neither the spiritual nor the personal, but attachments on the part of life.

(*SW* 4, 389)

In *Of Cosmogonic Eros*, Klages extends the meaning of the category of the 'erotic' to a much wider dimension of experience, both physical and metaphysical, than is the case of the conventional sense in which we usually use the word:

We all know from memory what it means to live as if in a dream: in the 'self-forgetfulness' of a rare happiness, or when we were completely 'lost' in the sight of the setting sun, completely 'absorbed' in the enticing song of a flute, entirely 'immersed' in the distant image of bygone days of youth. If breaking open announces the readiness of the unshackled soul to 'put out', to 'go into raptures', to 'roam', then an inner melting prepares the magic of its 'being transported'. Although the complete delight of eros can be connected with a breaking-open as well as with a melting loss of self, then there exists between the latter and its delight a palpable affinity, as result of which we cannot better picture to ourselves the sweetness of the erotic shudder than when we emphasize the soul's melting overflow, its devotion. If we consider this to be the essential characteristic of erotic delight, then we can recognize with little difficulty its share in, on the one hand, all moments of 'bliss' in the satisfaction of physical desires (whether in eating and drinking, whether in the sexual embrace), and in, on the other, all kinds of truest happiness, from 'blissful happiness', 'joyful bliss', 'rapture', 'delight', 'enchantment', just as even such spiritualized feelings of elation as 'rapture' and 'transfiguration'.

(*SW* 3, 397)

In *The Spirit as Adversary of the Soul*, Klages explores the interaction between the various polarities of existence in terms of a *gamos*, or symbolical marriage:

This activity which we call the soul continually takes place through the interaction of the poles of reality, and as the elements are born through their

160   *Selections from Klages*

gamos with the soul of the visionary, so their being present is based on the *flux* of action and, in respect of the earth, on the uninterrupted exchange between the earth and the cosmos.

(*SW* 2, 1141)

The role of eros in connecting these polarities of the world, and the precise sense in which it deserves to be described as 'cosmogonic', i.e. world-creating, are explored by Klages in his aptly entitled early work, *Of Cosmogonic Eros*:

Eros is called elementary or cosmic to the extent that an individual being, when seized by it, experiences that it has something pulsing and flooding through it like an electric current which, similar in its nature to magnetism, allows the most distantly apart souls, irrespective of their limits, to sense each other in the attraction connecting them, transforms the very means of all activity which separates bodies, space and time, into the omnipresent element of a supporting and swirling ocean, and in this way connects the *poles of the world*, regardless of their irreducible difference. And it is called cosmogonic because it is a state of fullness that pours itself forth, according to which the inner – immediately giving birth out of itself – immediately becomes something external, the world and the reality that appears. Very different from mere feeling it is at the same time the ceaseless *revelation* of what wells up from the most secluded part of the soul.

(*SW* 3, 387)

Consequently, in *The Spirit as Adversary of the Soul*, Klages explains that it would be a mistake to reduce eros to something that is (merely) sexual, when in fact, in his eyes, eros is (as befits something 'cosmogonic') so much more:

The path from the animal stage of mating to the primordially human stage [...] leads from the natural uniformity of the *sexual drive* to the confused profusion of forms of *eros* which, rooted in vision and ignited by the image, thus reaches also far beyond the limits which are set around the sexual drive, bringing about, in a thousand forms, the gamos of the soul with the secret of the world.

(*SW* 3, 1353)

This supra-sexual dimension of eros is explored in the emotional phenomenology of Klages's *Of Cosmogonic Eros*, in one of its densest and most compelling passages where Klages offers his definition of *Eros Kosmogonos*:

While the desire for satisfaction of the sexual drive is accompanied by the sexual union of two individuals (and, strictly speaking, two individuals of opposing sexual gender), there can be no limitation, not even speculative, on the occasions when the carrier of the soul enters into the fiery circle of erotic ecstasy. It can find perfection at the mere sight of a beloved being,

All-embracing love   161

whether a being of the opposite sex or of the same sex, it may be an animal, a plant: and it can find perfection no less in the scent of a fragrance, the taste of a wine, the sound of a musical note, the touch of a dripping twig. It can awaken in the waking state as well as in the most intoxicating dream. It celebrates its orgies under the rising winds of the spring storms, in the face of the star-sown firmament, in the hailstone shower, on the flaming mountain ridge, in the raging of the sea surf, under the lightning flashes of 'first love', but no less in the embrace of destiny, which crushes its carrier. It is desire at the same time for *rising up* and *going down*; desire, for which dying and death becomes painfully blissful transformation! In the eternal moment of its completion lies: *unshackled raving* or *crystalline reverie*.... So little does it resemble the condition of any kind of neediness that we should characterize what is an urge about it as a drive towards *overflowing*, to radiant *overflowing*, to extreme *self-squandering*. It is not neediness and lack, but exuberance of a welling fullness, a gold-bestowing flame and a pregnancy that will give birth to worlds. For this reason, wherever its ray falls, that spot glows in nameless beauty, wherever its foot steps, there a thicket of blossoms will flourish, and its embrace releases from things and people the god imprisoned within them! This is the most general composition of that *condition* that is called, in the symbolic language of the prophetic spirit of prehistory, *Eros Kosmogonos*.

(*SW* 3, 386)

In *Of Cosmogonic Eros*, Klages turns to various sources – to the classical story of Damon and Phintias, to the medieval *Song of the Nibelungen*, and to a story by the Brothers Grimm – to illustrate aspects of the vitalist modalities of eros:

Who has not in their youth had their enthusiasm fired by the story of Damon and Phintias,[62] or the relation of Hagen and Volker,[63] or the tale recognized around the globe about the brothers! Who could fail to recognize that in the fairy-tale an erotic band surrounds with maternal tenderness all the individuals, humans, animals, plants, stones and in particular all utensils! We recall, for example, the touching friendship of the dog and the sparrow, and the terrible revenge taken by the sparrow on the driver of a cart because he ran over his 'Brother Dog'![64] The eros of the Western world stands under the sign of 'blood brotherhood', of which the 'sacred band' of the Thebans is a world-historical example.[65] It created the poetry of the guilds and workers' associations, the mercenary soldiers and the travellers, and its influence can be felt in our day in the fraternal customs of our student leagues, whose song-filled symposia were able, until a generation or so ago, to preserve sufficient of it to make many a 'Philistine' think for a lifetime with wistful nostalgia of the 'good old student times'.[66]

(*SW* 3, 406)

162 Selections from Klages

In one of his most lyrical and exquisite passages in *Of Cosmogonic Eros*, Klages evokes the kind of special – indeed, unique – experiential moments that, for him, represent the erotic under the guise of the 'eros of distance':

> Let us give an account of an unspectacular experience, to which everyone in the age of their 'hopes and endeavours' will have been privy, even if he or she has long since forgotten it in the age of their accomplishments.
>
> In the lilac-scented summer night, in dimly flickering light, he was struck with an inexpressible vision of happiness by a gleaming ray from moist eyes, he was made to tremble and was transformed by a mysterious smile, the tense beguiling charm of the passing shape embraced him magnetically: he dissolved in a current of delight, and the flame of love, as if caught by a gust of the wind, touched and set fire to the encircling firmament. But alas for him, if he unwisely took this moment of fulfilment for nothing than a promise, confused the charm of the appearance with its bodily carrier and allowed himself to be seduced by a mystical gesture into a possessive love-relationship. The promise will *not* be fulfilled, which the unlimited minute appeared to grant, and he will find only too soon, painfully disappointed, instead of the divine shape that shone upon him a finite, a limited, a *measurable* being! What we with our human sense took to be a mere promise, was rather a deep draught from the goblet of the *eros of distance*, which transports one from the tangible world of things into a never-to-be-touched reality of images!
>
> *(SW 3, 411)*

It is impossible to overlook the tender melancholy attaching to the concept of the erotic as it is expounded by Klages in the pages of *Of Cosmogonic Eros*, as well as its powerful sense of nostalgia (in the etymological sense of the word, i.e. *nostos* = 'return home' + *algos* = 'pain'):

> We do not dispute that there is something uniquely gratifying when two mutually devoted lovers live their lives closely together; but we do dispute the repeatability of the overwhelming shudder of those *first* moments, and we propose the thesis that only first moments unlock the gate to the secret of the world, not the human pleasures, however warm, of domestic togetherness.
>
> *(SW 3, 60)*

In uncovering the mysterious, daimonic aspects of eros, Klages seeks, in *Of Cosmogonic Eros*, to show its all-embracing presence in a vitalist conception of life:

> For the epopt,[67] we said, bodiliness is a symbol of the soul of the world that pours forth images. Now, the person not merely in love, so to speak, but possessed in the depths of his or her soul by the most profound passion – think of Solveig's love for Peer[68] – is, in relation to the object of love, just

Writing and poetry 163

as much a mystical initiate with the eye of the world-creating god, before whom the cup bursts and the skin of the body begins to glow as the elementary soul shines through. While ignited by the uniqueness of the soul's being, such a person *penetrates* the humanity of the beloved with the shine of the gaze in which the soul's daimon resides. This – like the eros of antiquity and of the Germanic Middle Ages – does not exclude that the magic light reflecting the primordial image can go, wandering, from one person to another. Even the shortest period of erotic union would not interfere with the most fulfilled interiority, and precisely an exuberance that gives to the utmost would tolerate without contradiction even devotion to a hetaira.[69]

(*SW* 3, 472)

Writing and poetry: it's a kind of magic

In an impassioned paragraph, cited above (in the section on 'Life'), Klages invokes the powerful – indeed, daimonic – effect of ancient Indian palaces, the temple ruins at Karnak or Luxor, the pyramid of Cheops, the thermal baths of Caracalla, Roman aqueducts, the churches of Ravenna and Byzantium, the Alhambra, Romanesque castles and crypts, and northern Gothic. He cries out, as if in a fit of impatience: 'Here too let there be an end to "aesthetics"!' (*SW*, vol. 2, p. 1118). Yet Klages turns repeatedly to art, especially painting and poetry, to substantiate his vitalist theses; so much so, in fact, that some critics have suggested aesthetics is the paradigm of his philosophical system.[70] In certain key passages, Klages explicitly concerns himself with works of art, some visual, some literary. And at the heart of what could, without contradiction or exaggeration, be described as Klagesian aesthetics, lies the following thought – as formulated by Klages in *Expressive Movement and Formative Power* (and elsewhere):

What could not be a miracle, *wants* to become a work; what could not become a work, becomes a *deed*...

(*SW* 6, 287)[71]

In an early (and never completed) essay entitled *On Dream Consciousness*, Klages addressed in the form of a short, but significant, footnote the problem of the relation between the dream and the artist:

The dream begins to dissolve precisely when one tries to represent it. [...] This is the tragic aspect of the problem of the artist – to be sure, of the artist, not of the poet, whom the miracle of language enables to remain in the dream. The object of art is what is not an object, namely images [*Bilder*], which are to be revealed in the material of the world of perception, in sound, colour, or stone. The artist should make representable what can otherwise only be dreamed, should depict the appearance [*Erscheinung*] in the object of perception, should be able to want what is resistant to volition.

164　*Selections from Klages*

Here lies the source of the deep strife in the heart of all personal artistry and the harsh, combative quality of all art that is no longer, like the art of primordial times and of early antiquity, purely mythological and therefore purely poetic.

(*SW* 3, 179)

One of the writers in whom, inevitably, Klages took great interest was the canonical figure of Goethe.[72] That said, Klages's approach to Goethe was by no means an entirely uncritical one; reflected, for instance, in his essay entitled *Remarks on the Limits of the Goethean Human Being* (1917). One of the two fragments on Goethe dating back to 1903 explores Goethe's relation to Romanticism:

Goethe was in relation to art a representative of the active spirit, Romanticism in relation to life a representative of the visionary. Goethe *was active* in the area of vision – for all art is something visionary –, Romanticism *envisions* in all regions of action. Goethe's poetry can be described as a deed, the documents of Romanticism would correspondingly have to be called a miracle. A *totality* of life stands behind both: in the case of Goethe, Apollo, the god of individuation and also of materialization; in the case of Romanticism, the dream after-image of the wild hunter, the shadow, still reeling from drinking deep of the draught of transcendence, of Odin. The path opened by Goethe was continued by Platen and, in part, Mörike,[73] the path of Romanticism by all the rest of the poetry of the nineteenth century.

(*RR*, 323–324)

And in another fragment from 1903 Klages explores the significance of the figure central to one of Goethe's major works, *Faust*. The entirety of all 12,000 lines of Goethe's two-part masterpiece is compressed here into a single synthetic reading:

Goethe shows in his Faust the decline of the spirit of magic in the modern spirit of the deed. As is the case in probably every primordially born work of literature, Faust is already at the outset what he ends up being: a scholar and a philanthropist; except that initially he resists this and chooses suicide. But he commits suicide more profoundly through his futile career. Creating a dam for the sea or rather just an illusion of one, in the course of which the blinded Faust descends into the patriotic enthusiasm of the rival club celebration, is no more than the fulfillment of the thought of the valuelessness of life and its denial with which the tragedy opens. Inbetween there is his attempt to turn around and to return to magic. This is represented from the start through a misunderstanding of its meaning by the devil; and Faust then really misuses it for purely non-magical purposes: to impress a girl or to save a bankrupt king from ruin. Rightly condemned by the Earth Spirit and accompanied only by its imitator and unintentional fool, the devil, Faust races as an empty individualist through empty pleasures of all-too-human

Writing and poetry 165

desire, looks from the primordial realm to the ghostly play of shadows, first in the northern, then in the southern Walpurgisnacht – continually sinning, because he continually repents – and ends up as the magic-less, roguish egg-head who affirms profit, work, service to society. With a terrible logical consistency the lemures enter after the death of the 'worker' (masks from the realm of Jehovah!): first disguised with the make-up of the underworld as real lemures, but then in their fully masked form as hideously seraphic vampires, who run off with his soul into a fourth dimension. This was precisely the development of 'world history' in the nineteenth century. Even the homosexual impulse of the devil in the concluding scene serves as a significant hint at homosexuality in all its forms today.[74] – It is not entirely without good reason that the present age has founded Goethe societies.

(*RR*, 324)

One of the chief characteristics of Klages's interest in art is his intercultural approach to the works of all manner of places and epochs, as this passage from *The Spirit as Adversary of the Soul* reveals:

Notwithstanding the fact that among historical sculptors certainly none can be found who would not gladly see his name associated for ever with his most successful work, Klio saw fit wisely to remark that the most powerful of sculptures which, in order to be created, needed a human being, became *nameless*,[75] as if one should read from this fact that it is sacrilege or folly to want to explain from the wretchedness of *persons* something that only *through persons* springs from those same powers that brought into being the Niagara Falls, the deserts of Arabia, the geyser of Mount Hekla.[76] Who knows the planners of those miraculous buildings just mentioned [i.e. see above], who knows the musical composers of ancient chants and folk songs, who even knows the creators of the hymns of the Veda, the Indian and Homeric epics, the 'prophecy of Wala' [from the Edda]?[77] Even the poet of the medieval Song of the Nibelungs [i.e. the *Nibelungenlied*], who would not take second place after Ferdowsi,[78] is unknown to us, and as far as Shakespeare is concerned, the scholars still dispute whether he was really the author of 'Shakespeare's dramas'. In the meantime, whether one wishes to call it chance or not, one thing remains certain: what lives 'immortal' in every creation whether of stone or of words is never the 'heart and soul' [*Gemüt*] of the poet; and when Eichendorff says, 'The poet is the heart of the world',[79] he is announcing a truth to which of course the poet alone is privy: only *he or she* is a poet (in the most profound meaning of the word), in whom the 'heart of the world' has at some time or another taken up abode.

(*SW* 2, 1118)

In *Expressive Movement and Formative Power*, Klages pursues the idea that the animals of a landscape emerge from (and hence are in some sense expressive of) its 'soul':

166   *Selections from Klages*

Through the marriage – not merely metaphorical! – that is celebrated with its image, the soul of the landscape enters literally into a spirit capable of being impregnated by it, in order to weave out of it the veil of Maya of things in the form of giving shape, little needing any sideways glance at models and with the same *unconscious inevitability* as it produces plants and animals in the form of giving birth, namely: not through the imitation of those already existing, but out of the necessity of their 'nature'.

(*SW* 6, 289)

Tirelessly and with an increasing sense of urgency Klages promotes the idea, here in *The Spirit as Adversary of the Soul*, that what a phenomenological view of the world can reveal is its vitalist dimension. In this respect, he believes, a study of landscape has much to teach us:

The earth as, so to speak, a place of residence for elementary souls would correspondingly be crowned with works of sculptors dependent on nature, and their cosmically compelled effect would, on the other hand, be a fateful necessity awoken in a vision and reaching perfection in the birth of images. And this perfection would be in harmony with *that* completion that is produced by the unwakingly formative powers; for it is part of the secret of the 'blind' rule of earthly and sidereal powers alike that, unconcerned by torments and joys, they break off life after life of the individual beings sprung from them before their time, with frost and drought and flood and storm and fire and rain of ash and earthquake. They do not spare the strongest and most beautiful of their 'children', tirelessly giving birth again with inexhaustible generative power to *what is perfect*. In the natural world *outside* human beings one will not find a flower whose bold colours do not merge into one accord, or a tree whose leaves' forms do not superbly fit the linear characteristics of its branches, or a tree or a prairie whose stones and plants and animals do not chime symphonically together. Just as souls and world are *not* opposites but poles, whose oscillations in the process of envisioning are harmonically in phase, so too all human activity (as well as its lack of activity) does not break through the rhythm of the landscape, but crowns it with *commemorations of eternity*.

To these belong productions of human skill and ingenuity from houses to their walls, and to these belong no less, however, the so-called sacred groves, rivers, lakes, cliffs, mountain tops, trees, bays, animals or, in short, all locations that are dedicated to the Pelasgian sense of piety, and are as a result taken away from arbitrary caprice, for those works are only able to crown the landscape by leaving in it untouched what *must* remained untouched, if its rhythm is to roll on, undisturbed, through what has been created by human hand.

(*SW* 2, 1208)

In a crisp aphoristic formulation from *The Spirit as Adversary of the Soul*, Klages reminds us that all art, properly speaking, is symbolic:

Writing and poetry 167

Art, if it is to be more than a thinly reasoned showing-off with peeling surfaces, is devout, and accordingly symbolic, art.

(*SW* 2, 1263)

The extent to which Klages wants us to take art seriously is indicated in this plea (in *The Spirit as Adversary of the Soul*) that we regard it as in some sense magical:

Let there be no mistake: *either* the most powerful poetry and art of all times is sheer invention – no, a smoke screen –, *or* it is a magic means of opening up to us *real worlds*, to which we would on our own no longer find a way out of our dungeon of believing in facts.

(*SW* 2, 1185)

In his early sketches Klages plays extensively with the idea of magic, usually in the context of aesthetics. As the following extracts from *Rhythms and Runes* illustrate, magic is a way for Klages to talk about the power of art. (The date in brackets refers to the period from which the fragment in question dates):

Writing poetry as a form of life. [1900] – To write poetry is a form of ecstatic vitality. The life of the poet is writing inner poetry. Poetic experience is a magical experience of language.

(*RR*, 243)

The nature of the poet. – Although an individual being, the poet remains the moment into which the universe flows: he is animal, star, sea, plant; he is the eye of the element, and so in his core matriarchal and earthbound. The praxis corresponding to his inner vision is magic. – The astral (like the material) spirit is, by contrast, a single point that has been torn out. Both compel being from outside it, whether through astral or through material mechanics. – In the poet beings come and go, removed from his willpower; they transform themselves into him, the world speaks out of him. The voice of the rivers, the mountains, and the plains sounds forth from his lips. His fundamental experience is the shudder of words. What streams through him is the panta rhei[80] of what happens, he sings the soul of the storm, the sea, and the primordial tones.

(*RR*, 261–262)

Mechanical and magic philosophy. [1901] – The praxis of our philosophy is magic, it itself is the theory of magic. Academic philosophy is the theory of mechanics and its praxis is mechanics. – Magical philosophy denies the principle of identity,[81] and consequently unity, thing, permanence, repetition, mathematics; it denies concepts and causality, for causality is the objective parallel of logical connection. – It works with images and symbols, and its method is the method of analogy.[82] – The most important names

168   *Selections from Klages*

for it are: element, substance, principle, daimon, cosmos, microcosm, macrocosm, essence, image, primordial image, vortex, tangle, fire. – Its ultimate formulas are magic spells and have magical power.

(*RR*, 312)

In *Humankind and Earth* Klages reminds us that a work of art transcends the
conditions that produce it, including the life of its originator, the artist:

The life of the artist (= sculptor) is in the *service* of the work, so much so
that his work contains the essence of his life and of more than only *his* life.

(*Mensch und Erde*, 99)

Art takes us back to a time when there was no time, and in this sense it opens up
the primordial dimension of being, as Klages argues in *The Spirit as Adversary
of the Soul*:

If one assumes it to be the case that, while every individual being is a
microcosm, it is only after the intermediate realm of animals and not until
with humankind that these: distances, activity, the cosmos, begin to
awaken, then the images of ecstatic vision would be just as much the goal
and the perfection of what happens in the world as its creative, primordial
beginning over and over again, and this would be the sense comprised in
all image-drunken moments: *to be the means in objective form of their
renewal*. In this way one would have named the macrocosmic sense of all
human creativity and influence, *after* it had been rescued from the magical
rotating of a primordial time in which soul and world fused with each other
in rhythmically uninterrupted, mutually consecutive embraces. – It makes
essentially no difference whether one demonstrates this in buildings,
statues, paintings, in ornaments and items of everyday use, in writing and
'drawing', in musical compositions, songs and poems, in dances and
mystery plays, *or* whether one chooses language to do so.

(*SW* 2, 1190)

In *The Foundations of the Doctrine of Character*, Klages argues that it is not so
much our language that is lacking in vitality, but our experience of life. To this
experiental poverty, the poet can – through arts – offer a much-needed
corrective:

One often hears people talking about the poverty of language, and how we
lack the words for our most profound experiences: it might be more truthful
to speak of the poverty of experience, to which in countless cases a sheen
of significance is lent only by the richness of the words with which it is
adorned. It is only because the life that has become solidified in language
overtakes, in passion and in wildness as in spiritual impetus, the ultimate
peaks and troughs in the life of the individual – aside from the dark feelings

Writing and poetry 169

of one's early youth –, that it can, when set in motion again, still transport souls away from themselves with an almost daimonic, magical force and into otherwise unattainable vortices of more or less human activity, and, exactly as if blessed by the genius of language, a great poet leads us into an unknown wonderland.

(*SW* 4, 230)

In *The Spirit as Adversary of the Soul* Klages explains wherein the 'magic of language' (which he means in an almost literal sense) resides:

The magic of language, which all great linguistic masters (and, to the highest degree, poets) have at their disposal, consists in the renewal of primordial sounds by means of a lingustic repository, which is separated by many millennia from the pre-rational sources of language. The 'how', unteachable and unlearnable, has nothing to do with bold new constructions, nothing to do with seeking out obsolete words and phrases, but is based on a willingness to follow elementary rhythms.

(*SW* 2, 1159)

In the chapter in *The Spirit as Adversary of the Soul* entitled 'Elementary Symbols', Klages considers such symbolic elements as the moon, water, and (discussed in the extract below) the tree. In this chapter, Klages says he wishes to undertake, using an expression from Goethe's *Faust*, a kind of descent to the Mothers, down to the vitalist sources of the cosmos: 'Formation, transformation, / The eternal mind's eternal recreation' (ll. 6287–6288).[83]

Hardly any symbolism has become so deeply engrained in language and so extensively bound up with poetry as has the symbol of the plant. Does this mean that the plant is being turned into a human or is the human being turned into a plant? In old Chinese lyric poetry the royal bride is said to be 'a tree clothed in silken leaves', each of her hands is a 'branch with five twigs', her coloured nails are compared to the blossoms, her teeth to 'moist pumpkin seeds'. In the Vedas, it is said of the singer that he 'sprouts song-like blossoms' as does a tree,[84] in the Mahabharata it is said of the heroine that she lies breathing on her husband's chest as does 'a flower when the morning refreshes it'.[85] In his world-famous verses [...] Homer espies the rising and falling of the human race in the springing up and falling of leaves;[86] and, as if the millennia had changed nothing, Schiller describes Wallenstein when he is abandoned by his followers as a 'tree without leaves'.[87] – Indeed, anyone who has, without any sort of poetic intent, spoken of 'lush' or 'rising' youth, of 'faded' or 'dry' old age, of 'blooming' health, of 'budding' innocence, of 'fully blossomed' beauty, *what* exactly has he or she been 'comparing': a plant with a human being or rather a human being with a plant? Without any doubt, the latter! And correspondingly, among those expressions that are truly poetic expressions there is

170 *Selections from Klages*

scarcely any other kind than the one where what is immediately comprehensible is precisely something plant-like, whereas what is human is something merely mediated that only acquires an illumination commanding our sympathy when it is related to the former. If in this way the human being has become a kind of plant, then we should not understand it as an anthropomorphization of the plant if it, too, has 'eyes', 'feet', a 'head' or 'hair', if it can 'speak' or 'sing', 'sigh' and 'moan', and if the tree, struck by a blow from the axe, 'bleeds' and 'cries out'. For such expressions presuppose a plant-*soul*, whose expressions are, after all, to be depicted no differently from those of the human mind and soul, to say nothing of the fact that [...] in such expressions the semantic meaning of the words undergoes a palpable change.

> As the sun begins to set,
> There's a last tree that stands
> As in the flaming morning glow
> On the furthest edge of the sky.
>
> It is a tree and nothing else,
> But if one thinks in the night
> Of the last, wonderful light,
> One thinks of it too.
>
> In the same way I think of you,
> Now that youth has left me,
> You hold for me its final gleam
> That remains for all time.[88]

The thrilling force of these lines by *Hebbel* springs from the way in which an entire human fate is united with the image of tree, viewed as if in ritual ecstasy, and certainly not the reverse! Not a tendency to personify the whole of nature, but precisely to renaturalize the human person, is what characterizes the experience of the poet; and for this very reason it participates in the symbolism of prehistory!

(*SW* 2, 1308)

In the passage above, Klages discusses a lyric text by the German poet and dramatist Friedrich Hebbel (1813–1863). Further on in *The Spirit as Adversary of the Soul*, Klages returns to another one of his favourite authors, Nikolaus Lenau, to exemplify his aesthetic theses:

If we wanted to try to articulate in sober words what is convertible into a form of judgement from a Pelasgian's experience of a tree, and in fact the experience of anyone who still retains the vestiges of primordial feeling, then it would not be this: the tree, too, has vicissitudes just like a human being, so it too must be something like a human; but rather it would be this:

Writing and poetry 171

I, too, a human being, am something that *grows* and *fades away* again; I, too, am held as if by my roots, untiringly fed by the earth from underground vaults and watered by the sky with light and rain from above; I, too, even if increasingly straying from the path and alienated from this reality of clouds, streams, rainfall, lightning, storms, trees, and forests (whose voices I can no longer understand, even if they still seem to me to have a kind of primordial familiarity), am not a rejected fellow member of a worldly home in *which all individual beings are connected with each other.* Losing myself and giving myself back to that home, I return, stripped of my self [*entselbstet*], back into the life of the tree that runs through its branches! 'Coming to oneself again' after what is, of course, a far more profound 'contemplation' than the kind that can be so feebly *said* in such sentences, the vitally connected attitude reflects the character, not confined by the limitations of personality, of the plant's *daimon*.

Convinced that authentic poetry springs together with authentic myth from *one* source, we call [...] on the genius of the poet for assistance. [...] We think of the incomparable forest poems of *Lenau* who, with a sure instinct, placed at their centre the figure of a magician, Merlin the wizard.[89] With that linguistic force which is peculiar only to an intoxication with images, the following short sample expresses not only the shudder provoked by the tree and by the weather, but at the same time, in its concluding stanza, their sense and essence.

> Full of thundery passion
> Into the storm Merlin
> Throws his cloak,
> So that the air cools,
> Lightnings bathe
> His naked chest.
>
> A network of roots
> Spreads from the oak to the ground,
> Hidden beneath, sucking
> Life from secret springs,
> That make the trunk swell toward the sky.
>
> Merlin lets his hair flutter in the wind
> To and fro in the stormy night,
> And the fiery, tawny lightnings
> Flash, anointing his head.
> Nature, as she is revealed,
> Intimately becoming his twin,
> Is drunk in by his heart, when bolts crackle,
> Kissing his dark hair.[90]

(*SW* 2, 1313)

172   *Selections from Klages*

Some of the greatest pages in *The Spirit as Adversary of the Soul* are devoted to an evocation and an analysis of the great Swiss Symbolist painter, Arnold Böcklin. His works are extensively exhibited in Munich – in the Neue Pinakothek and in the Sammlung Schack. In these miniature verbal portraits, Klages reveals himself as a true '*passeur d'enthousiasme*', to use the French expression: someone who shares his enthusiasm and, in turn, ignites enthusiasm in others. And this, in the true etymological sense of the word 'enthusiasm', i.e. to be *entheos*, i.e. full of or possessed by a god. (See Chapter 2, pp. 82–85.)

In *Expressive Movement and Formative Power* Klages explains the erotic – in the Klagesian sense – origin of all great art:

> It is in the heat of conception, not in the greatness of the spirit, that in future we shall search for the cause of what makes a masterpiece so overwhelming: in other words, how the vital fullness of the real child has its ground, not so much in the essence of its parents, as in the depth of their procreative passion. If one wants to call this inner life of the work of art its form, then form is unattainable to spiritual effort, and a 'style' carries the magic of form exactly to the extent that the rhythm in it masters its law.
>
> (*SW* 6, 259)

According to the argument of *Expressive Movement and Formative Power*, with its passion the soul is able to influence even the spirit:

> The ground of the *shaped* revelation of life is thus to be sought not in its fullness itself, but rather in the effectiveness of its pulse right up to the altitudinal levels of the spirit. Instead of saying that life has given its blood to the spirit, it would be just as correct to say that the spirit has descended into its waves; accordingly, the bringing-to-life of the spirit coincides with the spiritualization of what is alive.
>
> (*SW* 6, 312)

Elsewhere in *The Spirit as Adversary of the Soul* Klages explores the complicated relation between the work of art and the will of the artist. What art reveals, he argues, is another (and more vital) dimension to reality. Once again, Klages finds that sculpture is the best form of art in which to analyse the vital power of the images:

> If we remember that something only happens from vitality, and that the living being appears in being alive, then we shall easily find a link to another kind of search for reality, i.e. that of the sculptors (artists) and even the poets (to the extent they have to participate in the sculptural) who, at least within the more recent era of culture and above all since the so-called Renaissance, had also been compelled to become searchers for truth. – Just as with the drive-impulse [*Triebantrieb*] an effect is exercised on the body of the impulse carrier [*Antriebsträger*] by an attraction of the images which

results in an approach to the source of attraction or even a union with it, so the attraction of images exercises an effect as well on the soul of a human being capable of gazing into the distance, which would result in their objectification in solid matter. And just as the searcher for truth is bound to what happens by its reality, so it is the images themselves who bind the artist and, as it were, use his mind in order to come, through him, into appearance as a visible presence. In this way the sculptor finds himself confronted by an inner compulsion with the task of shaping – through composing, painting, chiselling, building, dancing, etc. – with the help of his will, something which would be a success to the extent that it comes into being, and equally would be a failure to the extent that it bears the traces of arbitrary caprice. If it is no longer granted to him to work in a kind of somnambulistic state, such as is the actual case for many an achievement of primitive peoples as well as of certain artistic periods in the past, then in him too a critical analysis would have to escape the tragic double impulse of having to think what escapes through being conceptualized, and having to will what escapes through being willed. This critical analysis, incessantly competing with image-bearing urgings (comparable to the birth-pangs of pregnancy), compels him again deliberately, step by step, once more to eradicate from what has been achieved those aspects where the form is a manufactured form instead of an organic form, and where there is a distorted gesture of the will instead of vital expression. [...][91] The fruits of the sufferings and joys of *this* critical analysis will not be denied by anyone. After all, it is works of sculpture whose achievement brings us back from the apparent reality of thought-things (=facts) to the reality of images, while what they do not achieve, manifesting itself in what is achieved as something *disturbing* it – from which no sculpture, however significant, since the 'Renaissance' is free – might with good reason remind us that a reality that is merely understood is a false reality! Now, even the expressions [*Niederschläge*] of a deep will-to-truth are works, namely: in the medium of the word, and both, the research scholar as well as the artist, deserve to be counted as sculptors! For what they achieve in the service, not of any curiosity, but of the voices from the depths of their soul, they achieve because they were able *with* the will to cancel out what had been willed, and if, correspondingly, we oppose the will-to-the-work to the will-to-the-deed as being incompatible with it, so we would like in doing this to have frankly revealed that the only possible life-*affirming* achievement of willing takes place in the *self-denial of willing*. What could not be a miracle, wants to become a work; what could not become a work, becomes a deed.

(*SW* 2, 621–623)

Finally, an aphoristic sentence brings to a conclusion a discussion in *The Spirit as Adversary of the Soul* of the relationship between speaking and writing – and links the intellectual ambition of Klagesian philosophy to its particular view of language:

174 *Selections from Klages*

Poetry that is pure, because completely free from communicative purposes, is pure monologue or dialogue with reality or it is – and here it approaches its limits – dialogue of the singer with this soul ('lyric'). But thinking is a silent dialogue of the ego with another ego in the same person and usually of a predominantly speaking ego with a predominantly listening ego, and moreover it is – nothing! No other people nas so early on in its prehistorical period thought so uninhibitedly as the Greeks; but nor was there one so hungry for conversations as they were. It is surely no coincidence that an intellectual system that is so vast as is the Platonic is carried out in the form of conversations that take place between sharply characterized speakers and in tones that are often almost dramatic! With the aid of this brilliant device Plato has created a memorial from which we can deduce that precisely the most powerful of our thoughts are those *speeches* which remain victorious in dispute with one's inner Peripatetic![92] [...] [T]he internalization of speaking received a powerful boost through the invention of writing. However, after many centuries in which books and card-indexes and writing tools belong to the scholar as leather and lasts and awls do the cobbler, the role of the silent conversation-partner has to a certain extent been replaced by those three things: the real scholar 'discusses' a paper and has forgotten that thinking is a conversation without a second person. In this way we entirely lost sight of the fact that of the little which the individual thinker brings to the thought of humankind, he owes by the far the best part to a language that thinks *through* him. 'To philosophize is an attempt at interpreting the magic of words.'[93]

(*SW* 2, 1166–1167)

Anthropology and the guidance of souls: we are truly blessed

As well as opening the reader's eyes to the cosmic dimension of life, the writings of Klages reveal him to have been a shrewed psychologist, a keen observer of human behaviour, and a steely-eyed analyst of character foibles and failings. In *On the Doctrine of Expression and the Doctrine of Character*, Klages reminds us of some the human, all-too-human negativities to which any anthropology, i.e. a study of humankind, must not close its eyes:

Before an anthropology in general could flourish, thinkers would need to have forgotten to be ashamed of vanity, selfishness, envy, malice, fear of death, and forgetfulness.

(*SW* 4, 14)

In *The Foundations of the Science of Character* Klages sketches the ambition of the kind of vitalist psychology he sought to develop and elaborate. As he puts it, psychology, i.e. the investigation of the psyche or the soul, involves an ability 'to see the sense of the phenomenal world' (*in der Erscheinungswelt ihren Sinn zu sehen*), or in other words to see *symbolically*:

Anthropology and the guidance of souls 175

What we are trying to understand has to be seen in opposition to whatever presupposition of all knowledge it is to which the name 'object' incontrovertibly bears witness. We still remain in the metaphor, which is actually more than a metaphor, if we add that being too close to an object does harm to an overview of it and that in order to philosophize one needs 'distance', however little we are otherwise favourably disposed toward a term which has, since Nietzsche, become one of the favourite words of our literary figures.[94] Being close holds the gaze to *one* point, isolates the object of close inspection, and inevitably leads to that atomism of thought of which orthodox science offered an example, whereas horizon-widening distance demands, as it were, a *gaze that can wander where it will*, which opposes to the belief in objective individualism the totality of an *image*.

Only the image, the vision, can stand firm in the dissolving acid of attention and can compel the mind with an irresistible power of persuasion. Distance, however, plunges the incomplete reality of only 'fixed' objects into the universe of contemplation, and lends the constantly differentiating daytime gaze of consciousness something of the synthetic foresight of the prophetic eye. *Truth becomes more profound in relation to the power of sight of the truth-seeking spirit.*

Now, psychology is concerned with what are in themselves non-sensory matters, and the individual person must find the material in himself or herself to interpret them. Thus the spirit must be able to gain a relation of unfamiliarity to the experience of the personality with which it is involved; to a certain extent, it has to de-humanize itself, in order to be able to look at what is human; indeed, it has to know how to distance itself to such an extent that the individual characteristics of the interior life suddenly combine into an image for it – an image, whose partial characteristics it can gauge in a similar way to how the bodily eye reads off the position of a particular place from a map. Images, however, whether dreamed or perceived, are temporal-spatial realities. Hence we get at the matter more precisely if, conversely, we say that a gift for psychology lies essentially in the ability *to see in the phenomenal world its sense*. To see the 'sense' in it means nothing other than to see a phenomenon *symbolically*. And indeed it is an indispensable characteristic of the *pathos philosophon*,[95] and moreover its point of intersection with that of the artist and the poet, that it comprehends things, following an inescapable compulsion, symbolically: in this respect it is, despite the magnitude of the difference, similar to the mentality of the 'savage'.

(*SW* 4, 421)

Rather than moving from the part to the whole, Klagesian psychology – so he maintains in *The Foundations of the Doctrine of Character* – moves from the whole to the part:

Summarized as a principle: one has to have the *entirety* before one can successfully attempt to examine its *parts*. One can dissect the former into

176 *Selections from Klages*

the latter, but not ever conversely assemble the former from the latter, unless one has already won from the former the guiding idea for the process of assemblage. New and fruitful thoughts are continually being sparked off at one point or another of that profound dividing line of the spirit, where the symbolism of phenomena ends and their symptomatology begins.

(*SW* 4, 422)

As Klages explains in *The Foundations of the Doctrine of Character*, we shall never find the soul in the brain, so the project of neuroscience would not have interested him. So where, we may ask, can we learn about the soul? In human form, Klages replies:

It is not in the the brain that we find the soul, but in form, and if it were permitted to us to express this as a paradox, then we would recommend, instead of studying the nerves of a human being, a study of his or her exterior!

(*SW* 4, 423)

In *On the Doctrine of Expression and the Doctrine of Character*, Klages demonstrates an almost uncanny intuition into the complexity of human character. Here, he explains how the character of our interlocutors can affect our own character; the relation between two people is not a simple causal one, but rather dialectical:

Every presence of a fellow human being has an effect that brings about a specific change on a human being's character. The one and the same character can actually become another, depending on the spectator in front of him or her. However many people a person usually comes into contact with, his or her soul will have just as many different physiognomies available. Let us explain this with some examples. – How one answers a particular question depends to a large extent on the person who is asking the question. We would not recount something that has happened to one listener using exactly the same words as we would when speaking to another. Anyone who observes more closely will discover that his or her entire behaviour toward different people displays permanently different uniformities. We are not talking here about conscious play-acting. Rather it is a question of changes that take place in one's being right down to the most involuntary depths of the heart and soul, and with such commanding force that, even if we become aware of them, the will nevertheless remains completely incapabable of preventing them. This has to do with among other things the fact that very sensitive natures, who themselves do not easily lose consciousness of what they are doing, can often lose their inner poise in the company of several people, each one of whom they may well *individually* like. Their being is constantly trying to adapt itself to *each* of them.

Anthropology and the guidance of souls 177

While it wants amid the clashing requirements to reach a compromise state which will satisfy all of them at the same time, it can easily 'lose' its 'self-control' or seek a quick exit in stony reserve. There is no doubt that this is the reason for the invention of certain social ceremonies.

(SW 4, 16)

In *The Doctrine of Expression and the Doctrine of Character*, Klages explores how we are never really in control of our emotions; this insight will have consequences for our understanding of ethics by showing how out instinctive reactions are in a sense 'beyond good and evil':

In general one operates with the assumption that how we conceive of admirable or reprehensible character traits determines the kind and degree of our feelings for a particular individual. But this is certainly not the case. Precisely in cases of immediate and intensive affection or dislike, a person who is gripped by these emotions is entirely unable to give an account of his or her feelings. If a rationale is sought, then one can be certain that it will bear the hallmarks of a self-justification in accordance with an existing ethical code. Any particular characteristic to which this tradition attaches its predicate 'good' or 'evil' with particular emphasis is used as a pretext to explain the mysterious origin of strong love or sudden hatred. In truth, the natural elective affinity of minds and souls is never produced through moral agreement, nor is it prevented or cancelled out through the strongest opposites in ethical behaviour.

(SW 4, 17)

Turning from sociology and ethics to linguistics, the study of language is for Klages intimately bound up with the study of psychology. In *The Foundations of the Doctrine of Character* he explains how close attention to linguistic detail reveals the persistence of a prehistorical dimension in our thought:

The fact that we can talk about the character even of lifeless things actually reveals a piece of our prehistorical past. Originally people believed that every object of perception had a soul, and they did so on the basis of immediate experience, something that still powerfully persists in children and sometimes even yearns to be revived in adults (as soon as the understanding's critical approach grows weary).[96] All perception originally consists in the apprehension of *living unities*, and the division of the world into a dead half and an ensouled half is the result of later (and, in the individual, never entirely completed) experience. Language has preserved for us this phase of prehistory by describing countless events in the non-human world of perception, indeed settled facts, as kinds of vital processes and activities: not only does the rain 'lash' the tree, but the path 'runs' across the field and the house 'throws' a shadow!

(SW 4, 204)

178 *Selections from Klages*

During his time as a student in Munich, Klages attended the lectures of Theodor Lipps (1851–1914), a leading theoretical psychologist and a forerunner of the phenomenological approach to psychology. Lipps was a prolific writer, whose works include *Fundamentals of Logic* (1893), *Basic Course in Psychology* (1903), and *Aesthetics* (1903–1906); he translated Hume's *Treatise on Human Nature*, but he is best known for introducing the notion of 'empathy' into aesthetic, philosophical, and psychological discourse. But Klages, as this passage from *The Foundations of the Doctrine of Character* shows, rejected this Lippsian concept:

> If the world of perception is originally like a mirror which reflects back to human beings their own image a thousandfold, then we must be all the more cautious about ending up in the dead end of so-called theories of empathy.[97] What we actually feel *into* something has merely an illusory value, and only what we feel *out of* something has cognitive value. Anyone who has been to a pleasurable rendezvous, and now finds everyone that he or she encounters to be nicer and friendlier than usual, is feeling his or her own happiness and satisfaction into them, and is deceiving himself or herself precisely to this extent about his or her real states of mind. Rightly considered, what the fact of 'mirroring' [*Spiegelung*] shows us is something completely different. Knowledge of beings (or, put more briefly, understanding) is only possible in accordance with *some sort of* similarities between the person who knows and what is supposed to be known, and in the case of a growing sense of unfamiliarity gives way to an initially felt, and subsequently conscious, lack of understanding, as long as – thanks to mere empathy – a misunderstanding fills the gap! For this reason we cannot readily know whether, for instance, the 'savage', when he prays to stones, trees, and animals, isn't in fact much rather manifesting a deeper understanding than we have. For to the extent that he is *less of a person* than we are, he might also enjoy a *much more rooted vitality*; in which case his judgments, or rather behaviours, would have sprung from a much greater similarity and closer affinity, and would in this way have expressed something of the essence of the stones, trees, and animals, even if in the language of myth, to which, because we have become alienated, access for us later human beings remains closed.

> (*SW* 4, 208)

In one of his early works, *Handwriting and Character*, we find Klages speculating on the polaristic relation between vice and virtue:

> Every evaluative character trait, usually called 'virtue', has its danger or 'preferential weakness'. The enthusiastic person is threatened by the accumulation of illusions, the down-to-earth person by dryness, the enterprising person by recklessness, the industrious [or go-ahead] person by impatience, the frivolous [or happy-go-lucky] person by fickleness, the

Anthropology and the guidance of souls   179

thoughtful person by indecisiveness, the calm [or unruffled] person by ponderousness.

(*SW* 7, 356)

In *The Foundations of the Doctrine of Character* Klages reminds us that our character is not 'ours', in the sense of something we make, but it is 'ours' in the sense of what we 'are':

Just as each person does not for instance make his or her character, but discovers it as a fact of nature, irrespective of whether he or she knows how to use it, so along with precisely this character he or she is endowed with a certain degree of capacity for depth, breadth, warmth, fervour, interiority, amplitude, magnificence, etc., of *experience*, of which he or she may fall short thousands of times, but will never be able to exceed.

(*SW* 4, 218)

In *The Psychological Achievements of Nietzsche*, Klages offered an encomium – and a critique – of this significant philosophical figure in twentieth-century thought. His monograph also contains, however, more general observations of a psychological nature, including the following. Here Klages addresses a perennial issue in interpersonal relations, and one frequently encountered today – the problem of envy:

Since we know about life only and exclusively through our own experience, we are justified, indeed duty-bound, to say that someone who experiences more profoundly, more fully, more fervently, more ardently, more excessively is a *more vitally rich* person, and the envy directed towards this person by someone who is less endowed is a *vital* envy. If, however, I feel and think that I know: that for a particular person there blossom crimson seas, wells that guard secrets, shining ethereal heights, and from all of these I am excluded, excluded because of a lack of organs of the soul for them, just as a lack of bodily organs excludes the deep-sea fish from the wonders of the kingdom of the air, and the alpine bird from the wonders of the deep sea; and if I am not able to admire or to love that person for this reason, then no compensation will allow me to escape my envious hatred toward him and as a result I must seek *to eradicate him from the world*.

(*SW* 5, 119)

What, in the passage above, Klages offers as a general observation, he exemplifies in a more anecdotal form in this passage from *The Foundations of the Doctrine of Character*:

Suppose an inwardly barren stock market speculator, feeling bored on a beach by the Southern Ocean, catches sight of another person whom the image of the sea is obviously delighting. *What* this person is experiencing, he

180   *Selections from Klages*

doesn't know, and what he can deduce of the experience by analogy with his own feeble sources of enjoyment is certainly falsely deduced; but the fact, obvious even to him, that this person is experiencing pleasures denied to him is sufficient to turn him into a malicious opponent of the other's way of life and into a rival whose enmity is all the more intense because it is *only* in the breaking of resistances that he is able to experience at least *something*.

(*SW* 4, 220)

In *On the Doctrine of Expression and Doctrine of Character*, Klages investigates the notion of the 'ideal', an important notion in philosophy from Plato via early modern philosophy, German Idealism, and British Idealism, to the present day.[98] This analysis reveals a thoroughly Nietzschean scepticism about the genealogy of 'ideals':

Ideals are elements of the character, but detached from the natural context of all other elements and hence stripped of their actual shackles. The path of their strongest development is, apart from demands of contemporary taste, obviously determined by a *law of compensation*, by virtue of which such drives create most abundantly those ideals which are in the real world satisfied the least. With their dreams human beings reimburse themselves for all sorts of renunciations and losses. Their ideals are in actual fact the wealth of their poverty.

(*SW* 7, 221)

In *On the Doctrine of Expression and Doctrine of Character*, Klages engages with Zarathustra's cry, 'Become hard!', by pointing to its origin in a German historical legend:

Only someone who is in charge of himself or herself and is entirely under his or her own control is able to do great deeds and, by means of them, is able to realize higher goals; but let him or her examine how many opportunities for happiness fall victim to this ability! It is not by chance that the legendary black-smith spurs the landgrave with his mawkish mild manners on to deeds through the repeated cry, 'become *hard*!'.[99] Just as gentleness is on close terms with hardness, so (according to the no less weighty testimony of language) strength of will and disciplined strength are on close terms with hardness, even culmi-nating in that calculating coldness of the heart for which there remains of all the desires and pleasures of the earth just this one: the attainment of success. To chart safely a path between this Scylla and Charybdis is, of all the many paradoxical tasks of ethically orientated humanity, one of the hardest.

(*SW* 4, 515)

In *The Foundations of the Doctrine of Character*, Klages points to a fundamental difference between humans and animals, relating to our consciousness of the inevitability of death:

Anthropology and the guidance of souls   181

Animals do not die, they simply come to an end; human beings, however, do die, because they are accompanied at every step by the *thought* of having to come to an end: that is the loss of 'eternal life'!

(*SW* 4, 353)

Why, Klages asks in *The Foundations of the Doctrine of Character*, are human beings able to endure pain, but not the thought of death? At the root of the problem, he believes, lies the overvaluation, not of life, but rather of the consciousness of transience:

A human being can tolerate in his or her life pains hundreds of time much more extreme than those which death usually involves, *without* any fear of death, and in this kind of bravery the human being is fundamentally superior to the animal; but what can fill even the bravest at least temporarily with an inexpressible horror of death, and drives human beings time and again into all sorts of belief in immortality, is the thought of saying goodbye for good, of *taking leave for ever,* for every living being clings to life, and it is no small matter to know in advance: you will leave all of this, and you will never see it again. The ineluctable tragedy of death, imposed among all beings only on human beings, is the *consciousness*, granted to them alone, *of transience in general*, and the fear of death is rooted not so much in a fear of dying as rather in the thought of existence, which as such resists cessation!

(*SW* 4, 355)

Over time, we all change, and yet there is something about us, the 'person', which does not. For Klages, this observation points to the role of the ego in constituting our identity, and in *On the Concept of the Personality* he ponders the relation between ego and soul:

The character of a human being can change over the course of time, and it can often really change itself so hugely that we have to admit that we would not be able to recognize how it was earlier; but this does not prevent us from taking its carrier [*Träger*] to be exactly the same 'person' as before! What is it, then, that we possess as something eternally one and the same, whether we find ourselves in the wealth of hopeful youth or in the poverty of abstinent old age, and in turn as being in everything the same, whoever bears the name of the human being?! To this there can be only one answer: the ego! Only the human being experiences and has to learn to think and say: I am I. Only the human being experiences and knows: I *was* it and I *shall be* it. For planted in this experience is the axis of the supra-temporal, and thus, *in relation* to time, permanently identical, ego. Only a human being can, full of melancholy, see how a happy yesterday disappears; full of anxiety, how a gloomy tomorrow is threatening; because something within, untouched by the flow of time, remains always the one

182   *Selections from Klages*

and the same: his or her ego. As far as the animal and the infant are concerned, both live in the fullness or emptiness of the moment; grown persons live almost uninterruptedly 'in former times' or in a 'some day in the future', because only in them has something become firmly established which can be related to what is most distant in time: an unchanging, identical ego that persists *alongside* time. *Persons are carriers of life, in whom the soul has become a satellite of the ego.*

(*SW* 4, 545)

So on this account of the personality, as Klages presents it in *On the Concept of Personality*, it is the site of intervention where the spirit 'binds' soul:

The essence of the personality lies in each particular form of the relation of unrepeatable, individual souls with the unchanging, persistent spirit: *personality is soul bound up by spirit.*

(*SW* 4, 550)

The Foundations of the Doctrine of Character contains some of Klages's most logically and rhetorically dense writing on questions of personality and character, approached through his signature conceptual prism of the relation between spirit and soul:[100]

The deed belongs only to the spirit, it 'conquers', 'rules', and 'overcomes', but things happen to and are done unto the soul. And just as the deed is related to the arrow and the ray, so the god of the self, Apollo, is, on the one hand, the god of light (and only the spirit appears, according to German usage, 'awake' or 'awakened') and, on the other, 'darkened and deranged', while such formulations as 'suffering of the soul', 'pain of the soul', and 'torture of the soul' testify to the (humanly lesser) pathos of the soul. The gender analogy between spirit and man, between soul and woman has a profound basis and recurs in Greek in the similar opposition of *ó noũs* and *i psyché*.

According to such a view, every personality is composed in its determinative core of two substances and all differences in character types derive from the variably mixed ratio of spirit and soul. The former carries the urge for preservation, whose effects are the perception of objects and the will, the latter carries the urge to sacrifice, the drive to unselfing and to flow away in a vision. The soul can be experienced without the spirit, it may pulse rhythmically in the atmospheric 'elements' and predominate, at least in the animal kingdom. The spirit without the soul, by contrast, can be neither thought nor represented, for it lies instead as something acosmic outside any consciousness and can only be detected from its incessant effects on what is elemental within ourselves, which under its ray freezes and disintegrates. It is the 'absolute' or 'eccentric' *exterior*, the soul is the natural *interior*, correspondingly it is related to darkness and to the night, as

Anthropology and the guidance of souls 183

the former is to twilight-free clarity. Out of the struggle between both of them, in the hermaphrodite-like area of personal being, arises a specifically *human* consciousness with the distinctive symptom of a feeling of self. The philosophy of the Romantics called it 'daylight consciousness' and its opposite pole 'night-time consciousness',[101] manifested in us only in exceptional situations, but in animals in entire phenomenal categories such as a mysterious sense of place, in so to speak magical instincts and supra-rational instincts of care....

Because spirit and element (or spirit and life, or spirit and soul) dislike and oppose each other as if by a law of nature, the former can want initially to 'liberate' itself from the latter, to shake it off entirely, in which case the final goal of its efforts would lie *outside* the world or *supra naturam*, something whose personality form is (in the strictest sense) a spiritual character, which stamps its mark on the Middle Ages in the form of self-castrating monks and on Buddhism as esotericists turning within themselves. In the humankind of today it has lost its significance and so is excluded from our discussion. The same applies in precisely the opposite mixed ratio to the element which not only vigorously opposes, but smashes in ecstasy the spirit, an element for which an example, albeit one grown alien to us, can be found in the 'primitive peoples' and an entirely misunderstood expression found in a mysticism which deserves this name. – Because in both interwoven forms the conflicting substances *diverge from each other*, the result is not so much a wealth of various kinds of personality but rather an *annullment* by them of personality. Despite the basic differences in their dominant substances, both spirit-ruled and elemental epochs demonstrate a certain retreat of 'original characters' and of feelings of personality and, correspondingly, an excess of general (and in this respect, so to speak, universal) life aims, which resemble each other in the drive to explode the limits of individual being. On the spirit-related side this is sought through asceticism, 'self-overcoming', even doing violence to oneself and in general through a disciplined renunciation of individual will; in which respect, for instance, the inhabitants of Tibetan cloisters of the present day are – on the elementary or vital side, through stimulation to intoxication – not essentially different from those of medieval Christianity, which, similarly skilled in certain techniques, likes to make use of masses whipped up in ceremonial excitement, comparable to those elsewhere in the orgiastic cults of antiquity and especially those of Dionysos. *Both* life tendencies still intersect today in the cultic practices of Islamic dervishes.

On the other hand, an immeasurable diversity of characters is immediately revealed to us when we turn from a *divergence* of these substances to the *convergence*. The spirit can turn *to* what is elemental, and what is elemental can turn *to* the spirit: each with the need, dwelling deep within, to become like the opponent, which leads to the development of two unforeseeable processes. Without one exactly getting lost in the other, in varying degrees of completeness either the spirit is superimposed on what is

184 *Selections from Klages*

elemental, or the elemental on the spirit, each sacrificing an essential part of its own character. In an effort to bind the flux of what happens in the unity of the ego and to dictate its own 'law' to what is in the world, the spirit becomes 'reason', that is, the carrier of logic, which bit by bit takes over and atomizes everything and is nevertheless never able to solve a riddle. An excess of calculating reason, in any amount one pleases, forms the basis for a third kind of character types with their inevitable numerous sub-types. Next to this arises as a fourth and final kind that of the *impassioned* character, in which what is elemental strives, by binding it through the image, to *dissolve* the spirit in the image, for its part assuming the form of *feeling*, and this is just as unlikely as the cognitive drive is (albeit it for different reasons) ever to reach its goal.

Both these classes, with a wealth of sub-classes and at the same time becoming highly diverse with usually only a little difference in emphasis, denote such segments of *personality* of history as the later Greek period, the Renaissance, the second half of the eighteenth century, and without exception they embrace all the great figures of historical humankind. Anyone who looks with an unprejudiced eye at such ages of great individual human beings, and especially at these individuals themselves – with their tireless straining of the will, their periodically occurring fits of deep despondency (to be interpreted as a response of violated 'nature') and a self-torture which is usually only concealed with difficulty – will reject as untenable the legend of the deed and its happiness-bringing effect, and no longer entertain doubts about the divisive double-nature of the personality. Yet it should not go unmentioned that the convergence of these two substances does not necessarily mean their mutual opposition [or working *against* each other], for occasionally there can be a less painful cooperation [or working *with* each other]. Just as the former gives rise, in all kinds of different degrees, sometimes to the badly centred and unstable, sometimes to the uneven, dissonant, contradictory, and finally to the 'torn' personality, so the latter gives rise to the harmonic, balanced, smooth personality which, as a compensation for the loss of full immediacy of its vital expressions, has developed a *style*[102] and, in the dispute which can never actually be resolved between the primordial potencies, represents as it were the short pause of ceasefire. In this way there arises that happy *seeming* of synthesis and totality, by means of which, among others, someone like Goethe can captivate – and deceive – the naïve spectator.

(*SW* 4, 369)

As this aphoristic declaration in *The Spirit as Adversary of the Soul* confirms, Klagesian philosophy – in contradistinction to the Platonic, Scholastic, Cartesian, and modern empirical traditions – places a priority on *Gefühle* or feelings:

Feelings are the wealth of humankind and the poverty of the gods.

(*SW* 2, 1060)

Anthropology and the guidance of souls 185

Yet it would be a mistake to read Klages's philosophy or psychology as a simplistic irrationalism or recidivism. As he makes clear in *The Spirit as the Adversary of the Soul*, we have, one way or another, to come to terms with the spirit, however deleterious (as indeed in his view it is) it may be:[103]

> It ought to be unnecessary to say it, but in the interest of clarity let it be said: one can*not* exclude, whichever means one uses, the spirit from life, or make it ineffective, or force it back into submission to life, let alone in any way return to the past. How could such beliefs do honour to a thinker who never grew tired and never will of impressing on his readers that nothing which has ever happened will ever be repeated!
>
> In saying this, it is *not* disputed that the way of life of each and every person who has engaged deeply with knowledge of the spirit's struggle against the tragic divinity of life would, in essential respects, be different *without* it, and so as a result the way of life of humankind in its entirety, to the extent that such knowledge became, if not common property, at least the property of its ruling classes. For this to happen would just as little require any kind of programme as a programme is needed for someone to shun or to remove what is destestable, to nurture and to protect what is honoured and loved. Faced with the lack of judgement of the masses, perhaps teachers and leaders would erect signposts; yet it remains certain that 'a knowing one' will find them for each of his or her decisions, the greatest as well as the smallest, in his or her own interior.
>
> (*SW* 2, 1424)

Indeed, Klages eschews any mystical retreat from the dilemma of how to accommodate spirit and soul, as from any existential problem in life. In *The Spirit as Adversary of the Soul*, he demonstrates an at times remarkably pragmatic outlook:

> It is not the case that any intervention in life is in itself necessarily a violation of life, but the *unilateral* intervention, which disturbs its rhythm instead of carrying it on, is. Anyone who builds a roof has to fell trees; anyone who sets up a gravestone, breaks up stones; this *would* be a sacrilege done to the image of the world on the part of someone who acted in consciousness of the masterful power of the spirit and had only conceived the idea of doing it as an individual; by contrast, it is a permissible, and even required, collaboration with the weaving-loom of destiny[104] on the part of someone who – abandoning himself or herself to the voices of the soul – is, in somnambulistic compulsion, only fulfilling with his or her own doing the earth's desire for growth; from which the thoughtful reader might conclude why it could be necessary to find out from divine signs where a house, a temple should be built, and to win the participation at the location's inauguration of its 'genius loci' through simultaneously propitiatory and protection-seeking sacrifices. Then again: anyone who nurtures a flower, waters it, kills its

186 *Selections from Klages*

pests, is unquestionably intervening in the weaving of Maya, but not in order to eradicate caterpillars and bugs, but in order to bring flowers into full bloom. This kind of activity is given by *eros* the quality of an image, and what turned it into a supreme value *is* precisely what life itself has 'proposed' as its culmination; for only in the elective character of love does the creative drive of the telluric powers *awaken*!

(*SW* 2, 1369)

Turning now to Klages's theory of education, there is clearly a link between his anthropology and what, in educational terms, achievement or success might mean, as the following passage from his essay *On the Relation of Education to the Essence of Humankind* suggests:

If we consider which educational goals emerge from the fact that the human being's soul is driven to envision and to shape, then the first we must mention is: *perfection*. – Bees, termites, birds construct perfect dwellings for themselves; but only in human beings is it innate to *strive* for perfection in everything achieved. This is particularly true of all the previously acknowledged special goals.[105] In itself the will is will-to-power and it recognizes only the *degree* of achievement; a willing carried by the soul, by contrast, evaluates according to *kind* (quality) and, *if* we can distinguish different grades, according to the degree of perfection. Our knowledge of the essence of the human being is not a critique of the will (as is sometimes misunderstandingly supposed), but rather a critique of the despotism of the will, which sacrifices the values of the blood to the illusory value of the greatest number (with the unlovely name, 'record'), robs human beings of their senses through an ever greater spurring on to perform, leaves their soul desolate, and brings the pulse rate of vital processes to a standstill.

Because the human being as a personal individual being is tainted with ambition and the craving for honours, education must know how to make these qualities work for it; and it achieves this by stemming *that* ambition which only wishes to do better than others, but encouages the *other* which wants to do better through a greater perfection of achievement.

(*SW* 3, 726–727)

In his conclusion to *The Spirit as Adversary of the Soul*, Klages talks about a specific kind of ambition, which he describes as follows: 'To carry out everything one does as perfectly as possible' (*GWS*=*SW*, vol. 2, p. 1424). And he continues in this passage with a reflection on how, as a vitalist, one should lead one's life:

The moments of great experience come or they do not come, and *if* they have come, then they go again: no willing, no activity could ever compel them. Everything that is *perfectly* achieved gives us the gift of a minute of happiness, which is by far not the highest and most profound happiness,

Anthropology and the guidance of souls 187

but which is a real happiness and is moreover the only one that was granted human beings to *obtain*. We are not speaking here of the sheer exuberance of heroism, nor of the sidereal intoxications or the creative ecstasy of inventive geniuses, but about the possible wealth of every kind of activity you could think of. After all, an achievement can be more or less perfect, whether it is called building houses or putting soles on boots or mending pots or checking the bookkeeping or doing the dusting; and a successful achievement always repays, like a grateful being (it *is* a being!), the person who works and brings it about with a friendly look, which is more warming than all the joys of being an observer and next to which the empty desire for success grows pale. In the reappearance even of the slightest fabric made with one's own hands, related shapes blossom and gleam, gently seeking our love, from the entirety of the past.

(*SW* 2, 1424–1425)

So what are the implications of a vitalist outlook for a programme of education? What would constitute a vitalist pedagogics? In *On the Relation of Education to the Essence of the Human Being*, Klages lists three objectives as lying at the heart of education, as he sees it, the first two being these:

To awaken a sense for the richness and the beauty of the German language, to enhance its written as well as its spoken usage in line with our great masters of the word, and to practise it, partly through lively exchange, partly through cultivating the extemporaneous lecture, appears to us to be the most valuable of *those* educational goals which are aligned with a perfection of achievement. We need hardly add that it helps as nothing else does to preserve and to foster the *inheritance of our ancestors*.

As a second major goal of the conduct of souls, let us name the development of a *respect for all that is vital*, whether it be plant, animal, or human being, or whether it be something in which all three meet and join together into a profoundly stirring totality, the landscape of the homeland. Anyone who lacks respect for what is vital has no sense of piety, however often he or she may go to church; anyone who carries this respect in his or her heart and practises it, *does* have a sense of piety, even if he or she does not know the catechism off by heart. In this respect the true spirit of community is rooted, that spirit of community which is not simply put on display, but which is constantly present as a power at work is feeling, judging, acting. One has only to cast a glance at the innumerable kinds of selfishness such as greed for profit, arrogance, envy, professional snobbery, and a know-it-all attitude, and one is immediately convinced that none of these would be compatible with true respect for what is vital. From it and through it, the threads are woven between soul and soul, between soul and landscape, between the individual soul and the soul of the people. – As the fabric of the community is created in this way, the gaze becomes keener for every *false* thread or, to speak plainly, for all reprehensible arrogance, for all

188 *Selections from Klages*

lower forms of egotism, and not least for the phantoms that pretend to be humanitarian ideals and to the present day have cost humanity dear. Education in respect for what is vital is one and the same as education in being strict with oneself.

(*SW* 3, 728)

In his essay on education and on vitalist pedagogics, Klages gives us a third educational goal, one which involves the educator as much as the person being educated. For Klages, the most effective aspect of education in a vitalist perspective is to teach – by example:

The third goal of the education of souls that we would like to mention is by far the one most difficult to attain: we are talking about the *exemplary character* of the educator. All exemplary models in history are surpassed in effectiveness by one visible in the present! Nothing makes a stronger impression on the soul of a human being in general and, in particular, on the soul of a child, than *that* fellow human being whom they love and feel themselves compelled to admire. To emulate this person is the fervent endeavour of a child. There are three qualities which, aside from wisdom, mark out the *great* educator: *truthfulness, courage, and moderation.* Only the fewest can boast about fully possessing these qualities. For once, however, the saying of the old Romans is true: *in magnis et voluisse sat est.*[106]

(*SW* 3, 729)

Gender issues constitute an area where, from our contemporary perspective, many a twentieth-century thinker falls down; one thinks, for instance, of Freud. Now it is unnecessary to accuse Klages of essentialism, for he is a fervent proponent of the notion of essence! Although the division between masculine and feminine in this passage from *The Foundations of the Doctrine of Character* might strike us as stereotypical or outmoded, we should perhaps pay closer attention to what Klages says about the mismatch latent in 'mutual erotic affection'. Characteristically for Klages, the emphasis in his notion of the feminine lies on the idea of unattainability:

The typically masculine form of forming a partnership with life is an ability for excitement and creative enthusiasm, which sacrifices itself in the work and for the cause; the typically feminine form is *personal* love and motherliness, which is ready to sacrifice its own will for the object of love; as a result, in mutual erotic affection there should be good reason for the highest veneration to be professed – by the woman, for the distant flight, unattainable for her, of the intoxicated spirituality of the man, and by the man, for the profundity and selflessness of the woman, which he cannot attain.

(*SW* 4, 405)

Anthropology and the guidance of souls 189

Rather than worry about 'sin', Klages urges us to think more about avoiding 'sacrilege'. And as one might expect from a vitalist thinker, a 'sacrilege' – so he explains in *The Spirit as Adversary of the Soul* – is 'a sacrilege against life':

> At least within 'civilization', in other words, under the influence of the Christian degeneration of the blood,[107] the conception of the immoral person has experienced that extreme intensification which took shape in the concept of 'sin'. Just as it is certain for a moral consciousness that there is sin, so it is certain for the vital consciousness that there is *sacrilege*.[108] Every sin is a sin against the spirit,[109] every sacrilege is a sacrilege against life! 'Sin against a wild animal' or 'sin against a tree' would be laughable: 'sacrilege against a wild animal' and 'sacrilege against a tree' are, on the other hand, something one can still understand to a certain extent even today. 'Sin' corresponds roughly to the Greek *amartia*, 'sacrilege' exactly to the Greek *ubris*.[110] Hubris consists ultimately in the criminal revolt of the ego-shaped spirit against the childlike belonging even of humankind to the realm of the Great Mother. That is why, just as in opposition to sin there is 'virtue', which 'elevates' its bearer in this life or in the next, so in opposition to sacrilege is the *sacrifice*,[111] which destroys its bearer: *not* 'to the glory of God', but instead, that there may shine more brightly the aura of – the gods!
>
> (*SW* 2, 1365)

In the final analysis, Klages argues in a short text entitled *Letter on Ethics* of 1918, education should be about the 'conduct of souls', an expression he uses in an avowedly non-clerical sense. Its aim, he suggests, is to nourish the soul, to provide it with miracles, with love, and with examples to follow. In short, the role of education is to provide the basis for a heroism of daily life:

> If there is a judgement that turns against sacrilege, there must also be a judgement whose consequence is *care for life*. I don't like to call this education because, as we have seen, the word has already been used by the moral individual in the service of *his* conduct of the soul. About the word itself, however, I am not so concerned, as long as the matter itself is clear. – No life-affirming guide of souls can imagine that he or she is able to change something or improve it. From a fir-cone there grows a fir-tree, from a beech-nut a beech-tree, and it is not the person who plants the seed and tends the shoot who is the producer of its growth and the sculptor of its form. But a plant needs light and moisture, and it will become magnificent or not so magnificent, depending on the extent to which I ensure there is a supply of both. The vital guidance of souls does not consist in the setting-up of laws and in the generation of a sterilizing belief in a threatening 'Thou shalt', but in the provision of spiritual nourishment. If the term 'care of souls' didn't have slightly clerical overtones, there would none better to characterize the activity of an esoteric guide of souls.

190 *Selections from Klages*

What, then, are the main sources of nourishment for the soul? *The miracle, love, and the example.* The miracle can be found by the soul, for instance, in the landscape, in poetry, in beauty. So one should provide it with the landscape, poetry, beauty, and see how it blossoms as a result. Love in the broadest sense of the word, to which there also belong veneration, worship, admiration, indeed every kind of heartfelt recognition, truly brings effective warmth only from someone who loves. The eternal image of this guidance of souls is the image of the loving mother with the beloved child. So one should give the soul all the shining beams of maternal love, and see how it blossoms as a result. The examples are gods, poets, and heroes. One should let the soul be blessed by the sight of the heroes, and see how it blossoms as a result. And if it does not blossom at any of these three, then it is lacking in the power to bloom, and no guide of souls can conjure one up. For this is the secret of the soul, *that it only becomes richer in giving.*[112] Not the love which one receives, but the love which, through received love, became ignited within oneself, *this* is what nourishes the soul. And all the miracles and examples of the world remain merely a – theatrical representation, if they are not able to awaken in the soul the secret miracle and the secret hero.

(SW 3, 672)

In this aphoristic sentence (from *The Spirit as Adversary of the Soul*), Klages draws on Schuler's notion of the '*Blutleuchte*', a strange but powerful (and easily misunderstood) term signifying the vitalist energy of life:

Just as the essences of reality are renewed through the birth of images, so the blood beacon[113] of the creative soul is renewed among other things by the reflection of its primordial image in the mirror of the selflessly loving soul.

(SW 2, 1214)

Playing on the biblical question, 'what does it profit a man if he gain the world and lose his soul?', Klages here (in his essay *On the Essence of Consciousness*) urges the reader to remain always open to vital – and vitalist – possibilities, and in this way to save, not so much one's own individual soul as soul itself:

Hold yourselves ready and worthy of the moment of conception; and if it should never come, at least you did the only thing you could in order to – save your *soul*!

(SW 3, 299)

Final thoughts

The path of life. – After endless searching it has, tremblingly, been found: the meaning and essence of the colourful exterior of things. What shines through in a magical way is the *second world* as a metaphysical reality. Powers and effects are a puppet show for the blindness of our thought –

behind it lies the vital universe, rustling in the wing-beats of the gods: this I *lived* in the storm of youth, this I *lost* in the age of assailing doubt, this I *know* in my autumnal thought.

(*RR*, 255)

The primordial imagistic dimension of the world. – Every part of the world can at any moment become the complete possession of the soul, it can submerge into the colour of essence. These are the moments when one looks through into the world of eternity.

(*RR*, 244)

Life and being.[114] – Life is flux, persistence is death. Life becomes petrified and ends up believing in the reality of things, in the delusion of permanence. The universe has the reality of an incessant process. Only in the play of enduring and transient forces is there a pledge of life.

(*RR*, 249)

Seeking and finding. – Only someone who does *not* seek, will find; for only such a person is led by the procession of the gods.

(*RR*, 253)

Spirit and soul. – Only when the spirit sleeps does the soul awaken. It sleeps most deeply when the senses are sleeping. But in the waking state there can also be a sleep of the spirit. In everything one does there are moments when it occasionally dozes off and the soul, emergent, opens its eyelids. The richer our life is in such moments, the more it is pervaded by this sleep of the spirit, the more profoundly we are alive and refreshed in every moment. This is shown by the way the eyes, moist and dark, gleam.

(*RR*, 264)

Science and reality. – Let us reflect on how far removed from science is the way in which a child sees things. The spring around which it plays, the tree whose branches and leave rustle in front of the parental house, perhaps the church tower from which – sometimes welcome, sometimes not – the hour is rung out: it is all gleamingly surrounded by the dark sorrow of its fleetingness. However many towers and trees and spring the earth may possess, not one of them could be exchanged with the singular image. Has science ever even *asked* about this reality? Does the botanist care about the beauty of the flower whose nature he wishes to explore, and in the end, does he think about how its life is unrepeatable?

(*RR*, 276)

Mnemonic verse. – The image that falls into the senses,
That and nothing else is the sense of the world.

(*RR*, 280)

192 *Selections from Klages*

Work and miracle. – Deed, work, system belong to them spirit. What could not be a miracle, wants to become a work. – Unconsciously the maternal ground of the spirit creates from the shining crimson blood; the sculpting power, however, is masculine, sun-like, spiritual.

Miracle, work, and deed. – Previously I had written: What could not become a deed, wants to become a work. Now I know what is right! What could not become a miracle, wants to become a work; what could not become a work, becomes a deed: that is the right order!

(*RR*, 256 and 289)

Life is everything that I ever wrote, or ever will write, the gold leaf of life!
(*Ludwig Klages: Die Geschichte seines Lebens: Die Jugend*, 331)

Notes

1 Frederic Wertham, 'Progress in Psychiatry III: The Significance of Klages' System for Psychopathology', *Archives of Neurology and Psychiatry*, 24, no. 2 (1930), 381–388 (p. 382).
2 'On the Relation of Education to the Essence of Humankind' (1935/1936), in *SW*, vol. 3, pp. 723–730. The publication history of this essay, which first appeared in two issues of *Der Neue Volkserzieher*, a publication of a *gleichgeschaltete* organization, is given by H. E. Schröder in his commentary (*SW*, vol. 3, pp. 805–807). For further discussion of the application of Klages's pedagogical theories, among others with reference to the founder of 'expressive gymnastics' (*Ausdrucksgymnastik*) Rudolf Bode (1881–1970), the American psychologist Robert E. Ornstein (b. 1942), and the analytical psychologist C. G. Jung (1875–1961), see W. Kuckartz, *Ludwig Klages als Erzieher*, Bonn: Bouvier Verlag Herbert Grundmann, 1978.
3 Nietzsche, *Basic Writings*, ed. and tr. W. Kaufmann, New York: Modern Library, 1968, p. 214; and G. C. Lichtenberg, *Schriften und Briefe*, 4 vols, ed. W. Promies, Munich: Hanser, 1967–1974, vol. 2, *Südelbücher*, p. 412 (K 76). In his *Nachlass* fragments, subsequently published as *The Will to Power*, Nietzsche goes so far as to argue that 'the mistake lies in the fictitious insertion of a subject', that 'the "subject" is not something that creates effects, but only a fiction' and that 'the "subject" is not something given, but something added and invented and projected behind what there is' (§632, §552, §481); *The Will to Power*, ed. W. Kaufmann, tr. R. H. Hollingdale and W. Kaufmann, New York: Vintage, 1968, pp. 337, 297, 267.
4 R. H. Stephenson (ed. and tr.), *Goethe's 'Maxims and Reflections': A Selection*, Glasgow: Scottish Papers in Germanic Studies, 1986, p. 121; F. Nietzsche, *The Gay Science*, ed. and tr. W. Kaufmann, New York: Random House, 1974, p. 167.
5 For instance, male bees die after mating. In fact, in some insects and arachnids, sexual cannibalism is a common practice (the female eats the male after mating). What Klages is keen to distinguish is the death of the individual in the process of life and its deliberate extermination as a result of the fatal intervention in life of the spirit or *Geist*.
6 For further discussion of the notion of sacrifice, which has fascinated such twentieth-century thinkers as Georges Bataille (1897–1962), Jacques Derrida (1930–2004), Jean-Luc Nancy (b. 1940), René Girard (1923–2015), and Slavoj Žižek (b. 1949), see D. K. Keenan, *The Question of Sacrifice*, Bloomington and Indianapolis: Indiana University Press, 2005; and P. D. Bubbio, *Sacrifice in the Post-Kantian Tradition: Perspectivism, Intersubjectivity, and Recognition*, Albany, NY: State University of New York Press, 2014.

Notes 193

7　The famous 'Rider's Song' (*Reiterlied*) brings to a close the first part, *Wallenstein's Camp*, of Schiller's trilogy of plays about the famous Bohemian general, Albrecht von Wallenstein (1583–1634): *Und setzt ihr nicht das Leben ein, Nie wird euch das Leben gewonnen sein* (cf. Friedrich Schiller, *The Robbers; Wallenstein*, tr. F. J. Lamport, Harmondsworth: Penguin, 1979, p. 214).

8　In his theory of similarity, Klages is moving into philosophical territory that would later be explored by the French philosopher Gilles Deleuze (1925–1995) in his *Difference and Repetition* (*Différence et répétition*) of 1968; see Deleuze, *Difference and Repetition*, tr. P. Patton, New York: Columbia University Press; London: Continuum, 2004.

9　For discussion of the image of 'dancing in chains', see Chapter 1, note 90 (on p. 48).

10　These lines are taken from the poem 'Restless' ('Rastlos') by Wilhelm Jordan (1819–1904) in his collection *Strophen und Stäbe* (1871). The original German reads:

> Und so zeigt
> Diese Welt
> Nur was steigt
> Oder fällt…

11　Klages alludes here to the myth of Castor and Pollux (or Polydeuces), twin brothers who were, on some accounts, said to have been born from an egg, the result of the union between Zeus, disguised as a swan, and Leda. One of the twins (Pollux) was immortal, the other (Castor) mortal, so they took it in turns to spend time in the realms of the living and the dead, as Pindar explains in his tenth Nemean Ode:

> In alternate changes the twin brethren spend the one day beside their dear father Zeus and, the other, down in the hollow earth in the depths of Therapnê, thus fulfilling an equal lot, since, when Castor was slain in war, Polydeuces preferred this life to being wholly a god and dwelling in heaven.
> (ll. 55–59; in Pindar, *The Odes*, tr. J. Sandys, London; New York: Heinemann; Putnam, 1927, p. 421)

One of the sections of Klages's *Nachlass*, containing his early writings from the period 1889 to 1891, is entitled *Battles of the Dioscuri* (*Dioskurenkämpfe*), see *RR*, pp. 111–215; and in *Of Cosmogonic Eros*, Klages cited a poem by Annette von Droste-Hülshoff (1797–1848) which uses the Dioscuri motif (*SW*, vol. 3, p. 486); cf. H.-P. Preußer, *Pathische Ästhetik: Ludwig Klages und die Urgeschichte der Postmoderne*, Heidelberg: Winter, 2015, p. 89, fn. 31.

12　Jakob Böhme, inscription in a family album (*c.*1612); see A. von Franckenberg, *Gründlicher und wahrhafter Bericht von dem Leben und dem Abschied des in Gott selig ruhenden Jacob Boehmes*, in Jacob Böhme, *Sämtliche Schriften*, ed. W.-E. Peuckert and A. Faust, 11 vols, Stuttgart: Frommanns, 1955–1961, vol. 10, *Historischer Bericht von dem Leben und Schriften Jacob Böhmens*, p. 20. The original German reads:

> Wem Zeit wie Ewigkeit
> Und Ewigkeit wie Zeit,
> Der ist befreit
> Von allem Streit.

13　M. P. Hall, *The Secret Teachings of All Ages: An Encyclopedic Outline of Masonic, Hermetic, Qabbalistic, and Rosicrucian Symbolical Philosophy* [1928], New York: Tarcher/Penguin, 2003, p. 129.

14　T. Taylor, *A Dissertation on the Eleusinian and Bacchic Mysteries* [1790], in *Oracles and Mysteries* [Thomas Taylor Series, vol. 7], Frome: Prometheus Trust, 2001, pp. 58–127 (p. 77). For further discussion of the Eleusinian Mysteries, see

194 *Selections from Klages*

W. F. Otto, 'The Meaning of the Eleusinian Mysteries' [1939], in J. Campbell (ed.), *The Mysteries: Papers from the Eranos Yearbooks*, Princeton, NJ: Princeton University Press, 1955, pp. 14–31; George E. Mylonas, *Eleusis and the Eleusinian Mysteries* [1962], Princeton, NJ: Princeton University Press, 2015; C. Kerényi, *Eleusis: Archetypal Image of Mother and Daughter*, tr. R. Manheim, Princeton, NJ: Princeton University Press, 1967; R. Gordon Wasson, Albert Hofmann, and Carl A. P. Ruck, *The Road to Eleusis: Unveiling the Secret* [1978], Berkeley, CA: North Atlantic Books, 2008; and H. P. Foley (ed.), *The Homeric 'Hymn to Demeter': Translation, Commentary, and Interpretive Essays*, Princeton, NJ: Princeton University Press, 1994, pp. 70–75, 'Background: The Eleusinian Mysteries and Women's Rites for Demeter'. For a general discussion of the religious background formed by ancient Greek mystery cults, see M. B. Cosmopoulos (ed.), *Greek Mysteries: The Archaeology and Ritual of Ancient Greek Secret Cults*, London and New York: Routledge, 2003; J. Larson, *Ancient Greek Cults: A Guide*, New York and London: Routledge, 2007; and H. Bowden, *Mystery Cults in the Ancient World*, London: Thames & Hudson, 2010.

15 The ecstatic is a category investigated by Klages at various points in his extensive writings, including those writings of his early years which Klages himself edited and published in 1944 as *Rhythms and Runes* (*Rhythmen und Runen*); in his major essay of 1914, 'Of Dream Consciousness' (see *SW*, vol. 3, pp. 231–232); and in *The Spirit as Adversary of the Soul* (*SW*, vol. 2, pp. 235, 260, 266, 286, 760, 1190–1196). By far his most extensive discussion, however, is in *Of Cosmogonic Eros*, where Klages devotes two chapters to the 'condition' (*Zustand*) and then to the 'essence' or 'nature' (*Wesen*) of ecstasy. For further discussion, see Paul Bishop, 'I Must Get Out (Of Myself) More Often: Jung, Klages, and the Ecstatic-Archaic', in Paul Bishop and Leslie Gardiner (eds), *The Ecstatic and the Archaic: An Analytical Psychological Inquiry*, forthcoming.

16 *Teletae* refers to initiation in sacred Mysteries. Cf. 'In his last book of his *Metamorphoses*, the Latin author Apuleius several times uses the loanword *teleta* for the mysteries of Isis and Osiris' (F. L. Schuddeboom, *Greek Religious Terminology – Telete and Orgia: A Revised and Expanded English Edition of the Studies by Zijderveld and Van der Burg*, Leiden: Brill, 2009, p. 69). For the use of the term *teletai* in Porphyry, cf. I. Tanaseanu-Döbler, *Theurgy in Late Antiquity: The Invention of a Ritual Tradition*, Göttingen: Vandenhoeck & Ruprecht, pp. 88ff.

17 A. Machen, *Hieroglyphics*, London: Grant Richards, 1902, p. 11.

18 E. M. Cioran, *Aveux et anathèmes*, Paris: Gallimard, 1987, p. 60: *L'orgasme n'a jamais été un événement philosophique.*

19 The *epopteia* or mystical vision was the final stage of the initiation rites celebrated at the Eleusinian Mysteries. Cf.:

> *Epopteia* – the most important mystical vision that culminates the Eleusinian mysteries, a beholding of the secret symbols or epiphanies of the gods; *epopteia* is the highest stage of initiation; *epoptai* (beholders) are those who came back to watch the rituals again; in a similar way, the philosophical purification and instruction culminates in *epoptika* – the direct revelation of truth and contemplation of the Forms, or divine realities.
>
> (A. Uždavinys, *The Golden Chain: An Anthology of Pythagorean and Platonic Philosophy*, Bloomington, IN: World Wisdom, 2004, p. 296)

20 The *hieros gamos* is a 'mystical marriage' or 'sacred ceremony', the symbolic ritual of union or marriage between two deities, usually god and goddess. For further discussion, see A. Avagianou, *Sacred Marriage in the Rituals of Greek Religion*, Berne: Lang, 1991.

21 For further discussion of this work, see P. Bishop, 'Traum und Lebensphilosophie: Ludwig Klages und eine andere Entdeckung des dunklen Kontinents', in M. Guthmüller

Notes 195

and H.-W. Schmidt-Hannisa (eds), *Das nächtliche Selbst: Traumwesen und Traumkunst im Jahrhundert der Psychologie*, vol. 1, *1850–1900*, Göttingen: Wallenstein, 2016, pp. 374–397.

22 See E. Rohde, *Psyche: Seelencult und Unsterblichkeitsglaube der Griechen*, 2nd edn, 2 vols in 1, Freiburg im Breisgau: Mohr, vol. 2, p. 27, note 2.

23 Although the term 'logocentric' is usually associated with the deconstructionism of Jacques Derrida, specifically his 1967 study *Of Grammatology* (*De la grammatologie*), it was, in fact, first coined by Klages. For further discussion, see M. Frank, *Gott im Exil: Vorlesungen über die Neue Mythologie, 2. Teil*, Frankfurt am Main: Suhrkamp, 1988, pp. 9–10; and H.-P. Preußer, 'Logozentrismus und Sinn: Indikatoren eines Paradigmenwechsels: Ludwig Klages – Jacques Derrida – George Steiner' [1999], in *Pathische Ästhetik: Ludwig Klages und die Urgeschichte der Postmoderne*, Heidelberg: Winter, 2015, pp. 63–78.

24 The Euphorbiacaea, sometimes called euphorbia, is a name for the spurge family of flowering plants.

25 The Asteraceae or Compositae are a family of flowering plants, often referred to as as the aster, daisy, composite, or sunflower family.

26 Compare with the question posed by the German naturalist and physician Gottfried Reinhold Treviranus (1776–1837) in his *The Phenomena and Laws of Organic Life* (*Die Erscheinungen und Gesetze des organischen Lebens*) (1831–1833): 'How does the animal know to recognize in water the means to extinguish its thirst, or the carnivore recognize its nourishment in meat and the herbivore its nourishment in plants?' (vol. 1, p. 15; cited in *GWS=SW*, vol. 1, p. 206).

27 By 'magic', Klages does not mean conjuring a rabbit out of a hat or other forms of abracadabra, but rather the use of rituals, symbols, and other forms of 'magical thinking' (i.e. an associative, rather than causal, kind of thinking. For further discussion of 'magic', see *RR*, p. 312: 'The praxis of our philosophy is magic, it itself is the theory of magic'.

28 For further discussion, see H. Kern, *Von Paracelsus bis Klages: Studien zur Philosophie des Lebens*, Berlin: Widukind/Boss, 1942, with its studies of Paracelsus, Gottfried Wihelm Leibniz (1646–1716), Johann Georg Hamann (1730–1788), Johann Gottfried Herder (1744–1803), Goethe, the period of German Romanticism, Johann Gottlieb Fichte (1762–1814), Ernst Moritz Arndt (1769–1860) (a German patriotic writer), Georg Friedrich Daumer (1800–1875) (a German poet and philosopher), Nietzsche, Julius Bahnsen (1830–1881) (the founder of characterology and the author of *Contributions to Characterology*, 1867), and finally Klages himself.

29 Klages is referring to the (late) German Romantic writer Joseph von Eichendorff (1788–1857). The phrases cited by Klages are typical Eichendorffian motifs. For an introduction to the key themes of Eichendorff's works, see A. Menhennet, *The Romantic Movement*, London: Croom Helm; Totowa, NJ: Barnes & Noble, 1981, pp. 95–107; and R. Cardinal, *German Romantics in Context*, London: Studio Vista, 1975, pp. 135–143.

30 Klages cites here from the section 'Nach Falconet und über Falconet' in *Aus Goethes Brieftasche* (1776) which discusses the work of the French sculptor Étienne Maurice Falconet (1716–1791); see Goethe, *Werke* [*Hamburger Ausgabe*], ed. E. Trunz, 14 vols, Hamburg: Wegner, 1948–1960, vol. 12, pp. 21–30 (pp. 23–28); translated in *Goethe on Art*, ed. J. Gage, Berkeley and Los Angeles: University of California Press, 1980, pp. 17–20. For further discussion of this unusual text by Goethe, see W. D. Robson-Scott, *The Younger Goethe and the Visual Arts*, Cambridge: Cambridge University Press, 1981, pp. 53–56.

31 See Eichendorff's novel *Ahnung und Gegenwart* (1815), chapter 3.

32 *gamos*=marriage, cf. *hieros gamos*, the sexual union or marriage between a god and a goddess.

196   Selections from Klages

33 Compare with Nietzsche's remark in *Thus Spoke Zarathustra*, 'You must have chaos within you to give birth to a dancing star' ('Zarathustra's Prologue', §5; Nietzsche, *Thus Spoke Zarathustra*, tr. R. J. Hollingdale, Harmondsworth: Penguin, 1969, p. 46).

34 Novalis (1772–1801), 'Das allgemeine Brouillon', §295; in *Werke, Tagebücher und Briefe*, Bd. 2, *Das philosophisch-theoretische Werk*, ed. H.-J. Mähl, Munich: Hanser, 1978, p. 527.

35 Nikolaus Lenau (1802–1850), 'Sturmesmythe', from his collection *Reiseblätter*; in N. Lenau, *Sämtliche Werke und Briefe*, ed. W. Dietze, 2 vols, Leipzig und Frankfurt am Main: Insel, 1970, vol. 1, pp. 262–263. The original German reads:

> Stumm und regungslos in sich verschlossen
> Ruht die tiefe See dahingegossen,
> Sendet ihren Gruß dem Strande nicht;
> Ihre Wellenpulse sind versunken,
> Ungespüret glühn die Abendfunken,
> Wie auf einem Totenangesicht.

36 See *The Spirit as Adversary of the Soul*, book 5, part 1, section 1, chapter 57, 'From the Prehistory of the Discovery of the Images', where Klages had discussed the work of Philippus Aureolus Theophrastus Bombastus von Hohenheim, better known as Paracelsus (1493–1541). Here Klages had cited a passage from Paracelsus's *Astronomia Magna or the whole Philosophia Sagax of the Great and Little World*, book 1, 'Probatio in Scientiam Nigromanticum', where Paracelsus discusses the art of necromancy: 'The elementary body is tangible, but the sidereal body is not tangible. [...] Therefore, when visible the elementary body is tangible, and the sidereal body, intangible' (*GWS=SW*, vol. 2, p. 885). For the context to Paracelsus's remarks, and his distinction between an 'elemental' and a 'sidereal' (subtle or astral) body (both of which are mortal, as opposed to the 'illumined' body or resurrected flesh, which is immortal), see Paracelsus, *Selected Writings* [1951], ed. J. Jacobi, Princeton, NJ: Princeton University Press, 1988, pp. 18, 103, 155, and 217 (cf. p. 249); and Paracelsus, *Essential Readings*, ed. N. Goodrick-Clarke, Berkeley, CA: North Atlantic Books, 1999, p. 112. For further discussion, see F. Hartmann, *The Life and the Doctrines of [...] Paracelsus*, New York: Lovell, 1891, chapter 4, 'Anthropology', pp. 82–129 (esp. pp. 103–110).

37 As Heinz-Peter Preußer has suggested, Klages takes over from Paracelsus a dualism of elemental and sidereal body, and transforms it into a dualism of physiological sensation and spiritual vision/contemplation or imagination ('Logozentrismus und Sinn', in *Pathische Ästhetik*, p. 65; cf. *GWS=SW*, vol. 2, p. 885). According to Klages,

> it is bestowed on the body – to sense the spatio-temporal Here and to act on it in accordance with the laws of mechanics; by contrast, on the soul – to contemplate [*schauen*] through spatial and temporal distances and *to stand in a reciprocal relation* to the placeless Everywhere of the soul's images once more,

a thought which brings together 'divination, dream interpretation, and magic customs' (*GWS=SW*, vol. 2, p. 885).

38 The significance of the notion of 'atmosphere' has been recently rediscovered in philosophical discourse about architecture; see G. Böhme, *Atmosphäre*, Frankfurt am Main: Suhrkamp, 1995; G. Böhme, *Aisthetik: Vorlesungen über Ästhetik als allgemeine Wahrnehmungslehre*, Munich: Fink, 2001; G. Böhme, 'Atmosphere as the Subject Matter of Architecture', in P. Ursprung (ed.), *Herzog & de Meuron: Natural History*, Zurich: Lars Müller, pp. 398–406; and P. Zumthor, *Atmospheres: Architectural Environments – Surrounding Objects*, Basel: Birkhauser, 2006.

Notes 197

39 For the use of this expression, see St Paul's First Letter to the Corinthians, chapters 1 and 2. Here Paul distinguishes between the *pneumatikoi* (the 'spirituals'), the *psychikoi* (the 'souled'), and the *sarkikoi/sarkinoi* (the 'fleshly', the 'worldly'), identifying the 'spirituals' with the 'perfect'. Some Gnostic systems use a similar set of distinctions (see, for instance, Irenaeus's *Against Heresies*, vol. 1, book 1, chapter 7) but, confusingly, Klages appears to reverse the force of the opposition between 'pneumatics' and 'psychics' as used by Paul. For the Pauline terminology, see the footnote in W. A. Meeks and J. T. Fitzgerald (eds), *The Writings of St Paul*, New York and London: Norton, 2007, p. 26.

40 For a discussion of the notion of 'nimbus' in the work of Klages, see G. Moretti, 'Nimbus: Nota sulla quesione dell' "aura" in Ludwig Klages', *Rivista di Estetica* 53, no. 1, 2013, 149–159.

41 The oak is a sacred tree in many pagan religions. According to Strabo, the sacred grove of the Celts of Asia Minor was full of oaks. In his *Historia Naturalis*, Pliny the Elder describes a festival during which druids climbed an oaktree, cut a spring of mistletoe, and sacrificed two bulls. And a sacred oak stood in the centre of the precinct of the Oracle of Zeus in Dodona, Epirus; the rustling of its leaves was interpreted as oracular pronouncements by its priests.

42 Klages takes this definition from Friedrich August Ludwig, *Clavis virgiliana, sive, explicatio vocabulorum difficuliorum plerumque omnium, formularumque dicendi complurium quae in Virgilii operibus occurrant*, 2 vols, Berlin: Frölich, 1805, part 2, *Aeneis*, p. 77.

43 See *The Iliad of Homer*, tr. R. Lattimore, Chicago and London: University of Chicago Press, 1951, pp. 380–381.

44 The Greek word for chaos derives from *khaos* = 'vast chasm', 'void'.

45 Subsequently the term 'aura' has become popularized through the work of Walter Benjamin, although the origin of the notion in this sense is to be found in Klages; for further discussion, which brings out the extent of Benjamin's indebtedness to Klages, see M. B. Hansen, 'Benjamin's Aura', *Critical Inquiry* 34, Winter 2008, 336–375.

46 See Stendhal (1783–1842), *On Love* (1822), chapter 17.

47 See Nietzsche, *On the Genealogy of Morals*, III, §6, where he contrasts Stendhal's definition of beauty with Kant's definition of it as 'disinterested pleasure'; in *Basic Writings*, pp. 539–542.

48 The Porta Nigra is a large Roman city gate in the city of Trier, so named because of the darkened colour of its stone.

49 See the paintings by the German Symbolist painter Arnold Böcklin (1827–1901), especially his paintings *Triton and Nereid* and *In the Play of the Waves*.

50 The Via Appia (Appian Way) connected Rome to Brindisi in south-east Italy and was one of the most important routes in the time of the Roman republic.

51 Flowing through central Russia, the Volga is Europe's longest river.

52 Cf. the use of the phrase 'deceptively remote distance' in the novella by Wilhelm Raabe (1831–1910), *Prinzessin Fisch: Eine Erzählung*.

53 See the quotation from Novalis above (in the section 'The Reality of Images' on p. 145).

54 Derived from the Greek words *idios* = 'one's own' and *pathos* = 'suffering', an idiopathy is literally 'a disease of its own kind', i.e. a disease of apparently spontaneous origin or whose pathogenesis is at any rate unknown.

55 See Klages, *Of Cosmogonic Eros*, chapter 6 (*SW* 3, p. 470).

56 In using this expression, Klages is alluding to the famous Mothers Scene in Goethe's *Faust*, Part Two: '*Kein Weg! Ins Unbetretene, / Nicht zu Betretende*', 'No road! Into the unacceded, / The inaccessible' (ll. 6222–6223; J. W. von Goethe, *Faust: A Tragedy*, ed. C. Hamlin, tr. W. Arndt, 2nd edn, New York and London: Norton, 2001, p. 177).

57 For the putative etymology of 'matter' from Middle English *matere* via Old French from Latin *materia* = 'timber, 'substance', and ultimately *mater* = 'mother', cf. Jung,

198 *Selections from Klages*

Collected Works, ed. Sir H. Read, M. Fordham, G. Adler, and W. McGuire, 20 vols, London: Routledge & Kegan Paul, 1953–1983, vol. 9/i, §170 and §195; vol. 16, §344–§345.

58 In traditional Catholic piety, the souls in Purgatory are known as the 'poor souls'. Following the principle enunciated in 2 Maccabees 12:46, 'It is a holy and wholesome thing to pray for the dead, that they may be loosed from their sins', novenas were held for the relief of the poor souls in Purgatory and, on All Souls Day (2 November), the Mass was offered for them.

59 The sacrament of Extreme Unction, nowadays called the Anointing of the Sick, was traditionally administered in the Roman Catholic Church by anointing the five organs of the external senses (eyes, ears, nose, lips, and hands) with oil; it often forms part of the last rites, administered to someone who is dying.

60 An allusion to Goethe's poem 'Comfort in Tears' ('Trost in Tränen'), which includes the lines, 'Why, who would seek to woo the stars / Down from their glorious sphere? / Enough it is to worship them, / When nights are calm and clear' ('Die Sterne, die begehrt man nicht, / Man freut sich ihrer Pracht, / Und mit Entzücken blickt man auf / In jeder heitern Nacht') (*Works of J. W. Goethe*, ed. N. H. Dole, 14 vols, London and Boston: Niccolls, 1901–1902, vol. 9, *Poems*, p. 54).

61 In this sentence, Klages alludes to a line from a poem by Conrad Ferdinand Meyer (1825–1898), 'Chorus of the Dead' ('Chor der Toten'), which includes the lines: 'And what we discovered in valid reflections / Remains to earthly changes connected' ('Und was wir an gültigen Sätzen gefunden, / Dran bleibt aller irdische Wandel gebunden') (C. F. Meyer, *Gedichte: Ausgabe letzter Hand*, ed. K.-M. Guth, Berlin: Contumax, 2015, p. 199).

62 Damon and Phintias (or Pythias), see the story related by Aristoxenus, Cicero (*De Officiis*, 3.45), Diodorus Siculus (*Bibliotheca historica*, 10.4) and, subsequently, Schiller in his poem 'The Guarantee' ('Die Bürgschaft'), expounding the virtues of friendship, loyalty, and trust.

63 See the medieval German epic, *Das Nibelungenlied*, for the two figures of Hagen, the warrior, and Volker, the minstrel.

64 See the story by the Brothers Grimm, 'The Dog and the Sparrow'. The sparrow takes its revenge by pecking open the bungs of the wine-casks on the cart, causes the driver to strike both his horses dead, and sets in trail a sequence of events leading to the driver being struck dead by his wife.

65 The sacred band of Thebes was an elite troop of soldiers consisting of 150 pairs of male lovers.

66 Cf. the first line of a student song entitled *O alte Burschenherrlichkeit*, after the first line in its opening stanza; dating back to around 1825 and attributed to Eugen Höfling, the song reactivates the ancient topos of *Ubi sunt* ('Where are they ...?', i.e. those who lived before us) and casts a nostalgic glance back at the friendship and fellowship of the students' duelling societies.

67 An *epopt* was an initiate into the highest level of the Mysteries of Eleusis.

68 The reference is obviously to the verse-play by the Norwegian dramatist, Henrik Ibsen (1826–1906), *Peer Gynt* (1876), based loosely on a Norwegian fairy-tale. Ibsen was a figure appreciated by the George Circle and the *Kosmikerkreis* alike (see Richard Faber, 'Die politisch-religiösen Ideendichter Ludwig Derleth, Stefan George und Henrik Ibsen'), especially Alfred Schuler (see G. Dörr, 'Naturalismus, Paganismus, Esoterik: Zu Alfred Schulers Ibsen-Rezeption', in R. Faber and H. Høibraaten (eds), *Ibsens 'Kaiser und Galiläer': Quellen–Interpretation–Rezeption*, Würzburg: Königshausen & Naumann, 2011, pp. 147–180 and 181–210). See also P. Bishop, '"Mein eigenstes wärmstes Herzblut will ich presigeben": Alfred Schuler's Reception of Henrik Ibsen and its Context', *Oxford German Studies* 28, 1999, 152–194.

69 The *hetairai* were in ancient Greece the courtesans of noble or rich citizens. See, for instance, the poem by Rainer Maria Rilke (1875–1926), 'Tombs of the Hetaerae'

Notes 199

('Hetären-Gräber'), in *The Selected Poetry of Rainer Maria Rilke*, ed. and tr. S. Mitchell, London: Picador, 1974, pp. 44–47. In the Jungian tradition, the hetaira belongs (along with the amazon, the mother, and the medium) to four feminine 'types'; see T. Wolff, *Structural Forms of the Feminine Psyche*, tr. P. Watzlawik, Zurich: C. H. Jung Institute, 1956.

70 Compare, for instance, the following remarks by Michael Pauen on aesthetics as the 'secret paradigm' of Klages's philosophy: 'Klages never wrote an aesthetics, yet art is the secret paradigm of his philosophy' (M. Pauen, *Dithyrambiker des Untergangs: Gnostizismus in Ästhetik und Philosophie der Moderne*, Berlin: Akademie Verlag, 1994, p. 135); 'Aesthetic experience thus informs not just the *images* in which Klages's theory is later expressed but the *content* of this theory [...]' (p. 152);

> The theory of images shows that his later writings maintain the primacy of the aesthetic which the programme of a "magic philosophy" that expresses itself in images and symbols had proposed. [...] The images are "real" not least because of their aesthetic character
>
> (p. 177);

'Klages's frequent references to "images" and "symbols" shows that it is above all aesthetic experience against which conceptual knowledge is measured. [...] Aesthetic experience and Symbolist poetics thus flow immediately into Klages's epistemological critique and metaphysics' (p. 182).

71 For the genesis of this aphorism, see *Rhythms and Runes*, pp. 256 and 289; it is also repeated in *The Spirit as Adversary of the Soul* (see *SW*, vol. 2, pp. 513 and 623).

72 Klages devoted two substantial essays to analysing the significance of Goethe, cf. 'On the Limitations of the Goethean Human Being' (1917) and 'Goethe as a Psychologist' (1928). A similar interest in the figures of Goethe and Schiller is demonstrated by one of the few 'disciples' of Klages, Werner Deubel (1894–1949); see his essays 'Goethe as the Founder of a New World Outlook: A Sketch' (1931) and 'Outlines of a New Image of Schiller' (1934), in W. Deubel, *Im Kampf um die Seele: Wider den Geist der Zeit: Essays und Aufsätze, Aphorismen und Gedichte*, ed. F. Deubel, Bonn: Bouvier, 1997, pp. 118–162 and 163–199. For further discussion, see P. Bishop, 'The "Schillerbild" of Werner Deubel: Schiller as "Poet of the Nation"?', in N. Martin (ed.), *Schiller: National Poet – Poet of Nations: A Birmingham Symposium*, Amsterdam and New York: Rodopi, 2006, pp. 301–320.

73 August von Platen-Hallermünde (1796–1835), known as Graf (Count) Platen, and Eduard Mörike (1804–1875), a Lutheran pastor in Swabia, have affinities with Romanticism, but differences as well. According to Wittgenstein, Mörike 'really is a *great* poet and his poems are among the best things we have [...] the beauty of Mörike's work is very closely related to that of Goethe's' (*Wittgenstein in Cambridge: Letters and Documents 1911–1951*, ed. B. McGuinness, Oxford and Cambridge, MA: Blackwell, 2012, p. 65), which bears out Klages's judgement.

74 How should one approach Klages from a LGBT perspective? Does Klages need queering? While a text such as the section in *Rhythms and Runes* entitled 'Homosexual Characteristics' (*RR*, pp. 366–367) suggests Klages would have little time for the identity politics of the gay movement, one might recall that the circle around Stefan George was, if not homosexual, certainly homoerotic in inclination, and Klages's colleague, Alfred Schuler, was openly gay. For further discussion, see M. Keilson-Lauritz, *Von der Liebe die Freundschaft heißt: Zur Homoerotik im Werk Stefan Georges*, Berlin: Verlag rosa Winkel, 1987; and M. Keilson-Lauritz, 'Stefan George's Concept of Love and the Gay Emancipation Movement', in J. Rieckmann, *A Companion to the Works of Stefan George*, Rochester, NY: Camden House, 2005, pp. 207–243.

75 Klio = Clio, one of the nine Muses and the one who is responsible for history.

76 Hekla is in the south of Iceland and the site of an active volcano; see C. S. Forbes, *Iceland: Its Volcanoes, Geysers, and Glaciers*, London: Murray, 1860, pp. 260–280.

200 *Selections from Klages*

77 See the text known as the *Völuspá* (variously translated as 'The Wise-Woman's Prophecy', 'The Prophecy of the Seeress', and 'The Seeress's Prophecy'), part of the collection of Old Norse poems known as the *Poetic Edda*.

78 Ferdowsi, or Hakim Abu'l-Qasim Ferdowsi Tusi, is the greatly revered Persian poet who wrote the epic work, *Shahnameh*, the Persian 'Book of Kings', the world's longest epic poem created by a single writer.

79 *Der Dichter ist das Herz der Welt*; see Eichendorff's poem, 'To the Poets' ('An die Dichter'), discussed by Menhennet in *The Romantic Movement*, pp. 104–105.

80 The principle of *panta rhei*, 'all things flow', is associated with the worldview of the pre-Socratic philosopher Heraclitus. (Although the phrase cannot be found in this form in any of the surviving fragments of Heraclitus, it is traditionally ascribed to him and can be derived from, among other sources, Simplicius's *Commentary on Aristotle's 'Physics'* (23.33) and from two passages in Plato's *Cratylus*, 'all things flow and nothing stands' (401d) and 'all things are in motion and nothing at rest'; he 'compares them to the stream of a river, and says that you cannot go into the same water twice' (402a) (Plato, *Collected Dialogues*, ed. E. Hamilton and H. Cairns, Princeton, NJ: Princeton University Press, 1989, pp. 438 and 439). For further discussion, see J. Barnes, *The Presocratic Philosophers*, London and New York: Routledge, 1982, pp. 49–52; and D. W. Graham, 'Heraclitus: Flux, Order, and Knowledge', in P. Curd and D. W. Graham, *The Oxford Handbook of Presocratic Philosophy*, Oxford and New York: Oxford University Press, 2008, pp. 169–188).

81 At this point, Klages inserts an editorial footnote:

> This should not be taken literally, but is intended to express the following: it denies that identities occur in reality. – What is not disputed is reference in thought to reality (without which one could not speak meaningfully about 'reality' at all), but rather the *conceptuality* of reality. – Precisely this intellectual theme is worked out in the present author's writings and confirmed by his conclusions.
>
> (*RR*, p. 312, footnote)

82 Analogy is a form of reasoning which has been described (by Pierre Grimes) as the doorway into Platonic metaphysics, and (by the scientist Joseph Priestley) as 'our best guide in all philosophical investigations' (cited in P. Bartha, 'Analogy and Analogical Reasoning', *Stanford Encyclopedia of Philosophy*. Available http://plato. stanford.edu/entries/reasoning-analogy. Accessed 12 November 2016. Even and especially in early Greek philosophy, analogy was a valid method of philosophical reasoning; see G. E. R. Lloyd, *Polarity and Analogy: Two Types of Argumentation in Early Greek Thought*, New York: Cambridge University Press, 1966.

83 See *The Spirit as Adversary of the Soul*, book 5, part 2, section 5, chapter 73; *SW*, vol. 2, p. 1301. The Mothers Scene can be found in *Faust*, Part Two, Act 1, 'Dark Gallery' (Goethe, *Faust*, ed. Hamlin, tr. Arndt, pp. 176–179). For a discussion of the significance of this mysterious, controversial, and in some respects highly parodic scene, see J. R. Williams, 'The Problem of the Mothers', in P. Bishop (ed.), *A Companion to Goethe's 'Faust', Parts I and II*, Rochester, NY: Camden House, 2001, pp. 122–143.

84 See Rig-Veda, X.71 [897], in *Rig-Veda*, tr. H. Grassmann, 2 vols, Leipzig: Brockhaus, 1877, Part 2, p. 358. In the translation by Ralph T. H. Griffith of Book 10, Hymn 71, 'Jnanam', these lines read (ll. 10–11):

> All friends are joyful in the friend who cometh in triumph, having conquered in assembly. / He is their blame-averter, food-provider: prepared is he and fit for deed of vigour. / *One plies his constant task reciting verses*, one sings the holy psalm in Sakvarî measures. / One more, the Brahman, tells the lore of being, and one lays down the rules of sacrificing.
>
> (*The Hymns of the Rig Veda: Translated with a Popular Commentary*, tr. R. T. H. Griffith, vol. 2, 2nd edn, Benares: Lazarus, 1896, pp. 435–436)

Notes 201

85 The story of Nala and Damayanti is part of the massive Indian epic, the *Mahābhārata*; a likely source for Klages's reference is the version presented by Friedrich Rückert (1788–1866), the German poet and Orientalist; see *Nal und Damajanti: Eine indische Geschichte* [1828], tr. F. Rückert, 2nd edn, Frankfurt am Main: Sauerländer, 1838, pp. 285–286: 'And Damayanti, again in pleasure / Lying on her husband's chest, / Breathed like a meadowfull of flowers, / When the morning dew falls upon it' ('Und Damajanti, wieder in Lust / Ruhend an ihres Gatten Brust, / Athmete wie die Blumenau, / Wenn sie besucht der Morgenthau'). Cf. *The Mahābhārata*, vol. 2, *2. The Book of the Assembly Hall; 3. The Book of the Forest*, ed. and tr. J. A. B. van Buitenen, Chicago and London: Chicago University Press, 1975, p. 361: 'Damayanti of the beautiful face laid her face on his chest and, overcome with emotion, the long-eyed woman heaved a sigh'.

86 See *The Spirit as Adversary of the Soul*, book 5, part 2, section 5, chapter 73; *SW*, vol. 2, p. 1325. Here Klages cites the following lines from the *Iliad*, book 6, ll. 146–149, where Glaukos of Lykia, on the side of the Trojans, says to his opponent Diomedes, one of the companions of Odysseus: 'As is the generation of leaves, so is that of humanity. / The wind scatters the leaves on the ground, but the live timber / burgeons with leaves again in the season of spring returning. / So one generation of men will grow while another / dies' (*The Iliad of Homer*, tr. Lattimore, p. 157).

87 See *Wallenstein's Death*, Act 3, Scene 13, where Wallenstein, dressed in armour, speaks the following dramatic monologue: 'My leafy branches you have hacked away, / A naked trunk I stand! But here within / My inmost marrow spring the vital power / That put forth shoots, and gave a world its birth' (Schiller, *The Robbers; Wallenstein*, tr. Lamport, p. 390). For further discussion, see B. Lange, *Die Sprache von Schillers 'Wallenstein'*, Berlin: de Gruyter, 1873, pp. 148–149.

88 Hebbel's poem 'The Last Tree' ('Der letzte Baum') belongs to his poems from the period 1857–1863; see F. Hebbel, *Werke*, ed. H. Geiger, 2 vols, Wiesbaden: Vollmer, [1973], vol. 2, *Gedichte und Prosa*, pp. 254–255.

89 For discussion of the mythologem of Merlin in relation to Klages, see Kuckartz, *Ludwig Klages als Erzieher*, pp. 160–171.

90 Lenau, *Vermischte Gedichte*, 'Waldlieder', No. 5; in N. Lenau, *Sämtliche Werke und Briefe*, vol. 1, pp. 426–428. The figure of Merlin the magician is at the centre of the fifth (and longest) poems in this cycle: 'An initiate, in harmony with the "eternal laws" of existence, Merlin is for Lenau the ultimate poet-priest-magician', for 'in nature and the inner realm, Merlin attains the spiritual power, unity, insight, solace, and release that the despairing Lenau so ardently seeks' (R. G. Dahms, entry on 'Lenau, Nikolaus', in N. J. Lacy, G. Ashe, S. N. Ihle, M. E. Kalinke, and R. H. Thompson (eds), *The New Arthurian Encyclopedia*, updated paperback edition, New York and London: Garland, 1996, p. 277). For an appraisal of Lenau's work, see R. Dove, 'The Rhetoric of Lament: A Reassessment of Nikolaus Lenau', *Orbis Litterarum* 39, no. 3 (1984), 230–265.

91 At this point, Klages inserts an excerpt from his 1902 monograph on the work of Stefan George:

Creativity has become terrible and ruinous. Adverse to arbitrariness it should willingly realize itself. The spirit breaks and hammers unformable masses in its masterful fire. Torn between powerlessness and cruelty, it ploughs fragmentary seeds and digs the furrow deeper into a bloodthirsty soil. Therefore a martyr's fire plays around the features of these latecomers from the distant past, and as if over hollow-eyed ravines they seem to cross over on dizzying footbridges.

(L. Klages, *Stefan George*, ed. M. Großheim, Bonn: Bouvier, 2008, p. 30)

92 At this point Klages adds the following foonote:

Incidentally it was not involuntarily that Plato had recourse to the dialogue form but consciously and deliberately. Thinking, according to Socrates in the *Theaetetus*,

202   *Selections from Klages*

is 'a discourse that the mind carries on with itself about any subject that it is considering' and it seems to do nothing else when thinking than 'talking to itself, asking questions and answering them'. 'So', he goes on, 'I should describe thinking as discourse, and judgment as a statement pronounced, not aloud to someone else, but silently to oneself'.

(*GWS=SW*, vol. 2, p. 1472; cf. *Theaetetus*, 189e–190a; in Plato, *Collected Dialogues*, pp. 895–896)

93   See the fragment of 1915 entitled 'On the aura of words' in *Rhythms and Runes*:

Because of the aura of the concept contained in the word, it is possible for concepts to turn into gods (cf. Nemesis, Dike, Ananke) and for every epoch, every thinker, poet, orator, etc., and in the end every speaking individual to have favourite words which have a meaning only for them, which lead and mislead their entire thought, which – despite the broadest legacy of definitions – do not reveal their extra-conceptual nimbus to other age-groups and personalities, and which for this reason can never be fully understood. – What, for instance, was the meaning, which today we can no longer access, of the word 'will' for Schopenhauer, the 'absolute' and the 'infinite' for Schelling, the 'a priori' for Kant, the 'pneuma' for the Gnostics! Strictly speaking, philosophy is just as untranslatable out of its language and its time as poetry is; and hence the bitter troubles and the difficult art of the philosophical stylist to rescue the extra-conceptual meaning content simultaneously grasped in the visionary moment in the magic of linguistic expressions. To philosophize is an attempt at interpreting the magic of words.

(*RR*, p. 365)

94   Here Klages is probably thinking of the expression *Pathos der Distanz*, 'pathos of distance'; see Nietzsche, *Beyond Good and Evil*, §257; in *Basic Writings*, p. 391. For further discussion, see R. Diprose, 'Nietzsche and the Pathos of Distance', in P. Patton (ed.), *Nietzsche, Feminism and Political Theory*, London: Routledge, 1993, pp. 1–26.

95   In book 2 of Plato's *Republic*, Socrates introduces the philosopher (*philosophos*) and equates him or her with the lover of learning (*philomathēs*), noting that the truly philosophic character trait (*pathos philosophon*) is to distinguish 'friendly from hostile looks by nothing other than having learned the one and being ignorant of the other' (*Republic*, 375e; 376c; 376b, in *The Republic of Plato*, tr. A. Bloom, New York: Basic Books, 1968, p. 53). See E. A. Havelock, *Preface to Plato*, Cambridge, MA, and London: Belknap Press of Harvard University Press, 1963, p. 307. In an autobiographical sketch from 1867–1868, Nietzsche reflects on the meaning of the phrase for education:

I had in mind the goal of becoming a truly practical teacher and above all awakening in young people the circumspection and self-reflection that enables them to maintain a focus on the why?, the what?, and the how? of scholarship. One will not fail to spot a philosophical element in this way of looking at things. The young person should first attain that condition of amazement that has been called *philosophon pathos kat exochêen*. After life has been reduced before him to lots of puzzles, he should consciously, but with strict resignation stick to what it is possible to know and to choose according to his abilities from among this huge field. How I came to this point of view is something I shall now explain. It is here that for the first time the name of Schopenhauer appears in these pages.

(F. Nietzsche, 'Account of My Two Years in Leipzig', in *Werke in drei Bänden*, ed. K. Schlechta, Munich: Hanser, 1968, vol. 3, pp. 127–148 [here: pp. 132–133])

96   Compare with Freud's remarks on animism in, for example, *Totem and Taboo* (1913), chapter 3, 'Animism, Magic, and the Omnipotence of Thought' (*Totem and*

Taboo: Some Points of Agreement between the Mental Lives of Savages and Neurotics, tr. J. Strachey, London: Routledge and Kegan Paul, 1961, esp. pp. 75–77).

97 Here we can clearly see how Klages sought to engage with the thought of Theodor Lipps (1851–1914), who developed the notion of empathy or *Einfühlung*. Lipps was an important influence on Klages's intellectual development, and Klages's reception of Lipps is a chapter in the so-far unwritten history of German thought in the late nineteenth and early twentieth centuries.

98 For further discussion, see J. Dunham, I. H. Grant, and S. Watson, *Idealism: The History of a Philosophy*, Durham: Acumen, 2011; D. Boucher (ed.), *The British Idealists*, Cambridge: Cambridge University Press, 1997; and D. Boucher, 'The Scottish Contribution to British Idealism and the Reception of Hegel', in G. Graham (ed.), *Scottish Philosophy in the Nineteenth and Twentieth Centuries*, Oxford: Oxford University Press, 2015, pp. 154–182.

99 See the legend, told by Johannes Rothe in 1421, concerning Ludwig II, Landgrave of Thuringia, and his encounter with a blacksmith in Ruhla, who called in the landgrave to take a stance against the nobles who were harassing the people. In 'Of Old and New Law-Tables', §29, Zarathustra proclaims: 'This new law-table do I put before you, O my brothers: *Become hard!*' (*Thus Spoke Zarathustra*, tr. Hollingdale, p. 231).

100 Some earlier commentators on Klages emphasized those passages which seem to suggest we might come to live in harmony with spirit or *Geist*. Hans Eggert Schröder, for instance, argued that the Klagesian concept of personality embodied that successful integration of the spirit with the demands of life (H. E. Schröder, 'Vom Sinn der Persönlichkeit: Ein Beitrag zum Menschenbild von Ludwig Klages', *Psychologische Rundschau* 8, 1957, 207–217 [pp. 208 and 215]; and 'Über den Geistbegriff bei Klages', *Schweidewege* 4, 1974, 113–120). Similarly, Hans Kasdorff considered it might be possible to develop a fruitful relationship between soul and spirit (H. Kasdorff, *Ludwig Klages: Gesammelte Aufsätze und Vorträge zu seinem Werk*, Bonn: Bouvier, 1984, pp. 109 and 25). More recently, however, critics have drawn attention to the reliance of Klages's theoretical methodology on an argumentative rhetoric of inversion (R. Müller, *Das verzwistete Ich: Ludwig Klages und sein philosophisches Hauptwerk "Der Geist als Widersacher der Seele"*, Berne, Frankfurt am Main: Lang, 1971, p. 55; and Pauen, *Dithyrambiker des Untergangs*, pp. 136–137). This rhetoric tends to exclude any easy reconciliation, although Klages recognizes that a form of *modus vivendi* can sometimes be found.

101 Compare with the title of the study by Gotthilf Heinrich von Schubert (1780–1860), *Views from the Nocturnal Side of Natural Science* (1808). In his study of George, Klages had written:

> The pagan world is the world of nocturnal consciousness, which participates like a plant in the fate of the planet that streams forth invisibly in magnetic currents. It does indeed require space and time, but not light. It works its effect more powerfully through the pores of the skin than through the eyes in one's head and it is revealed most powerfully of all when all the senses are asleep: *for then awakens the body that is the soul.*
>
> (*Stefan George*, ed. Großheim, p. 70)

102 In this emphasis on style Klages aligns himself with two of his great predecessors: Nietzsche, for whom 'one thing is needful' – 'to "give style" to one's character' (*The Gay Science*, tr. Kaufmann, §290, p. 232); and before him, Goethe who, in a famous essay of 1789, distinguished between 'Simple Imitation, Manner, Style' and defined style as 'rest[ing] on the most fundamental principle of cognition, on the essence of things – to the extent that it is granted to perceive this essence in visible and tangible form', for which reason style is the 'highest possible level' of art and 'the highest achievement of humankind' (J. W. Goethe, *Essays on Art and Literature*

204 *Selections from Klages*

[Goethe Edition, vol. 3], ed. J. Gearey, tr. E. von Nardroff and E. H. von Nardroff, New York: Suhrkamp, 1986, pp. 71–74 [p. 72]).

103 For further discussion of the complex question of the relation between spirit and soul, the reader is referred again to Schröder, 'Vom Sinn der Persönlichkeit' and Schröder, 'Über den Geistbegriff bei Klages', as well as H. Kasdorff, 'Das Gegen-und Miteinander von Geist und Seele' [1976], in *Ludwig Klages: Gesammelte Aufsätze und Vorträge zu seinem Werk*, Bonn: Bouvier, 1984, pp. 109–134.

104 For the notion of the weaving-loom of destiny (or 'the spindle of Necessity'), see Plato, *Republic*, book 10 (617b–d and 620c–621a). The image of weaving ties in with Klages's understanding of the Mothers Scene in *Faust*, Part Two, and constitutes a significant image in his thought.

105 See the discussion earlier in Klages's essay 'On the Relation of Education to the Essence of Humankind', where he considers various educational goals, namely: 'objectivity, ability to organize, logical thought, powers of reasoning, conceptual recall, ability to generalize, specific scholarly critical skills', but also 'contemplative powers, resourcefulness, and independence of judgement' (*SW*, vol. 3, p. 276).

106 'In great endeavours, even to have had the will is enough' (Propertius, *Elegies*, book 2, no. 10, l. 5; cf. Propertius, *Elegies*, ed. and tr. G. P. Goold, Cambridge, MA, and London: Harvard University Press, 1990, p. 133: 'In mighty projects even to have wished is enough').

107 Cf. Nietzsche, *On the Genealogy of Morals*, III, §17, where 'degeneration of the blood, malaria, syphilis, and the like' are identified with the 'German depression after the Thirty Years' War, which infected half of Germany with vile diseases and thus prepared the ground for German servility, German pusillanimity' (*Basic Writings*, p. 567).

108 The word 'sacrilege' derives etymologically from *sacrilegus*, formed from *sacer*='sacred' and *legere*='to take possession of'.

109 Klages is playing here on the biblical passage about 'the sin against the Holy Ghost' (Mark 3: 28–30).

110 In ancient Greek 'hubris' refers to an action that shames or humilates a victim (see Aristotle, *Rhetoric*, 1378b).

111 The word 'sacrifice' derives from *sacer*='sacred', 'holy', and *facere*='to do', 'to perform', i.e. to make something sacred.

112 Klages's rhetoric here is reminiscent of the title of a chapter, 'Of the Bestowing Virtue', in Nietzsche's *Thus Spoke Zarathustra* (*Thus Spoke Zarathustra*, tr. Hollingdale, pp. 99–104), and his words echo the conclusion of another chapter entitled 'Of the Sublime Men': 'This indeed is the secret of the soul: only when the hero has deserted the soul does there approach it in dreams – the superhero' (p. 141).

113 A term used by Klages's friend, Alfred Schuler, in his private lecture series given in 1917–1918 under the title *On the Essence of the Eternal City*. In his first lecture 'On the Essence of the Telesma' Schuler told his audience:

> Turning my eye inwards I catch sight of a vibrating fullness of light / innumerable shining flows delighting in their exchange / an eternally uninterrupted marriage in the aether. This substance / which I take to be / identical with / what is called the 'great telesma' [i.e. the esoteric force mentioned by Hermes Trismesgistos in the *Tabula Smaragdina* or *Emerald Tablet*] and described in an analogous way / I consider to be the transfiguring / blissful-making power / which is located in the blood. To the extent it makes the flow of blood shine / I call it essential life. This definition came to me of its own accord at the same time as the experience. The possession of the beacon is thus our participation in absolute life. [...] [S]uch a beacon is connected with currents from the cosmos / in which they must also be dispersed. / Whoever stands in the light of the beacon experiences these currents as cold showers coming out of the cosmos / whereas the essence / wedded to the

Notes 205

blood / glows in blissful warmth. – The substance which shoots forth from the universe is what I call cosmic. Eros Kosmogonos seems to me to be a late symbolization of this descent.

(A. Schuler, *Cosmogonische Augen: Gesammelte Schriften*, ed. B. Müller, Paderborn: Igel, 1997, pp. 220–221; cf. *Gesammelte Werke*, ed. B. Müller, Munich: Telesma-Verlag, 2007, pp. 262–263)

Some commentators have seen a connection between Schuler's ideas and the tradition of Gnosticism (see F. Wegener, *Alfred Schuler, der letzte Katharer: Gnosis, Nationalsozialismus und mystische Blutleuchte*, Gladbeck: KFVR, 2003, pp. 39–40); others have noted an affinity with ideas found in the work of Rainer Maria Rilke (V. Durr, *Rainer Maria Rilke: The Poet's Trajectory*, New York: Lang, 2006, chapter 5, 'Death and "the Open"', pp. 108–146, esp. pp. 121–122).

114 Compare with the remark of Georg Misch (1878–1965) that the defining characteristic of vitalist philosophy is 'the shift in philosophical principles from the concept of being to the idea of life' (*Lebensphilosophie und Phänomenologie: Eine Auseinandersetzung der Diltheyschen Richtung mit Heidegger und Husserl*, 2nd edn, Leipzig: Teubner, 1931, p. 4), cited in a recently republished work by Philipp Lersch (1898–1972), *Lebensphilosophie der Gegenwart* (1932), who applies this shift to the work of Klages; see *Erlebnishorizonte: Schriften zur Lebensphilosophie*, ed. T. Rolf, Munich: Albunea, 2011, pp. 41–123 (p. 89, n. 112).

Further reading

Graphology

Saudek, R., 'The Methods of Graphology', *British Journal of Medical Psychology* 7, no. 2 (June 1927), 221–259.

Stein-Lewinson, T., 'An Introduction to the Graphology of Ludwig Klages' *Journal of Personality* 6, no. 3 (March 1938), 163–176.

Psychology (characterology, expression)

Allport, G. W., [review of] 'Klages, Ludwig. *The Science of Character*. Translated by W. H. Johnston. [...]', *Psychological Bulletin* 30, no. 5 (May 1933), 370–371.

Kunz, H., 'Die Metaphysik von Ludwig Klages und ihre Bedeutung für die Persönlichkeitsforschung', in *Die Psychologie des 20. Jahrhunderts*, 15 vols, Zurich: Kindler, 1976–1981, vol. 1, *Die europäische Tradition: Tendenzen, Schulen, Entwicklungslinien*, ed. H. Balmer, Zurich: Kindler, 1976, pp. 353–381.

Sprott, W. J. H., [review of] '*The Science of Character*. By Ludwig Klages. Translated by W. H. Johnston. [...]', *Mind* [NS] 38, no. 152 (October 1929), 513–520.

Wertham, F., 'Progress in Psychiatry III: The Significance of Klages' System for Psychopathology', *Archives of Neurology and Psychiatry* 24, no. 2 (1930), 381–388.

Aesthetics

Baer, L., 'The Literary Criticism of Ludwig Klages and the Klages School: An Introduction to Biocentric Thought', *The Journal of English and Germanic Philology* 40, no. 1 (January 1941), 91–138.

Pfeiffer, J., 'Dichtung und Metaphysik: Zur Deutung des Dichterischen bei Ludwig Klages' [1951], in *Die dichterische Wirklichkeit: Versuche über Wesen und Wahrheit der Dichtung*, Hamburg: Meiner, 1962, pp. 114–152.

Intellectual background and context

Alksnis, G., *Chthonic Gnosis: Ludwig Klages and his Quest for the Pandaemonic All*, Munich: Theion Publishing, 2015 (a republication of the first academic thesis on Klages in the English-speaking world, completed in 1970).

Bishop, P., 'The Reception of Friedrich Nietzsche in the Early Work of Ludwig Klages', *Oxford German Studies* 31, no. 1 (January 2002), 129–160.

Further reading 207

Bishop, P., 'Ein Kind Zarathustras und eine nicht-metaphysische Auslegung der ewigen Wiederkehr', *Hestia: Jahrbuch des Klages-Gesellschaft* 21, 2002/2003, 15–37.

Bishop, P., 'Stefan George and the Munich Cosmologists', in J. Rieckmann (ed.), *A Companion to the Works of Stefan George*, Rochester, NY: Camden House, 2005, pp. 161–187.

Bishop, P., 'A Biocentric Approach to Weimar Aesthetics: Friedrich Schiller and Ludwig Klages', *Publications of the English Goethe Society* 75, no. 2 (September 2006), 95–108.

Bishop, P., 'The Battle between Spirit and Soul: Messianism, Redemption and Apocalypse in Klages', in W. Cristaudo and W. Baker (eds), *Messianism, Apocalypse and Redemption in 20th Century German Thought*, Adelaide: ATF Press, 2006, pp. 181–194.

Bishop, P., 'The Philosophical Contribution of Ludwig Klages', in Gunnar Alksnis, *Chthonic Gnosis: Ludwig Klages and his Quest for the Pandaemonic All*, Munich: Theion Publishing, 2015, pp. 9–43.

Bishop, P., 'Traum und Lebensphilosophie: Ludwig Klages und eine andere Entdeckung des dunklen Kontinents', in M. Guthmüller and H.-W. Schmidt-Hannisa (eds), *Das nächtliche Selbst: Traumwesen und Traumkunst im Jahrhundert der Psychologie*, vol. 1, *1850–1900*, Göttingen: Wallenstein, 2016, pp. 374–397.

Block, R., 'Selective Affinities: Walter Benjamin and Ludwig Klages', *Arcadia* 35 (2000), 117–136.

Falter, R., *Ludwig Klages: Lebensphilosophie als Zivilisationskritik*, Munich: Telesma, 2003.

Furness, R., *Zarathustra's Children: A Study of a Lost Generation of German Writers*, Rochester, NY: Camden House, 2000 (contains a chapter on Klages, as well as a chapter on Alfred Schuler; an indispensable starting-point for reading Klages in English).

Ganzoni, W., *Die neue Schau der Seele: Goethe – Nietzsche – Klages*, Vienna and Stuttgart: Braumüller, 1957.

Gianni Ardic, C., *La Fuga degli dèi: Mito, matriarcato e immagine in Ludwig Klages*, Milan: Jouvence, 2016.

Großheim, M., *Ludwig Klages und die Phänomenologie*, Berlin: Akadamie Verlag, 1994 (contains detailed discussions of Klages in relation to, among others, Martin Heidegger, Edmund Husserl, and Max Scheler).

Großheim, M. (ed.), *Perspektiven des Lebensphilosophie: Zum 125. Geburtstag von Ludwig Klages*, Bonn: Bouvier, 1999 (a collection of papers demonstrating a rich variety of approaches to Klages's thought).

Hammer, S., *Widersacher oder Wegbereiter? Ludwig Klages und die Moderne*, Heidelberg and Berlin: Hüthig, 1992.

Hinton Thomas, R., 'Nietzsche in Weimar Germany – and the Case of Ludwig Klages', in A. Phelan (ed.), *The Weimar Dilemma: Intellectuals in the Weimar Republic*, Manchester: Manchester University Press, 1985, pp. 71–91.

Honneth, A., 'L'esprit et son objet: Parentés anthropologiques entre la "Dialectique de la raison" et la critique de la civilisation dans la philosophie de la vie', in G. Raulet (ed.), *Weimar ou l'explosion de la modernité*, Paris: Éditions Anthropos, 1984, pp. 97–112.

Kaltenbrunner, G.-K., 'Der Konservative als Seelenforscher, Kosmiker und Untergangsdenker', in *Der schwierige Konservatismus: Definitionen – Theorien – Porträts*, Herford and Berlin: Nicolai, 1975, pp. 247–265.

Kasdorff, H., *Ludwig Klages: Gesammelte Werke und Vorträge zu seinem Werk*, Bonn: Bouvier Verlag Herbert Grundmann, 1984.

208 *Further reading*

Kasdorff, H., *Ludwig Klages: Werk und Wirkung: Einführung und kommentierte Biblio-graphie*, 2 vols, Bonn: Bouvier, 1969–1974 (everything you ever wanted to know about the reception of Ludwig Klages but were too afraid to ask: a massive reference-guide to the extensive secondary literature, and a testimony to Klages's importance in the twentieth century).

Kotowski, E.-V., *Feindliche Dioskuren: Theodor Lessing und Ludwig Klages: Das Scheitern einer Jugendfreundschaft (1885–1899)*, Berlin: Jüdische Verlagsanstalt, 2000.

Kozljanič, R. J., *Lebensphilosophie: Eine Einführung*, Stuttgart: Kohlhammer, 2004 (contains a chapter on Klages, as well as discussions of Friedrich Schlegel, Arthur Schopenhauer, Carl Gustav Carus, Friedrich Nietzsche, Henri Bergson, Wilhelm Dilthey, Georg Simmel, Otto Friedrich Bollnow, and Hermann Schmitz).

Kunz, H., *Martin Heidegger und Ludwig Klages: Daseinsanalytik und Metaphysik*, ed. H. Balmer, Munich: Kindler, 1976.

Lebovic, N., *The Philosophy of Life and Death: Ludwig Klages and the Rise of a Nazi Biopolitics*, New York: Palgrave Macmillan, 2013.

Martella, V., *Dialectics of Cultural Criticism: Adorno's Confrontation with Rudolf Borchardt and Ludwig Klages in the 'Odyssey' chapter of 'Dialektik der Aufklärung'*, doctoral dissertation, Justus-Liebig-Universität Gießen, 2012.

Müller, R., *Das verzwistete Ich – Ludwig Klages und sein philosophisches Hauptwerk "Der Geist als Widersacher der Seele"*, Bern and Frankfurt am Main: Lang, 1971.

Ninck, M., 'Zur Philosophie von Ludwig Klages', *Kant-Studien*, 36 (1931), 148–157.

Pauen, M., *Dithyrambiker des Untergangs: Gnostizismus in Ästhetik und Philosophie der Moderne*, Berlin: Akademie Verlag, 1994 (contains an important chapter on Klages's 'pagan gnosis' as well as discussions of Schopenhauer, Ernst Bloch, Martin Heidegger, and Theodor W. Adorno).

Preußer, H.-P., *Pathische Ästhetik: Ludwig Klages und die Urgeschichte der Post-moderne*, Heidelberg: Winter, 2015 (a collection of scholarly articles on Klages by a distinguished academic commentator).

Prinzhorn, H., *Die Wissenschaft am Scheidewege von Leben und Geist: Festschrift für Ludwig Klages zum 60. Geburtstag*, Leipzig: Barth, 1932 (papers by nearly thirty contributors to a *Festschrift* on Klages's sixtieth birthday).

Reschka, R., 'Der tödliche Pfeil: Ludwig Klages' Kultur- und Zivilisationskritik', in *Philosophische Abenteurer*, Tübingen: Mohr Siebeck, 2001, pp. 187–212.

Schröder, H. E., *Schiller – Nietzsche – Klages: Abhandlungen und Essays zur Geistes-geschichte der Gegenwart*, Bonn: Bouvier Verlag Herbert Grundmann, 1974 (a collection of papers by one of Klages's most prolific commentators on a range of related subjects).

Schröder, H. E., *Ludwig Klages: Die Geschichte seines Lebens*, vol. 1, *Die Jugend*, 2nd edn; vol. 2/i, *Das Werk: Erster Halbband (1905–1920)*, 2nd edn; vol. 2/ii (ed. F. Tenigl), *Das Werk: Zweiter Halbband (1920–1956)*, Bonn: Bouvier, 1996; 1992 (a comprehensive and, to date, most authoritative biography of Klages's life and work).

Stauth, G., 'Critical Theory and Pre-Fascist Social Thought', *History of European Ideas* 18, 1994, 711–727.

Stauth, G. and Turner, B. S., 'Ludwig Klages (1872–1956) and the Origins of Critical Theory', *Theory, Culture and Society* 9, no. 3, 1992, 45–63.

Tenigl, F., *Ludwig Klages: Vorträge und Aufsätze zu seiner Philosophie und Seelenkunde*, Bonn: Bouvier, 1997.

Further reading 209

Klages in translation

Klages, L., *The Science of Character: Translated from the Fifth and Sixth Editions*, tr. W. H. Johnston, London: George Allen & Unwin, 1929 (the first and only complete work by Klages to have been translated into English).

Klages, L., *The Biocentric Worldview: Selected Essays and Poems*, tr. J. D. Pryce, London: Arktos, 2013 (a selection of some of Klages's most important essays which appears, however, in a publishing house with its own political agenda).

Klages, L., *Cosmogonic Reflections: Selected Aphorisms*, tr. J. D. Pryce, London: Arktos, 2015 (a follow-up volume to the above – a selection, with an arguably political slant, from Klages's writings with some problematic translations).

Klages, L., *Dream Theory* (currently in preparation).

Index

Page numbers in **bold** indicate figures and in *italic* indicate tables.

Abraham, Karl 33
Ackerknecht, Erwin 7–8, 16, 20, 39
activity 94–95
Adler, Alfred xviii, 21
Adorno, Theodor W. 39, 93
aesthetics 85–86, 87–88, 103–104,
    144–147, 156, 163–174, 199n70
Allgemeine Zeitung 70
Allport, Gordon W. xiii
Althaus, Hilde 18
analogy 167, 200n82
Anaxagoras 122, 125
ancestral worship 155–158
anthropology 174–190
anti-Semitism 3, 32–33, 35
Aphrodite 104, 105, 118n115
apocalyptic rhetoric 91–94
Apollo 164, 182
Apollonianism 6, 111n39, 114n64,
    143–144
Apuleius 194n16
Aristotle 78, 89, 111n48
Arktos (the centaur) xviii
art 41–42, 49n117, 81–85, **82**, 163–174
atmosphere 147, 196n38
Augustine 62, 67, 108n9, 109n25
aura 147, 149, 151, 189, 197n40, 197n45,
    202n93
automatic movement 56
Axel, Erwin (pseudonym) 52

Baader, Franz von 79
Bachofen, Johann Jakob xv, 9, 19, 79, 92,
    94
Baeumler, Alfred xviii, 19
Baeyer, Adolf von 3
Bahr, Hermann 15

Baldur 87
Barth, Johann Ambrosius 17, 38, 40
Baudrillard, Jean xix
Baur, Ferdinand Christian 11–12
beat *see* rhythm and beat
Beauvoir, Simone de 105
Beckmann, Max 21
Beneke, Friedrich Eduard 100
Benjamin, Walter xii, xxiiin5, 89, 93,
    115n67, 197n45
Benn, Gottfried 22
Benoist, Alain de xix
Bergson, Henri 15
Bernhard, Putti 4
Bernoulli, Carl Albrecht 18, 19
Bernoulli, Carl Johann 19
Bernoulli, Christoph 16, 20, 29–30, 72
Bertram, Ernst xiv, 7, 10, 21
Bilder see images
Binet, Alfred 5
birth and death 132–134
Blätter für die Kunst 10
Blavatsky, Helena 11
Bleuler, Eugen 8
Bloch, Ernst xviii, 92, 101, 113n60
Blutleuchte 190, 204n113
Böcklin, Arnold 81–85, **82**, 151–152, 172
Bode, Rudolf 7, 19, 33, 192n2
Boehm, Franz Josef xviii
Boehringer, Robert 10
Böhme, Jakob xvi, 131–132, 193n12
Bollnow, Otto F. 93
Bousset, Wilhelm 12
British Idealism 180, 203n98
Bruck, Arthur Moeller van den 32
Bucke, Richard Maurice 44n19
Burkhardt, Jacob xv

Index 211

Busse, Hans Hinrich 5–6, 13
Buxtehude, xii
Buytendijk, F. J. J. 93

Carpenter, Edward 44n19
Carus, Carl Gustav 9, 20, 79, 94, 106, 107n1, 112n51
Cassirer, Ernst 93
Castor and Pollux 193n11
catastrophe 99, 132–133
Cathars 11
Catilinarian conspiracy 58, 108n10
Ceres 133
Chaboseau, Augustin 11
character 9, 55, 56–62, *61*, 94–95, 176–184
characterological types 94–95, 183–184
Charron, Pierre 22
Cicero 106
Cioran, E. M. 135
'conduct of souls' 189–190
consciousness: of death 180–181; and ego 121–122; genesis of 70–73
Cortázar, Julio: *Hopscotch* xi
Cosmic Circle 4–5, 10–11, 12–13
cosmic consciousness 44n19
cosmogonic role of eros 160–161
cosmos *see* universe
Crépieux-Jamin, Jules 5
cultural critique 9
Curtius, Ludwig 5

Dacqué, Edgar xii
daimon/daimonic 63, 81, 85, 101, 111n42, 117n93, 117n94, 117n96, 144, 147–148, 150, 156–157, 162–163, 168–169, 171
Damon and Phintias 161, 198n62
dancing 131
Darwin, Charles 124
Däubler, Theodor 22
Davies, Peter xviii
death 132–134, 155–158, 180–181
Deleuze, Gilles 193n8
Delius, Frederick 21
Delphi 90, 111n43, 112n51, 112n52
Demeter of Knidos 53, 107n2
Derleth, Ludwig 10, 22
Derrida, Jacques xvii, 40, 195n23
Deubel, Werner xiv, xxivn16, 19–20, 39, 199n72
Deussen, Julius 20, 39
Deutsche Psychologie 17
Diederichs, Eugen 20
Dilthey, Wilhelm xiii, 21
Dionysianism 143–144

Dionysos 26, 183
Dioscuri, the 2, 131, 193n11
distance 151–154
distance learning programmes 16
Dix, Otto 21
Döhmann, Heinrich 20
Donath, Alice 8
Donath, Gustav 8
dreams 100, 116n88, 163–164
drive-impulses 25, 67–68, 69, 76–77, 86
driving forces, system of 60–61, *61*
Droste-Hülshoff, Annette von 193n11
dualism 89, 196n37

ecological concerns 124–125
ecstasy 103–104, 134–139, 144–145, 156–157
Edda, Norse Poetic 111n46, 165, 200n77
education, theory of 186–188, 189–190
ego: and consciousness 121–122; and identity 181–182
Eichendorff, Joseph von 143–144, 195n29
Einhorn, Alfred 3
Einstein, Albert 71
elementary souls, images as 99–103
Eleusinan Mysteries 133–134, 194n19
emotional expression 52
empathy 178, 203n97
Encausse, Gérard 11
environmentalism 9, 39, 124–125
envy 179–180
epopteia 136, 137, 194n19
eros of distance concept 105, 154, 162
eros and the erotic 105, 154, 157, 158–163, 172
Eros Kosmogonos 160–161
Eriugena, Johannes Scotus 109n24
essence of life 113n61
eternal recurrence, doctrine of 27
ethics 64, 121, 177
eugenics 5, 32–33
Eugster, Jakob 16, 72
Evola, Julius xix
Ewald, Gottfried xv
existentialism 39
expression, science of 9, 51–56
expressive movement 54–56

facial expression 52
Falconet, Étienne Maurice 195n30
Faust (Goethe) 17, 28, 104, 114n63, 164–165, 169, 200n83
Faye, Guillaume xix
feelings 60, 76–77, 84, 121, 122, 177, 184

212 *Index*

feminine 188
feminism 40, 105, 118n116
Festschriften: in honour of Klages 28–30, 38
Feuerbach, Ludwig 2
Fichte, Johann Gottlieb 100
Fink, Eugen 102
First World War 10, 14–16
Fischer, Otto 7, 41, 49n117
Förster-Nietzsche, Elisabeth 6, 19, 21
Fortlage, Karl 99–100
Foucault, Michel 40
Frankfurt School 39, 93
Frankfurter Allgemeine Zeitung xvi, xvii
Freud, Sigmund 8, 21, 33, 62, 188, 202n96
Freytag, Gustav 30–31, 38
Freytag, Gustav Willibald 7, 8–9
Frobenius, Leo xii

gamos ('symbolical marriage') 159–160, 194n20
Gattiker, Hermann 16
Gebsattel, Viktor Emil von 7
Geist see opposition of spirit and soul
gender issues 188
genius loci 101–102, 147, 185
George, Stefan xviii, 10, 12–13, 21, 32, 34, 199n74, 201n91, 203n101
George Circle 10, 34
German Graphological Society 5
German Idealism 163, 180
German Romanticism 78–79
Germanic mythology 2
Germanic tribes 2
Gianni Ardic, Chiara 43n7
Glöckner, Ernst 7
Gnosticism xv, 11–12, 44n22, 148–149, 197n39, 202n93, 205n113
gods 102–103
Goethe, Johann Wolfgang von 6, 17, 52, 103, 104, 107, 114n63, 118n102, 121, 122, 143–144, 164–165, 169, 184, 199n72, 203n102
Goethe Medal for Art and Science 28
Görres, Johann Joseph von 79, 109n23
Graphologische Monatshefte 17, 52, 55, 74
graphology 3, 5–9, 53–55
Grau, Alexander xvii–xviii
Greek mythology 2
Grimes, Pierre 200n82
Grimm, Brothers 161, 198n64
Großheim, Michael xxiiin5, 74, 108n5, 110n33, 115n67
Grundmann, Herbert 40–41

Guénon, René xix
Gundolf, Friedrich 10

Habermas, Jürgen xvi–xvii, xxivn24, 114n66
Hager, Wilhelm xxiii
Hamann, Johann Georg 40
handwriting *see* graphology
Hanse, Olivier 43n11
happiness, specific 103–107
Hardenberg, Friedrich von *see* Novalis
hardness 180
Harnack, Adolf von 12
Hartmann, Franz 11
Hartmann, Nicolai xvi, xvii
Hattingberg, Hans von 7
Hebbel, Friedrich 170
Hegel, G. W. F. 2, 97–99, 100
Heidegger, Martin xvi, xvii, 22, 24, 39, 47n78, 93, 100, 102
Hellingrath, Norbert von 7, 15
Heraclitus 78, 100, 101, 102, 115n80, 200n80
Hercules 92
Herodotus 92
heroism of daily life 189
Hesse, Hermann xi
Hestia: Jahrbuch der Klages-Gesellschaft xix
hetairai 105, 118n116, 198n69
Heuss, Theodor xvii, 40
Heymel, Alfred Walter von 7
Hilgenfeld, Adolf 12
Hindenburg, Paul von 28, 32
history, theory of 91–93, 97–99
Hitler, Adolf 32
Hodur 87
Hoffmann, Hermann xv
Höfling, Eugen 198n66
Hölderlin, Friedrich 15, 100, 114n62
Hönel, Harald (ed.): *Ludwig Klages – Explorer and Herald of Life* 38
Homburger, August xv
Homer 92, 201n86
homosexuality 165, 199n74
Horkheimer, Max xviii
Huch, Friedrich 19
Hufeland, C. W. F. 79
Humboldt, Wilhelm von 40
Hume, David 178
Hunziker, Gertrude 16

Ibel, Rudolf 41
Ibsen, Henrik 198n68
Idealism 180, 203n98

Index 213

ideals 180
identity 181–182
idiopathic 153, 197n54
images: as elementary souls 99–103;
reality of images doctrine 73–88, 103,
134–151; and rhythm and beat 128–130
immortality 155–156, 158
impulse movement 56
inanimate objects 139–140
instincts 62, 76, 86
Institute for Scientific Graphology 5
International Congress for Philosophy 9
International Society for Medical
Psychology and Psychotherapy 8
Isis (and Osiris) 16, 194n16
Italy 36–38

jargon 39
Jaspers, Karl xv–xvi, 7, 22, 24–25, 47n79,
47n80
Jensen, Adolf Ellegard 93
Jonas, Hans 12
Jordan, Wilhelm 2, 130–131, 193n10
judgment 96, 119n117
Julian, Emperor of Rome 102
Jung, Carl Gustav xii, xiii, xv, xviii, 14,
15, 21, 33, 61, 94
Jünger, Ernst xviii
Jünger, Friedrich Georg 93

Kafka, Franz 14
Kahn, Eugen xv
Kampmann, Martina 18
Kampmann, Niels 18, 19
Kant, Immanuel 17, 110n36, 197n47,
202n93
Kasdorff, Hans xx, xxiii, 73, 74, 108n4,
115n77, 120, 203n100
Kehrer, Ferdinand Adalbert xiv
Kern, Hans xx, xxiii, 18, 19, 20, 39, 120,
195n28
Keyserling, Hermann von xi, 120
Kierkegaard, Søren 97
Kiesewetter, Carl 11
Kingsley, Peter 111n40
Klages, Friedrich Ferdinand Louis 1
Klages, Helene 1, 14
Klages, Ludwig: celebrity and honours
28–32, 33, 38; childhood 1–3; education
2–3; family 1–2; First World War 10,
14–16; graphology 5–9; Italy 36–38;
lecturing 6–9, 30–32, 33, 35–36; literary
style 120; and National Socialism
32–35, *35*; and Nietzsche 20–28; old

age 39–42; post-Second World War
reception 38–39, 40; private classes 16;
Sämtliche Werke (complete works)
40–41, 103; Schwabing 3–16;
Switzerland 16–20
Klages, Ludwig, *The Spirit as Adversary
of the Soul* 16, 17–18; aesthetics
145–147; Apollonianism and
Dionysianism 143–144; art 165,
166–167, 168, 169–174; atmosphere
147; birth and death 132–134;
Blutleuchte 190; catastrophe 99,
132–133; consciousness 70; ecstasy
134–135, 136; elementary souls
101–102, 117n92; Eleusinan Mysteries
133–134; eros 160; essence of life
113n61; feelings 184; *gamos* 159–160;
Gnostic themes 12; on Heraclitus 100;
index 19; judgments 119n117; new
edition 40; nimbus 149; opposition of
spirit and soul 89, 90–91, 185–186;
planetary soul 149–151; on Plotinus
105; reality of images doctrine 78–81,
87, 150–151; rhythm and beat 127–128,
131; sacrifice 126–127; sacrilege 189;
specific happiness 105–106; theory of
the will 65–66, 70; time 153, 154; value
139; vitalist outlook 186–187
Klages, Ludwig, works: *Attempt at a
Synthesis of Menthone* 3; 'The Basic
Law of Expression' 55; 'Conceptual
Critique' 17; 'Consciousness and Life'
70–71, 121; 'Development of
Personalism' 63–64; 'The Drives and
the Will' 62, 65; *Expressive Movement
and Formative Power* 55, 64–65, 75,
127, 138–139, 163, 165–166, 172; 'The
Expressive Movement and its
Diagnostic Exploitation' 75; *The
Foundations of the Doctrine of
Character* 59, 94–97, 138, 141–143,
158–159, 168–169, 175–176, 177, 178,
179–181, 182–184, 188; *Foundations of
the Science of Expression* 55, 56, 124,
128–130, 174–175; *The Foundations of
the Study of Character* 18, 57, 75–77,
85, 87–88; 'From the History of the
Doctrine of Character' 57–58;
Handwriting and Character 85–86,
178–179; *Humankind and Earth* 70,
123–125, 126, 168; 'Humankind and
Earth' (lecture) 92–93; *Introduction to
the Psychology of Handwriting* 18,
53–54; 'Letter on Ethics' 16, 189–190;

214 *Index*

Klages, Ludwig, works *continued*
Of Cosmogonic Eros 16, 17, 18, 89–90,
102, 119n117, 122, 125–126, 135–136,
144–145, 147, 151–158, 159, 160–163;
'On the Characterology of the Criminal'
64; *On the Concept of the Personality*
74, 181–182; *On the Doctrine of
Expression and the Doctrine of
Character* 174, 176–177, 180; 'On the
Doctrine of Life' (lecture) 72–73; *On
Dream Consciousness* 40, 71, 136–138,
163–164; 'On Sympathy' 74–75; *On the
Essence of Consciousness* 16, 18, 134,
139–140, 148–149, 190; *On the Essence
of Rhythm* 39–40, 130–132, 140–141;
On the Nature of Consciousness 81, 88;
*On the Relation of Education to the
Essence of Humankind* 120, 186,
187–188, 192n2, 204n105; 'On the
Source of Immediate Feelings of
Affection' 74–75; *On the Study of
Expression and the Study of Character*
55; 'On the Theory and
Symptomatology of the Will' 62, 65;
'On the Theory of Writing Pressure' 75;
Primer of the Study of Character 57;
'Principle Issues in Lavater' 52;
Principles of Characterology 57, 59;
The Problems of Graphology 32, 55;
*The Psychological Achievements of
Nietzsche* 18, 22–28, 179; 'Remarks on
the Limitations of the Goethean Human
Being' 16, 164; *Rhythms and Runes*
36–38, 41, 81, 92, 103, 116n81,
167–168, 190–192, 202n93; *The Science
of Character* 60; 'Why Does It Bring
Ruin If One Lifts the Veil of Isis?' 16
Klages, Marie Helene (née Kolster) 1–2
Klinger, Max 21
Koffmane, Georg 12
Kolbenheyer, Erwin Guido 15
Kolster, Ida 2
Kosmiker 4–5, 10–11, 12–13
Kotowski, Elke-Vera 2
Kozljanič, Robert Josef xx, xxvn38,
115n68, 116n91, 117n94, 117n95,
119n120
Krantz-Gross, Annelise xx
Krebs, Pierre xix
Kretschmer, Ernst xiv
Krieck, Ernst xviii
Kronfeld, Arthur xiv
Kubin, Alfred xii, 19, 93
Kühn, Sophie von 4

La Mettrie, Julien Offray de 96
La Roche, Emanuel 16, 72
La Rochefoucauld 22
Lampe, Jorg 20
landscape 123–124, 149–150, 165–166,
187, 190
landscape painting (Chinese) 41–42,
49n117
landscape painting (French) 110n38
Lange, Johannes xv
Langelüddeke, Albrecht xvi
language 40, 60, 79–80, 173–174, 177;
magic of 169
*Language as a Source of the Study of the
Soul* (*Language as the Source of
Psychology*) 40, 62, 65, 66–69
Larisch, Rudolf von 8, 19
Lavater, Johann Kaspar 52
Lawrence, D. H. xviii
Lebensphilosophie xviii, xx, 121, 205n114
Lebovic, Nitzan xviii, 4, 35
Lechter, Melchior 10–11
Lenau, Nikolaus 145–147, 170–171,
196n35
Lersch, Philipp 93, 205n114
Lessing, Gotthold Ephraim 94
Lessing, Theodor 2–3
Lévi, Eliphas 11
Lichtenberg, G. C. 121–122
Lichtenberger, Henri 28
life 121–127, 132–134, 139–140, 155–158
linguistic turn 40
Lipps, Theodor 107, 178, 203n97
Lipsius, Richard Adelbert 12
logocentrism 139, 195n23
Loki 87
Lotze, Hermann 107
love 158–163
Löwith, Karl xi–xii, xvii, 28
Lukács, Georg xviii

magic 142–143, 144, 167–174, 195n27
Magna Mater ('Great Mother') 1, 134
Mahābhārata 169, 201n85
Mahler, Gustav 20
Mann, Thomas 10, 14–15, 21
Marc, Franz 21
Martella, Vincenzo xxvn35
masculine 188
Mead, G. R. S. 12
mechanical beat *see* rhythm and beat
mechanization of humankind 96–97
Meinecke, Friedrich 15
Meiner, Annemarie 40

Index 215

Meiner, Arthur 40
Meiner, Wolfgang 40
menthone 3
Merlin 171, 201n89, 201n90
Metzger, Wolfgang 93
Meyer, Camilla 16, 18
Meyer, Conrad Ferdinand 16
Meyer, Georg 5
Michon, Jean Hippolyte 5
Minoan art 41–42
miracle 163–164, 173, 189–190, 192
Misch, Georg 205
Mombert, Alfred 22
Montaigne, Michel de 22, 97
moral customs 64
Morgenstern, Christian 22
Mörike, Eduard 164, 199n73
movement, human 54–56
Müller, Werner 93
Müller-Guex, Hermann 16
Münch, Gerhart xii
Musil, Robert 4, 8, 43n13
Myers–Brigg Type Indicator® 94
Mystery religions of antiquity 133–134
mysticism 65, 78, 109n23, 146, 183, 185
mythology 2

Nachlass (Klages) 38, 92; *see also* Klages,
    Rhythms and Runes
Nachlass (Schuler) 11, 35, 38
National Review xvii
National Socialism xvii, 32–35, *35*
natural selection 124
Naumann, Friedrich 15
Neander, Johann August 11
Neff, Berthold xviii
neologisms 120
Neoplatonism 103, 106, 133
Neue Pinakothek, Munich 81, 172
Neue Volkserzieher, Der 192n2
'New Right' xix
New Statesman xvii
Nibelungenlied, Das 161, 198n63
Nibelungs, The (Jordan) 2
Nietzsche, Friedrich 17, 19, 20–28, 46n72,
    47n74, 48n90, 60, 79, 100, 106, 121,
    122–123, 127, 179, 192n3, 203n102
nimbus 147, 148–149, 151; *see also* aura
Ninck, Johannes 8
Ninck, Martin 28, 38, 93
nostalgia 162
Novalis 4, 21, 152

occultism 11

Odin 163
Oken, Lorenz 79
Oliver, Revilo P. xviii
Olshausen, Wolfgang 31–32
Olympian gods 102–103
Onfray, Michel xx
opposition of spirit and soul 89–94,
    182–186
orgy 24–25, 183
Otto, Walter F. 7, 93, 102
Overbeck, Franz 19
overturnings 99, 132–133

paganism xviii, 12, 35, 102, 105, 156,
    197n41, 203n101
painting 81–85, **82**, 172
Palágyi, Menyhért 9, 19, 43n16, 60,
    71–72, 107; *Natural Philosophical
    Lectures: On the Fundamental
    Problems of Consciousness and of Life*
    71–72
Pannwitz, Rudolf 22
pantheism 102–103
Papus, Henri 11
Paracelsus 195n28, 196n36, 196n37
Pasqually, Martinez de 11
Passavant, J. D. 79
past and present 151–154
pathos 94–95, 111n48
Pathos der Distanz ('pathos of distance')
    202n94
Pauen, Michael xxivn5, xxivn6, 44n23,
    103–104, 199n70
Paul of Tarsus (Saint) 148, 197n39
pedagogics, vitalist 187–188
Pelasgians 41, 89, 92, 105, 113n52,
    113n56, 125–126, 136, 158, 166, 170
perception 80–81, 100–101, 148–149, 178
personality 9, 55, 56–62, *61*, 94–95,
    176–184, 203n100
Persephone 133
phenomenology 39, 101, 103, 108n5, 128,
    135, 160, 166, 178
Phlegethon xii
planetary soul 149–151
Platen, August von 164, 199n73
Plato 22–23, 24, 62, 78, 92, 111n42,
    111n43, 136–137, 154, 174, 180,
    200n80, 201n92, 202n95
Playing in the Waves (Böcklin) 81–85, **82**
Plehn, Rose 36
Plotinus 78, 103–105, 154
Plutarch 78, 90, 106, 111n43, 112n51
poetry 163–174

216 *Index*

polytheism 102–103
Pompeii 37–38
Porphyry 103–104, 194n16
post-structuralism 39, 40
Pound, Ezra xii–xiii
pre-Socratic philosophers 100, 106, 108n6, 122, 200n80
Preußer, Heinz-Peter 111n48, 196n37
Preyer, Willhelm T. 5
primordial image 86, 95, 101–103, 113n53, 130, 134, 147–149, 151, 153–154, 163, 168, 190
Prinzhorn, Hans xii, xvi, 18, 19, 20, 28, 29, 39, 57; *Science at the Crossroads between Life and Spirit* (ed. Prinzhorn) 28–30
Prodicos of Ceos 92, 104, 113n58
Promethean age 92
Propertius 204n106
Protagoras 22, 78, 108n6
proximity 151–154
Pryce, Joe xviii
pseudoscience 5, 9
psychoanalysis 21, 33, 62
Psychodiagnostic Seminar 6–7, 15
psychology xii–xiiv, xvi, 17, 22, 28, 40, 46n63, 53, 56–57, 62, 66, 100, 174–175
Purgatory 198n58

queer theory 199n74

race 32–33, 35
reality of images doctrine 73–88, 103, 134–151
reflex movement 56
Reichardt, Martin xvi
Reinhart, Georg 18
Reizenstein, Richard 12
religion 155–158
Renaissance 78, 92
Reventlow, Franziska zu 4–5
rhythm and beat 127–134
Rhythmus (journal) 33
Riezler, Walter 7
Rig-Veda 200n84
Rilke, Rainer Maria 12, 198n69, 205n113
Robertson, Ritchie xviii
Romanticism 78–79, 143–144, 164
Rome 4, 12, 36–37, 63, 108n10, 152, 197n50
Römermann, Marie 14, 30
Rosenberg, Alfred xviii, 33–34
Rothacker xvi–xvii
Rosenfeld, Hans-Friedrich 20

Rückert, Friedrich 201n85

Sachs, Hans xiii
sacrifice 126–127, 192n6
sacrilege 189, 204n108
Saint-Martin, Louise Claude de 11
Salin, Edgar 10
Sammlung Schack, Munich 172
Saucke, Alice 18, 19
Saucke, Kurt 18, 19
Saudek, Robert 6
Saussure, Ferdinand de 40
scepticism 24–25, 180
Schablonisierung 94–99
Scheler, Max xii, xvii, 93
Schiller, Friedrich xiv, 21, 87, 108n12, 109n26, 126–127, 193n7
Schindler, Heinrich Bruno 79
Schlegel, Friedrich 106
Schmeer, Hans 28
Schmitz, Oscar A. H. 10
Schneider, Kurt xv
Schopenhauer, Arthur 78, 106, 110n39, 136, 154
Schöppe, Wilhelm 20
Schröder, Hans Eggert xx, 17, 33, 39, 41, 72–74, 75, 86, 134, 203n100
Schubert, Gotthilf Heinrich von 20, 79, 203n101
Schuler, Alfred 11, 12–14, 15, 19, 22, 35, 38, 79, 190, 204n113
Schultz, Johannes Heinrich xiv–xv
Schultz, Wolfgang 12
Schuon, Fritjhof xix
Schütze, Martin xiii–xiv
Schwabing, Munich 3–16
sculpture 6, 87–88, 165, 172–173
Second World War 38
Seele see opposition of spirit and soul
Seesemann, Kurt 20
self-assertion 60–61, *61*
self-devotion 60–61, *61*
Seneca 97, 106, 115n73
sensing experience 100–101
sexuality 105, 160–161
similarity 127, 128, 130, 132
Simmel, Georg 15, 21–22
Simon, Hermann xiv
sin 189
sleep 99–100, 116n88
Socrates 22, 24, 116n89, 117n96, 201n92, 202n95
Sombart, Werner 15
Sophism 22–23, 92, 108n6

Index 217

soul: definition of 154; guidance of 189–190; planetary 149–151; reality as reality of souls 140–141; *see also* opposition of spirit and soul
specific happiness 103–107
Spengler, Oswald xi, xii, 32, 34
Spir, Afrikan 3
spirit *see* opposition of spirit and soul
spirituality 155–158
Sprott, Walter John Herbert xiii, 62
Stauffenberg, Alexander von 10
Stauffenberg, Berthold von 10
Stauffenberg, Claus von 10
Steiner, Rudolf 7, 21
Steinitzer, Heinrich 7
Stendhal 151–152, 197n46
Stettin 7–8
Strauss, Richard 20–21
Strelow, Heinz-Siegfried xx
structuralism 39, 40
struggle for existence 124–125
style 184, 203n102
Süddeutsche Zeitung xviii
sudden turns 99, 132–133
Switzerland 16–20
symbol xiv–xvi, 19, 40, 77, 92, 116n80, 119n117, 133–134, 142–143, 166–167
symbolic dimension of life 139
symbolic elements 169–170
symbolical marriage 159–160, 194n20
symphony of rhythms 127–134

Taylor, Thomas 133, 193n14
teaching 188
teletae 16, 194n16
Tenigl, Franz 41
Theosophists 11–12
Third Reich 32–35
Thucydides 92
Tieck, Ludwig 4
time 151–154
Toller, Ernst 15
too late (always already) 91
Traditional Martinist Order 11
tragedy 126–127
trinity of separated poles 125–126
Troeltsch, Ernst 15

universe 71–72, 123–126; as alive 125–126

Valéry, Paul 17
value 139
Velde, Henry van de 21
Verwey, Albert 10
vice and virtue 178–179
Vienna 8
Viennese Psychoanalytic Society 8
virtue and vice 178–179
visionary experience 100–101
vital plenitude 139
vitalism xviii, xx–xxi, 93, 105–106, 121–124, 127, 143, 158, 161–163, 166, 174, 186–190
vitalist pedagogics 187–188
Vogtländer, Else xv
Völkischer Beobachter 49n108
Voltaire 48n90, 127
voluntary movement 54–56
Voss, Richard 36

Wartime Support Centre for Intellectuals 15
Weber, Max 15
Wedekind, Herta 7
Wegener, Franz 11
Weizsäcker, Viktor von 93
Wellek, Albert 93
Wertham, Frederic xiv, 60
Wilamowitz-Moellendorf, Ulrich von 102
will, theory of the 9, 62–70
Wille und Macht (journal) 33
Willermoz, Jean-Baptiste 11
Winterthur 8
wisdom 120–121
Wittgenstein, Ludwig 40, 199n73
Wolff, Toni 105, 118n116
Wölfflin, Heinrich 7
Wolfskehl, Karl 10
Wolters, Friedrich 10
Working-Group for Biocentric Research 33, 39
world, as living being 122–123, 125
Wotan 93
writing 163–174

Zeit, Die 41
Zeitschrift für Menschenkunde 74
Zeitschrift für Pathopsychologie 71

Taylor & Francis eBooks

Helping you to choose the right eBooks for your Library

Add Routledge titles to your library's digital collection today. Taylor and Francis ebooks contains over 50,000 titles in the Humanities, Social Sciences, Behavioural Sciences, Built Environment and Law.

Choose from a range of subject packages or create your own!

Benefits for you
- Free MARC records
- COUNTER-compliant usage statistics
- Flexible purchase and pricing options
- All titles DRM-free.

Benefits for your user
- Off-site, anytime access via Athens or referring URL
- Print or copy pages or chapters
- Full content search
- Bookmark, highlight and annotate text
- Access to thousands of pages of quality research at the click of a button.

REQUEST YOUR **FREE** INSTITUTIONAL TRIAL TODAY

Free Trials Available
We offer free trials to qualifying academic, corporate and government customers.

eCollections – Choose from over 30 subject eCollections, including:

Archaeology	Language Learning
Architecture	Law
Asian Studies	Literature
Business & Management	Media & Communication
Classical Studies	Middle East Studies
Construction	Music
Creative & Media Arts	Philosophy
Criminology & Criminal Justice	Planning
Economics	Politics
Education	Psychology & Mental Health
Energy	Religion
Engineering	Security
English Language & Linguistics	Social Work
Environment & Sustainability	Sociology
Geography	Sport
Health Studies	Theatre & Performance
History	Tourism, Hospitality & Events

For more information, pricing enquiries or to order a free trial, please contact your local sales team:
www.tandfebooks.com/page/sales

Routledge
Taylor & Francis Group

The home of Routledge books

www.tandfebooks.com